I0332110

A ROMAN DIARY AND OTHER
DOCUMENTS

A ROMAN DIARY
AND OTHER DOCUMENTS
RELATING TO THE PAPAL INQUIRY
INTO ENGLISH ORDINATIONS
MDCCCXCVI. BY T. A. LACEY

WIPF & STOCK · Eugene, Oregon

Wipf and Stock Publishers
199 W 8th Ave, Suite 3
Eugene, OR 97401

A Roman Diary and Other Documents
Relating to the Papal Inquiry into English Ordinations
MDCCCXCVI
By Lacey, Thomas Alexander
Softcover ISBN-13: 978-1-7252-9930-6
Hardcover ISBN-13: 978-1-7252-9931-3
eBook ISBN-13: 978-1-7252-9932-0
Publication date 2/1/2021
Previously published by Longmans, Green, and Co., 1910

This edition is a scanned facsimile of
the original edition published in 1910.

GALLIS
ANGLVS
INDESINENTER
CONIVNCTVS

PREFACE

THIS volume can hardly be called a book. "Encore ne saurait-on composer jamais un livre," says a recent French writer with native or acquired sense of form, "en remaniant des correspondances." Still less can you make a book by merely amassing a diary, letters, and some fugitive pieces of fourteen years ago. That is all that I have done. Then let the result stand, not as a book, but as a collection.

Why is the thing done? It needs justification, and this is the apology. Fourteen years ago, I took part in a certain course of action which was misunderstood at the time, and which is persistently misrepresented even to-day. Full explanation was impossible, because others with whom I had been acting were tied to silence, and I could not fairly use my greater freedom. How long the obligation lay upon them I do not know precisely, but some of them have now begun to speak, without doing much to dispel misconceptions, and thus set me free to speak for my own part.

This volume, then, contains my part of the record of what happened when the late Pope, Leo XIII, opened up to fresh investigation the old question of the English ordinations. A narrative newly

x A ROMAN DIARY AND OTHER DOCUMENTS

written might have some advantage of form; but there is more safety in the mere production of what was written at the time. The collection is not quite chaotic, for it has a nucleus in the diary which I kept during two months of active work at Rome. This Diary is printed just as it was written, for it is produced as evidence.

There is much in it that gives me little satisfaction, much that is trivial, some evidence of bad temper, and some unpleasant indications of ignorance. It has been found necessary, for obvious reasons, to withhold some names, and half-a-dozen passages of a purely personal character, containing in all about two hundred and fifty words, have been omitted as affecting others than myself. Some things I should like to omit on my own account, but they are retained in order that the evidence may be entire. The Diary is intended to show what was done, what was said, and what was thought; to indicate also, by its silences, what was not done. For this purpose it must be produced as a whole; excerpts would be useless. Severe demands are therefore made on the patience of the reader.

The Diary must be left intact, but it seems reasonable to illustrate, and sometimes to correct it—sometimes also to apologize—in the margin. Reading it after these fourteen years, I observe with surprise how many things are noted which I have completely forgotten, how many which I vividly remember are unrecorded. I have not hesitated to draw upon my memory for illustration; but such

PREFACE

reminiscences cannot, of course, be considered evidence in the same measure as the notes made at the time. I have collected some extracts from letters for further illustration. This section of the volume might easily be enlarged; but it is hard to know where to stop, and it seems safer to draw the line rigidly at letters written by myself or addressed to me.

No excuse is needed for the addition of the text of Mr. Gladstone's Memorandum. The fifth section is concerned with the correction of a mistake, and, one may hope, with the settlement of a tiresome and foolish controversy. The sixth is needed for the explanation of some allusions; it deals with documentary matter the importance of which has been greatly exaggerated, but it also contains something about Reginald Pole that is not without a certain interest even now. This should be true also of the note on the Provincial Council of Mainz, which may possibly stir up someone to edit in convenient form a document of the Reformation period that will repay study.

Of the section *De Re Anglicana* enough has been said in the Introduction, but it may be necessary to explain how I came by the *Risposta*. One morning in September, 1896, the post brought me, without any indication of its source, a packet containing the uncorrected printer's proofs of this pamphlet. One hesitated; but the matter cried aloud for public comment, and I swallowed my scruples about using what was thus placed in my hands. Perhaps I was

xii A ROMAN DIARY AND OTHER DOCUMENTS

hasty in assuming its genuineness. But public notice was taken of it, and it was not disavowed. The text is now published for the first time. My copy, as I have said, is an uncorrected proof ; finding it impossible to obtain any other, I have to rely on this, correcting it to the best of my ability. One incorrigible sentence has been left obelized.

The remaining sections are aftermath. Let me have pardon for thinking it worth while to recall from oblivion some writings in which I dealt with the Bull *Apostolicae Curae* and its defenders. One final paper is added, in which an historical precedent was adduced to show that a pontifical utterance of this kind may pass out of sight.

At the suggestion of the publishers there have been added to the volume Appendices containing the Bull itself and the *Responsio Archiepiscoporum Angliae.* Monsignor Moyes, unmindful of ancient enmities, has been good enough to supply an authentic copy of the former. Some doubt was expressed about the inclusion of the latter, on the ground that it might seem to link up the action of the English hierarchy too closely with the adventure on which Father Puller and I were engaged. But the other contents of the volume make it plain, beyond the possibility of cavil, that we had no official sanction. My own bishop would not even grant me formal leave of absence. The benison of the Archbishop of York, which we valued highly, was purely personal. Moreover, the arguments of the *Responsio* are of another order than

PREFACE   xiii

those which we employed. I have explained in the
Introduction what was the weakness of the position
which we personally occupied. The answer of the
English hierarchy was free from that weakness,
and it is hardly desirable to recall the incidents of
the controversy without at the same time putting
the question on its true and permanent footing. For
this reason I am glad that the Bishop of Salisbury,
who controls the copyright of the *Responsio*, has
kindly allowed its inclusion. He has not, however,
read my volume, nor was he in any way responsible
for the action described in it.

I have also been enabled to give the text of a
letter of Leo XIII, acknowledging the Archbishops'
Responsio, a document hitherto, I understand,
ἀνέκδοτον. It may be defective, though the ladies
of the Cambridge Type-writing Agency in the
Adelphi have devoted much skill and industry to
the deciphering of a clumsy manuscript. The copy
in my hands was without signature, but I have no
reason to doubt the authenticity of the letter. A
fourth Appendix contains a Bibliography, as complete as I can make it, dating from the time when
the question was raised in a new form by M. Portal.

I have to thank the editors of the *Guardian* and
of the *Contemporary Review* for leave to reproduce
some articles. By favour of the Society for Promoting Christian Knowledge, the volume also contains two brief dissertations, originally published as
tracts of the Church Historical Society. In every
case the text has been carefully revised, but the

xiv A ROMAN DIARY AND OTHER DOCUMENTS

arguments have been left as written, though sometimes guarded or corrected in the margin. I am indebted to Mr. Henry Gladstone for permission to print matter from Mr. Gladstone's pen, and to Mr. Tilney Basset for a copy of a letter of my own, drawn from the stores at Hawarden. To those who have been kind enough to read the proofs thanks are due for much help, but I will not name them lest they should seem to be responsible for things of which they disapproved. My friend Miss Christian Burke has relieved me of the grievous labour of preparing an Index.

HIGHGATE, *October 14th,* 1910

CONTENTS

		PAGE
PREFACE	. .	ix
I.	INTRODUCTION	3
II	A ROMAN DIARY	29
III	LETTERS .	87
IV.	MR. GLADSTONE'S MEMORANDUM .	139
V	THE ROYAL MANDATE FOR BARLOW'S CONSECRATION . . .	153
	I MEMORANDUM DELIVERED TO CARDINAL MAZZELLA . . .	153
	II. LETTERS TO THE EDITOR OF THE *TABLET* .	157
VI.	JULIUS III AND PAUL IV . .	171
	I. PAUL IV AND ANGLICAN ORDERS .	171
	II. CARDINAL POLE'S DESCRIPTION OF THE ENGLISH ORDINAL	177
VII	THE COUNCIL OF MAINZ, A D. 1549 . .	187
VIII.	THE PAMPHLET *DE RE ANGLICANA* AND ITS CRITICS . .	195
	I. *DE RE ANGLICANA* . . .	195
	ii. RISPOSTA ALL'OPUSCOLO *DE RE ANGLICANA*	210
	iii. THE *RISPOSTA* EXAMINED . . .	240
IX.	THE SOURCES OF THE BULL *APOSTOLICAE CURAE*	253
	I. EXAMINATION OF THE BULL .	253
	II. THE GORDON DECISION . .	272
X.	THE THEOLOGY OF THE BULL *APOSTOLICAE CURAE*	285
XI.	THE INTERPRETATION OF THE ENGLISH ORDINAL	311
XII	GREGORY IX AND GREEK ORDINATIONS . .	331

xvi A ROMAN DIARY AND OTHER DOCUMENTS

APPENDICES

I. SANCTISSIMI DOMINI NOSTRI LEONIS DIVINA PROVIDENTIA PAPAE XIII LITTERAE APOSTOLICAE DE ORDINATIONIBUS ANGLICANIS . . . 341

II. RESPONSIO ARCHIEPISCOPORUM ANGLIAE AD LITTERAS APOSTOLICAS LEONIS PAPAE XIII DE ORDINATIONIBUS ANGLICANIS . 354

III. RESPONSIO LEONIS XIII AD ARCHIEPISCOPOS ANGLIAE 395

IV. BIBLIOGRAPHY . 398

INDEX . . . 409

INTRODUCTION

A ROMAN DIARY
AND OTHER DOCUMENTS

I

INTRODUCTION

IN the spring of the year 1894 I undertook, with some reluctance, the task of writing a Latin dissertation dealing with the question of English ordinations as discussed from the Roman point of view. The questions involved were tolerably familiar to me, but I had always treated them from the standpoint of those who are ordinarily content to accept as a matter of course the sacramental validity of the sacred ministry exercised in the Church of England. In the course of controversy doubts, historic or theological, were from time to time suggested, needing resolution; the kind of apologetic demanded for this purpose was inevitable; but to throw oneself into a hostile position, to argue upon the assumptions there treated as indisputable, and to wrest from them an affirmative conclusion, was a new employment from which one might naturally shrink. But the work seemed to be needed. The fresh discussion of the subject started by the Abbé Portal in the previous year showed that debate was not impossible; it was not a question merely of controversy, but rather of

3

4   A ROMAN DIARY AND OTHER DOCUMENTS

mutual understanding ; a desire for such understanding was in the air, and Leo XIII was said to be
passionately bent on furthering the reconciliation of
all professing Christians. If we were to render help,
it was useless to go on arguing exclusively from our
own assumptions ; we must place ourselves at the
standpoint of those from whom we were separated,
and see whether we could not compel them on their
own principles to abridge the differences between
us and them. This accordingly was attempted.

I have not to tell the whole story of the movement. When that is written, it will be known what
hopes were not unreasonably entertained, and what
considerations led to the selection of the question of
ordination as the best subject of discussion. I am
concerned only with my own part in the movement,
and with certain misconceptions which it seems well
to remove. It was an accident that brought me in.
A dissertation was required, and it must be in Latin.
Other men were at least as well qualified to handle
the matter, but I was supposed to have some special
skill in handling the language. The need was
explained by a correspondent well acquainted with
the ground. " La cour de Rome," he wrote, " ne
sait pas l'anglais ; elle n'est informée de vos affaires
que par un petit nombre de truchements, qui, autant
que je les connais, sont loin d'avoir l'esprit très
ouvert. En latin vous serez lus ; en anglais, vous
seriez interprètés." In Latin, then, our argument was
to be presented. Mr. Edward Denny, who had
recently published an admirable treatise on the
subject, was associated with me ; we made his
Anglican Orders and Jurisdiction the basis of our
work, and a pleasanter partnership there could

INTRODUCTION 5

hardly have been. In November the book was all
but finished, and the Bishop of Salisbury, after
reading some parts of it in manuscript, supplied
a preface which lifted both the Latinity and the
argument to a higher plane.

Early in the year 1895 our *Dissertatio Apologetica
de Hierarchia Anglicana* issued from the Cambridge
University Press, and was criticized with conspicuous fairness in reviews and journals from one
end of Europe to the other. The Abbé Boudinhon,
one of our earliest reviewers, described the book in
the *Canoniste Contemporain* as " Un modèle de
discussion courtoise et approfondie, qui impose à
l'adversaire le même sérieux dans les recherches et
les preuves, les mêmes sentiments de modération et
de loyauté." In the *Zeitschrift für Katholische
Theologie* the Jesuit Father Emil Lingens acknowledged our merits more cautiously but no less
effectively. " Die Verfasser," he wrote, " beide
anglicanische Geistliche, zeigen sich auch ernstlich
bestrebt, ihrer Gegner mit wahrer Achtung und
ohne jegliche Bitterkeit zu behandeln." It was
clear that part of our object was attained ; we had
achieved the tone of sympathetic discussion. The
result was seen in much correspondence, which fell
for the most part into my hands, and it thus came
about that the book was very unfairly attributed
more to me than to Mr. Denny.

During the year 1895 things moved apace. It
seemed no small matter that Mgr. Gasparri, professor of Canon Law at Paris, took up our question.
He had published, two years earlier, a solid treatise
on the whole theory and practice of Ordination,
in which he had dismissed with even more than

6 A ROMAN DIARY AND OTHER DOCUMENTS

ordinary lightness the claims of the English Church to possess a valid ministry. We made much use of his work in writing *De Hierarchia*, and did not fail to comment on his deplorable treatment of our own question. This brought other critics upon him, and he took chastisement in the most cheerful spirit, freely confessing ignorance of a matter lying outside his own province, and making serious efforts to retrieve his mistake. Visiting Rome in the month of April, he reported that he had brought our book under the notice of certain Cardinals who were intending to study the question, and gave the first warning that much more would turn upon the rite than upon historical circumstances. From this time onward he and M. Boudinhon worked together, not agreeing in all details, but developing in the main the same argument for the validity of the English Ordinations.

In April appeared the Apostolic Letter *Ad Anglos* of Leo XIII. In September it became known that the Pope was resolved to open up our subject to the fullest investigation. He had demanded and received from the Abbé Duchesne, from Mgr. Gasparri, and from the Jesuit De Augustinis, professor in the Collegio Romano, memoranda which were more or less favourable to our contention ; how favourable the last of them was we did not ourselves know until a later day. There was activity on the other side, Cardinal Vaughan working hard in a way not fully understood until his biography by Mr. Snead-Cox was published. Dom Gasquet explored the Vatican Archives and produced two documents of considerable importance, which compelled a careful

INTRODUCTION

reconsideration of one part of our argument. In December M. Portal began the issue of the *Revue Anglo-Romaine*, with a benediction from Cardinal Bourret and an imposing list of contributors. It was a heavy task to keep going this weekly review of forty-six large pages, and those of us who shared the burden had some desperate struggles—not always successful—with the printer's proofs. It lived barely one year, and it is entombed in three massive volumes containing a remarkable body of original articles and selected documents. Policy, and human weakness, forbade exclusive attention to a single subject, and its pages were lightened or burdened by various displays of irrelevant erudition : some of M. Loisy's earlier and more orthodox essays in criticism obtained a narrow publicity by its means. Gasparri dealt with our own special question in a couple of masterly articles, written and published before he was summoned to Rome for the impending Commission. Father Puller contributed another. One that was signed with mysterious asterisks, the unfavourable conclusion of which did not obscure its friendly tone, fell from the pen of a learned Cardinal resident in Rome. I wrote on a subject in regard to which I was very inadequately equipped, and yet Duchesne was good enough to say that he thought I had made out a fair case for the contention that the Popes of Rome and Alexandria — possibly also the Bishop of Antioch—were at one time consecrated with imposition of the Gospel-text in place of the imposition of hands.

These labours occupied the winter. In March

8 A ROMAN DIARY AND OTHER DOCUMENTS

the Commission appointed by the Pope to investigate the question assembled in Rome. We had no communication of any kind with De Augustinis, and knew only that he was inclined to our side. With the three appointed on Cardinal Vaughan's advice—Dom Gasquet, Canon Moyes, and the Franciscan Father David Fleming—we had been engaged in open controversy, and with one of them I had had some private correspondence of no importance. With Mgr. Gasparri and the Abbé Duchesne we had closer relations. They now demanded help in detail. Duchesne was drawn to Father Puller, whose full and accurate erudition was exactly of the kind that commanded his confidence ; Gasparri had been in communication with me for some time, and asked me to keep him supplied with information.

The result was that Father Puller and I went to Rome to give the help desired. Mr. Snead-Cox has said in his Life of Cardinal Vaughan[1] that we acted with one side of the Commission, "much as solicitors who work with counsel." That is partly true, but it may suggest a serious falsehood. We did work as solicitors work when instructing counsel : we supplied information, we prompted arguments, we held consultations. But we were not solicitors ; we were managing the affairs of no clients; we were promoters of no cause ; we had engaged no advocates. To suggest that we were so employed is to revive an old misunderstanding. From more than one side we were represented as going to Rome with a petition for the recognition of our Orders. At an earlier stage of the movement Cardinal

[1] Vol. II. p. 195.

INTRODUCTION 9

Vaughan had privately written of "Halifax and his party" in this sense: "They are most anxious to get some kind of assurance about their Orders, at least the statement that they are possibly valid!"[1] A more complete misconception there could hardly be. We did desire a favourable decision at Rome; we worked for it and we prayed for it; but we did not desire it for our own assurance. Nothing of that kind was needed. What we desired, what we worked for and prayed for, was the removal of a practical obstruction hindering the concord of Christians. It was not on our side alone that the need of this relief was felt. There were others, eager advocates of Christian union, whose efforts were hampered by their uncertainty about our Orders. They could not ignore, as we could, the practice actually current in the Roman Church. For their sake, no less than for our own, the obstruction must, if possible, be demolished. The Pope was willing to examine the obstruction. That was enough for us; we would give our help. It was not, in truth, an action *inter partes:* there were no petitioners, no respondents. It was an investigation, enjoined by the Pope on his own counsellors, *ad informandam conscientiam.* We worked as solicitors work, but not always. It is not a solicitor's business to furnish the court with evidence that tells against his own client: he leaves that to the other side. Father Puller and I did furnish the Commission with some evidence that told against our own contention. It annoyed us a little when men praised us for this. It did not seem to us a remarkably virtuous act. We were

[1] *Ibid.,* p 182

10 A ROMAN DIARY AND OTHER DOCUMENTS

engaged in an honest investigation and we could not have acted otherwise.

Yet there was something more than the merely superficial aspect of things to encourage the misconception of which I complain. Our conduct of the argument looked that way. I have explained the difficulty which I had in entering on the argument, the necessity of looking at things from a standpoint that was not my own. I forced myself to do this, with so much success that for two years or more the alien standpoint became habitual to me. Father Puller was made of sterner stuff. Portal used to introduce him at Rome as "un Anglican intransigeant;" he would then put me forward as "M. Lacey—qui transige." That was a pleasantry, but there was some truth in it. We were agreed in this, that it was useless to put before the Papal Commissioners arguments which would carry no weight with those to whom they were addressed.

This difficulty may call for some further explanation. How can the validity of an ordination be discussed? There are two ways. There may be a question about the due and proper use of an acknowledged rite. Such questions not infrequently arise in the administration of the Roman rites of Ordination, which are so intricate in themselves, and so hedged about by judicial decisions and theological opinions, that mistakes may easily be made calling for conditional or even unconditional repetitions of an ordination. Mgr. Gasparri was a consummate expert in questions of this kind. There is a question of another kind concerning the general validity of Orders conferred by a doubtful rite or under

INTRODUCTION 11

doubtful conditions. That was the question as presented to the Commission. How is such a question to be discussed? There is only one way in which the value of a mode of ordination can be determined. It is determined by the practice of the Church. The matter must be considered on the Catholic hypothesis; and the Catholic hypothesis, in its simplest form, is that Holy Order is a gift of God, conferred by means of the ministry of the Church. But there is no prescribed form of this ministration having divine authority, or even human authority of an exclusive and immutable character. The ordinary baptismal formula is taken to be of this kind—even though Nicholas I did seem to acknowledge baptism "in the Name of Christ" as sufficient—and therefore the validity of a baptismal rite is easily determined. There is no corresponding formula for ordination. What, then, is the warrant for Holy Orders? It is found in the mere fact that they are conferred by the Church. The Church, by the hand of a qualified minister, ordains a man; therefore he is duly ordained. There is no prescribed form. On the hypothesis of the fundamental equality of bishops, any diocesan bishop can validly ordain in any form which he chooses to employ. Innocent IV, in the days when he was no more than a prominent canonist, expressed the opinion that in default of any direction from a superior authority it might be sufficient for a bishop to lay his hand on a candidate's head, saying "Sis sacerdos," a form which would be equally appropriate for the inauguration of a Flamen Dialis. In the case of a mere eccentricity like this there might be room for doubt, but

12 A ROMAN DIARY AND OTHER DOCUMENTS

such flights of fancy are of only academic interest;
bishops do not indulge in them. With all freedom
of action, a freedom for many ages almost untram-
melled, they have adhered to certain general lines
of ritual in ordination. But in the absence of any
prescribed form, and of any appointed standard of
sufficiency, it is impossible to mark out narrow
limits of variation. Any rite seriously used by a
bishop of the Catholic Church, with the grave intention of perpetuating the sacred ministry as it has
come down from apostolic times, may be taken as
adequate. But he must be a bishop of the Catholic
Church. The same assurance will not wait upon
the action of a bishop standing apart in isolation, or
attached to a notoriously heretical community. On
this head, if the matter be regarded from the standpoint of those allowing the full claims of the Papacy,
there is a sharp distinction to be observed; those
bishops only who are in communion with Rome
will then be regarded as belonging to the Catholic
Church; a form of ordination used by one of them
with the Pope's consent, express or implied, is a
form used in the Church, and is therefore of un-
questionable validity; another form used by a
bishop not in communion with Rome may be valid,
but has no warrant in itself arising out of that use;
it must be examined by reference to the standard
of Roman practice.

Now, what was our position? We believe the
Church of England to be an integral part of the
Catholic Church of Christ. We therefore as a
matter of course believe our Orders, received
in that Church, to be valid. There can be no
general question. There may be an individual

INTRODUCTION   13

doubt whether a particular person has been properly
ordained, but there can be no question of the
sufficiency of the ritual commonly used. It is used
by the Church, and that is conclusive. Neither are
we to be troubled by obscure historical difficulties
in proving the transmission of Orders. We are
affected neither by Macaulay's challenge to prove
the direct Apostolic descent of any one bishop in
Christendom, nor by a lack of documentary evidence
concerning a particular bishop here and there. Belief
in the Church implies belief that God's providence
will guard what is necessary, and that God's grace
is large enough to cover unknown accidents. Without this assurance sacraments would be mere traps
for the unwary. We have this assurance, and
we are untroubled.

But the canonists and theologians with whom we
were working did not share this assurance. On the
contrary, they were convinced that the English
Church, whatever might be said in its favour, was
in a state of schism, and that the English Ordinal
had been brought into use by schismatic bishops.
The validity of the rite, therefore, could not be
assumed ; it was not to be regarded as *prima facie*
a rite of the Catholic Church. Even if there were
no presumption against it, there must be a strict
examination of its merits. It might prove good :
other rites of Ordination used by schismatics and
heretics had been allowed by the judgment of the
Church, and so might this. But how was it to
be examined ? To what standard should it be
brought ? There was only one answer. It must be
compared with other rites allowed by the Church ;
if it agreed sufficiently with them, it could be

14 A ROMAN DIARY AND OTHER DOCUMENTS

declared valid; if not, there was another conclusion.

To this examination Monsignor Gasparri and M. Boudinhon addressed themselves with all the precise and verbal accuracy of experienced canonists. They collected all the rites of Ordination which churches in communion with Rome are known to have used. It is obvious that nothing which is absent from any one of these can be considered essential. When everything that is peculiar to one or more of them has been set aside, there remains a residue common to all. Nothing more than this can be considered essential. Does the English rite, then, contain what is found in this common residue? If so, it suffices.

The weakness of this method, as seen from our point of view, is obvious. It assumes that the English Church is not a part of the Catholic Church of Christ, but an alien body to be judged by comparison with the true fold. If we were using the method, we should have to include the English rite along with the Latin, the Greek, the Nestorian, and the Coptic, among those collated for the purpose of finding a standard. It could not be brought to the standard for judgment: it would itself form part of the standard. I sometimes pointed this out to our friends, only to be put off with a polite smile. In truth, since we had undertaken the task of convincing the Roman authorities on their own ground, we were obliged to argue as if the English Church were schismatic. We were consequently in a false position; we probably conveyed a false impression; we probably caused some searching of hearts among our own people; we were probably not unaffected

INTRODUCTION 15

ourselves. I can say for myself that, after facing this way for more than two years of continual debate, I had to get back with something like a wrench to my true orientation. Our friends and opponents are not to be blamed for adopting this method. I do not know how else they could have acted; and I would point out that we should be obliged to use the same method in similar circumstances. Let it be supposed—a not improbable supposition—that the authorities of the English Church have to decide whether they will accept as valid the ministry of the Swedish Church. If they hold the Swedish Church to have been throughout the last four centuries an integral part of the Catholic Church of Christ, then *cadet quæstio:* the Swedish Ordinations will be Ordinations of the Catholic Church.[1] If, on the contrary, they hold that the Swedish Church has been schismatic or of doubtful orthodoxy, it will be necessary to inquire whether a genuine ministry has been preserved; and this can hardly be done without ascertaining, among other things, whether the Swedish rites of Ordination are sufficiently in agreement with other rites, including our own, to be warrant of a genuine episcopate and priesthood. For such practical purposes the method seems to be imposed.

But I am now concerned to point out a more serious flaw that vitiates the method if it be pushed beyond its proper limits. It was only by using it and testing it that I became aware of this, and

---

[1] It is obvious that the general treatment of the subject of Holy Order will have to be considered *inter alia* in determining the question whether the Church under review be orthodox or not.

16 A ROMAN DIARY AND OTHER DOCUMENTS

the fruit of such wearisome labour should have some value. A first essay of criticism is contained in this volume. In the course of a lecture delivered at Sion College in November, 1896, I showed the precariousness of the method as used by M. Boudinhon. From a comparison of rites he concluded that a certain thing was necessary in the ordination of deacons. I sprang upon him the Canons of Hippolytus, in which was a form for the ordination of a deacon lacking that very thing. At that time those Canons were commonly supposed to be an authentic Roman document of the third century ; M. Boudinhon at once bowed to their authority, and varied his judgment on the essentials of diaconal Ordination. An acute critic afterwards showed the particular instance to be faulty ; but, as illustrating a defect of method, the incident retains its value. M. Boudinhon's previous conclusion had been based on imperfect evidence. But the evidence will always be imperfect. It can never be known that all the rites used in the Church from the beginning have been ascertained and collated. It is safe to infer the validity of a rite from its agreement with the common element in the known rites of the Church, but it is not safe to pronounce a rite invalid for lack of this agreement : there may have been a rite of the Church, now forgotten, with which it would agree. Imposition of hands appears to be a common element in all the known rites of Ordination ; but if I was right in my contention that the bishops of Rome and Alexandria were at one time consecrated without imposition of hands, it would be impossible to pronounce ordinations certainly invalid for lack of that ceremony. Thus the

INTRODUCTION

method may establish the adequacy of a rite, but can never establish its inadequacy. The argument may be used dialectically to demonstrate the necessity of acknowledging certain ordinations; it cannot be used for the purpose of determining the abstract essentials of Ordination, and therefore it cannot be pressed in the negative sense to the exclusion of any rite as defective. Mgr. Gasparri and M. Boudinhon did not always observe this limitation, and others less wary have ignored it to their logical undoing.

We then could use this argument dialectically, and be unaffected by any failure to convince those to whom it was addressed. We were not solicitors, but we were in a sense advocates. Certain theologians were urging a change in the practice of the Roman Church. We were not directly concerned, for we had no intention of submitting any question about our own ordination to the judgment of Rome; but for the general good of the Church we desired that change, and we therefore joined in the argument. We had to argue on the ground taken. It was with justifiable pride that I received from a man like M. Paul Fabre his commendation of *De Hierarchia*: "C'est une étude historique; ce n'est pas un plaidoyer;" but in one way he was wrong. We tried to make it good history, but it was certainly a plea; if anyone, by an allowed misuse of terms, calls it a piece of special pleading, I shall not complain. We were bound to the conditions of the argument; we had to set aside our own convictions, and argue from the convictions of others.

These things I recall in reading the notes that I made each day of our work in Rome, and I

c

18 A ROMAN DIARY AND OTHER DOCUMENTS

no longer wonder that Father Puller and I were accused of putting in jeopardy the dignity of our own priesthood. It was a risk which had to be run. I do not remember any consciousness of the peril at the time, but I look back and understand the generosity which impelled Mr. Gladstone to thank us "for undertaking so bravely an arduous work."

Another charge of contrary tenour has more recently been laid against us and those who were engaged with us. We have been accused of trying alternately to bully and to cajole the Pope into giving a decision favourable to our claims. Our aim, it is hinted, was to frighten him by representing an adverse decision as fatal to hopes of union, so that he should at the worst keep silence. The memorandum with which Mr. Gladstone intervened was "a magnificent bribe," an attempt to move the aged Pontiff by holding out the prospect of what was nearest to his heart—the reconciliation of England to the Holy See. Is there any foundation for this presentment of the story? How it is to be reconciled with the supposition that we were timorously seeking a resolution of our own doubts, I will let others determine. We afforded some grounds for that charge; did we afford any for this? I think we did, though the charge can easily be rebutted. Memory and the written records alike tell me that Father Puller and I adopted an attitude in Rome that must have seemed arrogant to those accustomed to another manner. We certainly had not the air of suppliants. Both the "Anglican intransigeant" and the other "qui transigeait" spoke very plainly of the effect which an adverse decision would have. It was useless, we said again

INTRODUCTION 19

and again, to talk to the English Church about reconciliation with Rome until the question of the Ordinations was settled in a favourable sense. That might be a very short step towards reconciliation, but it was the indispensable first step. This was specially noticeable in the latter part of our visit. I am still puzzled to know why the Cardinal Secretary of State pressed us to stay in Rome when the sessions of the Commission were ended ; but it was evident then, as now, that we were no longer to be concerned with meticulous inquiry into questions of detail. Something else was required of us. We found that we were expected to enlighten some very eminent persons whose knowledge of English churchmanship was much smaller than their interest in its development. We made no secret of our independent spirit ; perhaps we made unnecessary display of it. Duchesne may have thought so. When we demurred to his suggestion that we should visit various Cardinals, on the ground of our lack of credentials to "les grands," he replied in his most caustic manner, "Mais qui y a-t-il à Rome de plus grand que vous?" I was very much nettled, and made no note of the remark in my Diary ; I can remember it now with amusement. There were occasions when I, at all events, carried independence of demeanour too far. My insularity, my more than transalpine barbarity, betrayed me once into a deplorable breach of etiquette in Cardinal Rampolla's antechamber. I tender belated apologies to a magnificent person, of whose rank and station I am ignorant, but whose pained and bewildered expression I cannot forget. To a certain forcefulness of manner, offensive to Italian

20 A ROMAN DIARY AND OTHER DOCUMENTS

taste, I plead guilty; I do not acknowledge any dream of enforcing a decision by a suggestion of politic motives. Our only object was to lay the truth bare, to show plainly that no doubts on the matter in question were entertained among ourselves, and to leave no room for mistakes about the way in which an unfavourable decision would be received. If Leo XIII was deceived on this head, the fault was not ours.

The one incident of the campaign which hurts me in retrospect is the treatment of my pamphlet, *De Re Anglicana*. The pamphlet was, on the face of it, a partial statement, and it was open to legitimate criticism. I could have borne it patiently if I had been told that I saw my surroundings in too rosy a light, that my optimism deceived me, that my knowledge was at fault, that I lacked a sense of proportion, or even that I was carried away by the spirit of party. The reply would have been obvious, that I probably knew more about the subject than my critics. But I encountered criticism of another sort. In a secret paper I was accused of deliberate fraud, of saying things in the ears of Cardinals at Rome which I should not dare to say in the open air of England. It was a charge of conscious and intentional falsehood, and it was delivered as a stab in the dark. The calumny was easily answered when known. My pamphlet was not formally published or put on sale, but a hundred copies were printed and freely circulated not only in Rome, but also in England and America. I sent one, as a matter of course, to my own bishop at Ely. As soon as the accusation came to my ears, and before it was made public, I placed others at the

INTRODUCTION

great public libraries in England. It was myself, indeed, who made the accusation public. I was angry, and I retorted in kind; more fiercely, perhaps, than I ought to have done. I had the less right to be angry, as I now see, in that I had nursed similar suspicions and made similar charges against others. This volume contains evidence of it. I would gladly forget the whole matter, but even after this lapse of years I cannot pretend to be anything less than indignant. I no longer suspect my critics of bad faith. Doubtless they were, like me, suffering from nervous tension. But the facts remain: the documents are in this volume; they are part of the record, and must not be suppressed.

When I read my Diary with the deliberate judgment of a later day, two things strike me as remarkable. The first is the disproportionate attention paid by the Commission to unimportant points. It seems to be all about Barlow. We were hardly prepared for this, and much work had to be done with materials not in hand. In dealing with these materials I made one bad blunder, which is recorded and corrected in this volume. Father Puller must have had little or no share in this, as it lay in a department where I usually wearied myself alone. It was pure weariness: only those who have gone through the whole of the stupid business about Barlow can understand the futility of the objections raised, the obscuring of a clear case by needless side issues, the ruin of the sense of proportion which the discussion causes. Lingard settled the matter once for all, with his broad common sense and historic perception: it never

22 A ROMAN DIARY AND OTHER DOCUMENTS

should have been moved again. It was threshed out unmercifully in the Commission of 1896, and I make bold to say that anyone who attempts to stir the old objections again should be held convict of dishonest intent. When I handed to Cardinal Mazzella one of the documents—that about which I had gone astray—he put it aside with the remark that it was of no importance. This was unkind, in view of the trouble we had taken over it, but it was true. The documents about Barlow, and the absence of documents, are of no importance. These arguments are for the dustbin.

The second thing that strikes me is the dry and jejune character of my notes. I put this down partly to fatigue. Never in my life have I been so hard worked as during those two months. It should be remembered that, apart from the labours of the Commission, we had to keep going the weekly issue of the *Revue Anglo-Romaine*, a sufficient task in itself. There were labours of translation also, the most irksome of employments. The differing genius of the two languages became painfully apparent as we strove to render into French clarity the English allusiveness of Newman, the rich imagery of Wiseman, or the majestic involutions of Mr. Gladstone's mind. We had some trouble with a young Lazarist, helping us with Wiseman, who wanted to bring the Children of Israel into conflict with "des Golias" during their wandering in the wilderness ; one giant was as good as another for him, but we could not allow Wiseman to be represented as confusing the Anakim with the Philistines of Gath. Our method of translating Mr. Gladstone's Memorandum is not to be re-

INTRODUCTION 23

commended. Puller and I first rendered it into what we considered to be French, and Portal then revised our rendering into what he considered to be French. The difficulty was first to ascertain the meaning of the original, and then to find some possible way of expressing that meaning in French. "Ça ne peut pas se dire en français," Portal would say brusquely and despairingly. Puller and I wrangled for twenty minutes over the meaning of one sentence. I then gave way, not because I was convinced, but because I was the younger. Such were our labours.

A short visit to Monte Cassino brought welcome but inadequate respite. The note in my Diary, "Nightingale singing all night," recalls the sleeplessness of fatigue, which beset me the first night that we spent there. I was up at my window constantly, until the purple masses of the engirdling mountains were outlined in gold. Father Puller called me from a passing slumber at half-past four to go to Mattins; I responded with alacrity, just turned over once on my bed, and found him standing over me again with the news that it was past eight o'clock. I remember the listlessness and distaste with which I made some few visits to the usual objects of interest in Rome. In such great weariness, a degree of spiritual dryness and a certain shortness of temper were inevitable. They are reflected in the Diary. Moreover, I was making only notes to aid my memory. I should not like it to be thought that any of those engaged in our work were absorbed in externals and mindful only of the machinery of the Church. I kept no *journal intime* of aspirations, of hopes and prayers. Nor would

24 A ROMAN DIARY AND OTHER DOCUMENTS

it be seemly to enlarge on these things in retrospect. I will recall only the day when we were allowed to attend a Mass celebrated by M. Portal in the Crypt of St. Peter, at the tomb of the Apostle ; the vision of the man rapt in his holy office ; the burning words of faith and hope which he addressed in a brief discourse to the worshippers. But for this I should never have understood the deep springs of his busy activity.

These things dwell in my mind more than disputations. My memories of Rome are in the main religious memories. I love the Church of Rome, and I do not know that my love has been diminished by the failure of efforts that were made and of hopes that were entertained fourteen years ago. There have been worse rubs since, which leave me still of the same mind. For Rome is various ; there is a worst to be known, and there is a best that hardly can be known. We saw Leo XIII celebrate Mass—with what tremulous devotion, with what sense of the unseen, those who remember him need not be told. A minor prelate of the Court said Mass afterwards. As we descended the stairway, I heard a member of a religious order exclaim : " Si je disais ainsi la Messe devant mon supérieur——!" It was a faithful son of Rome who said that things would not mend until four Monsignori had been hanged in the Campo de' Fiori every morning for a considerable spell. Having made the acquaintance of a certain distinguished prelate, I may myself claim to have waded in some of the deepest waters of Popery. This brilliant churchman, for brilliant he was, enlarged to me on the marvellous elasticity

INTRODUCTION 25

of the Church of Rome, her power of utilizing all that is great and good in human nature; she could find room for "hommes d'état, hommes de science, hommes d'affaires," and so on through a dozen categories. A minor prelate, who was sitting by, softly interjected "hommes de vertu." The other laughed lightly, and allowed "hommes de vertu aussi, evidemment;" but I could tell by his angry flush that the shaft went deep. When I asked why Leo XIII tolerated this man, whose reputation would spell ruin for any "homme d'affaires," I was told that he would not willingly quarrel with the French Republic, and that he ran some risk of this even by refusing to make the man a Cardinal. Here is one aspect of Rome. There is another aspect. I shall venture to repeat what I wrote soon after the death of George Tyrrell. I had accused Rome of breeding heretics, and a devout soul, a simple Oblate of St. Benedict, answered me with a passionate reference to "that holy and heavenly faith which is the soul of Rome, and her very self: that faith which is the joy and consolation of her countless sons and daughters." Tyrrell, he said, in this sense died within Rome's holy pale. I allowed the appeal, and explained ·—

"I was thinking of another Rome, a Rome which is locally situate in the middle part of Italy, and which thence stretches forth tentacles of amazing grip—oh! how they draw!—the Rome of saints and martyrs and stupendous sinners; the Rome of Popes and Cardinals and Monsignori; the Rome of convents and bells, of colleges and schools; the Rome of scarlet-clad seminarists and purple prelates; the Rome of the Propaganda and of the Holy

26 A ROMAN DIARY AND OTHER DOCUMENTS

Office, of Curia and Basilica; the Rome of Medici and Farnese, of Consalvi and of Antonelli; that labyrinth of history, that *colluvies gentium*, matron and courtesan, murderess and saver of men, preacher of righteousness and worker of iniquity, sea of grace and sink of corruption, commixture of all contraries, great of soul and immeasurably small, scaling heaven and stumbling in the mire—the Church of Rome, the marvellous work of God and the baffling work of man. This it is that breeds heretics; and no wonder!

"That mystical Rome, that hidden soul, which my friend the Oblate loves, and which folded the dying Tyrrell in her arms while the other Rome spat and cursed—this Rome lurks in the narrow streets beside the Tiber, leads about priests in shabby cassocks and here and there a prelate in glossy mantle, prompts the ragged children who say their prayers at San Clemente, guards in spotless purity the cornette of the daughter of St. Vincent, sits in meditation beside the shrine of San Filippo, sometimes slips into a vacant chair at a Sacred Congregation or peeps over the shoulder of a Pope to guide his pen, is always active somewhere, sends out messages to the ends of the earth, and gathers in devotions from all lands. This also is great and wonderful, a marvellous work of God and a satisfying work of man. And this does not breed heretics."

A ROMAN DIARY

II

A ROMAN DIARY

1896. *March* 20. Letter from M. Portal. Mgr. Gasparri and Duchesne are nominated by the Pope to the Commission on Anglican Orders. Gasparri asks for information. Were any bishops, who had been consecrated according to the Ordinal, afterwards reconciled by Pole? Was Cranmer consecrated according to the old Pontifical or by the new Order? It would be well for me to go to Rome.

March 22. Letter from Lord Halifax in the same sense and inclosing more from Portal. Halifax wants Father Puller and me to go.

March 25. Up to town on Halifax's invitation to meet Father Puller, Portal, and the Archbishop of York. The Archbishop failed us. Knox Little, Riley, and Birkbeck also present. Father Puller and I agreed to go.

March 27. Saw the Bishop of Ely and got his consent verbally.[1] Letter from Halifax. The Archbishop of York has consented to write a letter about it to Portal, which he may show in the proper quarters.

Ap. 7. Left home 8 a.m. Met Puller at Holborn Viaduct Station. Started for Dover 11 a.m. Calais, Paris, Dijon.

[1] *I.e.* to a long absence from my parish. See Letters of March 27th and 30th, and of April 10th.

29

30 A ROMAN DIARY AND OTHER DOCUMENTS

Ap. 8. Through Mt. Cenis tunnel. Turin ; fine view of Mt. Blanc. Genoa.

Ap. 9. Arrived Rome 6.15. Portal met us at station, and took us to our rooms at 36 Via del Tritone. A French pension au quatrième. Afterwards he took us to the Lazarist house in Via di San Nicola da Tolentino, when we were introduced to the Superior, a venerable old man with full white beard, Archbishop in partibus, and formerly Vicar Apostolic in Persia, Mgr. Thomas. After déjeuner we drove—still with Portal—to St. Peter's ; thence to the Farnese Palace to see Duchesne, who lives there as head of the French School,[1] occupying with his school and library the upper story, the first floor being the embassy. He asked about the quotation from Daniele Barbaro in *de Hierarchia,* not being able to find it in the *Archivio Veneto.* I explained that I borrowed the reference from Dom Gasquet. He was much amused, and said he would challenge Gasquet on the subject. I explained to him about the book of Barlow's attacking the Protestants, which is in the Cambridge University Library.[2] He wished to have it sent at once, to arrive on Monday. Puller talked much with him about Pope Victor's action in the Paschal controversy. Telegraphed to Wood to send the copy of Barlow. Afterwards to see Gasparri. He is a very dark, youthful-looking man. Lives on the fourth story of a dingy house in the Via della Pace. Salon with brick floor ; no carpet

---

[1] The "École de Rome," or Institute of Archæology, maintained by the French Government, of which he had been appointed Director in 1895.

[2] Since published, with an Introduction by the Rev. J. R. Lunn under the title *Bishop Barlowe's Dialoge*

A ROMAN DIARY 31

save a small rug by the sofa. He is full of Ferrar's case. The enemy are maintaining that Ferrar was consecrated according to the Ordinal, in order to adduce him as an instance of a bishop consecrated by the Ordinal, who might nevertheless have conferred *minor* orders—an instance such as is needed for their interpretation of the Breve *Regimini* of Paul IV.

The Commission consists of Cardinal Mazzella, president, Dom Gasquet, Moyes, and a certain Father David representing one side; Duchesne, Gasparri, and de Augustinis on the other side, specially appointed by the Pope, and last an unknown Spaniard.[1] Father Scannell also has been summoned.

Ap. 10. Mgr. Gasparri came to see us in the morning, with two questions : (1) about Ferrar's Consecration, and (2) about certain Legatine acts of Pole's, supposed to involve the invalidity of the Edwardine Orders.

(1) Showed him the text of the Register, and Estcourt's discussion of it. He seized the point at once, that the Register points to no changes in the rite of consecration, but only in the Mass which followed. We found that according to Maskell an episcopal consecration was finished, as the Register suggests, *antequam Missa celebraretur.* The interest of this question is due to the fact that the Commission is discussing the meaning of the Brief of Paul IV, *Regimini.* The Pope spoke of men advanced "ad ordines tam sacros quam non sacros ab episcopo non in forma Ecclesiæ ordinato."

---

[1] He was sufficiently well known as a theologian, the Capuchin Fr. José Calasanzio de Llevaneras, afterwards Cardinal.

32 A ROMAN DIARY AND OTHER DOCUMENTS

Gasparri asks what bishop consecrated by the new rite ever advanced clerks "ad ordines non sacros." The other side reply *Ferrar*, making him out to have been consecrated by the Ordinal.

(2) On the other question we discussed the deprivation of bishops, and degradation a solo presbyteratu.[1]

Discovered to-day that I was mistaken about the reference to *Archivio Veneto*. It should have been *Venetian State Papers*.[2] Wrote to Duchesne explaining.

In the afternoon drove with Portal to S. Pietro in Montorio to see the panorama of Rome, and afterwards walked in the gardens of the Villa Pamphili Doria. A good deal of talk about the nature of Excommunication.[3]

Ap. 11. Called on Gasparri at 8.30 to take him a copy of the register of Ferrar's consecration, and some notes. The session of the Commission at 10 a.m. Afterwards I walked alone to Forum, Colosseum, Campidoglio, etc., and was strangely unimpressed. Everything seemed so very familiar.

Afternoon: Sir Walter Phillimore called on us. Then came Duchesne, bringing two Jesuit fathers, Lapôtre and another, who is a Bollandist. Finally

---

[1] In relation to the statement of Foxe and others that Ridley, Ferrar, and Hooper were degraded from the priesthood only, and not from the Episcopate. *De Hierarchia*, pp. 160, *seqq.*

[2] An extraordinary mistake in *De Hierarchia*, p. 81 n. I think one of us must have been burrowing in the *Archivio* to see if we could find anything to add to what Mr Brown had calendared, and the one title was substituted for the other in our note

[3] Others joined us. I remember one remark. A certain priest said, " Il faut convenir que l'église de Rome ne retire jamais ce qu'elle a une fois dit." I replied, " Non, elle n'en change que le sens." " C'est ça," he answered eagerly, and then seemed to wish he had not been quite so prompt

A ROMAN DIARY 33

came Portal, who carried off us and Phillimore to the Villa Medici and the Pincio. Duchesne reported that our information had been very useful at the morning session, and had fully established the fact that Ferrar was consecrated according to the Pontifical.

Rather over-tired to-day: too much walking.

Ap. 12. *Low Sunday.* Heard Mass sung at the German college. Beautiful plain-chant: Missa de Angelis: very dignified and reverent ceremonial. One of the young Lazarists accompanied us. Afterwards went with Portal to call on Father Scannell at the Collegio Inglese, he having left cards on us the previous day. Did not find him at home. Looked into the Pantheon and heard Mass at noon. At last a building which surpasses all expectation.

Afternoon. Duchesne and Gasparri came by appointment and we did three hours' hard work investigating the cases alleged by Moyes as showing that Pole rejected the Edwardine Orders. Duchesne is satisfied that Pole made no distinction between the men ordained by the two rites, but Gasparri is of the contrary opinion.

Afterwards we called on the Oxenhams in the Piazza del Popolo.

Ap. 13. I spent the morning at the Biblioteca Nazionale consulting Wilkins' Concilia: found that Pole in the second Legatine Constitution referred to the *Decretum ad Armenos*, without, however, quoting it in full. Hence probably the mistake made by Dixon in his History.[1] From this copy of Wilkins all the pages containing the Bull

---

[1] I cannot now make out what the mistake was. See Vol. IV, p. 462.

D

34 A ROMAN DIARY AND OTHER DOCUMENTS

Regnans in excelsis, except the first, have been removed. Father Puller went to the Vatican Library and found the *Venetian State Papers* with Daniele Barbaro's report; also verified, in Gairdner, the letter of June 12, 1536, in which, according to Estcourt's copy, Barlow was called "*elect* of St. Davye's;" but in Gairdner's he is called "Bishop, then elect of St. Asaph, now of St. David's."[1]

Afternoon in the Biblioteca Casanatense, where I looked up *Degradation* in Reiffenstuel. Nothing much to the purpose.

Afterwards a long discussion with Portal on *Unity*, planning out an article for the *Revue Anglo-Romaine.*

The Secretary to the Commission, son of the Spanish Ambassador and of an English mother, is very fierce against us. Mgr. Merry del Val his name.[2]

Calling on Gasparri we were introduced to Father Scannell, who promised to go with us to the Catacomb of St. Priscilla.

Ap. 14. Letter from E. G. W., enclosing bibliographical account of Barlow's Dialogue; characteristically complete. The first edition, published in 1531, rather too early to be of much service to us. Afterwards I went to the Biblioteca Nazionale, while Father Puller translated Wiseman's letter with Portal for the *Revue.* At the Biblioteca Nazionale I found a German-Latin translation of Pearson on the Creed, but no Hammond, Field, or Bilson, no Beveridge except the defence of the Apostolic Canons, and no Barrow except the Mathematical Treatises.

---

[1] See below, April 17th, and Letters of April 14th, May 18th and 24th.
[2] Now Cardinal Secretary of State

A ROMAN DIARY 35

Afternoon to Catacomb of St. Priscilla; Duchesne, Portal, Canon Bright, Scannell, Father Puller, and I.[1] All came to tea with us afterwards.

Duchesne reports that out of forty cases alleged by Moyes, in which Pole or those acting under his authority had refused to recognise the Edwardine Orders, he has demolished thirty-eight *and a half.* This has much impressed de Augustinis.

Ap. 15. Gasparri has seen Cardinal Rampolla, spoken about us, and obtained permission to show us anything and consult us. Apparently some one had been objecting.

Worked most of the day at the article on Unity. Visited S. Ignazio and the Minerva.

At dinner a young Belgian next to me, M. de Bossierre, "cameriere segreto di spada e cappa" to the Pope. He was educated in England, and speaks English almost perfectly. Very friendly, and thought he could get permission for us to say Mass at the Tomb of the Apostles. After dinner we had him in to tea and explained our position and the object of our visit.

[1] I must add something from memory. Dr Bright, who lacked conversational French, leaned on Puller's interpretation of Duchesne's interesting disquisitions. When we reached the resting place of Pope Marcellinus, on whose difficult history he was a leading authority, he became excited, and burst into a disquisition of his own The scene rises before me the low vaulted passage, the smoking tapers, Bright's wonderful face thrust forward over Puller's shoulder, the pale little abbé standing silent in resentful astonishment, Scannell's burly form shaking with suppressed laughter. Duchesne presently whispered to me " Qui est-ce donc?" I thought he knew who our companion was, and answered simply, "Bright." " Et puis?" he asked, raising his eyebrows I explained, with some astonishment, that he was Professor of Ecclesiastical History at Oxford. "Ah! *Briecht!*" exclaimed Duchesne, and begged for an interpretation of the discourse Suppose the name to be German, long drawn out, and my clumsy phonetics may serve their turn

36 A ROMAN DIARY AND OTHER DOCUMENTS

M. Chabot, a French priest and Lecturer on Oriental studies at the Sorbonne, called with Portal in the afternoon. Also Mr. Oxenham.

Ap. 16. Visited S. Maria Maggiore. Afterwards worked at my article. Dined with Sir Walter Phillimore at the Hôtel d'Italie. The Phillimores are occupying the rooms which the Marion Crawfords have just vacated.

Ap. 17. Worked at my article most of the day. Father Puller heard an *Armenian* Mass at S. Ignazio.

Telegram from Father Waggett saying that the copy of the letter of June 12, 1536, in the Harleian collection, which Gairdner refers to, agrees with Estcourt's copy in speaking of Barlow as *elect* of St. David's.[1]

M. Portal saw Cardinal Rampolla to-day, and found him most friendly, but he avoided speaking of the Archbishop of York's letter.

Puller and I visited St. Peter's in the afternoon ; prayed at the altar of St. Gregory the Great. Observed the extraordinary likeness of Alexander VII (Chigi) to Napoleon III. Afterwards we called with M. Portal on the Sœurs de Charité.

Ap. 18. Visited with Puller San Lorenzo Fuori. The stone on which he was martyred shown behind the Confession. The tomb of Pius IX beyond.

A. S. Barnes left his card. No address. Puller went to the Benedictines of S. Anselmo in their house in Bocca di Leone, with introduction from Birkbeck, and obtained permission for us to attend their Mass to-morrow.

Sir Walter Phillimore saw Cardinal Rampolla ;

[1] *Supra,* April 13.

A ROMAN DIARY

half an hour's conversation, which he then came and reported to us. N.B.—The Cardinal receives at 6 p.m. The Cardinal was rather shy of speaking on the question of Orders, but called attention to the impartiality of the Commission. Phillimore spoke of the growing desire for union—of the English Church Union—of the Bishop of Lincoln and his good works and saintliness—of the Lincoln trial and the Bishop's refusal to plead before the Privy Council. Also of political matters. Dillon, etc. The Pope, said the Cardinal, had put pressure on Dillon to keep the peace.

Ap. 19. *Sunday.* Mass at the Benedictines in Bocca di Leone. A young English monk from Ampleforth looked after us and provided us with graduals ; Dom Cuthbert Mercer by name. This is a house of the congregation of Beuron,[1] and most of the monks are from Maredsous. They sing the Solesmes chant, with much less precision than at the German College, where it seems the Ratisbon books are used. Terce immediately before Mass, Sext after, both said *sine nota.* Terce at nine o'clock.

After Mass we were invited to an interview with the Abbot Primate of the Benedictine Order, Dom Hemptinne,[2] who arrived in Rome last night. He is Flemish, and speaks English well. A long and pleasant conversation, with nothing of great importance. He remarked that in England *we* are in some respects bolder than *they*, e.g. in wearing the clerical habit.

---

[1] A Benedictine friend tells me that I was mistaken here. This house, now the Convent of Sant' Anselmo sull' Aventino, does not belong to any special congregation of the Benedictine Order, but is an international house of studies.

[2] Dom Hildebrand de Hemptinne, formerly Abbot of Maredsous.

38   A ROMAN DIARY AND OTHER DOCUMENTS

At an early Mass at San Claudio, where the Blessed Sacrament is continually exposed, I saw a priest make the oblation *per unum*, and say the Canon after Consecration extensis brachiis in modum Crucis.

Afterwards to the English College, where Mass was just ending. Scannell showed us the refectory and library : found Hammond's Practical Catechism there. Discussed with Scannell the difference between a decision allowing Anglican priests to minister in the Roman Church, and one admitting the validity of our Sacraments, but not allowing ministrations on the ground of *praxis*. The latter would not in any way prove a barrier to re-union. Adversely it would affect *converts* only, with whom we have no concern. Scannell frankly says he does not believe in the validity, but he is working for *no decision at all*.

Afternoon, Portal came, and I discussed this same point with him. He pointed out that a decision *confirming* the *status quo* would be mischievous, but if no decision at all is given no harm is done, though the *status quo* is maintained in practice.

At three o'clock Duchesne, with his friend M. Fabre, an historian of merit, Gasparri, Sir W. Phillimore, and Scannell arrived. A long discussion on Barlow, detailing the facts about the absence of evidence and the arguments of Moyes thereon. We made the contention that of all the instruments which may have existed, some which *must* have existed are lost, as the Congé d'élire,[1] Restitution, etc. ; the disappearance of some is fully accounted

---

[1] But see below, April 28th.

A ROMAN DIARY 39

for, e.g. Barlow's own Register and the Act book of the Convent of Canterbury; there remains unaccounted for only the memorandum of consecration in Cranmer's Register. Phillimore was very helpful in explaining the force of the Act regulating the election, etc. He holds that the same instrument *must* have ordered both confirmation and consecration; but Barlow was confirmed; *ergo* his consecration was ordered by the king.[1]

Lent Scannell *de Hierarchia*, and Fr. Sydney Smith's pamphlet.

Ap. 20. With Portal we visited the Sulpicians, and had a long and interesting conversation with them, the whole community being present. M. Fabre was again there, and M. Fournier, professor of law in the Institut of Grenoble.

Ap. 21. In the morning Mgr. Gasparri came with questions about Barlow—precedence in Parliament and such like. Mr. Lunn's copy of Barlow's Dialogue arrived with many notes. He explains some of the *answers* of 1540 by supposing that "*consecration*" was spoken of in a restricted sense of the *inunction*. We looked into this, going through all the answers as given in Burnet. The

---

[1] See *Letter* of May 7th. The Act provides as follows : "The king's Highness, by his letters patent under his great seal, shall signifie the said election, if it be to the dignity of a bishop, to the archbishop and metropolitane of the Province where the see of the said bishoprick was void, if the see of the said archbishop be full and not void : and if it be void, then to any other archbishop within this realm or in any other the king's dominions ; requiring and commanding such archbishop, to whom any such signification shall be made, to confirm the said election, and to invest and consecrate the said person so elected to the office and dignity that he is elected unto, and to give and use to him all such benedictions, ceremonies, and other things requisite for the same" (25 Henry VIII, cap. 20). See below, May 12th, and pp. 157–68.

40 A ROMAN DIARY AND OTHER DOCUMENTS

theory seems very probable. Many of the doctors distinguish *consecration* and *ordination cum impositione manuum.* Others say that *consecration* is not mentioned in Scripture, but only appointment with imposition of hands.

A ridiculous book arrived, written by one Dr. MacDevitt, and published with imprimatur of the Archbishop of Dublin. He gives the Nag's Head fable with embellishments, and has some curious views on the theology of Orders, adopted apparently as telling heavily against Anglican Orders. The significance of the book is that while piling up arguments of the most grotesque kind for invalidity the author concludes for *conditional* re-ordination, and tries to make out that this is the existing practice.

Ap. 22. Heavy rain all day. I found that some of my information given to Gasparri was inexact, and drew up a memorandum showing that the king's mandate for confirmation and consecration of a simple bishop went to the Archbishop alone, who must then proceed according to *jus commune*, which moreover had just been confirmed by statute (Act of Submission of Clergy). Therefore Cranmer, having received the Mandate for Skyp and again for Bulkely, had to see that he was consecrated by three true bishops according to *jus commune.* Neglect of this would bring him and all concerned under the pains of præmunire.

Gasparri came in the morning, bringing notes of some things put forward by Moyes at the previous sitting of the Commission. Moyes alleged fourteen possible *documents* in Barlow's case, nine dealing with appointment, and five with consecration. All

A ROMAN DIARY 41

the former, he said, were extant; all the latter
wanting. Moyes now gives references for the
extant documents. Among them are the *Congé
d'élire*, and the *Literæ certificatoriæ de electione
peracta*. For these he gives a reference to the
Patent Rolls. Referring to Moyes' own articles
in the *Tablet*, we find that these are the documents relating to St. Asaph. Again for the *in-
thronization* he refers to the well-known private
letter of John Barlow to Cromwell, *alluding* to
the installation, as if it were an official instrument.

I drafted a memorandum showing that in point
of fact the *only* documents extant are 1° those
entered in Cranmer's Register,[1] and 2° the Concessio
temporalium; and that in face of the disappearance
of so many documents, which certainly existed, it is
impossible to infer anything from the absence of
some others.

Observed and showed Gasparri that in the
Sarum Pontifical the Consecrator does not impose
hands at the *Oratio ad instar præfationis*, but
afterwards at the prayer *Pater Sancte, omnipotens
Deus*.

Afternoon, we and Portal went to see Duchesne
at the Farnese Palace. Told him of our discovery
about Moyes' references. He was very amusing,
full of stories about the Commission and other
things. He had been arguing that the Bulls both
of Julius III and of Paul IV were favourable to us.
Moyes retorted that they must be read together
and were then unfavourable. "Then," said
Duchesne, "put them together and there is one

[1] Inaccurate. See below, April 28th, and further developments.

42 A ROMAN DIARY AND OTHER DOCUMENTS

Pope for you, take them apart and there are two Popes for me."

* * * * *

He entrusted to us the Memoirs of Moyes and Co.[1] and of de Augustinis, and his own.

Abstract of de Augustinis, written in Italian.

1. In the year 1684 no papal decision against Anglican Orders had been given, and in 1685 a case submitted to the Holy Office was " Dilata."
2. Gordon's case was purely personal, and the decision was not grounded on his Supplica.
3. The Bull and Brief of Paul IV do not refer to the Anglican rite.
4. Paul IV did not condemn Cranmer for changing the essential form of Orders. He had offended only *sentiendo et docendo* against the Sacrament of Order.
5. Men ordained according to the Anglican rite were received by Pole *in suis ordinibus.*
6. The Nag's Head Fable is rubbish and Parker's Register is genuine.
7. Hodgekyn validly consecrated Parker.
8. Barlow was unquestionably a true Bishop.

The Rite.

9. Traditio Instrumentorum is no essential part of Ordination, but only a declaratory ceremony.

---

[1] I regret this rudeness of style, here and elsewhere.

A ROMAN DIARY   43

10. Council of Mainz in 1549. "In collatione
    Ordinum, quae cum impositione manuum
    veluti visibili signo traditur, doceant rite
    ordinatis gratiam divinitus conferri, qua ad
    ecclesiastica munera rite et utiliter exer-
    cenda apti et idonei efficiantur."

11. Council of Trent, 1562, demonstrates the
    sacramental nature of Order by a reference
    to St. Paul's words, "Admoneo te ut resus-
    cites gratiam Dei quae est in te per imposi-
    tionem manuum mearum."

12. The form in the Anglican rite must not be
    considered to be the *Accipe Spiritum Sanctum*
    alone, "ma con esse si congiunga l'Orazione
    che le precede, e di cui esse sono quasi la
    conclusione. È nella Orazione che si ha
    propriamente la forma sacramentale dell'
    Ordine, secondo l' insegnamento della Scrit-
    tura e della Tradizione." [1]

13. He analyses the rite for the consecration of
    a Bishop and determines that the *Signum* is
    massimamente determinato. The elect is
    presented *to be consecrated* Bishop, and then
    prayer is made that the heavenly grace may
    descend on him so that *as Bishop* in the
    Church, and according to God's institution,
    he may serve faithfully to the glory of
    God's name and the good of the same
    Church.

---

[1] "But with these words is conjoined the Prayer which precedes
them, and of which they are in a sense the conclusion. The sacramental form of Ordination consists properly of Prayer, according to
the teaching of Scripture and of tradition"

44 A ROMAN DIARY AND OTHER DOCUMENTS

14. The concluding words about the *spirit of soberness*, etc., cannot be taken to destroy this determination.

15. If, juxta communem sententiam, the words *Accipe Spiritum Sanctum* alone are sufficient to make a Bishop, much more are they sufficient when determined as in the English rite.

16. He briefly analyses the rite for the ordination of Priests, and shows that it contains the necessary *sign*, namely, imposition of hands with a corresponding form, and this is determined by the concluding words, "Whosesoever sins, etc.," by the preceding prayer, and by the general drift of the rite.

Objections.

17. "The rite was drawn up and introduced by heretics, with an heretical intention, therefore it cannot be valid." Answer: If it contains a sufficient matter and form the intention of the compilers is of no account; for the Arians baptized validly though they used the formula with heretical intention, and St. Thomas (3, 64, 9) says that faith is not necessary to the minister of a Sacrament.

18. "The Anglicans have corrupted the sacramental rite of the Church; therefore they confer no true sacrament." (Summa Th. 3, 60, 7, ad 3.) Answer: They have altered only accidentals, not essentials. By *verba sacramentalia* St. Thomas means the *form* of the Sacrament.

A ROMAN DIARY

Intention of the Minister.

19. It is *not* required that the Minister should intend to produce the *effect* or *end* of the Sacrament. Thus a man who does not believe that a Sacrament confers grace or imprints character may nevertheless validly minister the Sacrament. Quotes Sum. Theol. 3, 64, 9, ad 1, and 10, ad 3 ; also Bellarmine against Tilman and Kemnitz showing that the Council of Trent required not that a man should intend "quod ecclesia intendit, sed quod ecclesia facit."

20. He takes the case of a Bishop saying, " I do not intend to ordain you to be sacrificing priests," and shows that this declaration does not destroy the intention to do what the Church does. " He who simply wishes and intends to ordain a priest, in spite of such a declaration, does in fact ordain him as he is according to the divine power conferred on him—that is to say, with the power of offering the holy Sacrifice." This he defends by the decree of the Holy Office about Baptism conferred with a similar declaration, 18 December, 1872.

21. What *is* necessary? " To constitute ecclesiastical ministers by a sacred rite, and to do what has been done from the beginning of the Christian Society."

22. The expression of this intention is found in the Preface to the Ordinal, and is illustrated by various extracts from the rites.

46 A ROMAN DIARY AND OTHER DOCUMENTS

23. " Conchiudiamo : Le Ordinazioni anglicane, su cui non ha ancora pronunziato giudizio dottrinale la Santa Sede, sono valide per esser fatte da Ministro idoneo, con rito valido, con la intenzione di fare quel che fa la Chiesa." [1]

In an appendix he argues that Julius III ordered Pole to receive those ordained by the Edwardine Ordinal " non servata forma Ecclesiae *consueta.*"

We have also Duchesne's own memoir. He unkindly refers to Gasparri as holding to the Nag's Head Fable in his Tractatus de Sacra Ordinatione.

Here is a gem : " Barlow, pour conformer sa conduite aux idées de son prince, aurait dû, non pas se refuser à l'ordination, mais se la faire conférer par Henri VIII.

" Je regrette que la frivolité des objections m'entraine à des observations aussi peu graves."

Duchesne tells how he used with great effect in the Commission an argument which I supplied a few days ago. Pole, on the receipt of the Brief *Regimini,* must have verified the consecration of all bishops promoted during the Schism, to make sure they had been consecrated *in forma ecclesiæ*, in order that the ordinations they had performed might stand good. In doing this he must have either verified Barlow's consecration, or found that he was not consecrated ; and in the latter case it would certainly have been heard of. Moyes replied that there was no proof that Pole did so. " Then,"

---

[1] "We conclude · The English Ordinations, on which the Holy See has not yet given a doctrinal judgment, are valid by reason of their being effected by a competent Minister, with a valid rite, with the intention of doing what the Church does."

A ROMAN DIARY   47

said Duchesne, "he was a very unfaithful representative of the Pope."

I told Duchesne of Mr. Lunn's suggestion about
the Answers of 1540. He was much struck by it,
and at once noticed that the word *consecrare* is
especially used in the Pontificals in connection with
the anointing. "Consecrentur istae manus," etc.

Ap. 23. Visited the Sœurs de Charité in their
house in the Trastevere maintained by Prince Doria
Pamphili.

Ap. 24. Mgr. Gasparri came to us with questions.
Still Barlow. He wished to establish definitely the
fact that the bishops sit in the House of Lords
according to the order of consecration.

To-day Gasparri saw the Pope, spoke to him of
the help we were rendering and our attitude
generally. The Pope spoke of us as being *at the
door*, "et je vais l'ouvrir à deux battants."[1] The
question is, What does that really mean?

Barnes called. He is wearing the ecclesiastical
habit, but has taken no further steps, and seems to
be awaiting anxiously the result of our Commission.
He had heard gossip about a speech of Lord
Halifax, in which he said, "If an adverse decision
be given, so much for Rome and the hopes of
reunion." This he thought unfortunate language,
as it would go straight to the Pope. It is a
grotesque rendering of Halifax's words, and it is
apparently being put in circulation here.

We visited with Portal two other houses of the
Sœurs de Charité—the Ophthalmic Hospital below
S. Onofrio maintained by Prince Torlonia, and the

[1] Italian was presumably spoken, but the conversation was reported
to us in French.

48 A ROMAN DIARY AND OTHER DOCUMENTS

Children's Hospital, "i Bambini" in the old Convent of S. Onofrio. Also the church, with Tasso's tomb, and a beautiful St. Anne of Pinturicchio, and in the convent a Lionardo.

After dinner I went to the Farnese to restore Duchesne his copies of the Memoirs, and had a long talk with him about the possibilities of the Commission. It seems that the actual decision of the Holy Office in Gordon's case was based not on his own Supplica at all, but on the report of Genetti, or even on a direct examination of the rite. They took the *forma essentialis* to be exclusively the *Accipe Spiritum Sanctum*, and declared this insufficient, on the express ground of its not being a prayer. For this reason Duchesne thinks it is impossible in the Commission to argue in favour of the validity on the ground of this form. Only the prayer which precedes can be treated as the form. In the presbyteral ordination he is himself satisfied that this contains a prayer for the ordinand, but it is slight and obscure : that for the episcopate is beyond challenge. We spoke of the practical difficulty of an affirmative decision as affecting the internal practice of the Roman Church. Duchesne also pointed out the difficulty of deciding dogmatically on the matter and form when the Council of Trent had declined to do so. I suggested that this had been done to all intents and purposes by acknowledging the validity of the Greek rite. He thought a *practical* decision might be come to, saving the actual praxis by requiring conditional reordination,[1] but expressly leaving open the theo-

---

[1] "I cannot understand," he said, "why you should object to this. It is no more than your own St. Chad endured, for the sake of peace."

A ROMAN DIARY 49

logical question. I pressed the danger of any decision, short of an absolute affirmative, which could even be represented to English people as final, and as settling the terms of a future reconciliation. We cannot ever press for reunion if our people are made to think that it would involve even conditional reordination. The utmost that could be made tolerable to our people would be an arrangement by which Anglican priests, wishing to exercise their office within the Roman Church, should have to undergo some sort of *sanatio*.

MM. Fabre and Fournier then arrived, and we drifted into a most animated discussion about the origin and character of the "mouvement centralisateur" of the ninth century, a great deal of which I could not catch. Duchesne seems to think that it was forced on the Popes, Leo IV alone (or with Nicholas I) actually favouring it.

* * * * *

Ap. 25. A letter from Mr. Gladstone sent on from Lord Halifax. Writing wonderfully firm. He will write for the *Revue* an article on the Armenians. M. Portal has seen Cardinal Rampolla again to-day, speaking about Mr. Gladstone among other things.

A priest of the diocese of Lyon, opposite to us at table, who was amazed to see us eating "maigre" yesterday,[1] came in after dinner and was still further astonished. He gave us many particulars of the usages still prevailing at Lyon: e.g. recitation of the *Te igitur* with arms extended *in modum crucis;* the oblation *per unum;* concelebration by five

---

[1] A Rogation Day, not observed with abstinence at Rome.

E

50 A ROMAN DIARY AND OTHER DOCUMENTS

priests, or by a bishop with six priests; position of the subdeacon at the gate of the choir until after the Epistle.

Ap. 26. We dined with the Lazarists at noon. Afterwards with M. Portal to San Teodoro, where was Quarant' ore. The "Sacconi," a noble confraternity attached to the church, were in attendance, covered from head to foot with a sack, having two holes for the eyes.

Mgr. Gasparri came, reporting that Moyes declared the Congé and Assent for Barlow at St. David's were in the Records. Telegraphed to E.G.W. to search.

Ap. 27. In the morning went to the Vatican Gardens with M. de Bossierre, the Bishop of Bayonne and his Grand Vicaire also in the company.

In the afternoon I worked in the Casanatense on Launoy's collection of definitions of the Church.

Afterwards we went to tea with Barnes. Talk quite colourless. After dinner to see the Pearkes at 57 Via Sistina.

In the sitting of the Commission on Saturday N. challenged A.'s statement about the Barlow documents. B. intervened, declaring that he had seen the documents. "You say so?" said N., "Yes." "I believe you," said N. with a little emphasis.[1]

Ap. 28. Father Puller went to a theological lecture at the Minerva with the young Lazarists. I to the Casanatense.

---

[1] This petulance was quite unjustified, as the sequel shows. The documents were found, as noted below, and there was no cause for any reticence about them. I should like to expunge the story, as well as the names, but it would not be fair to suppress evidence of our own suspicious temper

A ROMAN DIARY   51

Afternoon. Duchesne and M. Fabre came. Duchesne afterwards took us to call on Cardinal
Hohenlohe at Sta Maria Maggiore. A most
pleasant old gentleman. The *Revue* was lying on
his table.

Telegram from Wood explaining the mystery
about the Barlow documents. The *Patent Rolls*
contain nothing about Barlow's promotion to
St. David's. The reference given by Moyes is
for St. Asaph. But the *Privy Seals* records contain Congé and Assent for St. David's.[1]

Both of us to the Farnese to see Duchesne and
report on telegram. Fabre and Fournier there.
All agree that the discovery does not much help
Moyes, since the actual *instruments* are missing,
and his argument requires that they should actually be found, and not merely evidence of their
existence.[2]

N. stated and developed the thesis that the
Council of Chalcedon "a fait beaucoup de mal
à l'Église." What is called Monophysitism is,
according to him, only an Oriental way of stating
the truth.

Ap. 29. Visited the Lateran.

Ap. 30. In the morning Gasparri came. We
could not get anything out of him about the effect
of the telegram at the meeting of the Commission
yesterday.

The question now was about the rite. Was it

---

[1] The significance of this last was not yet understood. See
below, May 6th and 12th, and the letter of April 29th to W.H.F.

[2] This was unfair. Canon Moyes' argument required nothing of
the kind. Moreover, the documents in the Privy Seals, though this
we did not understand at the time, to all intents and purposes were
the instruments in question. See below, pp. 153, *seqq.*

52 A ROMAN DIARY AND OTHER DOCUMENTS

true, as recently stated in the *Tablet* by A. G. Clark, that the prayer, "Almighty God, giver of all good things, etc.," in the rite for the consecration of Bishops, was sometimes said by another than the Consecrator? I pointed out that the corresponding prayers in the rites for diaconal and presbyteral ordination since 1662 have been said as the Collect of the Mass, and so of course are said by the ordaining Bishop. Formerly they were said after the Litany, as is still the case in the consecration of a Bishop. In all cases the rubrick directs the Bishop or the Consecrator to say the Litany with this prayer. But is this rubrick adhered to in practice?

Our impression was that in the actual practice, though the Litany is commonly said by a priest, yet the special suffrage and the prayer in question are always said by the ordaining or consecrating Bishop.

It was agreed that we should write to the Archbishop of York, now at Florence, to ask for information as to the existing practice.

Gasparri contends that these prayers are unquestionably sufficient as *forms*, that there is sufficient moral union between them and the imposition of hands, on the ground of the unity of the whole rite as maintained by De Lugo and many others, and that, therefore, if it is certain that they are always said by the proper Minister, there can be no question as to the validity of the rite.

Father Puller wrote to the Archbishop.[1]

M. Portal came with an important letter from Lord Halifax about Mr. Gladstone. Mr. Gladstone

[1] See below, May 8.

A ROMAN DIARY 53

is quite willing under certain conditions, e.g. if asked
to do so, to write a letter either to the Pope or
to any one else, for publication at an opportune
moment. A draft of a letter to the Pope, on which
Lord Halifax and Mr. Gladstone were agreed,[1] was
enclosed. We talked this over. M. Portal thought
he must see Cardinal Rampolla and sound him.
But he would put it that Mr. Gladstone would
certainly do *something:* the only question was
what?

He waited on the Cardinal after Ave Maria, and
returned to us about half-past nine to report. The
Cardinal was keenly interested. It would not
do for Mr. Gladstone to write to the Holy Father a
letter intended for publication, but it would have
a good effect if he would write such a letter to some
one else; Lord Halifax, for example. To the
Abbé's idea of Mr. Gladstone's coming to Rome
he would not commit himself: he must think it
over.

*   *   *   *   *

In the afternoon we went to the new Benedictine
Convent of St. Anselmo on the Aventine, by
appointment with Dom Janssens the Prior, who
showed us all the buildings now nearly completed.
A significant remark fell from him. Talking of the
Abbate Tosti and the bad odour into which he fell
through some injudicious remarks upon the Roman
question, he said, " The relations between the
Vatican and the Government make a very difficult
question." It is plain that he at least regards it as
not a very simple one.

---

[1] This, my impression at the time, was incorrect. [Marginal note
of June 12th, 1896.]

54 A ROMAN DIARY AND OTHER DOCUMENTS

May 1. Father Puller found at the Casanatense the Acts of the Council of Mainz in 1549, in which the matter and form of Order are treated exactly as in the English Ordinal[1] : for a priest the matter being imposition of hands, and the form, "Accipe Spiritum Sanctum, quorum remiseris, etc." Moreover, this is spoken of as occurring at the *beginning* (principio) of the rite.[2]

This is interesting either as (1) having suggested the arrangement in the Ordinal of 1550, or as (2) evidence of contemporaneous opinion.

We went on to Gasparri with the information, and to ask where a copy of a Mainz Pontifical can be found. He could give no information.

In the evening we all went to Duchesne's. He was as amusing as usual. He, too, thinks this Council of Mainz important. He could only suggest the Vatican Library as a place in which to find the Pontifical.

He described the procedure in Commission. The Cardinal President puts questions. Gasparri, being a prelate, speaks first—and generally says all there is to be said. Then come the seculars, then the Jesuit, the Benedictine, and the Franciscans. N.'s mode of arguing, he says, is exactly like that of the Donatists in the great conference at Carthage, which Duchesne—alone probably—has read right through : the same wearisome insistence on trivial points, the same determination never to acknowledge a mistake.

---

[1] It is a curious thing that at the time neither of us remembered reading of this in the *Memoir* of De Augustinis. See above, p. 43. We imagined it to be a new discovery. I am not sure that De Augustinis brought out all the points.

[2] See below, pp 187–92

A ROMAN DIARY

Cardinal Mazzella speaks English perfectly, and Gasparri is the only member of the Commission who cannot read it.

May 2. Father Puller went to the Vatican Library but could not find a Mainz Pontifical. If there is one at all it is in the Palatine Library, which is all in confusion.

Mr. Crowe, correspondent of the *Daily Telegraph* and the *Tablet*, called and found me in with M. Portal, and tried hard to get some matter for an article on the Commission. We told him he might safely say that an entirely adverse decision is impossible,[1] but we had no more information to give.

Called with M. Portal in the afternoon on Mgr. N. Duchesne also appeared. Mgr. N. talked freely about the personnel of the Curia. He had a wild story about the Pope's brother, Cardinal Pecci, having been expelled from the Society of Jesus simply because he insisted on growing his beard. He described very vividly the condition of the Vatican on the night of the Giordano Bruno demonstration : cannon loaded in the Court of S. Damasus, every one in panic, the Pope going to exposition of the Blessed Sacrament in the Sistine Chapel, and saying " There is our artillery." He had much to say about the goodness of Cardinal Galimberti, though he detests his policy—naturally, as being a Frenchman. The Cardinal's health is mending to-day.[2]

---

[1] I do not know whether he used this valuable information. We honestly believed it to be true

[2] Our friends thought, I do not know on what ground, that Cardinal Galimberti would be a mainstay of their cause. He was Prefect of the Congregation for the Reunion of the Churches. Politically, he was understood to favour the triple alliance

56 A ROMAN DIARY AND OTHER DOCUMENTS

May 3. Holy Cross day and Sunday. Went to
the great function of Sta Croce in Gerusalemme.
The Cardinal Vicar celebrating. The great altar
standing in the middle of the transept of the Basilica,
people thronging almost up to it ; most difficult to
find room to kneel down. Picturesque peasants
and little children were skirmishing in front. Round
the apse sat several Trappist monks [1] mostly wearing
chasubles over their habits, some with cotta also.
Two bishops who wore copes and white mitres.
The Cardinal in the throne of the apse, a bishop
in cope assisting at the throne, a prelate in
violet cassock and cotta acting as ceremoniarius.
At the Credence were four servants in livery and
gowns, eight boys in cottas, looked after by two
men also in cottas. The four chaplains—clerk of
the crosier, of the book, of the mitre, and of the
candle, were in red copes. Terce was sung by the
clergy in the apse, the Cardinal wearing his scarlet
cappa clausa and biretta. He was then vested, and
the Mass proceeded. The choir was in a tribune
beside the altar. The effect was most picturesque
when during the Gloria and Credo the Cardinal sat
in his throne, and the four chaplains sat on the
steps below him wrapping their copes about them.
At the offertory three members of some confraternity in strange blue habits offered a candle to the
Cardinal on the throne. One of the small boys
drank of the wine and water before it was offered.
The hand-washings were all served by the livery
servants. At the Sanctus the boys brought torches

---

[1] I think this must be wrong There was once, and may be still,
a Cistercian Convent attached to the Basilica, but probably not of the
reform of La Trappe.

A ROMAN DIARY

and knelt on the nave side of the altar, where the incense also was served. The choir sang the Benedictus actually during the elevation. The whole ceremony lasted over two hours, after which the Cardinal went up to a tribune high in the transept and made ostension of the relics. No attempt was made to fence the people in any way, and the thurifer and others had to push their way through to get to and from the Sacristy, while when the Cardinal and the Ministers retired a narrow lane was made for them to pass through.

Father Puller received a letter from Frere [1] giving account of certain *reordinations* by Bonner, and King of Oxford, in Mary's reign, before the arrival of the Legate. There is no indication in the registers that these are reordinations, but the conclusion is arrived at by noting that the same names appear in the registers as ordained between 1550 and 1553. On the other hand, there are men ordained during these years who retain benefices without any mention made of reordination. Frere is inclined to draw the inference that in some cases reordination was resorted to on the ground of private scruples, but that there was no settled policy.

We determined to place this evidence at once in the hands of Duchesne. M. Portal came with a letter from Lord Halifax, saying that the Bishop of Stepney was sending an account of these matters

---

[1] In reply to one written by him on April 27th about a report which had reached him from Mr Birkbeck He wrote . "If you have discovered facts which prove that Bonner did repudiate Edwardine Orders, we should feel bound to communicate such facts to our friends on the Commission. They have acted so very loyally towards us, that, besides the general obligation of perfect openness in such matters, we are specially bound to be open with them."

58 A ROMAN DIARY AND OTHER DOCUMENTS

to the *Times*. We went to Duchesne's; found him not at home; then on to St. Peter's, where was a baptism. Back to Duchesne's, whom we now found at home, very tired and pining for some mountain or sea air. He took our information very seriously.

May 4. Neither Friday's nor Saturday's *Times* has the Bishop of Stepney's letter. But in the latter is confirmation of the report that the Bishop of Peterborough is to go to Moscow, appointed by the Archbishop of Canterbury with the consent of the Queen, to represent the Church of England at the Czar's Coronation.

We called on Mgr. Gasparri, and gave him a short paper which I have drawn up respecting Frere's information. (i) We have merely identity of *names* in the registers, nothing to show clearly identity of persons. (ii) Some ordained by the Edwardine rite are shown to have retained their benefices, no mention made of reordination; therefore either there were no reordinations, or else different cases were differently treated. (iii) All was done before the coming of the Legate, and by individual Bishops—especially Bonner. But Bonner rehabilitated Scory: therefore he either reordained none, or treated different cases differently.

M. Portal, finding that Gasparri knows Mgr. Agliardi, the special nuncio for the Moscow coronation (they were professors together at the Propaganda), told him about the Bishop of Peterborough's mission, and asked him to speak of it to Mgr. Agliardi; it would be a good thing to bring them together at Moscow.

Cardinal Galimberti in a very serious condition, with little or no prospect of recovery.

A ROMAN DIARY 59

May 5. Morning, I went to the Vatican galleries with the two Pearkes. Afternoon, Father Puller and I to the Colosseum.

May 6. Went to Mass at St. John by the Latin Gate, sung by the Chapter of St. John Lateran, or rather *for* them by a small and very bad choir. Very few people there. The floor of the church was strewn with leaves of box.

After breakfast M. Portal came with important information. The Commission will probably finish its work to-morrow, meeting again only once next week to draw up the *procès-verbal.* They hardly touch at all on the question of intention, merely stating a few general truths. Apparently things have been hurried. All graver considerations are to be reserved for another Commission of Cardinals, either of the Holy Office, or that of the Reunion of the Churches, or a special one appointed *ad hoc.* Nothing is yet known. Mgr. Gasparri is inclined to raise the question of Baptism, some one having described a careless case of *sprinkling* to him as if typical. He will probably have no opportunity of doing this, and will immediately return to Paris. Duchesne, he added, wished to see us.

We went on to the Farnese. Duchesne had much to say. We must on no account leave Rome when the Commission is finished. The report will be submitted in about a fortnight to the Cardinals. Until we know what Cardinals, nothing can be done. He described various Cardinals. Rampolla, "très saint homme," bent on doing all he can to further the Pope's policy, but likely to be influenced theologically by Mazzella. About Mazzella his mouth is shut. He has learnt what he knows in

60 A ROMAN DIARY AND OTHER DOCUMENTS

the Commission, and so can say nothing. Galimberti, alas! is dying. Another—name I forget—might as well die for any good he can do.

* * * * *

They are nearly all of the old school. They will ask what is the *intention of the English Ordinal?* What was the meaning of its compilers? Either heretical opinions or the change of the rite alone would not present much difficulty, but the combination is awkward. We must be on the spot to meet it. After all, a majority of the Cardinals will not decide. It will be not *maior pars*, but *sanior pars.* Of that the Pope will judge himself.

He pressed us to go at once to see Cardinal Mazzella and Father de Augustinis. We stuck at the former, but went to call on the Jesuit. He received us kindly, and was very—Jesuit. He did not at all know why we were in Rome, and when we spoke of the Commission seemed doubtful as to what commission we meant. However we forced the subject, and he talked a little, but to little purpose. He could not understand why so much is made of a secondary question ; the main question, after all, is that of the authority of the Pope. Yes, I said, but secondary questions often bar the way to the consideration of primary ones. Until the question of Orders is out of the way we can hardly get our people even to listen to talk about reunion.

M. Portal went to Cardinal Rampolla, got from him a definite expression of a wish for a letter from Mr. Gladstone, told him about the mission of the Bishop of Peterborough to Moscow and the

A ROMAN DIARY   61

probable mission of certain Russian Bishops to the Lambeth Conference next year. The Cardinal asked very kindly after us, and wanted to know if we had produced any documents, a question which enabled M. Portal to enlarge on our prompt production of some *adverse* evidence, with which he was much impressed.

After dinner a great surprise. A telegram from E. G. Wood, saying that he has found the *mandate to consecrate Barlow*.[1] We all went straight off to Duchesne with the telegram for him to produce at the Commission to-morrow. The question is, Where has it been found? If in the Privy Seals, did Moyes know of it, and is that the reason why he was so unwilling to give the reference to the Privy Seals for the Congé and Assent?[2]

May 7. By the first post came a copy of the Bishop of Stepney's letter to the *Times*, under cover of one from Collins. The Bishop had written about it to Cardinal Vaughan, who at once asked for a copy, which was sent him.

*   *   *   *   *

I at once took it to N., whom I found at work since five o'clock preparing his *votum*. Parts of this he read to me. He also asked for particulars of what the Bishop of Peterborough had said about Elizabeth's reply concerning the Council of Trent, and I gave him them from memory.[3]

By the next post came a letter from Frere stating

---

[1] See below, May 12th, and *Letter* of May 8th

[2] I am sorry to put on record this imputation of bad faith, for which there was not the smallest foundation, but as a matter of fact some of us did talk so, and I must not falsify the record. See above, April 27.

[3] See Letter from W H. F., May 11th, and note.

62 A ROMAN DIARY AND OTHER DOCUMENTS

that the Literae certificatoriae about Consecrations are preserved in the Privy Seals and Signed Bills, and calendared in the Domestic State Papers; but they are very imperfect. E.g. Repps' consecration is thus recorded, but the letter about Sampson is wanting. Sent this on to Gasparri at the Vatican while the Commission was actually sitting.

In the afternoon we visited Sta Maria in Trastevere, Sta Cecilia and S. Bartolomeo in Insula. At S. Cecilia we saw the caldarium and the stone of the martyrdom, but could not look at the shrine of the high altar as Quarant' ore was going on.

The Commission has held its last meeting. At present we have to wait and see to what Cardinals the matter will be referred. Portal has seen Cardinal Vincenzo Vannutelli to-day, and arranged for us to go and call upon him.

Frere writes that he has a conviction, growing stronger as he works out the evidence, "that in the first blush of Marian revulsion they were inclined to dispute the orders of the English Ordinal," but he is coming to suspect more and more, and hopes to prove, "that this doubt was a steadily diminishing quantity: possibly even that the influence of Pole or even Rome was exerted against it, and that the reordinations which prevailed in the early months were afterwards discouraged."[1]

May 8. Called on Mr. Oxenham, and met there Mr. Bliss, who is working for the English Government in the Archives of the Vatican.

Cardinal Galimberti dead.

Duchesne saw Cardinal Rampolla, who expressed a wish that we should stay in Rome for the present,

[1] See his final conclusions in his book, *The Marian Reaction*

A ROMAN DIARY 63

and hold ourselves in readiness to give information to the Commission of Cardinals which is now appointed. He also wishes us to wait upon him, but before this to see some other Cardinals also. Duchesne suggests the two Vannutelli, Mazzella, and Segna. Letter from the Archbishop of York, who is at Florence, giving assurance that the prayer after the Litany in the Consecration of Bishops is, by the unvarying use of both provinces, said by the Archbishop himself.

May 9. Finished my article *de Unitate*.[1] In the afternoon we called with Portal on Cardinal Vincenzo Vannutelli in Via Giulia. He received us rather effusively. Portal knew him when he was nuncio at Lisbon. He gesticulates extraordinarily in talking. He told us that he is on the Commission : that means that it is a *special* Commission, unless perhaps he has replaced Galimberti on the Commission for Reunion. He had not much to say except in laudation of the English people and the great part we have to play in the work of civilization. We talked a little about the relations of Anglicans and Romans at Zanzibar—Smythies consulting the Roman Bishop about his Swahili Catechism, and so on. He said we might certainly call on his brother Cardinal Serafino Vannutelli.

[1] The first part of this appeared in the *Revue Anglo-Romaine*, Vol. II, p. 529. The second and much longer part should have followed, but was suppressed in consequence of the publication of the encyclical *Satis cognitum*. It was suggested to M. Portal from a high quarter that he could not decently publish it immediately after the utterance of the Pope on the same subject. The whole was afterwards translated into English, and appeared under the title *The Unity of the Church as Taught by English Theologians*, being published by S.P.C.K. for the Church History Society.

64 A ROMAN DIARY AND OTHER DOCUMENTS

Telegraphed for copies of *de Hierarchia* to present to Cardinals.

May 10. *Sunday.* Went to High Mass at St. Peter's. Music good. Behaviour of crowd atrocious.

Sketched out with N. the plan of a Supplement to the *de Hierarchia,* dealing with the points in which the Cardinals are interested.

In the afternoon we called on Duchesne. The Abbé Daniel was there, Recteur of Dinant in Brittany. He was well acquainted with N. of P. before his fall, and we talked much about that. With Duchesne we had a long talk about the primitive arrangements of the Roman Church, as illustrated by the Canons of Hippolytus. He thinks that originally, when the Roman Church was the only Church for Italy, there probably was a Presbyterium consisting partly of bishops, partly of priests, or that possibly all the priests had episcopal powers ; and that a similar arrangement prevailed at Alexandria, of which the well-known passage of St. Jerome expresses a tradition.

May 11. Began the Supplement and worked hard at it all day.

May 12. Letter from Wood enclosing documents. The Mandate to Consecrate is what is usually known as the Royal Assent : but a full explanation of the whole process of issuing Letters Patent shows that this is the original Sign Manual which set the whole thing in motion, and that the king gave this order only, which was afterwards expanded in the routine of the office to the usual form.[1]

---

[1] See below, pp. 153–68.

A ROMAN DIARY 65

Father Puller and I called on Cardinal Segna, who was exceedingly pleasant, talking very frankly about our subject, and stating various objections which I noted for the Supplement. He lives in a very humble apartment, 102 Ripetta. He is just going to preside over the General Chapter of the Capuchins.

Worked hard at the Supplement. Also prepared a letter about the Mandate to be printed for Cardinal Mazzella.

May 13. Worked hard at the Supplement all day. The Abbé Zorn de Bulach came to dinner; he is brother to two ladies staying here; is attached to the Accademia Ecclesiastica, and works in the Congregation of the Council. A friend of Merry del Val. He seemed to know nothing about our question beyond the merest gossip.[1] Went to the Archives.

May 14. *Ascension Day.* Father Puller and I called in the morning on Cardinal Mazzella at the German College, giving him the Archbishop of York's letter, and a passage from Pilkington received this morning from Mr. Ross-Lewin to the effect that the Edwardine priests were reconciled in Mary's time by unction only.[2] He was stiff and grumpy, but speaking English seemed to express himself with great difficulty. He could not think why so much fuss was made about Orders. The *Pope* was the great question.

---

[1] He had very edifying views about Julius II; explained that he was converted after his election to the Papacy, and thenceforward said Mass every day. I asked whether he did so on the day of the storming of Mirandola, but of this event the abbé appeared to know nothing.

[2] See below, Letter of May 15th.

F

66 A ROMAN DIARY AND OTHER DOCUMENTS

Worked all day, and much of the night, at the Supplement.

May 15. Father Puller called on Cardinal Serafino Vannutelli—one of the most *papabili*—and found him most pleasant. He has to do with the question, but confesses himself sadly ignorant of English affairs.

Finished the Supplement[1]—about sixty hours' work since Sunday.

Portal at once charged me with a new pamphlet —suggested by the ignorance of Cardinal Vannutelli—a brief outline of the present state of the Church of England, with a clear explanation of *parties.* This to be finished before Monday.

May 16. Worked hard all day at the new pamphlet.

*　　*　　*　　*　　*

May 17. Heard a prône for the first time in Rome; at the Church of the Holy Apostles, at eight o'clock. Very few people attending.[2]

Dined with Mr. Nancrede at the Hotel d'Allemagne. Miss Patteson (sister of the Bishop of Melanesia) there. Miss Nancrede, a fixture in Rome, had much to say about identifications of Marion Crawford's characters generally recognized in society. E.g. Corona, a certain Vittoria Colonna (Duchessa di Sermoneta?), Astrardente, one of the

---

[1] *Dissertationis Apologeticae de Hierarchia Anglicana Supplementum,* auctore T A Lacey. Romae, ex typographia Pacis, Philippi Cuggiani, 1896

[2] I had told Portal that I wanted to attend a parochial service. "Il n'y a pas d'offices paroissiales à Rome," he replied. A Roman gentleman explained that the one function of a *parochus* in Rome was to give faculties for other priests to celebrate marriages. This was probably morose.

A ROMAN DIARY
67

Principi Orsini lately dead; Spicca, an attaché at the Russian Embassy; Ghisleri, Crawford himself!

Finished the new pamphlet, or rather memoir, *de Re Anglicana*,[1] in the small hours—a week's work over the two, not much, if any, less than ninety hours.

May 18. At 8.20 left for Monte Cassino. Arrived Cassino 11.15. Déjeuner at albergo in town, which is a queer tangle of dirty houses, the streets all paved with flagstones. In church a seated figure of St. Germanus, robed in silk cope and mitre. Walked up to the Monastery, an hour and a quarter. The Prior, Dom Amelli, showed us the archives and several manuscripts, one having some writing by St. Thomas in the margin. The Convent, he explained, is suppressed, but the monks go on as Canons of the Church, which is regarded as Cathedral of the Abbot's diocese. The best of the printed books of the library have been taken away by the Government. The Archives and Manuscripts remain as national monuments, of which the monks are custodians. So also is the whole building. They can alter nothing, or even repair, without leave. They cannot take a book out of what remains of the library without a permission. For whatever land they have in hand they pay rent. They are, however, forming a new private library—about 30,000 volumes so far—very casually made up, mostly by gifts. Here, too, they have their printing shop.

Supper in the refectory at 8—soup, eggs, cheese, fruit. Compline 8.45 in the Tower of St. Benedict,

[1] Below, pp. 195-209.

68 A ROMAN DIARY AND OTHER DOCUMENTS

sc. in the chapel where he died, this being the anniversary of its dedication.

May 19. Mass in the same chapel, where all the offices are said this week. Coffee and roll afterwards in a room off the kitchen, where these are served every morning for those who desire it. Dinner in refectory at 12. Soup, two dishes of flesh meat, cheese, and *raw beans.* Dom Dunstan Sibley from Fort Augustus showed us everything, and was very attentive. They have a diocesan seminary, a general seminary, a *petit séminaire,* and a school for lay boys. Monks are at the head of all departments, but there are some twenty secular priests as well engaged in tuition.

In the evening we went to see the Abbate Tosti, who is very feeble and palsied. He has permission to say Mass in his cell *seated.* He talked enthusiastically of the Bishop of Brechin, and preached us quite a sermon on the duty of submission to the Pope.

Nightingale singing all night.

May 20. Up at half-past four to attend Mattins in the Tower—Nocturns and Lauds. Prime and Terce are said before Mass at 7.45. Between these two offices the monks all say their Mass. To-day, however, a Black Mass was sung in the Basilica at 8—the Office of the Dead preceding, and Prime and Terce followed, whether with another Mass I did not hear, in the Tower. The monks sang the Mass in their choir behind the high altar very devoutly. They can see practically nothing of the priest at the altar.

At 9 left the monastery, Dom Dunstan walking halfway down the hill with us. Train at 10.40, arriving in Rome 1.30.

A ROMAN DIARY

Found proofs to correct.

May 21. Worked several hours with Portal revising for *Revue*.

May 22. Visited Sta Agnese in Piazza Navona, or Circo Agonale, and saw the vaults, formerly substructure of the Circus, where the child was exposed to shame.

Prepared statistical appendix to memoir, *de Re Anglicana*.

Visited Sta Agnese fuori le Mure. Part of the church was rebuilt by "Jul. Card. S.P. ad Vinc. Sixti iiii Pont. Max. nepos"—one of his few good works. Baldaquin, built by Paul V, makes a curious narrow front to the altar. The throne is in the apse, but the altar is placed with back towards it. Visited also Sta Costanza, close by.

Evening, 8 o'clock, called on Cardinal Parocchi at the Palazzo del Vicariato. More than an hour in antechamber. Saw him in a room with a big table arranged as for committees. He was extraordinarily kind. Gave him a copy of *de Hierarchia*, which he apparently had not seen. He pressed us to come again. Expressed a great admiration for England, and acknowledged that such a country, with such a history, must have ecclesiastically a considerable provincial independence.

May 23. To the Lateran for the great function. The Offices were sung up to None in the Chapel of the Choir. Then the Canons and Singers went to the choir before the apse, where an altar was dressed before the throne. The *Patriarch of Antioch*, Mgr. Casetta, who is vicegerent of the Cardinal Vicar (odd arrangement) officiated. The assistants wore chasubles cut away just below the waist in

70 A ROMAN DIARY AND OTHER DOCUMENTS

front, full-length behind. The Prophecies were sung from a lectern in the middle, the Patriarch sitting on the Faldstool before the Altar and rising to say the Collects. He was then vested in cope, and all went in procession by the long corridor to the Baptistery, singing the psalm *Quemadmodum.* Then came the blessing of the font, all the clergy standing round the inner part of the Baptistery, i.e. the ancient piscina. The procession, singing the Litany, returned by the corridor on the other side of the Apse, and Mass was sung. Three hours altogether.

In the afternoon Scannell called, a priest of the English College accompanying him. He explained that he had been keeping out of our way because of the fashion he was spied upon. He spoke as if he were certain there would be a negative decision of the question. It was impossible, said Portal. " C'est l'impossible qui arrive," said Scannell. Still he was very friendly and pleasant, and appears to be much disgusted with the *Tablet.*

May 24. *Whitsunday.* I went to S. Nicola da Tolentino at eight o'clock and heard the Armenians sing their Office.[1] Two seniors in black, the juniors some in red gowns with blue yokes, others in blue with red yokes. At last one of the seniors was vested in a sort of cope, with red and white perpendicular stripes, and went to the lectern accompanied by two candles. At this point I had to leave.

Then to S. Clemente ; where the Mass was exquisitely sung by seven or eight Dominican fathers : the priest behind the Altar, the Gospel

---

[1] A College of Armenians in communion with Rome has for some time enjoyed the use of this church.

A ROMAN DIARY 71

sung from the Ambon. Benedictus immediately
after Sanctus. Then perfect silence until the end
of the Canon, the Fathers all in prostration. They
bow from the waist on entering and leaving, and
during all the Collects. The priest sat for the
Epistle, reading from a book held before him ; stood
throughout Gloria and Credo. Oblation per unum,
and *Unde et memores* said brachiis extensis in
modum crucis. Afterwards a delightful Irish lad,
a lay brother, showed us the lower church [1]

Afternoon. Portal came full of news. Letter from
Lord Halifax enclosing a copy of one he has written
to Cardinal Rampolla respecting a memoir by Mr.
Gladstone,[2] which we are to translate into French
and give to the Cardinal.

Duchesne has been offered an honorary Doctorate
by Cambridge.

We went on to the Farnese. M. Fabre there and
le père Lapôtre.

*　　*　　*　　*　　*

Father Puller drew them into a talk about vernacular services, and all were in favour of saying
the Mass in the vulgar tongue, N. also in favour
of saying the Canon aloud. He would also like

[1] He told with perfect simplicity and humanity the story, depicted
in a fresco of the tenth century, of the mother recovering her child
from the chapel beneath the sea   "That is a beautiful story," I said
"There's not many believes it, sor," he replied sadly.   I heard Puller
murmuring something about "evidence," but I dug my elbow into his
side to silence the historic conscience, and so we left the boy happy
in our acceptance of the legend   After Mass, the sacred ministers
came down from the altar and sat on a bench between the ambones,
while *Veni Creator* was sung. ·One of us made some remark about
this unusual ceremony, and the boy exclaimed enthusiastically, "Yes,
just like the Apostles on the day of Pentecost !" *O sancta simplicitas!*

[2] Addressed to the Archbishop of York. For the text, see below,
pp. 139-49.

72 A ROMAN DIARY AND OTHER DOCUMENTS

to have the task of reforming the Breviary. He would do away with all the arrangements of hours, responses, etc., for private recitation, leaving them intact for common recitation. For private recitation he would appoint simply so many psalms each day, and lessons from the New Testament. He thought there was a great deal of the Old Testament not worth reading. He could undertake the task in one year if alone : if he had one colleague it would take three years; if ten colleagues, a century.

May 25. A good deal of work over Mr. Gladstone's letter. Complete holiday in the city. Crowds of peasants and others driving about in carriages. The holiday delays publication of our pamphlets.

May 26. Feast of St. Philip Neri : more complete holiday even than yesterday. Called on Nancrede in the afternoon. At night went to the Quarant' ore at St. Peter's. Wonderful effect of about a hundred candles on the high altar ; no other lights in the church except an odd candle standing here and there on a high standard.

May 27. Mr. Gladstone's letter finished, and taken by Portal to Cardinal Rampolla, who was delighted with it. *De Re Anglicana* came from the printer finished. At night Mr. Turton (New Zealander) and I went to the Colosseum by moonlight.

May 28. Breakfast with M. Duchesne, who has decided to come to Cambridge. Père Delehaye, the Bollandist, there : also Père Rivière, Jesuit—who is writing a history of the Society—M. Fabre, M. Portal, and two laymen.

Duchesne let out that the Description of the Rites

A ROMAN DIARY 73

by Pole was *not* before the Commission. He thinks the evidence of its having been before Julius III is of great importance.[1]

Evening. I went to call on the Cardinal Vicar with copies of the pamphlets, but was too late.

May 29. Visited the Lateran Museum under Duchesne's guidance.[2] I was too tired to enjoy it much. Finished revising my article on Unity for the *Revue*—a tremendous task—and on Portal's advice substituted a new ending, glancing at the Vatican Council, and avowing that the *Pastor Æternus* is no insuperable bar to union.

Evening. I called on the Cardinal Vicar. I spoke pretty fully of the state of things in England; he asked particularly if it were certain that *we* can get behind the prejudices of the people and bring them on gradually to Catholic truth. He did not actually make the comparison, but obviously meant to ask if we can do it more effectually than the Romanists. I illustrated the progress made by showing that it is easy now to speak in public about reunion and about the Holy See in a way which would have been impossible twenty years ago. Portal describes the Cardinal Vicar as very intelligent, very pious, but thoroughly suspicious of the reunion movement. He could not keep me long, as he had several people to see, and the Ordinations to-morrow; but he asked me to call on him again before leaving Rome.

---

[1] See below, pp. 177-81. I do not seem to have noted in the Diary my work on this in the Archives, or the aid rendered by Mr. Bliss, which ought to be acknowledged here.

[2] Duchesne stood rapt in admiration before one of the immense canvasses painted on commission for Pius IX At last he gave forth his criticism : "C'est un beau cadre."

74 A ROMAN DIARY AND OTHER DOCUMENTS

May 30. Father Puller went to the Ordinations at St. John Lateran. Began at seven o'clock. Ended at 12.5.

I went round, leaving cards and pamphlets on all the Cardinals in Rome.

May 31. *Trinity Sunday*. Heard the Armenian Mass at S. Nicola da Tolentino. The clerks in red or blue, as last Sunday, stood in semicircle before the altar. Priest in white cope, with square standing collar and white silk embroidered cap, entered with deacon and subdeacon in red silk tunics, the deacon bearing the censer, preceded by two candles and two *jangles*, circles of little bells on the top of staves. Arrived at the altar, the priest censed the altar, and turning round censed also each clerk in the semicircle. The normal position of deacon and subdeacon was at the ends of the semicircle ; the candle-bearers took their place in the semicircle, vested like the others, the jangle-bearers at each end of the altar, where they jangled incessantly. After the censing the priest blessed all with a crucifix, a ceremony incessantly repeated. Then a red curtain was drawn across, between the clerks and the ministers of the altar, for a short time. The singing went on without a break.

The curtain withdrawn, one clerk out of the semicircle read a lesson. Then the deacon took the book of the gospels from a table on the gospel side of the sanctuary, where were also the sacred vessels and four candles burning. With the book he passed behind the altar, candle-bearers and jangles preceding, and the subdeacon with the incense accompanying. They came round the

A ROMAN DIARY

altar, and the deacon mounted to it at the gospel corner, where he sang the gospel facing round[1] the church, the priest standing by him and the subdeacon serving the incense below, the candle-bearers standing by the book.

After the Gospel much singing. Then the deacon took the sacred vessels, just as he had taken the Gospel book, round the altar. They were covered with a veil of gauze, jewelled. The priest received them, held them above his head, and then placed them on the altar; then rinsed his fingers. He then censed the oblations. Much singing followed, the deacon now standing behind the priest censing, and from time to time turning round and censing each of the clerks in the semicircle. The subdeacon sang all the time. Presently, as the canon proceeded, the subdeacon joined the deacon behind the priest, the candle-bearers stood on either side of them, and the jangle-bearers beyond, making a line of six. Then all knelt, singing the whole time, the priest's voice being occasionally heard. The actual consecration was *sung* by the priest. After the consecration of the host a long *amen* was sung by the deacon or subdeacon, repeated by the chorus. The priest genuflected. (N.B.—He said the *first* part of the canon brachiis extensis in modum crucis). After the consecration of the cup all rose at once, the priest genuflecting, and the singing was resumed: the deacon as before censing the altar and the choir incessantly. After some time the priest turned round holding chalice and host, and chanted several verses, the rest responding; during this all knelt. Then a white

---

[1] *Sic.* I suppose I must have meant *down.*

76 A ROMAN DIARY AND OTHER DOCUMENTS

curtain was drawn across, some of the chorus being within it. Presently it was withdrawn, and the priest had now put on his cap again. (It was taken off and laid on the altar at the Offertory.) He blessed, and then turning round read a good deal from a book held by two clerks : and so all departed. Afterwards a person in lay clothes, who had been assisting at the Mass in the nave, went up to the altar and in a very unceremonious way bustled the sacred vessels off to the credence and put out the candles. The Sacrament is reserved on the high altar, but no one takes any notice of it.

June 1. Called on Cardinal Serafino Vannutelli (34 Via di Monte Giordano). He was just back from Frascati and had not yet read the pamphlets. He was keenly interested in Mr. Gladstone's letter ; he had read about it in the *Univers ;* was it true? I asked him directly whether he was seised of our question. He said, not yet, but he expected to be so shortly : meanwhile he thought it was in the hands of some consultors. My interview was shortened by the announcement of a lady who was starting for Bologna in the morning. I went on to Cardinal Vincenzo Vannutelli (147 Via Giulia). He had read the pamphlets and found them clear. I would rather have had a request for explanation than the compliment. I spoke about Mr. Gladstone's letter. It was pretty obvious from his manner that he had seen it, but he too asked for information about it. He thought we ought not to leave Rome yet. I tried to find out why, but without success. I asked him if he could tell me what is the actual state of affairs. He told me that so far as he knew Cardinal Mazzella had presented his report to the Holy

A ROMAN DIARY 77

Father, who since then had spoken not a word about it to any one ; but he thought—emphasizing this as a mere personal impression—that the Pope might perhaps take occasion from Mr. Gladstone's letter to put something out of his own motion. My interview was shortened by the announcement of a lady who is leaving to-morrow for Bologna! Afterwards I went to the Cardinal Vicar, who saw M. Portal before me. As soon as I got into the room be burst out about some new discovery to the effect that St. Pius V had withdrawn, or wished to withdraw, the Bull *Regnans in excelsis*, but it had passed too soon into promulgation. We ought to work at this in the Archives, where we should find evidence, he said, of the friendliness of the Roman authorities of that time for Elizabeth. It was the same with Sixtus V, who detested the ecclesiastical policy of Philip.[1] This, he thought, when published, would deeply impress minds in England. He spoke warmly of the loyauté de soldat of the Archbishop of York.

[1] By the Cardinal's advice we called on the Jesuit, Padre Carini, who gave us a pamphlet which he had written on the subject *Monsignor Niccolò Ormaneto, Veronese, Vescovo di Padova, Nunzio Apostolico alla Corte di Filippo II Re di Spagna, 1572–1577* The revelation does not amount to much. Ormaneto, who had been in England with Pole, was so conscious of the difficulties hindering the proposed war against Elizabeth, so disgusted with the King of France for inviting her to be sponsor to his daughter in baptism, and with the Duke of Alva for making a treaty with her, that he was disposed to fall back upon the alternative plan of converting the Queen instead of deposing her. This seemed almost impossible, in view of her bad character and that of her principal minister, "sed apud Deum omnia possibilia" All this is detailed in his correspondence with the Cardinal Secretary of State, where he also explains that Pius V had been conscious of his mistake in publishing the Bull of Excommunication and Deposition. "Parlandone sua St^à dopo il fatto, volendo che si rimediasse a certi disordini che erano stati per occasione di quella bolla privatoria, la quale non si doveva mai pubblicare se nò quando andava l'esercito

78 A ROMAN DIARY AND OTHER DOCUMENTS

He also asked with considerable emphasis whether *we* could get behind the prejudices of the English people, and so draw them on to the Catholic Faith. He did not actually draw a comparison with others, which was, however, pretty obvious.[1] He blessed me most affectionately on dismissing me.

June 2. Visited the Palatine with Father Puller, also the Ara Coeli. Evening, dined with Oxenham.

June 3. Times of Monday arrived with Mr. Gladstone's memoir and short note by the Archbishop of York. We passed this on to the Voce della Verita.

June 4. Mgr. Guthlin (Lucius Lector),[2] talking with Mgr. Thomas, reported a conversation with Cardinal Steinhuber about the *de Re Anglicana.* "Look at these statistics," he said, "they are most remarkable. All these religious, and these retreats. Of course we cannot say at once that their orders are valid, but something will have to be done."

Later in the day we all called on Mgr. Guthlin. He is canonist to the French Embassy : he

---

in Inghilterra per far quella impresa, talchè in una mano si portassero le chiavi di S. Pietro, che era la privatione, et nel' altra la spada di S. Paolo, perchè l'essersi pubblicata la bolla privatoria senza far la conquista del Regno ha causato gran male, et la morte di molti huomini cat^{ci} et fatta quella Donna molto maggiore nimica della Sede Ap^{ca}." That is to say, the Bull should not have been published until there was a Spanish army well placed in England. The most interesting part of the record is the admission that the sufferings of the English Papists were a consequence of the Bull, Elizabeth having turned upon them in self-defence.

[1] His persistence in recurring to this theme was remarkable. See above, May 29th. I remember that he also talked much about the *Life of Cardinal Manning,* then recently published

[2] Author of *Le Conclave.*

A ROMAN DIARY

repeated his conversation with Cardinal Steinhüber in great detail.

We afterwards went to S. Maria in Capella to assist at the Procession of the Blessed Sacrament, which goes round the garden of the Convent, Benediction being given at two improvised altars. In the late evening I called on M. Duchesne. Mgr. Guthlin had been talking to him also about the remarks of Cardinal Steinhüber, which he thinks very significant.

He asked about the mission of the Bishop of Peterborough to Moscow: was he attached to the extraordinary embassy? I explained the circumstances, including the unwillingness of the Queen to give her consent. He and M. Fabre consider that the most interesting feature of the proceeding is the action of the Church apart from, but in perfect good understanding with the civil power.

This has been a remarkable Fête Dieu. For the first time since 1870 there have been processions of the Blessed Sacrament in the streets. This morning Duchesne himself carried it from a little church near the Farnese into the Piazza Farnese. In the afternoon was another procession in the Piazza di Spagna. There was no difficulty at all with the authorities or with the people. Duchesne puts together this, and the Mass the other day at the Ara Coeli,[1] and the speech made by the Marchese di Rudini in the Chamber on Tuesday in reference to the Pope's intervention with Menelik about the

[1] A Mass of Requiem for those killed in the disastrous Abyssinian campaign, which was attended by the King, the members of the Legislature, and the Roman municipality.

80 A ROMAN DIARY AND OTHER DOCUMENTS

prisoners, as three serious indications of the approach of a better state of things.

June 5. Called on Cardinal Segna, but got nothing out of him, except pious generalities. He seems to be very much at a loss to know why he was made Cardinal. When I tried to engage him more closely on the question of the day his French suddenly became very deficient.[1]

Afternoon, called on Cardinal Steinhüber. Found him extremely pleasant, but in no way encouraging. He had read the pamphlets with great interest, and was of course interested in Mr. Gladstone ; a confrère in the Society, Father Porter, Archbishop of Bombay, had often told him that he was sure Mr. Gladstone would die in the Catholic Church.

June 6. Father Puller called on Cardinal Serafino Vannutelli, who told him that a commission of Cardinals was forthwith to take up the question of the Ordinations. He would receive the dossier on Monday, and the first meeting would be on Wednesday or Thursday. Father Puller asked him directly whether it was a special Commission or the Holy Office. He replied, "I am on this Commission : I am also in the Holy Office." Father Puller concluded from his manner that it was *not* the Holy Office.

---

[1] I must have been in a very bad temper to make these slighting remarks on Cardinal Segna. His erudition, old-fashioned though it was, his kindliness, and his simplicity, ought to have made it impossible so to speak of him. I remember his words : " Le Saint Père m'a fait Cardinal, je ne sais pas pourquoi " ; and I do not know how they could be taken for anything but an expression of genuine humility. Others could tell why he was made Cardinal. His repeated courtesy to friends whom I afterwards commended to him, and notably to the late Mr. David Greig, in whom he found a kindred spirit, shames me into making this most inadequate apology.

A ROMAN DIARY   81

June 5. Forgot to mention that this morning we assisted at Mass in the crypt at St. Peter's, celebrated by M. Portal; seven Sisters of Charity from S. Onofrio also assisted.

June 7. Heard the Pope's Mass in the private chapel of the apartment at 8 o'clock. Afterwards two parties had private audience, but the Pope being very fatigued we did not manage to secure one. He came into the outer room and blessed us all, " For you and for your families."

Portal called on Cardinal Serafino Vannutelli, who told him that the instruction to the Commission was to study the documents for a month. He said among other things that we had made a good impression; we have made it evident that the question is a serious one. They are much struck by the absence of timidity or supplication in our manner. I suppose there is no "drop-down-deadativeness."

Afternoon, we called at the Farnese, and went on with Duchesne and M. Fabre to the Procession at Casa Torlonia, in which we joined.

June 8. Called in the morning on the Superior of the Sulpicians to say goodbye. Afterwards to the Vatican to see Cardinal Rampolla by appointment at one o'clock. Congregations were just breaking up. Cardinals Serafino Vannutelli, Segna, and Steinhuber met us in the antechamber and greeted us warmly. Father Puller and I went in first to the Cardinal. He was curiously nervous in manner, but most encouraging. He sent a message for Mr. Gladstone direct from the Holy Father, that he was much touched by the expressions used in the memoir. He said with great emphasis, " Le

G

82 A ROMAN DIARY AND OTHER DOCUMENTS

Saint Père s'est occupé beaucoup lui-même de votre question, et vous pourrez vous assurer qu'il la traitera avec la plus parfaite impartialité. Il ne cherche que la vérité, mais avec le plus possible de la charité." He repeated this several times, and added, "Voilà en deux mots notre politique." We got to the subject of Mr. Gladstone's work on Butler, and he then spoke in Mr. Gladstone's own words of the necessity of combination against unbelief.

Father Puller then left for Milan. Portal and I called at the Farnese, and afterwards at S. Maria in Capella.

Returning to the Pension we found Mgr. Marini, Substitute of the Rota, waiting for us. He is launching a review in connection with the movement for the reunion of the Eastern churches, of which he is going to print at once 10,000 copies; the inference is that he has very influential backing. He wants our co-operation.

We afterwards drove round the Villa Borghese, and after dining left Rome at 10.20 for Pisa and Genoa.

June 9. Soon after sunrise got a very good view of Pisa from the train; Duomo, Baptistery and Campanile, as well as of the river. It rained hard all day, and we got hardly any views of the Alps, but there was much fresh snow.

June 10. Arrived at Paris soon after seven and drove straight to the Lazarists. Afterwards called on M. Levé, the printer of the *Monde* and of the *Revue Anglo-Romaine.* He is terribly crippled with gout; a most pious and edifying man. Then to the Institut Catholique, which is installed in the

A ROMAN DIARY 83

old Carmelite Convent, where the massacres of September began. Saw Mgr. Gasparri, and with him called on Mgr. d'Hulst, the rector of the Institut. Talked with him of our doings in Rome, and of English affairs generally, presenting him with a copy of *de Re Anglicana*. He was much struck by the suggestion that the Irish are the great hindrance to the acceptance of Catholic teaching by the English,[1] and turning to Gasparri, said, "Like the Poles in Russia." We called also on M. Arthur Loth at the office of *La Vérité*, and on M. Tavernier at the office of *l'Univers*. The latter had just received from his correspondent[2] a telegram warning him not to be too keen in support of Portal. That means, they agreed, that some one is preparing a blow for Portal. We also called on l'Abbé Klein, but did not find him at home.

June 11. At the Community Mass at the Lazarists seven seminarists communicated, and also several lay folk. The normal thing on week-days, I was assured. M. Boudinhon came up from the country to-day to see me—a most cheery, jovial man. We read my *Supplementum* together, and he was keenly interested in the Council of Mainz, and in the description of the Ordinal by Pole. We then talked about the coming Encyclical.[3] Gasparri had a long interview with the Pope about it before leaving Rome, and had described what was coming to M. Boudinhon. The object of the Pope is to settle the question as to

---

[1] He had gathered this from the *Life of Manning*, and asked me whether it was true.

[2] *Sic.* I do not remember the particulars.

[3] The Apostolic Letter *Satis Cognitum*, of which I had already heard something from Mgr. Gasparri in Rome.

84 A ROMAN DIARY AND OTHER DOCUMENTS

the difference of *unicitas* and *unitas*, showing that the *Ecclesia una* is not numerically the same as the *Ecclesia unica*. This is important, as it will justify M. Boudinhon's theory about schism,[1] as not cutting off from the Church absolutely, but as depriving the schismatics of the legitimate exercise of their functions.

The Abbé Klein also called to see me. He was very pleasant, avoiding delicate ground, and asked me to find him an "installation" at Cambridge for himself and a pupil at the summer meeting.

A. and B. also called to see me. Left Paris at 9 o'clock, evening.

Got the *Monde* for to-morrow, containing a very remarkable communication from the Roman correspondent. He speaks of our hearing the Pope's Mass last Sunday, with comments which could hardly have been inspired by any one but Cardinal Rampolla. He adds that the Pope will shortly have ready an utterance on the Anglican question, which will *not* be a reply to Mr. Gladstone, as it was begun before Mr. Gladstone's letter appeared.

June 12. Arrived Holborn Viaduct 6 a.m. Went up to Highgate. Afterwards called on Lord Halifax, and stayed to dine with him.

---

[1] For which see his articles, *Primauté, Schisme et Juridiction*, in the *Revue Anglo-Romaine*, Tome II, pp. 97–107, and 160-71.

LETTERS

III

LETTERS

M. Portal to T. A. L.

19 *mars*, 1896.

MGR. GASPARRI est parti pour Rome, mandé par le Pape, pour assister aux séances où seront traitées les affaires d'Angleterre. Il me prie de vous demander s'il y a eu des évêques anglicans sacrés d'après l'ordinal de 1550 ou 1552 qui soient revenus à l'Eglise catholique. Ecrivez-lui le renseignement à Rome. Il ajoute : " Si la discussion s'engage à fond, j'aurai probablement besoin de quelques renseignements historiques. Veuillez en prevenir M. Lacey. Je lui écrirai, et priez le de se tenir à ma disposition, pour me répondre tout de suite." Mon avis est que vous devriez aller à Rome. Je viens de le télégraphier à Lord Halifax. En tout cas il y a urgence à agir de votre côté et à frapper un bon coup. Vous avez une occasion unique.

The Rev. E. G. Wood to T. A. L.

20 *March*, 1896.

It would be delightful to send you to Rome as envoy extraordinary ! But I am inclined to think that you will be of more use at home ; matters are

88 A ROMAN DIARY AND OTHER DOCUMENTS

not far advanced enough for personal questioning.
I think written rather than spoken words are safer
at present as regards the scientific aspect. Lord
Halifax's interviews are most useful, but the theological and historical work is, I fancy, best done in
writing. Let Gasparri know that he can telegraph
if need be for information, or submit any points or
questions that he may wish, or that he may be
directed to submit, either by letter or by telegram;
and if it be needful he could have the reply by
wire.

Lord Halifax to T. A. L.

March 21, 1896.

Please read these letters carefully and return to
me. You see Moyes, Gasquet, and Fr. David are
gone to Rome with a report from the Cardinal
against our Orders. Also Gasparri has been sent
for to Rome by the Pope. You see what the Abbé
says. He proposes that you and Puller should
write to the Pope and *ask* to give personal explica-
tions as to our Orders; and the last thing he does
is to telegraph that he thinks this urgent.

I have seen Fr. Puller. He is ready to go if the
Archbishop of York advises it—*privately*, of course.
The Archbishop, to whom I have written most
fully, is coming to London on Wednesday for two
days, so I shall see him. He is quite ready to
write the letter we want to be prefixed to " Puller's
admirable article."[1]

---

[1] This letter was printed as preface to Fr Puller's pamphlet, *Les
Ordinations Anglicanes et le Sacrifice de la Messe.*

LETTERS   89

T. A. L. to the Bishop of Ely.

March 27, 1896.

Enclosed are some letters which I will ask you to look over. You will see from them that the Commission of Cardinals[1] at Rome which is considering the question of Anglican Orders is busily at work, and Duchesne and Gasparri, who are appointed by the Pope as consultors, are insisting on having help and advice from us, asking especially for me and Fr. Puller.

I went up to London on Wednesday to see Lord Halifax, Fr. Puller, and M. Portal. The Archbishop of York was called away.

Fr. Puller and I have conditionally agreed to go, but we have declined to write the letter to the Pope suggested to us, asking in some sort of way for audience. We can go only as friends of Gasparri and Duchesne, to advise them and give them information. Anything more would look too much like a recognition of the right of the Roman Church to decide the question. For a like reason it was unanimously agreed that we should not ask for letters testimonial from our diocesans; though such letters would be strictly *en règle*, yet they might be misrepresented as commissioning us to represent the English Episcopate.

I am advised, however, to ask one favour from your Lordship. It is uncertain how long I may be detained, and I therefore ask for leave of absence from my parish. It has been suggested that I

---

[1] So I wrote, whether from inadvertence or from ignorance I do not remember.

90 A ROMAN DIARY AND OTHER DOCUMENTS

should ask you to give me a letter in Latin setting out briefly the facts, *that some theologians in Rome* (omitting all reference to the Commission), *who are discussing grave matters affecting the relations of the Roman and English Churches, have asked me to go there and help them with information*, and on that account granting me leave of absence. It has been suggested that if such a letter might be shown privately it would produce considerable effect as indicating approval of our proceedings broadly, without in the least compromising the English Episcopate by anything we may say or do, judiciously or injudiciously. Fr. Puller will, of course, take actual directions from his immediate Superior.

M. Portal has ventured to say that if we took formal credentials, that fact of itself would probably prevent any actual decision of the question in an adverse sense, but this does not seem to us a sufficient reason for so dangerously compromising the independence of our Church. On the other hand, such a letter as I ask for would certainly produce some effect in the same direction, and would be free from danger.

The object which Fr. Puller and I set before ourselves is not to obtain a favourable decision, but to hinder the giving of any decision at all.

*   *   *   *   *

LETTERS   91

The Rev. F. W. Puller to T. A. L.

March 27, 1896.

No doubt Lord Halifax will have told you that
the Archbishop of York has promised to write
a letter to Portal, which he will be able to show
"in the proper quarter." If the letter is a good
one, this will have an excellent effect.

Will you let me know what books you will be
able to take with you, so that I may not take
needless duplicates?

The Archbishop of York was very strong on the
duty of going to Rome, and he solemnly blessed
me with a view to the enterprise.

The Rev. F. W. Puller to T. A. L.

March 30, 1896.

*   *   *   *   *

Very probably you will think of a number of
other books which we ought to take with us. I
have not put down great Roman books, like
Franzelin, Thomassinus, Bossuet, De Lugo, etc.,
because we shall, I suppose, be able to get at such
books easily in Rome.

*   *   *   *   *

Probably it will not be desirable for us to be
presented to the Pope. It may be well, however,
to be provided with whatever is necessary, in case it
should seem to be desirable. I have no idea what
etiquette requires for such an occasion. In England
I believe that a priest goes to Court in cassock

92 A ROMAN DIARY AND OTHER DOCUMENTS

and academical dress, i.e. I suppose, in cap, gown, and hood. Can you throw any light on these vestiary matters?

The Bishop of Ely to T. A. L.

March 30, 1896.

I find it is as I thought. I cannot grant you license of non-residence (save for sickness and certain other specified causes) without the approval of the Archbishop of Canterbury.

I will ask his Grace for his approval. If he refuses it, you can at any rate go—unlicensed—for three months, and I will not summon you back into residence till you have finished your work.

Lord Halifax to T. A. L.

Easter Eve, 1896.

* * * * *

The Archbishop of York has written quite a good letter as a preface to Father Puller's Articles. In it he absolutely endorses Father Puller's interpretation of Article XXXI. Altogether it is marvellous. Two English ecclesiastics, one a religious, sent to Rome with the approbation and consent of the Archbishop of York and others to confer with representatives of His Holiness. It is marvellous in our eyes : God's work, and no one else's ; and therefore not to be talked about. Only to be thanking Him and praying Him for a good success every moment of the day.

* * * * *

LETTERS 93

The Bishop of Ely to T. A. L.

April 10, 1896.

As I told you, I can only grant a license for non-residence (except in the cases of sickness, etc., specified in the Act) with the consent of the Archbishop, and he will not grant one until a clergyman has exhausted the three months he can be away from his benefice without license. So I fear you must make your journey with nothing to show for it, unless and until it exceeds three months, when you can write to me again. But I think, under the circumstances, you had better stay away as long as is necessary unlicensed.

The Rev. J. R. Lunn to T. A. L.

April 11.

Mr. Wood telegraphed to me from Cambridge, asking me to send you the manuscript copy I have just made of Barlowe's *Dialogue.* I do so. I have made a few hurried notes, which I thought would be useful.

* * * * *

I take Barlow's celebrated statement to mean that, so far as entering the episcopate is concerned, a Royal nomination is as good as a Papal Bull. And I take his Answer to mean that *Unction* is not part of the matter of the Sacrament of Order, is not to be found in N.T., and therefore is not necessary. But *Appointment* is ; and what appointment consists in he does not specify, but supposes it well known.

94 A ROMAN DIARY AND OTHER DOCUMENTS

The Rev. E. G. Wood to T. A. L.

April 11, 1896.

I have referred to Wilkins about Pole's Legatine Constitutions. The words are :—

"Et quia contra Capitis Ecclesiae et Sacramentorum doctrinam potissimum hic erratum est, placuit doctrinam de Primatu Ecclesiae Romanae et de Septem Sacramentis, quae in Concilio Generali Florentiae sub Eugenio quarto explicata est huic decreto subjicere."

Pole also orders Peckham's Constitution as to Tabernacles to be appended. But neither in the Corpus nor in the Cotton MS. is either decree or constitution set out in full. But it appears to me that he is as much committed to the doctrine as to the Instruments as if the decree were set out in full.

T. A. L. to the Rev. E. G. Wood.

14 *April,* 1896.

Your bibliography of Barlow's *Dialogue* has arrived, and is in a way disappointing; 1531 is rather too early a date for our purpose. I should like to know if there are any variations in the two editions. If so, the new matter or the omissions would be very significant.

We have been working pretty hard. Duchesne and Gasparri come to us for three hours at a time. Scannell also has called on us and invited us to the English College, and offered to place any books at our disposal. * * * * * Moyes has

LETTERS   95

prepared a vast memoir, which is being treated
as the basis of the discussion. They ask him
whether he expects to stay in Rome till next
spring; but it is hoped that Cardinal Mazzella
will rule most of the matter out as irrelevant.
*   *   *   * De Augustinis was put on the
Commission after presenting to the Pope a memoir
in favour of validity. He is, I believe, the first
Jesuit who has taken this line, and he is the leading
professor at the Collegio Romano. *   *   *   *
Duchesne is absolutely convinced that we have
made out our case for the tacit reception of the
Edwardine Orders by Pole, in spite of the second
Legatine Constitution. That means of course that
the Decretum ad Armenos was not taken to define
what is essential for Orders, but merely what was
customary—the view of d'Annibale. I have found
Wilkins at the Biblioteca Nazionale—the old Jesuits'
Library.

So far they have established only one thing at
the Commission—that Ferrar was consecrated by
the Pontifical. Of course that has an important
bearing on the question of the Degradations[1];
but the immediate object of the discussion was a
trivial one. They were settling the meaning of the
Bull of Paul IV. Gasparri had raised his question
about the words *ordines non sacros*. What Bishop
consecrated by the Ordinal had ever conferred
ordines non sacros? Moyes replied, *Ferrar*. So
the question of his consecration came up; we gave
Gasparri all the particulars, and while doing so we
came across the important fact—unknown to either

[1] See above, *Diary*, April 10, *note;* and *de Hierarchia Anglicana*,
pp. 160-3.

96 A ROMAN DIARY AND OTHER DOCUMENTS

of us before—that according to the Sarum Pontifical
the consecration of a Bishop took place before the
beginning of Mass — precisely the arrangement
which in Ferrar's case was challenged by Estcourt
as an irregularity. We found this in Maskell, and
of course it was conclusive.   *   *   *   *
We have found out exactly what the Commission
is. It is a body of consultores to the Holy Office,
Cardinal Mazzella presiding. They will report to
the Holy Office, but it is said that the Pope is
going to reserve the whole matter to himself. So
we may tell our horror-stricken friends in England
that we are in immediate touch with the familiars
of the Inquisition. Nay more, we went down to-
day with two of them—Duchesne and Scannell—
into the catacomb of St. Priscilla, and emerged
with life and limb! Morever, we had Canon Bright
with us. Also a Jesuit, le père Lapôtre, who wears
a pointed beard, and looks like a most respectable
country parson.   *   *   *   *   Le père
Lapôtre is the author of a book on John VIII,
and he is just doing Formosus, so he is an authority
on reordination.

At the old Jesuits' Library they have singularly
few English books of the seventeenth century.
Of Beveridge only the Apostolic Canons ; of Pearson only the Creed in a vile Latin translation and
the little posthumous volume of chronologica ; of
Barrow nothing but the mathematical treatises ;
of Hammond and Field nothing. In the Vatican
Library Fr. Puller has found a nice little surprise
for our friends. The Bishop of Oxford had told
him of another copy of the famous letter of June 12,
1536, which is printed in Gairdner's *Letters and*

LETTERS

Papers of Henry VIII, vol. 10. He went to the Vatican Library to verify it, and finds that instead of describing Barlow as "Bishop then elect of St. Asaph, now elect of St. David's," as in Estcourt's copy, it runs "Bishop then elect of St. Asaph, now of St. David's." Now if this is the corrected copy, of which Estcourt's paper was a draft, the alteration is most significant; it almost establishes June 11, Haddan's conjecture, as the date of the consecration. The draft made before the consecration required correction. P. has written to the Bishop of Oxford to consult him on the subject.[1]

We have not, so far, the slightest indication of the time that will be occupied, but they are beginning to talk ominously of the difficulties which the heat of June is likely to raise if it is not finished by then!

The Rev. E. G. Wood to T. A. L.

April 15, 1896.

*   *   *   *   *

A line of argument strikes me; viz. that the compilers of the Ordinal intended to make the *Accipe Spiritum Sanctum* and the accompanying imposition of hands the form and matter of ordination to the priesthood, or, as we might say, the actual and essential ceremony of Ordination; and that they did so because they really desired to come as closely as possible to what they read in Scripture as to Ordination. Bear in mind the prevailing idea of being Scriptural. If so, it is clear evidence of their intention to do what our LORD did, and to

[1] See Diary, April 17th, and Letters of May 18th and 24th.

H

98 A ROMAN DIARY AND OTHER DOCUMENTS

perpetuate the ministry He had instituted. They may more or less have misconceived the nature of that ministry, but that would not invalidate their intention. Given an honest desire (1) to follow our LORD's institution, (2) to perpetuate the ministry He had instituted, (3) to follow as closely as possible in so doing the evidence of Scripture, surely we must grant that it would be impossible to do so more admirably than this is done in our Ordinal. The idea of ordination presented to us in Scripture is far more clearly actualized in our Ordinal than in any other Rite. To call such a Rite invalid seems to me on broad grounds a kind of wantonness, a thing akin to a cynical scepticism. The historical argument as to the *Accipe* does not affect the point.

The Rev. Edward Denny to T. A. L.

17 April, 1896.

Would it be possible for some one to look at the manuscript speech of O'Harte[1] in the Vatican? I wonder whether it is the sole speech he made on the subject. I think also the records relating to the committee appointed by the Council of Trent to consider the canons suggested by the Cardinal of Lorraine (*vide* Paleotto, *Act. C. T.*, pp. 359-61, quoted *De Hierarchia*, n. 253) should be examined, if possible. I still find a difficulty in understanding how Paleotto could have based the statement he

---

[1] This Irish bishop is reported by Le Plat and Raynald, on the authority of Paleotto, to have said in the Council of Trent that the only valid argument against the English bishops was "*quia non sunt a Pontifice Romano adsciti.*" Dom Gasquet found in the Archives a manuscript report of the speech that does not bear out this interpretation.

LETTERS

did about O'Harte's speech on the manuscript discovered by Dom Gasquet, considering the position which he occupied at the Council as Auditor, and also how the committee of nine (amongst whom was Paleotto) could have worded their fourth reason for rejecting the canon numbered vii. in the way they did, if O'Harte merely said what Dom Gasquet's manuscript contains.[1]

Duchesne's opinion about the Marian *praxis* is interesting. I suppose he regards the Paul IV documents in the same light as Scannell. I am glad Scannell is on the Commission. I was struck with his first letter to the *Tablet* on those documents. He seems to have a clearer head than Moyes.

T. A. L. to the Rev. E. G. Wood.

25 *April*, 1896.

*　　*　　*　　*　　*

Last Monday we spent a very pleasant evening with the Sulpicians, who, it seems, are very conservative and rather distrustful of Portal, but they were most pleasant and friendly and full of inquiries about our ways and doings in England. We have had some long sittings, all about Barlow ; but they are now getting on to the rite, and things will be more interesting. We have had the memoir of de Augustinis, and it proved exciting reading. * * * The general purport of the memoir has leaked out through an amazing indiscretion of Cardinal

[1] It was found impossible to act on these suggestions, and I therefore withdrew, in my *Supplementum*, the arguments that we had based in *De Hierarchia* on Paleotto's report. Mr Denny and I had previously made a similar withdrawal in a *Monitum* attached to copies of our book

100 A ROMAN DIARY AND OTHER DOCUMENTS

Vaughan's at St. Joseph's, Mill Hill, about which news speedily reached Rome; and it has made the greatest impression. * * *

The Gordon case, on examination, presents some unlooked for features. The Holy Office, so far from pronouncing on Gordon's *Supplica*, as the published accounts implied, seems to have brushed his flimsy reasons aside altogether, and with the rite fairly before them, to have concluded that *Accipe Spiritum Sanctum* was the sole *form* employed, and that it was insufficient, *not being a prayer*. The near conjunction of this *decision* with the *votum* of the Consultores in the Abyssinian case must stand as one of the puzzles of history. The result is that, as Duchesne was showing me last night, they cannot in the Commission argue on the *Accipe Spiritum Sanctum* at all, as they cannot go behind a decision of the Holy Office. Duchesne and de Augustinis accept the prayer in the priests' Ordination as oratio super ordinandos, on the ground of the words "as well by these thy ministers," but the others either deny or doubt this. We shall, I think, have a good tussle over the *oneness* of the rite. Moyes boldly attacks de Lugo, or rather I should say Fr. David does, for it seems he is the theologian.

The other great lion in the way is the reluctance to disturb the existing *internal* practice about Ordinations, and with this a reluctance to define what the Council of Trent deliberately left open. I have been arguing that the acceptance of Greek Orders has practically done the latter, but of course it does not affect the former question, since Greek uniat priests are not allowed to officiate with the

LETTERS
101

Latin rite. * * * I have suggested a *proprio motu*, in which the Pope seems to be able to talk about any subject whatever, so that he might recognize the validity as a theological fact, while ordering for practical reasons either the *supply* of the porrection, or conditional reordination, for any who may seek permission to exercise their ministry in the Roman Church. There is also the practical question of the minor orders and the subdiaconate. One can easily see that it would be intolerable to treat *us* in these respects more favourably than Latins themselves.

The Pope seems to be wonderfully eager. Gasparri saw him yesterday and told him how useful we were being. He added some not very well chosen words about "Anglicans" being "all but Catholics," and "at the very door." "Je vais l'ouvrir à deux battants," cried the Pope with vivacity. Well, in that case, one leaf at all events must be the recognition of Orders. I am pressing everywhere the point that a definite ruling for conditional reordination, though it would not really close the door, would make it impossible for us to do much for reunion, since our people would all be persuaded that we were intending every one, from the Archbishops downwards, to be reordained.

T. A. L. to the Rev. W. H. Frere.

April 29, 1896.

Will you undertake a certain search for us?

Moyes has been building up an elaborate argument against Barlow by showing that *all* the documents relating to his *appointment* are extant, and

102 A ROMAN DIARY AND OTHER DOCUMENTS

all relating to *consecration* are wanting. We have pretty well riddled it by showing that his "document" for the enthronization, for instance, is a mere vague allusion in a private letter, and that in order to produce the *Breve de restitutione* he has to confuse it with the *Concessio.* I further challenged the existence of the *Congé* and the *Assent,* knowing they were not on the Patent Rolls. Moyes averred their existence. He was asked by Gasparri for a reference. He gave " Patent Rolls, 27 Henry 8, p. 1, m. 11." Now this is the reference for the St. Asaph election, and he had already given it as such in his article in the *Tablet.* He was confronted with this, whereupon he said it was a mistake, and showed that elsewhere in the same article he spoke of the St. David's documents as extant. That was true, but he gave no reference.

* * * * *

We then telegraphed to Wood, who went to the Records and found that the Congé and Assent, though missing from the Patent Rolls, are extant in their preliminary form in the Privy Seals and Signed Bills.

* * * * *

A special request from Gasparri. The *Literae certificatoriae* from the Archbishop to the King declaring the fact of the Consecration, are they preserved anywhere in the Records? And if so, is the collection complete? They are, you know, generally entered in the Register, and they are usually recited in the Writ for Restitution; but I do not know whether the originals are filed anywhere.

LETTERS   103

T. A. L. to the Rev. E. G. Wood.

29 *Ap.*, 1896.

I wonder if you made out the drift of our telegram. Moyes has been building up an elaborate argument, etc.[1]

*　　*　　*　　*　　*

When this was reported I telegraphed to you. What Gasquet had seen was of course what is in the Privy Seals. I am ashamed to say I did not know these were kept, though I was studying not long since the process of issuing Letters Patent under the Great Seal. * * *

We called with Duchesne on Cardinal Hohenlohe yesterday. The old gentleman was most kind and cordial. He is now Archpriest of Santa Maria Maggiore, and lives in a cramped *appartement* in the palace of the Basilica. If only he could replace Cardinal Mazzella, says N., our affairs would soon be settled satisfactorily.

*　　*　　*　　*　　*

Lord Halifax writes to Portal that he has seen the Bishop of Clifton, thinking it might be useful, and that the bishop said, among other things, " You cannot imagine what would be the effect on our people of requiring them to believe that persons who have no belief at all in the real presence can have the power of consecrating the Eucharist!" Well may our friends here say that they do not understand the theology of the " English Catholics." Apparently they teach that the orthodoxy of the

---

[1] Continues almost word for word in the preceding letter.

104 A ROMAN DIARY AND OTHER DOCUMENTS

priest is essential to the validity of the Sacrament. Now one can appreciate their ideas about *intention* in the collation of Orders.

The Rev. W. H. Frere to T. A. L.

4 *May*, 1896.

I am on my way back from the Record Office where I have been on your errand. I must write the result in the train to avoid delay.

I have been through the Privy Seals and Signed Bills of June and July: they are all calendared in Vols. X and XI of the *Domestic Papers*, and I find nothing much of interest. I went carefully through the records of Warton of St. Asaph as Barlow's successor: and Sampson and Repps. The Archbishop's certificate of consecration exists only for the latter, and is filed in this collection: others would be *here* were they forthcoming. It says nothing about Sampson nor Barlow.

But one point comes out from these documents: in the Royal Assent for Warton, i.e. the Privy Seal and Signed Bill (both) issued preliminary to the Letters Patent, the Vacancy is described as being " Per liberam transmutacionem Will. Barl. ultimi episcopi ibidem electi." This last word does not occur in the analogous document of Assent to Sampson, which has—" Roberti Shirburn ultimi epi ibidem " only. This, so far as it goes, is evidence that Barlow was not yet consecrated on June 16.[1]

[1] Hardly so. It only shows that Barlow was not consecrated before his avoidance of St. Asaph. See below, Letter of May 8th to W. H. F.

LETTERS

I will look up in Rymer the Letters Patent which issued as the result of this Privy Seal document, and see if they throw any further light. This is all I have to report. It will answer Gasparri's question about Archbishop's certificates.

But here is a new point which has a double bearing. In the Register of the Dean and Chapter of Canterbury *Sede Vacante* after Cranmer's attainder, a valuable list is given of the Bishops deprived *and the causes*.

Defect of order is alleged against some, but not against Barlow : the cause there given is merely his resignation. In the other cases several reasons are given against the same person, e.g. marriage or defective title because of the *quamdiu* clause : it would have been easy to add defect of order in Barlow's case if it had been a reason felt to exist. But, on the other hand, it would have been easy also to allege *marriage*. Valeat quantum.

It confirms my conviction that in the first blush of Marian revulsion they were inclined to dispute the Orders of the English Ordinal (you have no doubt seen my letter to Fr. Puller) ; but I am coming to suspect more and more, and hope to prove, that this doubt was a steadily diminishing quantity ; possibly even that the influence of Pole, or even of Rome, was exerted against it, and that the reordination which prevailed in the early months was afterwards discouraged. I cannot say this is *proved :* but I see increasing hopes that it may be proved when I have got and digested all the evidence.

*　　*　　*　　*　　*

106 A ROMAN DIARY AND OTHER DOCUMENTS

From the Rev. E. G. Wood to T. A. L.

May 6, 1896.

I send you four documents, which I have marked A, B, C, D. The most important of these is A. I have transcribed it on a piece of paper the exact size of the parchment and line for line, and put the King's signature in the exact place. This is what is commonly called the Assent to Barlow's election to St. David's. Now observe this is the actual original with the King's autograph signature. It is the very document which the King himself had to do with. It is the Sign Manual, or Signed Bill. It is the foundation of all the other documents which followed, up to the actual letters patent with the Great Seal attached, which reached Cranmer. This Sign Manual unquestionably directs the Consecration of Barlow.

* * * * *

The Privy Seal is commonly called the Significavit. It is not a fresh act of the Royal authority ; it is contained, as it were, in the one act of Royal authority, viz. the Sign Manual. That is to say, the Privy Seal followed necessarily and automatically on the Sign Manual. The whole routine is fixed. Two copies were made of the Privy Seal. One ends, " Per breve sub sigillo privato." This was intended to be on record at the Privy Seal Office. The other ended, " Sub Sigillo Privato," and had the Seal actually attached. Moreover, it contained a preface addressed to the Lord Chancellor, directing him to issue the Letters Patent under the Great Seal. All these documents differed

LETTERS

slightly from one another, but they were all founded on the Sign Manual, which contained implicitly everything contained in the succeeding documents, which, as I have said, were only routine expansions according to common form.

*   *   *   *   *

I think it very important to insist on all this, so as to enable our friends to see that document A is verily and indeed the royal mandate to confirm and consecrate Barlow. Remember that in all grants (and these documents are technically grants) nothing but the Litterae Patentes, or in other cases the Litterae Clausae, went beyond the official precincts. But the whole series is one. The germ is the Signed Bill; then there is a process of evolution, the ultimate product which alone sees the light, being the Letters Patent or Letters Close. There is only one act, viz. the Royal signature to the Signed Bill. That is, so to say, the efficient cause, and it was given only once until we come to the Restitution of Temporalities, which starts a fresh series.

*   *   *   *   *

As to Gordon's case, I wish you could get copies of the records. The decree certainly says nothing about the validity of the rite. The document as reproduced by Lee, p. 301, from the *Weekly Register*, first recites Gordon's memorial, and then concludes :—

> "Lecto supradicto memoriali SS.D. noster Papa prae-dictus, auditis votis eorundem Emm, decrevit quod praedictus Joannes Clemens Gordon orator ex integro ad omnes ordines etiam sacros et presby-teratus promoveatur, et quatenus non fuerit sacra-mento confirmationis munitus confirmetur."

108 A ROMAN DIARY AND OTHER DOCUMENTS

Now of course the present Consultors cannot go
behind a decree of H.O., but surely they are not
bound by the *vota*. But would it not be possible
to beg that these *vota*, or rather copies of them,
might be produced, that we might have the
benefit of studying them? The more one thinks
of it, the more intensely difficult does it seem to
me to conceive how any rite in Christendom can be
valid if ours is not; it so clearly bears on its face
the evidence of the purpose to confer by laying on
of hands the gift of the Holy Ghost, to make the
man a priest. As to the question of precatory or
imperative, surely this is just on all fours with the
same question in regard to the Sacrament of
Penance, and indeed analogous to that of the
Western and Eastern form in Baptism.

[Enclosures.]

A.

To the King our Sovereign Lord.

*Pleaseth it your highness of your most noble and
abundant grace to grant your gracious letters patent
under your great seal in due form to be made according to the tenour ensuing.*

Henry R.

Rex reverendissimo in Christo patri Thomae
Cantuar. archiepiscopo totius Angliae primati salutem. Sciatis quod electioni nuper factae in ecclesia
Cathedrali Meneven. per mortem bonae memoriae
dom. Richardi Rawlyns ultimi episcopi ibidem
vacante de reverendo in Christo patre dom. Willelmo Barlow sacrae theologiae professore tunc
episcopo Assaven et Mon. de Bisham Sarum dioec.

LETTERS 109

commendatorio perpetuo in episcopum loci illius et
pastorem regium assensum adhibuimus et favorem,
et hoc vobis tenore praesentium significamus ut quod
vestrum est in hac parte exequamini. In cuius etc.
Teste etc.

B.

Henricus octauus dei gratia Anglie et ffrancie
Rex fidei defensor et dominus Hibernie ac in terra
supremum capud ecclesie anglicane Predilecto et
fideli Consiliario nostro Thome Audeley militi
Cancellario nostro salutem. Vobis mandamus quod
sub magno sigillo nostro in custodia vestra existeñ
literas nostras patentes fieri faciatis in forma
sequeñ. Rex etc. dilectis nobis in Christo decano
et capitulo ecclesie cathedralis Meneueñ salutem.
Ex parte vestra nobis est humiliter supplicat' vt
cum ecclesia vestra predicta per mortem bone
memorie domini Richardi Rawlyns vltimi episcopi
ibidem sit pastoris solacio destituta alium vobis
eligend' in episcopum et pastorem licentiam nostram
concedere dignaremur. Nos precibus vestris in hac
parte fauorabiliter inclinati licentiam illam duximus
concedend' Mandantes quod talem vobis eligatis
in episcopum et pastorem qui deo devotus ecclesie
vestre necessarius nobisque et Regno nostro vtilis et
fidelis exisĩ. In cuius rei etc. Dat' nostro sub Priuato
sigillo apud Manerium nostrum de West' xxvij° die
Marcii Anno regni nostri vicesimo septimo.

Extracted at Record Office. E. G. Wood, Ap. 30,
1896.
This is the Congé d'élire for Barlow to St. David's.
It is in the Privy Seal bundle for March.
It is the copy sent to the Chancery.

110 A ROMAN DIARY AND OTHER DOCUMENTS

C.

Congé d'élire for Barlow to St. Asaph.

This is exactly the same as that to St. David's *mutatis mutandis*—so it is not worth copying. It is on the Patent Roll 27. Hen. VIII, 2 pt. m. 20. (Rymer, xiv. 570.) It is dated Jan. 7, 1536, but on the Roll it is placed *after* the assent; it immediately follows it.

A Privy Seal.

D.

Assent to Barlow's election to St. Asaph.

Rex reverendo in Christo patri Thome Cantuar' arch' totius Angliae primati Sciatis quod electioni nuper factae in Ecclesia Cathedrali Assaph. per mortem bonae memoriae dom' Henrici Standish ultimi episcopi ibidem vacante de venerabili Willelmo Barlowe priore domus sive prioratus de Bisham ordinis Sancti Augustini Sarum diœcesis in episcopum loci illius et pastorem regium assensum adhibemus et favorem. Et hoc vobis tenore presentium significamus ut quod vestrum est in hac parte exequamini. In cujus &c. Teste Rege apud Westm' vicesimo secundo die Februarii (27 Hy. VIII, 2pt. m.20. Rymer xiv. 559).

This document is a Privy Seal.

LETTERS

Sir Walter Phillimore to T A. L.

May 7, 1896

*   *   *   *   *

How is Bishop Barlow? As to mandate for *confirmation and consecration*, you will have seen that in Gibson, ed. Oxford, 1761, p. 1327, the precedent given—a late one, I allow—temp. Will. 3, has Assent and the Mandate for both in one document. Oughton, *Ordo judiciorum*, has in his second volume of Formularies no instrument as to consecration of Bishops. But in the last title of Vol. II, Tit. cccxxxvii. (ed. 1738, p. 482), he has the *Forma confirmandi Episcopum*, which begins : " Imprimis . . . praesententur literae commissionales et patentes regiae de assensu regio etc. sub Sigillo Magno Angliae, et coram eo publice leguntur." These *literae commissionales et patentes* are clearly those of Royal assent and confirmation : that they include mandate for consecration appears from p. 484, *Observationes.*

(2) "Post electionem celebratam et . . . significantur haec a Decano et Capitulo Regiae Maiestati et domino Archiepiscopo.

(3) Deinde rescribere solet Archiepiscopo per literas suas patentes Dominus Rex de assensu Regio eidem electioni adhibito ; una cum Mandato pro Confirmatione et Consecratione dicti Domini Electi."

This is, of course, no earlier in date than the precedent in Gibson. But it shows that form to be *then* (and, if *then*, probably always) the usual form. I attach importance to the singular *mandato.*

112 A ROMAN DIARY AND OTHER DOCUMENTS

T. A. L. to the Rev. W. H. Frere.

May 8, 1896.

Thank you very much for your note about the literae certificatoriae, which is just what was wanted. The best thing for our argument would have been that they were not kept at all : the next best, that they were kept carelessly. The absence of Sampson's robs the absence of Barlow's of all significance.

Father Puller has told you that I have a telegram from Wood, announcing the discovery of the mandate to consecrate Barlow. We are impatiently awaiting a letter of particulars. This completes the demolition of Moyes' case, which consisted in showing that not only was Barlow's consecration not mentioned in Cranmer's Register, but that also all the documents in which it might have been recorded are missing, while all relating to his appointment, apart from consecration, are extant. It was a wonderful scheme of documents that he showed. The missing ones were five.

    i. Mandate to consecrate.
    ii. License of Chapter of Canterbury to consecrate away from Canterbury.
    iii. Register.
    iv. Literae certificatoriae.
    v. Barlow's own Register ;

besides *possibly* commission to Bishop to consecrate, and writ of restitution if that was granted after consecration. Moyes graciously waived these, as

LETTERS 113

there was not the ghost of a reason for supposing that either ever existed or could have existed. We have now got i.; ii. and v. are known to have perished; iv. you have shown to afford no presumption; and so we come back to the Register as the only real lacuna.[1]

The Canterbury Register giving the reasons for deposition of Bishops has been much used. N. transposed the entries, so as to make it appear that "*ut supra*" in each case included the "*invaliditatem*[2] consecrationis.*" We exposed this, and so dealt our first severe blow at his credit.

Observe that the description of Barlow as *ultimi episcopi ibidem electi*—i.e. of St. Asaph—proves nothing. Since he certainly was not consecrated to St. Asaph, he remained always ultimus episcopus *electus* of that see.

I should very much like to know what are the variations between the Privy Seal for the Custodia of St. David's and the Concessio as finally given; but there is no hurry for this unless—which is hardly possible—it should afford positive evidence. Estcourt's argument from the terms of the Concessio is quite given up even by Moyes.

Your hypothesis about the intervention of the Legate to stop reordinations is most interesting. I will tell Duchesne of it, subject, of course, to reserves, and not for use. Our prompt production of your evidence seems to have made a very good impression.

[1] We were at this time under the impression that Mr. Wood's telegram announced the discovery of a hitherto unknown document
[2] The word used was *nullitatem.*

I

114 A ROMAN DIARY AND OTHER DOCUMENTS

T. A. L. to the Rev. E. G. Wood.

10 *May*, 1896.

Your letter with the documents is not yet come. The telegram about the mandate of consecration was just in time for the last sitting of the Commission, completing the demolition of Moyes' case. The *last sitting*, for the Commission has come to an abrupt conclusion, about which we experience a curiosity which is not gratified. All the members have their mouths shut, and are forbidden ever again to write or publish anything on the subject of Anglican Orders. This must be annoying for Moyes. Gasparri is very content; he is heartily sick of the whole matter, and has charged Portal never again to mention the Anglican Church to him. It is wonderful that, being so little interested in the question, he should have gone into it so thoroughly. Probably he will not lose his reward, for he is likely to have a nunciature before long, and the purple may not be so very far beyond that.[1]

Well, we thought of packing up our traps, but a message from Duchesne stayed us, and on Friday he went to see Cardinal Rampolla to talk about us. The Cardinal told him that a Commission of Cardinals was nominated to take over the question, and it was most important that we should stay to give our help. So now, if you please, we are here not by invitation of Gasparri and Duchesne, but by command of the Cardinal-Secretary. He added

---

[1] He was appointed Delegate Apostolic for Peru, Ecuador, and Bolivia in 1898, and became Cardinal in 1907.

LETTERS 115

that he wanted to see us, but we must call on some other Cardinals first. Duchesne suggested some names—whether *proprio motu* or not I cannot say —and we began yesterday with Cardinal Vincenzo Vannutelli, whom Portal knew as Nuncio at Lisbon. He was most effusive, and let out at once that he was on the Commission. He is a young man,[1] and talks with the most extraordinary gesticulation, his hands flourishing away all the time at the level of his eyes. After this interview I telegraphed for copies of *de Hierarchia*, which we shall formally present to the Cardinals. I am also setting to work on a small supplement, which we shall print here, dealing with later developments of the question. I want to make use of de Augustinis' suggestion about the *forma*, and of course I must not let it seem that I have seen his paper, but most fortunately it happens that Chase has suggested the same idea to me, and I shall quote it as his.   *   *   *

I think—but without any certainty—that Gasparri's thesis of the entire unity of the ordination rite, and the consequent sufficiency of one or other of the prayers contained therein with the Imposition of hands, has prevailed in the commission of inquiry, and is likely to prevail elsewhere. If so a real advance in theology will be made, and the whole conception of ordination will become much simpler. They were very anxious to know if the prayer at the end of the Litany in the rite for consecrating Bishops is invariably said by the consecrator himself, and we have obtained from the Archbishop of York an assurance that it is so.

---

[1] A curiously false impression ; he was sixty years of age

116 A ROMAN DIARY AND OTHER DOCUMENTS

The Rev. W. H. Frere to T. A. L.

May 11, 1896.

I can only scribble a line : I copied out bits of the Simancas documents which I hope are right, but it is hard to excerpt from things one does not know.

I looked for the St. David's *Concessio* on purpose to compare it with the Privy Seal, but could not find it. Would such a thing go under Letters Patent at all, or merely under Privy Seal?

The case goes well about the re-ordinations. I find no later cases, though it is fairly clear that there were people in Edwardian Orders left in possession of benefices who therefore ought at least to have been pressed to present themselves if the re-ordination policy was a fixed one.

[Enclosure.]

Extracts from the *Calendar of Letters and State Papers relating to English Affairs, preserved principally in the Archives of Simancas. Vol. I, Elizabeth.*

1561. 22 *Jan. Bishop Quadra to the King.*

Since writing the enclosed letter, Henry Sidney, who is the brother-in-law of Lord Robert, came to see me. . . . Although he is not at all well informed on religious questions, he did not fail to admit that the state of the country was very bad and a way must be found to mend it. He told me a number of things in this respect which grieved me, and endeavoured to persuade me with solemn

LETTERS 117

oaths that the Queen and Lord Robert were determined to restore religion by means of a general *Concilio*. . . .

23 *Feb.* *The same to the same.*

. . . Robert came the next day. . . . He again made me great promises and assured me that everything should be placed in your Majesty's hands, and even as regarded religion, if the sending of a representative to the *Concilio* did not suffice, he would go himself.

17 *Mar.* *The King to Bishop Quadra.*

. . . What she might now do is to liberate the prelates and other Catholics she has imprisoned, agree to send her Ambassadors and Catholic bishops to the *Concilio* and submit herself unconditionally to its decisions. Besides this she should, pending the resolutions of the *Concilio*, allow Catholics to live as they please without coercion or violence. . . .

His Holiness writes us that he has appointed the Abbé Martinengo to carry the bull of the *Concilio* to the Queen, and has given him orders, when he arrives in Flanders, to be governed by the directions of the Bishop of Arras. . . .

25 *Mar.* *Bishop Quadra to the King.*

On the 23rd ultimo I wrote to your Majesty that the going of the Earl of Bedford to France was not alone to condole for the King's death, and endeavour to obtain a ratification of the peace, but also to try for a close alliance between the heretics there and the Queen. Since the Earl came back

118 A ROMAN DIARY AND OTHER DOCUMENTS

I have learnt that what has been done is to propose
to the Queen-mother and the King's Council that,
as there is a diversity of opinion on religion in
England, and various counsels have been given to
the Queen, she begged the French Queen to send
her opinion and advice as to how she should act.
They answered that nobody's opinion on so clear
a matter could be very needful to one so wise as the
Queen, who knew perfectly well how Christian and
Catholic the Kingdom of England had always
been, and how obedient to the dictates of the
Church. The Earl replied that the Queen's intention was to end these differences by sending her
theologians to the general *Concilio*, but that she
thought, in order that the *Concilio* should be held
with all-fitting security and freedom, it was necessary that it should meet on this side of the
mountains, and if the most Christian King would
look to this and endeavour to have some such
fitting place named, the Queen offered to unite with
him and form a firm alliance in order that the
business might be carried through with liberty and
security and without coercion being resorted
to. . . .

Cecil is entirely pledged to these unhappy
heresies. . . . He asked me whether it would be
well to have some theologians sent here on the
Pope's behalf to confer on the Christian doctrine.
. . . He afterwards asked me whether I would consent to meet the archbishop of Canterbury to open
negotiations for conciliation. . . . He again asked
me recently what we can do about religious affairs,
as the archbishop of Canterbury did not care to
come and speak with me for fear of being noted as

LETTERS 119

suspicious by the other bishops. . . . He complained of the style of the bull of the *Concilio* and the insulting words which were constantly being said and written about them as if they were not Christians and did not believe in God. The end of it was to beg me as a bishop and minister of so pious a Prince as your Majesty to endeavour to open a way to some fair understanding. . . . He asked me what were the articles I wished to be considered before all others, and I told him those concerning ecclesiastical government and policy, namely, the office of Pope and Bishops, the authority of *Concilios* and the distinction between spiritual and temporal powers. We discussed this at great length, and at last he said the following three things to me, I know not in what spirit. First, that the Queen would be willing to send her Ambassadors and theologians to the *Concilio*, even though it were convoked by the Pope, on condition that the meeting was at a place satisfactory to the other Princes, namely, your Majesty, the Emperor, and the King of France. He then said that she would be willing that the Pope or his legates should preside in the *Concilio* in such a way as did not infer that he was a ruler over it, but only as head or president of it. The third was that they would be in favour of judging questions of faith as well as others, according to the precepts of holy scripture, consensus of divines, and the declarations of ancient *Concilios*. He was very emphatic about these ancient *Concilios*, saying that he would only admit the first four. He then said that what I demanded was evidently to have a judge for matters of faith and to declare the separation of the

120 A ROMAN DIARY AND OTHER DOCUMENTS

temporal and spiritual powers, and he went on to say that as the English bishops are canonically ordained they must have seats in the *Concilio* amongst the others. I told him that in regard to that the justice of his claim could afterwards be considered, and then asked him whether in case the *Concilio* fell through, which it well might if the German Protestants were obstinate in their claims, he thought this reconciliation between this kingdom and the Catholics could be effected by means of a national *Concilio* with the same intervention and presidency of the Pope's legates. . . . I hear he is going about publicly saying that the Queen wishes to send representatives to the *Concilio*, and that the *Concilio* cannot properly be judge of questions of faith, nor is the Pope able to preside over it by right, which was the subject of our discussion.

I also know that he is treating these bishops harshly, and that he used insulting words to the bishop of Winchester the other day because he preached against the authority of the *Concilios*. I hear that the bishops frequently meet in the archbishop of Canterbury's house and are drawing up a profession of their faith to send to the *Concilio*.

12 April. The same to the same.

. . . I think that the Abbé Martinengo's visit will enable us to settle the business very comfortably. . . .

I therefore think that the coming of the Nuncio should be accelerated so that we may see the answers they give him before the Queen settles her own affair, which she could now do, having time, and

LETTERS   121

being popular in consequence of the news that she
is to be represented in the *Concilio*. . . .
Robert tells me that Cecil will be firm about
sending representatives to the *Concilio*, and there
are some amongst the bishops who are already
beginning to soften and bend to what the Queen
desires, although others are very stubborn. . . .

27 April. Bishop Quadra to Lord Robert Dudley.

. . . On the 22nd of January I received a visit
from Sir Henry Sidney, your brother-in-law. . . .
[He] assured me that the intention of the Queen
and opinion of your Lordship and all prudent men
was that she should be represented in the *Concilio*.
I had no difficulty in believing this, as it seemed just
and probable ; and I was confirmed in my belief
shortly afterwards by the Queen personally, who
told me with her own lips several times that she
wished to send representatives to the *Concilio*. . . .

May 5. Bishop Quadra to the King.

. . . .

The paper contained two principal points, namely,
that the Queen did not consider it well to admit
the Nuncio, inasmuch as it was against the law
and good policy of the country, and that in this
step she followed the precedent of Queen Mary,
who had prohibited the entrance of the Nuncio
who brought the Cardinal's hat to Peto from Pope
Paul IV.

The second point was that as the Queen understood the object of the Nuncio's coming was to
intimate to her the holding of the *Concilio*, she
informed me that she had decided not to give her

122 A ROMAN DIARY AND OTHER DOCUMENTS

acquiescence to such *Concilio*, nor to consent to the continuance of that which had commenced at Trent, both on account of the lack of freedom which apparently would exist, and because she had not been consulted, as she ought to have been, as to the place of meeting and other circumstances in the same way that other princes had been consulted.

She did not say, nevertheless, that she would not assist when a free and pious *Concilio* was held, by sending her ambassadors and learned persons of the Anglican Church to endeavour to agree to a consensus of doctrines in the Universal Church, as all princes should do. . . .

I am quite sure that these people, bad as they are, were not of the same opinion in the matter three months ago as they are now. . . .

May 6. Bishop Quadra to the Duchess of Parma and the Cardinal Bishop of Arras (De Granvelle).

. . . .

These people, however, are so satisfied with themselves that it is useless to point out their errors. As regards their willingness to join in a *Concilio* if it is what they call free, christian, and pious, and is arranged by the other great powers in union with England and in consultation with his Holiness, your Highness will bear this in mind so that, if there be any occasion to proceed with these negotiations, it must be understoood that the Queen claims to be treated like the rest, and to attend on the same footing as the others. Although the liberty and piety which they demand in the *Concilio* may be nothing more than dislike to any *Concilio* at all, as

LETTERS

they none of them want it, yet, if the other sovereigns agree, these people will be bound to attend by the answer they have given.

NOTE ON THE ABOVE.

The above excerpts from the Simancas correspondence were sent in answer to a request contained in a letter from Father Puller, dated May 7th. The Bishop of Peterborough had recently referred to the subject in a lecture on Queen Elizabeth. The use we made of them, profiting by a hint from Duchesne (Diary, May 6th), may be seen in the following passage taken from the *Supplementum*, pp. 33-5 :—

Restat quaestio de animo imponentis; Utrum intentione perversa ad verum ecclesiae ministerium obruendum ritus in usum reductus fuerit. Qui autem ritum imposuerunt? Anne auctores? Sed quinam illi? Paene ignoti sunt. Cranmer ex illis procul dubio erat. Ex aliis vix unus dignoscitur. R. P. Sydney Smith voluit ostendere Martinum Bucerum magnam in componendis ordinationibus partem habuisse.[1] Id autem ratione temporum facile refutatur. Nam Bucer in Angliam venit mense Iunio, 1549; et proximo mense Ianuario scripsit ad amicum : "Quod me mones de puritate rituum, scito hic neminem extraneum de his rebus rogari."[2] At novus ritus iam mense Octobri 1549 paratus est. Certe Bucer voluit ritum iam efformatum ex sententia sua reformare, distinctionem ordinum evertere, formam quae tunc essentialis putabatur eiicere, in eumque finem ritunculum inter scripta sua adhuc asservatum conscripsisse videtur ; sed frustra laborabat.[3]

Nec vero ab auctoribus ritum accepimus. Episcopi primo, potestati civili fortasse morem gerentes, sed tamen officio pastorali utentes, eum in usum receperunt, quorum

[1] Vide *The Tablet*, Jan. 18, 25, Feb. 8, 1896.

[2] Cit. apud Lawrence, *Bampton Lectures*, p 245. R P. Sydney Smith hanc epistolam anno 1551 scriptam esse ratione tenuissima affirmare voluit.

[3] Cum de hac re in dissertatione *De Hier Angl* n. 206 disseruimus, Bucerum istam ritus adumbrationem antequam ritus Eduardini parati essent scripsisse putabamus, id quod vix possibile nunc videtur.

124 A ROMAN DIARY AND OTHER DOCUMENTS

non paucos nulla haereseos simulatione suspectos Cardinalis Legatus postea agnovit et cum Ecclesia Romana reconciliavit. Sed neque ab illis nos ritum accepimus. Namque ritus, tempore Mariae reiectus, anno demum 1559 in usum reductus est. Si igitur de animo imponentis quaeratur, rogari debet quo sensu quave intentione id factum sit. Qui autem id fecerunt? Non exules qui postmodum ex conventibus Calvinistarum Helveticis et Germanicis reversi tantam rerum ecclesiasticarum in Anglia confusionem moliebantur. Isti enim adhuc aut non redierant, aut certe potestate non erant adepti. Qui igitur? Elizabetha, eiusque consiliarii ; Cecil, Parker, eorumque similes, qui domi, usque dum Maria regnabat, morati aut eis quae tunc fiebant tacite assenserant, aut saltem privati vitam tranquillam sine haeretico tumultu degerant. Ab his, cum plurium consensu, ritus Eduardinus in usum reductus est. Qua tandem intentione? Anne ut ministerium Ecclesiae everteretur ; ut novum aliquod ad mentem haereticorum conderetur?

Testentur ea quae deinde sequebantur. Testetur Calvinistarum reiectio, imo, si volueris, persecutio. Multum fuit illis cum nostris religionis commercium. Fateor : sed eo magis illustratur ex parte nostra Calviniani ministerii ac regiminis obstinata reiectio. Ac si in ea parte praxis et doctrina nostratum arctissime definiatur, non minus innotuit eorundem firmissima voluntas sese cum ceteris Catholicis coniungendi. Anno 1561 Pius IV consilium inibat de Synodo Tridentina instauranda   Litteras de ea re ad Elizabetham scripsit, urgitque ut oratores mitteret. Haec in dissertatione notavimus, sed deerat nobis certa de reginae Anglorumque voluntate notitia. Ea nunc suppeditat.   In litteris oratoris Hispani ad curiam Anglicam invenitur. De Quadra ad regem Philippum indesinenter scribebat de Anglorum in futuro Concilio participatione. Die 25° Martii 1561 narrat se cum Cecilio collocutum esse, qui ex parte reginae dixisset Anglos Concilio hisce conditionibus libenter interfuturos esse : si locus ex sententia principum Christianorum designatus foret ; si Papa, aut ipse aut per Legatos, ea lege praesideret ut non superior,

LETTERS 125

sed caput tantum Concilii et praeses videretur ; si definitiones de fide expraeceptis S. Scripturae, consensu doctorum, et regulis antiquorum Conciliorum fierent ; si episcopi
Anglicani, cum canonice ordinati essent, aequo iure cum
aliis episcopis in Concilio sederent[1] Quorsum haec? Utrum sincere dicta sint nescio. Utrum
regina consiliariique sui Concilio interesse revera voluerint,
dubium est. Attamen haec certe non verba sunt hominis
qui novam Ecclesiam condere, novum ministerium con-
stituere voluerit. Quod autem Cecil dixit, idem omnes
fere Anglicani senserunt. Ecclesiam Anglicanam, quae
inde a populi incunabulis originem habuit, quae tot
sanctorum meritis ornata per decem fere saecula una cum
gente increverat, eisdem legibus, eadem fide, eisdem Sacramentis, nova libertate praeditam, in multos annos con-
tinuare voluerunt. Audax erat conatus, tempora periculosa ;
ab illo unitatis centro unde tot sublevamina, tot iniurias
acceperant, discedentes, ab ipsa tamen unitate, ut sibi
suadebant, non discessuri, propriis viribus cum divina gratia
religionem ac veritatem sustentare statuerunt. Antiqua
retinere, non nova condere moliebantur. Dicere licet id
temere inceptum : sed eos nihil aliud voluisse res ipsae
testantur.

The Rev. Canon Ross-Lewin to T. A. L.

15 May, 1896.

The recent letter of the Bishop of Stepney may
lead some to suppose that re-ordination took place
during Mary's reign, at any rate in the diocese of
London. I think, however, the following passage
(quoted on a fly-leaf of this letter) will show that
some supposed deficiency, e.g. oil, was alone
supplied, and that, I imagine, only in some dioceses.

* * * * *

I have sent the passage from Pilkington to the
Bishop of Stepney, and he admits its force. The

[1] Ex Archiv. *Simancas* State Papers, Elizabeth ; 1561 ; p. 189.

126 A ROMAN DIARY AND OTHER DOCUMENTS

Bishops who supplied the lack of oil merely obeyed the injunction given to them.

*　　*　　*　　*　　*

"They would make men believe that the oil hath such holiness in it, that whosoever wanteth it is no priest nor minister. Therefore in the late days of popery our holy bishops called before them all such as were made ministers without such greasing, and blessed them with the popes blessing, anointed them, and then all was perfect; they might sacrifice for quick and dead." (Pilkington, *Exposition upon the Prophet Aggeus*, A.D. 1562. Reprinted in *Pilkington's Works*, Parker Society Ed., p. 163.)

The Rev. Edward Denny to T. A. L.

16 *May*, 1896

*　　*　　*　　*　　*

I examined last Friday the original at the Record Office of the Royal Assent to Barlow's election to St. David's, signed by the King, and compared it with (1) the like Assent to Sampson's election to Chichester on the Patent Rolls, and (2) the original Assent signed like the Barlow document by the King, to Repps' election to Norwich, and found the clause, "ut quod vestrum est in hac parte exequamini," in all three. So far as I understand the matter, the Royal Assent signed by the King is the sole document which emanated from the King himself in such a case; and this formed the foundation of the Letters Patent required by 25 Henry viii. c. 20, which could not without it be passed under the Great Seal. It seems to me a very important document, the weight of which cannot be destroyed by the non-discovery of the Letters Patent.

*　　*　　*　　*　　*

LETTERS

The Rev. E. G. Wood to T. A. L.

May 18, 1896.

I augur well from the reference to a Commission of Cardinals instead of the cause going in the usual course to the S.C. of the Holy Office itself for decree. I congratulate you both on your invitation from the Cardinal Secretary to remain in Rome. I wish that a Commission could be got to search for and Calendar all papers at the Vatican relating to English affairs from the time of the divorce down to the 3rd or 4th of Elizabeth. There must be papers there of importance, and perhaps some unexpected ones. The mere fact of that letter of Cromwell to Tuke (June 12, 1536) seems to me to indicate such a possibility. By the way, has Puller investigated that again? Would it be possible to get it photographed? I want to discover whether it is an original. If one could have a photograph, I could get an opinion as to the date of handwriting. If you cannot, then please see (1) whether it is on a separate sheet by itself, (2) whether there is any other writing on the sheet or any endorsement or address. Cut a piece of paper the exact size and shape. If possible, facsimile by tracing, if it would be allowed, Cromwell's signature.

I am also anxious that you should get a sight of the Abyssinian decrees.

(1) The document of April 9, 1704, given by Estcourt. He of course only actually reproduces the response of the Holy Office, May 1860, which quotes the "Risoluzione" of the S.C. S.O. of April 9, 1704. It will be desirable to inspect, if it could be managed (and I suppose Cardinal Rampolla

128   A ROMAN DIARY AND OTHER DOCUMENTS

could manage anything he chose in this way), the actual record, and ascertain whether it was the report of consultors or an actual decree. If not the latter, then whether there was a decree, probably a few days later. It seems so impossible to reconcile Cardinal Patrizzi's statement with the plain words of the Risoluzione.

(2) The decree of 1860.

(3) The Gordon Case. I cannot understand Duchesne's statement. The decree (April 17, 1704) says nothing about "Accipe, etc." Does he refer to any record of votes of Consultors? If so, when were such votes, or report founded thereon, presented to the Holy Office?

You observe the dates April 9 and April 17 in the same year. It seems to me absolutely impossible to suppose that in the space of a week the Holy Office could give two diametrically opposite determinations.

As regards "Accipe Spiritum Sanctum" being a valid form for the Priesthood, what can be said to the following?

The Episcopate is the plenitude of the Priesthood. The Priesthood is included in the Episcopate. The Episcopate can be validly conferred *per saltum*. But "Accipe Spiritum Sanctum" alone is, according to the Sententia Communis, a sufficient and valid form by itself for conferring the Episcopate. Therefore if a layman is consecrated by imposition of hands and the words "Accipe Spiritum Sanctum," only, with the intention to make him a Bishop, he is validly consecrated and becomes Bishop and Priest. Therefore the Priesthood was conferred by the form "Accipe, etc." Therefore "Accipe, etc." is a valid form for Priesthood.

LETTERS   129

T. A. L. to the Rev. E. G. Wood.

24 May, 1896.

Duchesne has a letter from the Vice-Chancellor of Cambridge asking him to come and receive an honorary degree (D. Litt.) on June 18. Great excitement thereanent among all our friends. He would like full information.

*   *   *   *   *

The letter on the back of which I am writing was sent to Cardinal Mazzella with your copy of the Mandate, which is now probably reposing permanently in the archives of the Holy Office, since everything has been prepared there ; but the *question* is not in the Holy Office. You may count on that, whatever the *Tablet* says. We know it because the two Vannutelli have told us that they are seised of it, and they are not in the Holy Office. So much the better.[1]

It is quite impossible to get at the archives of the Holy Office. One might as well ask to see Rothschild's books. Nor should we gain anything if we did. We know what the result in Gordon's case was, and the archives could reveal nothing more, for the decrees are never *motivés*. Mazzella explained the process to Portal. The vota of Consultors are read. The Prefect asks each Cardinal his decision—affirmative, negative, dilatanda, or what not,—no reasons being assigned. Then either a decision is given by the majority, or the question is marked *dilata*. In the former case it may or not be

---

[1] This may serve to show how extremely imperfect our information was.

K

130 A ROMAN DIARY AND OTHER DOCUMENTS

submitted to the Pope for confirmation. In the Abyssinian case in 1704 no decision was given, so presumably the question was marked *dilata*. What the Holy Office supplied to the Propaganda in 1860 was an unanimous votum of the Consultors, and the proceeding is regarded as a highly irregular and improper one. In Gordon's case the dossier is complete. Duchesne gave us a general idea of its contents.

I am ashamed of having left you in the dark so long on one point. I seem to have conveyed to you somehow the idea that Puller had found in the Archives a *copy* of the Tuke letter. It was merely Gairdner that he consulted in the library: when you first wrote about it I was utterly mystified.

My Supplementum will be out to-morrow or Tuesday. Our next business is to place a memorandum by Mr. Gladstone in the hands of Cardinal Rampolla. This will delay us here a little longer yet.

The Rev. E. G. Wood to T. A. L.

May 27, 1896.

I cannot say I am yet satisfied about the Abyssinian case. Cardinal Patrizzi at any rate called the pronouncement a "decree." Referring to what Bouix (*Tractatus de Curia Romana*, p. 154), says as to the procedure of the H.O., I cannot think that the Resolution was a document drawn up by the Consultors.

There are three kinds of meeting: (1) Consultors without Cardinals but with the Assessor; (2) the Cardinals without the Pope; (3) the Cardinals with

LETTERS 131

the Pope. These are respectively termed Congressus Feriæ II, Feriæ IV, and Feriæ V. In the second the Consultors are called in and "eorum sententia expetetur." Then the Cardinals "definitive pronuntiant ac decernunt," unless they consider the matter very grave, and so remit it ad Congressum Feriæ V, in which the Pope (who, and none other, is himself Prefect of the S.C.S.O.) presides; otherwise they decide without the Pope. I cannot but think that the resolution was *not* a votum of the Consultors. Moreover, I cannot help thinking that the procedure you describe is that of the S. C. Concilii, especially as regards the causes "*In Folio*" and not that of the Holy Office.

But any way, it seems quite clear that in 1860 the Holy Office adopted as its own the resoluzione of 1704. Whatever its value in 1704, surely the H.O. validated it and used it as the expression of its answer to the question laid before it in 1860. I cannot see that all that has been said touches that.

*　　*　　*　　*　　*

I do hope the Special Commission will not be in a hurry, but adjourn for some months. To judge by the tone of the *Revue*, I cannot say I think our friends even yet appreciate our position ; and, if so, how much less our adversaries. The note on p. 367 to the Abbé Klein's paper is not satisfactory. Conditional reordination, they must understand, is a thing we cannot even consent to discuss. Some paper in reply to Klein's would seem to me advisable. We shall gain nothing by being too "mealy mouthed."

132 A ROMAN DIARY AND OTHER DOCUMENTS

The Prior of Monte Cassino to T. A. L.

1 June, 1896.

Grates tibi refero ex toto cordis affectu pro libris quos dono misisti huic nostrae egerrimae bibliothecae, una cum epistola mihi gratissima.

Faxit Deus ut plures nostrae bibliothecae sint memores, tuumque bonum sequantur exemplum. Ipse vero centuplum tibi rependat, teque in multitudine pacis inhabitare faciat.

The Bishop of Ely to T. A. L.

June 26, 1896.

I met Duchesne at Lord Halifax's on Tuesday, and had some interesting talk, but nothing more about the Commission than you know already. I shall be glad if the result tends or helps toward the reunion of Christendom, though I cannot agree with Lord Halifax that one "fragment of the episcopate" should accept the judgment of the rest. Minorities are often in the right, as the old "Athanasius contra mundum" shows. And what we heard from Duchesne, which you also mention, of the position of Uniats—as you wisely call it, the *present* policy of Rome—does not incline one to *that* solution.

T. A. L. to Mr. Gladstone.

June 30, 1896.

I am taking the liberty of sending you copies of two pamphlets, which I had printed while in Rome. I intended to ask Father Puller to present them to you, but I had not copies ready to my hand

LETTERS   133

in time. The *de Re Anglicana* was not written
for publication, but I think you may be interested
in seeing it.

I have just seen the abstract of the new Encyclical
in the *Times*, furnished, I suppose, by Cardinal
Vaughan. An idea of what it would contain was
given me some weeks ago by Mgr. Gasparri, whom
the Pope consulted about it. He thought it would
prove a turning point in the theology of the Church,
and I think he was hardly exaggerating its importance. The main point which he led me to expect
was the distinction drawn between the *unicitas* and
the *unitas* of the Church. These phrases have been
used for some time in the Roman schools, but the
Pope gives them a new interest by showing that the
Church which is *unita* is not necessarily identical
in extent with the *Ecclesia unica*. It is no small
gain to have a definition from Rome that the
separated communions are really parts of the *Ecclesia
unica*. It follows that the *unitas* which according
to the Pope is to be found only in communion with
the Holy See is necessary, to employ the familiar
distinction, rather for the *bene esse* than for the
esse of the Church. Separation will affect, not the
efficacy, but only the legitimacy of the operations
of the episcopate. Add to this the important definition of the *magisterium* as residing not in the
papacy but in the episcopate, and the final assertion
that bishops are in no sense mere vicars of the Pope,
and it seems to me that the relations between the
Churches are once more brought within the sphere
of more or less friendly argument.

The daily papers—as one might expect—are
widely astray as to the bearing of the Encyclical.

134 A ROMAN DIARY AND OTHER DOCUMENTS

I hope that a few days' consideration will enable Englishmen to take a juster view of its importance and interest to themselves.

Mr. Gladstone to T. A. L.

July 3, 1896.

I thank you for your tracts, and I think we are all indebted to you and Father Puller for undertaking so bravely an arduous work, which I do not suppose could have been better performed.

I have read the Encyclical, and have not enough knowledge to see in it all that Mgr. Gasparri describes : but I see nothing at variance with his view, nor anything which ought to inspire dark anticipations as to the Pope's eventual utterance on the subject of Anglican Orders. I do not allow myself to be very sanguine about that utterance : but I read the Encyclical, with its strong self-assertion of the Papacy, as intended to clear the ground for whatever he may have to say, and to let his flock know that, whatever it may be, they have nothing to do but obey it.

The Pope has sent through Cardinal Rampolla to the Abate Tosti for transmission to me a very kind and gracious message.

We were much pleased with the Abbé Duchesne, whom Lord Acton conceives to be the most learned man in France.

The "Life of Manning" and the Duchesne movement are enough to make this a considerable year in the history of the Church.[1]

[1] Reproduced by permission from *Correspondence on Church and Religion of William Ewart Gladstone*, by D. C. Lathbury. Vol. II p. 73.

LETTERS

T. A. L. to the Rev. W. H. Frere.

Sept. 26, 1896.

*   *   *   *   *

The document published by Le Quien is worthless.
The Archives of the Holy Office are inaccessible.
I was told that not even the Pope himself can give
permission for any one to see them except a Consultor. But we did see at Rome what Moyes had
extracted from them relative to the Gordon case,
and Scannell—who was really friendly, though not
at all in favour of the validity, unless indeed he was
convinced by the course of the investigation—told
me that they had before them the whole dossier of
the case, and that there was unquestionably a
thorough examination of the rite and all its history
and its circumstances. A Consultor was sent to
England expressly to examine things closely, and
his report was most candid. Thus Scannell. On
these inquiries, and not at all on Gordon's Supplica,
the decision was based.

In the Commission, Cardinal Mazzella refused
to let the consultors go behind the Gordon decision :
they were consultors of the Holy Office and were
bound by all its decisions. This Duchesne told us.
It was almost certain that if the Pope sent the matter
to the Holy Office they would practically refuse to
re-open the points decided in the Gordon case.
Only if it was sent to a special Commission of
Cardinals was there any hope of this. It was sent
to the Holy Office—and behold the result![1] As
Portal says, the only question for them was, *whether*

---

[1] Written after the publication of the Bull *Apostolicae Curae.*

136 A ROMAN DIARY AND OTHER DOCUMENTS

there were grounds for revising the decision, and their answer was negative. I believe the only fresh investigation has been of the historical facts : about them the Bull observes a significant silence for the most part.

MR. GLADSTONE'S MEMORANDUM

IV

MR. GLADSTONE'S MEMORANDUM

Addressed to the Archbishop of York[1]

THE question of the validity of Anglican orders might seem to be of limited interest if it were only to be treated by the amount of any immediate, practical, and external consequences, likely to follow upon any discussion or decision that might now be taken in respect to it. For the clergy of the Anglican communion, numbering between 30,000 and 40,000, and for their flocks, the whole subject is one of settled solidity. In the Oriental Churches there prevails a sentiment of increased and increasing friendliness towards the Anglican Church, but no question of actual intercommunion is likely at present to arise, while happily no system of proselytism exists to set a blister on our mutual relations. In the Latin Church, which from its magnitude and the close tissue of its organizations overshadows all Western Christendom, these Orders, so far as they have been noticed, have been commonly disputed, or denied, or treated as if they were null. A positive condemnation of them, if viewed dryly in its letter, would do no more than harden the existing usage of reordination in the case, which at most periods

[1] See *Diary*, May 24th.

139

has been a rare one, of Anglican clergy who might seek admission to the clerical order in the Roman Church.

But very different indeed would be the moral aspect and effect of a formal, authorized investigation of the question at Rome, to whichever side the result might incline. It is to the last degree improbable that a ruler of known wisdom would at this time put in motion the machinery of the Curia for the purpose of widening the breach which severs the Roman Catholic Church from a communion which, though small in comparison, yet is extended through the large and fast-increasing range of the English-speaking races, and which represents, in the religious sphere, one of the most powerful nations of European Christendom. According to my reading of history, that breach is, indeed, already a wide one ; but the existing schism has not been put into stereotype by any anathema, or any express renunciation of communion, on either side. As an acknowledgment of Anglican Orders would not create intercommunion, so a condemnation of them would not absolutely excommunicate ; but it would be a step, and even morally a stride, towards excommunication, and it would stand as a practical affirmation of the principle that it is wise to make the religious differences between the Churches of Christendom more conspicuous to the world, and also to bring them into a state of the highest fixity, so as to enhance the difficulty of approaching them at any future time in the spirit of reconciliation. From such a point of view, an inquiry resulting in a proscription of Anglican orders would be no less important than deplorable.

MR. GLADSTONE'S MEMORANDUM 141

But the information, which I have been allowed through the kindness of Lord Halifax to share, altogether dispels from my mind every apprehension of this kind, and convinces me that if the investigations of the Curia did not lead to a favourable result, wisdom and charity would in any case arrest them at such a point as to prevent their becoming an occasion and a means of embittering religious controversy.

I turn, therefore, to the other alternative, and assume, for the sake of argument, that the judgment of the examining tribunal would be found either to allow upon all points the preponderance of the contentions on behalf of validity, or at the least to place beyond controversy a portion of the matters which enter into the essence of the discussion. I will for the present take it for granted that these fall under three heads :—

1. The external competency of the consecrators.

2. The external sufficiency of the commission they have conferred.

3. That sufficiency of intention which the 11th Canon of the Council of Trent appears to require.

Under the first head the examination would of course include, in addition to the consecration of Parker and the competency of his consecrators, the several cases in which consecrators outside the English line have participated in the consecrations of Anglican bishops, and have in this manner furnished independent grounds for the assertion of validity. Even the dismissal from the controversy of any one of these three heads would be in the nature of an advance towards concord, and would be so far a reward for the labours of His Holiness,

142 A ROMAN DIARY AND OTHER DOCUMENTS

Pope Leo XIII, in furtherance of truth and peace. But I may be permitted to contemplate for a moment, as possible or likely, even the full acknowledgment that, without reference to any other real or supposed points of controversy, the simple abstract validity of Anglican consecrations is not subject to reasonable doubt.

And now I must take upon me to speak in the only capacity in which it can be warrantable for me to intervene in a discussion properly belonging to persons of competent authority. That is the capacity of an absolutely private person, born and baptized in the Anglican Church, accepting his lot there as is the duty of all who do not find that she has forfeited her original and inherent privilege and place. I may add that my case is that of one who has been led, by the circumstances both of his private and of his public career, to a lifelong and rather close observation of her character, her fortunes, and the part she has to play in the grand history of Redemption. Thus it is that her public interests are also his personal interest, and that they require or justify what is no more than his individual thought upon them.

He is not one of those who look for an early restitution of such a Christian unity as that which marked the earlier history of the Church. Yet he ever cherishes the belief that work may be done in that direction, which, if not majestic or imposing, may nevertheless be legitimate and solid ; and this by the least as well as by the greatest.

It is the Pope who, as the first Bishop of Christendom, has the noblest sphere of action ; but the humblest of the Christian flock has his place of

MR. GLADSTONE'S MEMORANDUM 143

daily duty, and, according as he fills it, helps to make or mar every good and holy work.

In this character the writer has viewed with profound and thankful satisfaction, during the last half century and more, the progressive advance of a great work of restoration in Christian doctrine. It has not been wholly confined within his own country to the Anglican Communion ; but it is best that he should speak of that which has been most under his eye. Within these limits it has not been confined to doctrine, but has extended to Christian life and all its workings. The aggregate result has been that it has brought the Church of England from a state externally of halcyon calm, but inwardly of deep stagnation, to one in which, while buffeted more or less by external storms, subjected to some peculiar and searching forms of trial, and even now by no means exempt from internal dissensions, she sees her clergy transformed (for this is the word which may advisedly be used), her vital energies enlarged and still growing in every direction, and a store of bright hopes accumulated that she may be able to contribute her share, and even possibly no mean share, towards the consummation of the work of the Gospel in the world.

Now the contemplation of these changes by no means uniformly ministers to our pride. They involve large admissions of collective fault. This is not the place, and I am not the proper organ, for exposition in detail. But I may mention the widespread depression of Evangelical doctrine, the insufficient exhibition of the Person and work of the Redeemer, the coldness and deadness as well as the infrequency of public worship, the relegation of the Holy Eucharist to impoverished ideas, and to the place of one (though doubtless a solemn one) among its occasional incidents, the gradual effacement of Church observance from personal and daily life. In all these respects there has been a profound alteration, which is still progressive, and which, apart from occasional extravagance or indiscretion, has indicated a real advance in the discipline of souls, and in the work of God on behalf of man. A single-minded allegiance to truth sometimes exacts admissions which may be turned to account for the purpose of inflicting polemical disadvantage. Such an admission I must now record. It is not to be denied that a very large part of these improvements has lain in a direction which has diminished the breadth of separation between ourselves and the authorized teaching of the unreformed Church both in East and West, so that, while on the one hand they were improvements in religious doctrine and life, on the other hand they were testimonials recorded against ourselves and in favour of bodies outside our own precinct—that is to say, they were valuable contributions to the cause of Christian reunion.

With sorrow we noted that, so far as the Western Church was concerned, its only public and corporate movements, especially in 1870, seemed to meet the approximations made among us with something of recession from us. But it is not necessary to open further this portion of the subject; "redeunt Saturnia regna." Certain publications of learned French priests, unsuspected in their orthodoxy, which went to affirm the validity of Anglican ordinations, naturally excited much interest in this

MR. GLADSTONE'S MEMORANDUM 145

country and elsewhere. But there was nothing in them to ruffle the Roman atmosphere or invest the subject, in the circles of the Vatican, with the character of administrative urgency. When, therefore, it came to be understood that Pope Leo XIII had given his commands that the validity of Anglican ordinations should form the subject of an historical and theological investigation, it was impossible not to be impressed with the profound interest of the considerations brought into view by such a step, if interpreted in accordance with just reason, as an effort towards the abatement of controversial differences.

There was, indeed, in my view a subject of thought, anterior to any scrutiny of the question upon its intrinsic merits, which deeply impressed itself upon my mind. Religious controversies do not, like bodily wounds, heal by the genial force of nature. If they do not proceed to gangrene and to mortification, at least they tend to harden into fixed facts, to incorporate themselves with law, character, and tradition—nay, even with language ; so that at last they take rank among the *data* and presuppositions of common life, and are thought as inexpugnable as the rocks of an ironbound coast. A poet of ours describes the sharp and total severance of two early friends :—

> They parted—ne'er to meet again !
> But never either found another
> To free the hollow heart from paining—
> They stood aloof, the scars remaining,
> Like cliffs which had been rent asunder ;
> A dreary sea now rolls between.[1]

[1] COLERIDGE'S *Christabel*.

L

146 A ROMAN DIARY AND OTHER DOCUMENTS

Let us remember that we are now far advanced in the fourth century since the Convocation of Canterbury under Warham, in 1531, passed its canon or resolution on the royal governorship of the Church.

How much has happened during those centuries to inflame the strife, how little to abate or quench it. What courage must it require in a Pope, what an elevation above all the levels of stormy partisanship, what genuineness of love for the whole Christian flock, whether separated or annexed, to enable him to approach the huge mass of hostile and still burning recollections, in the spirit and for the purposes of peace.

And yet that is what Pope Leo XIII has done, first in entertaining the question of this inquiry, and secondly in determining and providing, by the infusion both of capacity and of impartiality into the investigating tribunal, that no instrument should be overlooked, no guarantee omitted, for the probable attainment of the truth. He who bears in mind the cup of cold water administered to "one of these little ones" will surely record this effort, stamped in its very inception as alike arduous and blessed.

But what of the advantage to be derived from any proceeding which shall end, or shall reduce within narrower bounds, the debate upon Anglican Orders? I will put upon paper, with the utmost deference to authority and better judgment, my own personal and individual, and, as I freely admit, very insignificant reply to the question.

The one controversy which, according to my deep conviction, overshadows, and in the last resort

MR. GLADSTONE'S MEMORANDUM   147

absorbs, all others is the controversy between faith and unbelief. It is easy to understand the reliance which the loyal Roman Catholic places upon the vast organization and imposing belief and action of his Church, as his provision for meeting the emergency. But I presume that even he must feel that the hundreds of millions, who profess the name of Christ without owning the authority of his Church, must count for something in the case ; and that, the more he is able to show their affirmative belief to stand in consonance with his, the more he strengthens both the common cause—for surely there is a common cause—and his own particular position.

If, out of every hundred professing Christians, ninety-nine assert amidst all their separate and clashing convictions their belief in the central doctrines of the Trinity and the Incarnation, will not every member of each particular Church or community be forward to declare, will not the candid unbeliever be disposed freely to admit, that this unity amidst diversity is a great confirmation of the faith and a broad basis on which to build our hopes of the future?

I now descend to a level which, if lower than that of these transcendent doctrines, is still a lofty level.

The historical transmission of the truth by a visible Church with an ordained constitution is a matter of profound importance according to the belief and practice of fully three-fourths of Christendom. In these three-fourths I include the Anglican Churches, which are probably required in order to make them up.

148 A ROMAN DIARY AND OTHER DOCUMENTS

It is surely better for the Roman and also the Oriental Church to find the Churches of the Anglican succession standing side by side with them in the assertion of what they deem an important Christian principle, than to be obliged to regard them as mere pretenders in this behalf, and *pro tanto* to reduce the "cloud of witnesses" willing and desirous to testify on behalf of the principle. These considerations of advantage must, of course, be subordinated to historic truth, but for the moment advantage is the point with which I deal.

I attach no such value to these reflections as would warrant my tendering them for the consideration of any responsible person, much less of one laden with the cares and responsibilities of the highest position in the Christian Church.

On the other hand, there is nothing in them which requires that they should shrink from the light. They simply indicate the views of one who has passed a very long life in rather intimate connection with the Church of this country, with its rulers, its members, and its interests. I may add that my political life has brought me much into contact with those independent religious communities which supply an important religious factor in the religious life of Great Britain, and which, speaking generally, while they decline to own the authority either of the Roman or of the National Church, yet still allow to what they know as the established religion no inconsiderable hold upon their sympathies.

In conclusion, it is not for me to say what will be the upshot of the proceedings now in progress at Rome. But be their issue what it may, there is,

MR. GLADSTONE'S MEMORANDUM 149

in my view, no room for doubt as to the attitude which has been taken by the actual head of the Roman Catholic Church in regard to them. It seems to me an attitude in the largest sense paternal ; and while it will probably stand among the latest recollections of my lifetime, it will ever be cherished with cordial sentiments of reverence, of gratitude, and of high appreciation.

W. E. GLADSTONE.

HAWARDEN, *May*, 1896

THE ROYAL MANDATE FOR
BARLOW'S CONSECRATION

V

THE ROYAL MANDATE FOR BARLOW'S CONSECRATION

I

Memorandum delivered to Cardinal Mazzella[1]

Eminentissime et Reverendissime Domine,

ABHINC paucos dies telegramma viro rev. L. Duchesne dedi, quo confrater meus E. G. Wood mihi renuntiarat se *mandatum regium* pro consecratione Barlovi repperisse. Hodie ipsius documenti apographum ab eodem E. G. Wood recepi, una cum expositione modi quo huiusmodi instrumenta tempore Henrici VIII expediebantur atque in archivis reponebantur, de qua re diligentissimam apud ipsa archiva inquisitionem instituit. Quae ille docuit in formam sequentem redegi. Iuxta statutum 25 Hen. VIII cap. 20, de electione et consecratione episcoporum anno 1533 factum, provisum est ut rex de electione certior factus *per litteras patentes sub magno sigillo praedictam electionem archiepiscopo ac metropolitae provinciae significaret ; rogando ac mandando ut archiepiscopus, cui talia significarentur, praedictam electionem confirm-*

[1] See *Diary*, April 19th, 22nd, 28th ; May 12th, and *Letters* of May 6th, 7th, 8th, and 16th.

154 A ROMAN DIARY AND OTHER DOCUMENTS

aret, et praedictam personam ita electam ad munus et dignitatem huiusmodi investiret et consecraret, eique omnes benedictiones daret, omnibusque caeremoniis aliisque rebus uteretur quae in hac parte necessaria forent.[1] Quae ut mature intelligantur necesse erit quaedam de modo Litterarum Patentium expediendarum exponere.

Primo igitur litterae brevissime redactae sub *Signatura Manuali* ipsius regis parabantur, quae ad *Custodem Sigilli Privati* intra octo dies mittebantur. Ille instrumentum completis clausulis parabat, cuius duo apographa facta sunt, alterum, cui rubrica erat *Per breve sub Sigillo Privato* in archivis Sigilli Privati conservandum, alterum cui rubrica *Sub Sigillo Privato* ipsumque sigillum impressum est. Hoc autem Summo Cancellario datum est, cum praefatione de Litteris Patentibus sub Magno Sigillo expediendis. Quo recepto ille instrumentum definitivum parandum curabat, cuius iterum duo apographa facta sunt ; alterum in *Rotulis Patentibus* apud archiva cancellariatus conservandum, alterum quod Magno Sigillo impressum tanquam *Litterae Patentes* ipsi personae missum est cui rex actu rescribere voluisset.

Ex dictis patet quinque instrumenta exstare

---

[1] The king's Highness, by his letters patent under his great seal, shall signifie the said election, if it be to the dignity of a bishop, to the archbishop and metropolitane of the Province where the see of the said bishoprick was void, if the see of the said archbishop be full and not void : and if it be void, then to any other archbishop within this realm or in any other the king's dominions ; requiring and commanding such archbishop, to whom any such signification shall be made, to confirm the said election, and to invest and consecrate the said person so elected to the office and dignity that he is elected unto, and to give and use to him all such benedictions, ceremonies, and other things requisite for the same.

MANDATE FOR BARLOW'S CONSECRATION 155

possunt, ex quibus certissimo appareat huiusmodi
Litteras Patentes expeditas fuisse. Haec sunt: 1°
Breve sub Signatura Manuali, quod in archivis
Sigilli Privati, sub titulo generali *Signed Bills* con-
servari solet : 2° Instrumentum *Per breve sub Sigillo
Privato* in eisdem archivis conservatum : 3° Instrumentum *Sub Sigillo Privato* a Cancellario receptum et in eius archivis repositum : 4° *Litterae
Patentes* sub Magno Sigillo actu emissae : 5° Apographum earundem litterarum in *Rotulis Patentibus*
conservatum. Ipsae igitur Litterae Patentes in
possessionem eius cui directae sunt tradebantur ;
alia instrumenta omnia in archivis reperiri debent.
Tempore autem de quo agitur depositiones in
archivis incuriosissime fiebant ; nec facile invenietur
casus in quo omnia huiusmodi usque hodie asser-
vantur. Quod si vel unum ex his instrumentis
inveniatur, alia necessario expedita fuisse manifestum
est.

Quid ergo de Barlovi promotione habemus?
Primum ex istis instrumentis, quod et aliorum
fons et origo est, adhuc in archivis invenitur.[1]
Tale est :

" Henry R.

Rex reverendissimo in Christo patri Thomae
Cantuar. archiepiscopo totius Angliae primati salutem. Sciatis quod electioni nuper factae in ecclesia
Cathedrali Meneven. per mortem bonae memoriae
dom. Richardi Rawlyns ultimi episcopi ibidem
vacante de reverendo in Christo patre dom.
Willelmo Barlow sacrae theologiae professore tunc

---

[1] " Privy seals Bundle," April, 1536.

156 A ROMAN DIARY AND OTHER DOCUMENTS

episcopo Assaven. et Mon. de Bisham Sarum dioec. commendatorio perpetuo in episcopum loci illius et pastorem regium assensum adhibuimus et favorem, et hoc vobis tenore praesentium significamus ut quod vestrum est in hac parte exequamini. In cuius etc. Teste etc."

Hoc igitur dato instrumento necesse erat ut Custos Sigilli Privati litteras iuxta morem completas redigendas curaret. In his autem clausulae quae sub Signatura Manuali brevius expressae erant plenis phrasibus expansae sunt. Inter alia sensus verborum "*ut quod vestrum est in hac parte exequamini*" a scriptoribus iuxta normam scribendi ita exprimitur :—" Rogantes et in fide et dilectione quibus vos tenemini firmiter vobis mandantes quatenus praefatum Willelmum Barlow Episcopum Menevensem electum confirmare et eundem Willelmum in Episcopum Menevensem consecrare ipsumque prout moris est episcopalibus insigniis investire, ceteraque peragere quae vestro in hac parte incumbant officio pastorali iuxta formam statuti in ea parte editi et provisi velitis diligenter cum effectu." Ex instrumento ita elaborato Litterae Patentes intra paucos dies expedirentur necesse erat, ut omnia secundum leges fierent.[1]

Nihil ex his nisi solum Breve sub Signatura Manuali repertum est. Sed ex hoc omnia dependent, et notissimum est ex registro Cranmeri eum Litteras huiusmodi Patentes recepisse, et iuxta earum tenorem Barlovi electionem die 21 Aprilis confirmasse. Quo die ad consecrationem perrexerit ignoramus.

---

[1] This paragraph is altogether inaccurate. For the correction of the mistake, see the two letters to the *Tablet*, here following.

MANDATE FOR BARLOW'S CONSECRATION 157

Haec si ad quaestionem aliquam dirimendam utilia fuerint Eminentiae vestrae humillime submittit

Eminentiae vestrae

Servus in Christo observantissimus

T. A. LACEY.

Romae in via dicta *del Tritone* 36
13 Maii 1896

II

Letters to the Editor of the " Tablet."

SIR,—I am now in a position to place before your readers the results of some further investigation of the Royal Mandate for Consecration. It may be well to recall the origin of the question. Father Sydney Smith in a pamphlet, and Canon Moyes in your columns, contended that in the case of Barlow all documents relating to election are extant, all relating to consecration are missing. Among others they showed the *Royal Assent* to the election as extant, the *Royal Mandate* for the consecration as missing. They took these to be two separate documents, the former required by old custom anterior to the Act of 1533, the latter required by the terms of that Act.

I replied in my *Supplementum* that these two are one and the same thing ; to speak more strictly, any writ of *Royal Assent* is also a *Mandate for Consecration.* I made one considerable mistake in the statement of my case, which I will correct lower down.

I have already shown that it is a mistake to suppose a writ of *Assent* to have been in use before

158 A ROMAN DIARY AND OTHER DOCUMENTS

the Act of 1533. For more than a century promotions had all been made by Provision, and there was no occasion for such a writ. The Act of 1533 (25 H. VIII, cap. 20) is, therefore, our starting point. By this Act the form of capitular election was restored, subject to the Royal License or *congé-d'eslire*. The election was to be reported by the Chapter to the King. The procedure then to be followed is carefully set out in the Act. "The King's Highness, by his Letters Patents under his great seal, shall signify the said election, if it be to the dignity of a Bishop, to the Archbishop and Metropolitan of the Province where the See of the said Bishoprick was void, if the See of the said Archbishop he full and not void : and if it be void, then to any other Archbishop within this Realm, or in any other the King's Dominions ; requiring and commanding such Archbishop, to whom any such signification shall be made, to confirm the said election, and to invest and consecrate the said person so elected to the office and dignity that he is elected unto, and to give and use to him all such benedictions, ceremonies, and other things requisite for the same, without any suing, procuring, or obtaining any Bulls, Letters, or other things from the See of Rome for the same in any behalf." The next section provides that the election of an *Archbishop* is in like manner to be certified to some Archbishop with two other Bishops, or to four Bishops.

In carrying out these provisions, what precedents had the King's advisers to go on ?

1. There was a writ in common use for the Royal Assent to the election of certain Abbots and

MANDATE FOR BARLOW'S CONSECRATION 159

Priors. This writ went to the Bishop of the diocese where the convent was situated, signifying to him the election, "ut quod vestrum est in hac parte exequamini." That is to say he was ordered to invest and institute the elect.

2. In earlier days, when capitular election was still in force but confirmations had been reserved to the Roman Court, the King signified his assent to the Pope, praying him to do his part. Such a letter of the year 1374 is extant, in which the King signifies to the Pope his assent to the election of Neville to York.

3. In the year 1416, during the Great Schism, no Pope was recognized in England. In consequence, the King, with the special consent of Parliament, authorized Chichele, the Archbishop of Canterbury, to confirm the election of Wakering to Norwich. The writs are extant. setting forth the reasons for the unusual course taken and ordering the Archbishop "omnia quae vestro canonico incumbunt officio in hac parte peragatis et exequamini" (Rymer ix., 337–338). Wakering's writ of Restitution recites that this has been done. The writs of Restitution recite the same procedure in the cases of Chandler of Sarum, and Lacey of Exeter, but the patents apparently are not extant (*Ibid.* 450–539).

These are the precedents. When we examine the writs actually issued during the years immediately following the Act we find an extraordinary variety of practice. Sometimes the above precedents, one and three, were followed pretty closely ; the vacation and election are recited, the King's assent is signified, and the Archbishop is simply

160 A ROMAN DIARY AND OTHER DOCUMENTS

directed to do his duty, "ut quod vestrum est in hac parte ulterius exequamini cum effectu." Minor variations in the wording are frequent, as was natural in a new writ, not of common use. This I will call the *shorter form.*

At other times an entirely new form was used, which adopted a good deal of the wording of the Act, the Archbishop being specifically directed to confirm and consecrate. Allowance made for variations, the following is the ordinary style : " Rogantes et mandantes quatenus praefatam electionem ipsumque N. electum confirmare et eundem N. consecrare, ipsumque prout moris est episcopalibus insigniis investire, ceteraque peragere quae vestro in hac parte officio pastorali incumbunt iuxta formam statuti in ea parte editi et provisi velitis diligenter cum effectu." I will call this the *longer form.*

Two Bishops however, Lee of Lichfield in 1534 and Fox of Hereford in 1535, had writs drawn in a form altogether exceptional. A third common form was afterwards introduced, directing confirmation and consecration in general terms, which appears to have completely ousted the shorter form.

The first and second of these forms — the shorter and the longer—are those which have been distinguished as the *Assent to the Election,* and the *Mandate for Consecration.* Both were supposed to be required. But on carefully reading the Act one sees that only one instrument is required, in which the King shall at once signify his assent to the election, and direct the Archbishop to proceed. As a matter of fact, in some cases one Patent was issued, in other cases two ; sometimes

MANDATE FOR BARLOW'S CONSECRATION 161

the shorter form alone, sometimes the longer alone, sometimes both; sometimes, as I have said, a special form.

Here I wish to acknowledge the mistake into which I fell when writing my *Supplementum*. I assumed that in no case were the two forms of the writ issued. My mistake was due to my misunderstanding part of the information sent to me, and this again was due to the fixed idea, derived from Father Sydney Smith's pamphlet, that the shorter form was a writ of common use, expanded for the purposes of the Act of 1533 into the longer form. I was clearly in error, since in some cases both were issued. But I have not yet been able to determine the true relation between the two, or the reason why, in some cases, both were issued. My contention, however, that they are not rightly distinguished as *Assent to Election* and *Mandate to Consecrate* is absolutely established by further investigation.

I have been trying, with the help of Rymer, Gairdner's *Catalogue*, and Cranmer's *Register*, to determine precisely what was done in each case during the first few years after the passing of the Act—the period of Barlow's promotion. The task is far from complete, but the facts already ascertained are sufficient to prove my contention.

The manner in which the copies of the writs appear in the Register is of capital importance. In the case of each promotion recorded—there are, as is well known, several omissions—the Register contains an elaborate and detailed account of the Confirmation, in which are incorporated, with other instruments, the Patents which we are considering.

M

162 A ROMAN DIARY AND OTHER DOCUMENTS

Afterwards the Consecration is recorded in a brief entry of about five lines—often omitted, as notably in the cases of Sampson, Reppis, and Barlow— without any details or documents. The Patents, whether one or two, whatever their form, are thus included in the Acts of the Confirmation, and they are all alike entitled in the margin, *Litterae Patentes regiae Majestatis super assensu suo.* One sees at once how inaccurate it is to describe any of them as specifically *Mandates for Consecration.* That term belongs indeed to a later period, when under Edward VI capitular elections were abolished, and the king appointed to a bishopric by Letters Patent, commanding the Archbishop simply to consecrate, the only duty remaining to him.

To the ordering of the Register which I have here described there is only one exception. Shaxton, promoted to Sarum in 1535, received two Patents, but the second was not issued until four days after his confirmation. This writ is therefore not included in the Acts of the Confirmation, but is copied in the Register after them.

So far I have shown only that the Longer Form is not specifically a Mandate for Consecration, as distinguished from the Shorter Form. But my position proves to be stronger than I thought. The combined evidence of the Records and the Register proves that the Shorter Form by itself was a sufficient mandate according to the terms of the Act. As I have said, in some promotions only one Patent was issued. Four of these, occurring within a few weeks, are Barlow to St. Asaph, Barlow to St. Davids, Sampson to Chichester, and

MANDATE FOR BARLOW'S CONSECRATION 163

Reppis to Norwich. In all these cases the *Shorter Form* only was used. Here are the references:

Barlow to St. Asaph. Patent dated February 22, 1536. Gairdner, 392 (45): Cranmer's Reg. 180 b.

Barlow to St. Davids. Dated April 20, 1536, G. 775 (27); Reg. 205 a.

Sampson to Chichester. Dated *die xi junii*, 1536 (an obvious error for *ix*, since he was confirmed with Reppis on June 10). G. 1256 (19); Reg. 189 b.

Reppis to Norwich. Dated June 9, 1536, G. 1256 (12); Reg. 209 a.[1]

In these cases Cranmer proceeded to confirm and consecrate on the authority of this Shorter Form alone. Setting aside Barlow, it is certain that he consecrated Sampson and Reppis on June 11. But he had no power to act at all, either to confirm or to consecrate, except on the authority of a mandate given in accordance with the Act. Therefore the Shorter Form is such a mandate.

The contention, then, which I put forward is supported by further investigation. The distinction between the *Assent to the Election* and the *Mandate to Consecrate* is unreal. The Royal mandate to consecrate Barlow was issued in one of the forms then current, and is now extant.

Upon the relation of the two forms to each other, and the reason why sometimes both were issued, I have found no further light. In view, however, of that which I have determined, this question is one of little more than antiquarian in-

---

[1] Inaccurate. See the next Letter.

164 A ROMAN DIARY AND OTHER DOCUMENTS

terest. If I have time to pursue it further, perhaps you will allow me to give your readers the result.

T. A. LACEY.

MADINGLEY, *August* 31, 1896.

SIR,—Insinuations of bad faith add neither dignity to a controversy nor strength to an argument, and so, while always regretting their appearance, I would rather be their object than their author; nor do I fear the general verdict.[1] There are, however, two suggestions of this kind which I would rather not pass over. The writer of your article has said that my reply involved the suppression of one hypothesis and "the tacit substitution of another." *Tacit !* I thought I had in the most express terms acknowledged the mistake to which he refers, and called attention to the explanation substituted. Again, after quoting the terms of the longer form of assent, you wonder "how Mr. Lacey could, with these words before him, deny that this

---

This was written, I must admit, in the true controversial style. I do not know what right I had to assume this tone of superiority. I had been correcting a mistake with elaborate detail, a procedure which almost inevitably engenders suspicion. But the detail was necessary, for a mere acknowledgment of the mistake would have been misleading. Stated simply, and without detail, the case was as follows : Two documents were known, commonly distinguished as the *Assent to Election* and the *Mandate to Consecrate.* Moved by the suggestion of Sir Walter Phillimore that the Act of Henry VIII required only one such document (*Diary,* April 19th), I made a further study of the matter with imperfect information at my disposal, came to the erroneous conclusion that the *Assent* was merely a preliminary draft of the *Mandate,* and too hastily communicated this conclusion to Cardinal Mazzella, publishing it also in the *Supplementum.* It was, of course, challenged. After my return to England I made a further examination of the documents at first hand, discovering that both were in some cases issued as Letters Patent, but that either of them was an effective Mandate for consecration within the meaning of the Act.

MANDATE FOR BARLOW'S CONSECRATION 165

writ was a Mandate for Consecration." You might indeed wonder, if I had done anything of the kind, especially as my whole contention is that either the longer or the shorter form is a sufficient mandate for consecration. What I said was that neither of them is *specifically* a Mandate for Consecration— that is to say, as the context clearly shows, for consecration as distinct from other incidents of the promotion.

Permit me to add that if I were all that you think me, still I should not, in treating this question, be tempted to the faults which you impute to me. This particular question has no interest for me but one purely scientific and historical. The case for Barlow's consecration is that which Lingard stated sixty years ago, and which nothing short of direct negative proof can shake. If I prove my contention up to the hilt I add nothing to the strength of that case. In this detached frame of mind I offer some criticisms on your last article.

1. To show that the shorter form of assent existed before the Act of 1533 you allege precedents from the thirteenth century. I should have expected something of the kind at that early period, though I frankly admit I should not have expected anything so exactly similar; but I did not think it necessary to push my quest so far back. The question is whether this form of writ was continuously in use before and after the Act. What bearing upon this question have precedents the latest of which belongs to the year 1327? You seem to allow that for two hundred years before the Act this writ was not in use. Any argument

166 A ROMAN DIARY AND OTHER DOCUMENTS

that might be drawn from continuous use therefore disappears.

2. You argue that the shorter form could not have been a *Mandate* because it was in use during the Middle Ages. " In pre-reformation times," you say, "no English king would, or could, have *commanded* the Primate to confirm or consecrate a bishop-elect, and such an attitude on the part of the lay power would have been foreign to the whole spirit of mediæval economy." It is news indeed to hear that mediæval kings were so tender of the susceptibilities of bishops. I think I could produce many startling instances to the contrary, but two may suffice. The period of the Middle Ages is rather elastic. Would you refer to the early days? There is in Marculfus an ordinary *Indiculus* of the Frankish kings directing the Metropolitan to consecrate a bishop : " Qua de re statuta praesentibus ordinamus ut cum adunatorum caterva pontificum, ad quos tamen nostrae serenitatis devotio scripta pervenit, ipsum ut ordo postulat benedicere vestra industria studeat " (Migne. *P. L.*, tom. 87, col. 704. Also in Labbe, tom. viii., col. 1865). Would you look rather to a later period? In the year 1416, Henry V, with the consent of Parliament, directs Chichele to confirm Wakering to Norwich in these terms : " Vobis mandamus quod ad confirmationem praefati clerici nostri virtute electionis sibi ut praemittitur factae absque excusatione seu dilatione aliquali procedatis, ac caetera omnia quae vestro canonico incumbunt officio in hac parte peragatis et exequamini " (*Close Rolls*, H. 5 ; m. 23. *Rymer*, ix., 338). With these quotations before you I am sure you will admit

MANDATE FOR BARLOW'S CONSECRATION 167

at once that this part, at least, of your argument must go.

3. But, indeed, it is useless to ask whether this writ *could* have been a mandate, if, as I showed, it was actually taken as a mandate. You, therefore, addressed yourself to my crucial cases. And first as regards Sampson, you argue that since Cranmer certified to the King, in express terms, that he had confirmed and consecrated him, therefore he *must* have received the longer form of Assent, ordering this in the same express terms. The statement of this argument really seems sufficient for its refutation, but I happen to have in hand a direct refutation. Cranmer confirmed Shaxton also on the authority of the shorter form only, and certified the confirmation to the King on March 18, 1535. The longer form of Assent was issued some days afterwards (Cranmer's *Reg.* 172 a). The certificate, then, clearly does not imply the issue of the longer writ. Again I am sure you will wish to acknowledge the mistake.

The double confirmation of Barlow himself on the authority of the shorter form must be put aside, you think—and you assume my agreement—because the question is about his *consecration*. But to argue thus you must assume that a writ might be good as a mandate for confirmation, and not good as a mandate for consecration. You can find nothing in the Act to justify this. On the contrary, the Act speaks of a single writ signifying the King's assent, and commanding the Archbishop "to confirm the said election, and to invest and consecrate the said person." A writ which was good for one was good for the other, unless, perhaps, in case one or the other were expressly and exclusively mentioned. The argument,

168 A ROMAN DIARY AND OTHER DOCUMENTS

then, stands thus. Cranmer confirmed Barlow on the authority of the shorter form of Assent. But he could not confirm him save on the authority of a mandate to confirm and consecrate according to the Act. Therefore the shorter form of Assent was such a mandate.

So far, then, from Barlow's own case being nothing to the purpose, I might have proved my contention on the strength of that case only.

There remains the case of Reppis. You reply that in his case the longer form was actually issued, and you give your reference to the Patent Rolls, 28 Henry VIII, p. 2, m. 27. I would not for a moment question your categorical assertion, but I have verified it, delaying this letter till I could do so, and I have a real pleasure in making the same acknowledgment of a mistake in this case which I invite you to make in others.

Yours faithfully,

T. A. LACEY.

MADINGLEY, *September* 23.

JULIUS III AND PAUL IV

VI

JULIUS III AND PAUL IV

I

IN the spring of the year 1895, Dom Gasquet discovered in the Register of Paul IV a Bull, unknown to all previous writers on our subject, dealing with the powers delegated to Cardinal Pole for the reconciliation of the English Church to the Holy See. This Bull *Praeclara carissimi*, and an explanatory Brief *Regimini universalis*, were put forward as (1) declaring the English Ordinal to be an invalid rite, and (2) being founded on a "full and minute" description of that Ordinal, furnished by Pole himself.

On the former head I wrote the following Notes, which were circulated at the Church Congress held at Norwich in that year. The substance of them was afterwards incorporated into the *Supplementum de Hierarchia Anglicana*, printed at Rome.[1]

PAUL IV AND ANGLICAN ORDERS

A good deal has been said about certain documents recently discovered by Dom Gasquet in the Vatican archives, which are put forward as containing a papal reprobation of Anglican Orders. They are a Bull of Paul IV, dated June 20, 1555, and a Brief, dated October 30, in the same year. Briefly and doubtfully referred to in the *Civiltà Cattolica* of last June, they have since been reproduced elsewhere. What do they contain?

[1] See *Diary*, April 10th, 12th, and 22nd.

171

172 A ROMAN DIARY AND OTHER DOCUMENTS

The Bull, we find, is a papal confirmation of the general dispensation given by Card. Pole on the reconciliation of the kingdom (printed in *de Hierarchia Anglicana*, App. vii.), in which the Legate confirmed a number of things done since the rupture with Rome, and formally undertook to receive in their several grades all who had been ordained, *licet nulliter et de facto*,[1] under conditions

---

[1] I apparently had not then noticed the interesting word *concernentia* in this Bull In the extant text of Pole's General Dispensation, incorporated in the Act 1 and 2 Phil. and Mar. cap 8 (Gibson, p 41), the Legate promises to receive "in suis ordinibus" all persons who had obtained "aliquas impetrationes dispensationes concessiones gratias et indulta tam ordines quam beneficia ecclesiastica, seu alias spirituales materias, praetensa auctoritate supremitatis Ecclesiae Anglicanae, licet nulliter et de facto obtinuerint" But in the Bull *Praeclara* the corresponding passage runs thus "quae [personae] diversas impetrationes dispensationes gratias et indulta tam ordines quam beneficia ecclesiastica seu alias spirituales materias concernentia praetensa auctoritate supremitatis Ecclesiae Anglicanae nulliter et de facto obtinuerant."

Thus the Bull, reciting the terms of the Dispensation, adds the word *concernentia*, which rectifies both the grammar and the sense. The word had evidently slipped out of the copy of the Dispensation engrossed in the Act of Parliament. But there is a further complication. An embassy was sent from England seeking confirmation of Pole's acts (*infra*, p. 176). There is in the Archives of the Vatican a *Summarium* of their petition (cited by Brandi, *Roma e Canterbury*, p. 56, under ref. *Arch. Vat Arm.* LXIV, *tom.* 28, fol. 199), according to which they desired the Holy See to confirm "dispensationes cum ecclesiasticis personis secularibus et diversorum ordinum, ut promoveantur tam in ordinibus quam beneficiis obtentis nulliter sub scismate." Then is added the note. "Obtulit Rmus Legatus se daturum aliis similem dispensationem." This seems to indicate that the copy of the General Dispensation brought to Rome by the embassy contained the puzzling and defective passage that appears in the English Statute. On examination, the mistake was presumably set right, and the passage as recited in the Bull *Praeclara carissimi* was corrected to its proper sense and wording by the addition of the word *concernentia*.

But the passage is cited by Leo XIII, in the fifth paragraph of his Bull *Apostolicae Curae*, without that crucial word. "Neque praetermittendus est," says the Pope, "locus ex eisdem Pontificis litteris, omnino rei congruens, ubi cum aliis beneficio dispensationis egentibus numerantur qui *tam ordines quam beneficia ecclesiastica nulliter et de facto obtinuerant.*" Moreover, an argument is drawn from it which depends on the inaccuracy. Paul IV did not speak of *Orders*

JULIUS III AND PAUL IV 173

imposed by the Royal Supremacy (praetensa auctoritate supremitatis Ecclesiae Anglicanae). In confirming this dispensation the Pope inserted a somewhat obvious safeguard to the effect that none should be so received who had not been ordained by a properly constituted Bishop. " Ita tamen ut qui ad ordines tam sacros quam non sacros ab alio quam episcopo et archiepiscopo rite et recte ordinato promoti fuerunt eosdem ordines ab eorum ordinario de novo suscipere teneantur nec interim in eisdem ordinibus ministrent." This clause has been claimed as excluding all ordained according to the Anglican rite. It is impossible to imagine on what grounds it is so interpreted. Nothing whatever is said about the rite

which had been obtained *nulliter*, but of faculties and dispensations *concerning Orders*, which were regarded as null and void because obtained schismatically. There is not merely a verbal error in the citation ; the passage is used argumentatively in a sense which it cannot bear.

This extraordinary mistake was commented on as soon as the Bull *Apostolicae curae* appeared, and the criticism called forth some replies. Father Brandi's treatment of it is a curiosity of controversy. In his commentary on the Bull, *La Condanna delle Ordinazioni Anglicane* (p. 27), he endeavoured, by means of the above mentioned *Summarium*, to justify the *sense* of the impugned quotation, and on the strength of that interpretation indignantly rebuked those who pointed out the inaccuracy of its *wording* A little below (p. 32), he quoted the text of Pole's Dispensation, with the note : " Nel testo della lettera riferita dal Gibson non si legge qui la parola *concernentia*, quella medesima parola che . . . un Anglicano ha accusato Leone XIII di aver omessa della sua Bolla " But Leo XIII was not quoting from Pole's Dispensation ; he was quoting from *Praeclara carissimi*, which does contain the word *concernentia*. The English Archbishops might well say in their *Responsio* · " Papam . ex exemplari minus perfecto litteras *Praeclara carissimi* citare et ex eo disputare." By way of comment on this rather obscure hint, Father Brandi mockingly asked whether the Archbishops had in their possession a " better text " than that which the Pope had used, suggesting its publication (*Roma e Canterbury*, p. 9). The " better text " is the authentic text published by Dom Gasquet in 1895.

174 A ROMAN DIARY AND OTHER DOCUMENTS

used in the supposed ordinations. The only defect alluded to is the defect of power on the part of the Bishop or other person ordaining. Nor is any ground for this defect specified. Neither does the Pope assert that any such persons actually existed. He lays down a general principle, which is a mere truism of theology.

It was, however, expressed in rather unguarded language. Any who might have been ordained *ab alio quam episcopo rite et recte ordinato* were to be rejected. But the phrase *rite et recte* is a very sweeping one. In the strict sense, no Bishop is *rite et recte ordinatus* who has not been promoted according to the detailed requirements of the Canon Law. But according to the Roman Canon Law, not a single Bishop promoted since the rupture with Rome had been *rite et recte ordinatus;* they were consecrated *minus rite.* On this account the language of the Bull seems to have engendered grave doubts and fears in England. What Bishops were *rite et recte ordinati?*

The object of the Brief which followed was to allay these doubts. "Cum sicut nobis nuper innotuit a pluribus haesitetur qui episcopi et archiepiscopi schismate in ipso regno vigente rite et recte ordinati dici possint," etc. The Brief has no other purpose, and it must be interpreted accordingly. The Pope defines, "Eos tantum episcopos et archiepiscopos, qui non in forma ecclesiae ordinati et consecrati fuerunt, rite et recte ordinatos dici non posse." All Bishops consecrated *in forma ecclesiae* are to be taken as genuine Bishops. Again the Pope does not in any way state, or even imply, that there actually were any Bishops who fell short of this

JULIUS III AND PAUL IV 175

requirement. He is merely defining the phrase used in the Bull. Neither does he in any way define what is the *forma ecclesiae*. Yet this passage again, so purely general in its application, has been alleged as a further and more explicit repudiation of the Orders conferred by the Anglican rite. But we have not yet done with the Brief. We must not stretch the direct purport and effect of such a document beyond its immediate scope, but we may inquire what is contained in it by necessary implication : and this, even if it be a mere *obiter dictum*, will have its own weight. Now the Pope, in order to make his meaning perfectly clear, adds to his definition of a genuine Bishop a formal decree that all clerks whatsoever ordained by such genuine Bishops, having received at their ordination the character of Order, and having been admitted by dispensation to the execution of their Orders, should be so received without question. Any who were not ordained by a genuine Bishop, he says, must be re-ordained; "Alios vero quibus ordines huiusmodi etiam collati fuerunt ab episcopis et archiepiscopis in forma ecclesiae ordinatis et consecratis . . . characterem ordinum eis collatorum recepisse, executione ipsorum ordinum caruisse, et propterea tam nostram quam praefati Reginaldi Cardinalis et Legati dispensationem eis concessam eos ad executionem ordinum huiusmodi . . . plene habilitasse, sicque ab omnibus censeri et per quoscunque quavis auctoritate fungentes iudicari debere, ac si secus super his a quoquam quavis auctoritate scienter vel ignoranter contigerit attentari irritum et inane decernimus."

There is no exception. All ordained by a

176 A ROMAN DIARY AND OTHER DOCUMENTS

genuine Bishop are to be received. There is no question of the rite used in their ordination. That is assumed to be sufficient. But many of the Bishops who were reconciled by Pole, and who were therefore unquestionably genuine Bishops, had for three years been ordaining priests and deacons according to the Anglican rite. These all, having been ordained by genuine Bishops, are according to the terms of the Brief to be received. Therefore by necessary implication the Pope approves, or at least tolerates, the Anglican rite of ordination.[1]

II

When writing the above Notes, I had no means of testing the statements made about the description of the Ordinal which Pole was said to have laid before Paul IV. The discovery of this document also stands to the credit of Dom Gasquet. He, or others working on his materials, came to the conclusion that it was forwarded to Rome by the hands of the ambassadors, Sir Edward Carne, Lord Montagu, and Thirlby, Bishop of Ely, who negotiated the confirmation of Pole's General Dispensation in the year 1555. It was inferred that Julius III commissioned Pole as Legate upon imperfect information, that Pole was doubtful about the extent of his powers for dealing with men ordained by the rites of the new Ordinal, that he

---

[1] So Gasparri concluded, as regards the ordination of deacons and priests only. He held that the Pope rejected the bishops consecrated by the new rite. (*De la Valeur des Ordinations Anglicanes*, p. 15, and *Revue Anglo-Romaine*, Vol. I, p. 488). In the course of a long correspondence that appeared in the *Tablet* during the latter part of the year 1895, the Rev. J. B. Scannell maintained, with characteristic erudition, that the Pope purposely, and with true Roman caution, left the question undecided. These letters seem to have led to his appointment to the Commission of inquiry in the following year.

JULIUS III AND PAUL IV

consulted the Holy See accordingly, and that the newly elected Paul IV resolved his doubts after a careful study of the rites in question. When I was in Rome I had an opportunity of examining the document, with the valuable aid of Mr. Bliss, and from the indications of its date I drew a different conclusion. The result was digested into the following note, which appeared in the *Guardian* of June 10th, 1896, the substance of it being also included in the *Supplementum* :—

CARDINAL POLE'S DESCRIPTION OF THE ENGLISH ORDINAL

Some months ago a writer in the *Tablet* spoke of a "full and minute" description of the Anglican rites of ordination existing in the archives at the Vatican. He supposed this to have been sent to Rome with the embassy of 1555, and drew the conclusion that Paul IV had it before him when writing the much-discussed Bull, *Praeclara carissimi*, and in consequence ruled out the Anglican ordinations as invalid. I do not propose to return to the vexed question of the interpretation of that Bull, but I think the readers of the *Guardian* may be glad to have placed before them the text of the description with a few remarks by way of introduction.

The description is contained in a miscellaneous collection of papers, bound in a volume labelled *Nunziatura in Inghilterra* 3, all of which, with the possible exception of a copy of the will of Henry VIII in Italian, belong to the period of Pole's Legation. It is interesting on two accounts : first, on account of its contents, or rather of what is omitted ; secondly, because of certain indications of its date.

178 A ROMAN DIARY AND OTHER DOCUMENTS

It is obvious that the writer who spoke of it as "full and minute" had not seen it. The *substance* only of the rite is avowedly given, all subsidiary matters being omitted. This expression must be interpreted with some liberality, since the oaths are given in full. Pole was obviously interested in these.[1] It is not altogether surprising that he thought it unnecessary to include the prayers, since in his time the essence of the rite was undoubtedly supposed to lie in the imperative formula; but we seldom come across so definite a relegation of the prayers to an insignificant position. There is another omission of greater moment. Pole speaks of the first and second Ordinal as being substantially the same. Yet the Porrection of the Instruments, retained in the former book, was struck out of the latter. Pole ignores this change. It is difficult, therefore, to suppose that he regarded this ceremony as the essential matter of ordination.

The suggestion that this description was sent to Rome in 1555 will not, I think, bear investigation. There are two copies, written in different hands, both Italian, on fine Italian paper. One bears as a watermark the Piccolomini arms. The other has a watermark which I will describe, as some one may be able to identify it. Within a circle is a goose, a Lombardic G within the circle, and a D of the same character above it. Neither paper has been folded or shows any signs of having

---

[1] It is noteworthy that the Venetian ambassador in England, Daniele Barbaro, wrote in 1550 of the new rites of ordination with a similar insistence on the oath : "Nor do they differ from those of the Roman Catholic religion, save that in England they take oath to renounce the doctrine and authority of the Pope " (*Venetian State Papers*, Vol. V, p. 349.)

JULIUS III AND PAUL IV   179

been sent as a despatch. The second copy, page
104, deserves close attention. It is written on a
gathering of two folio sheets. The description
begins on the first *recto*, and concludes on the
second *recto*. On the *verso* of this begins another
document in the same hand. This is an Italian
version of the proclamation put out in the name of
Jane Grey, "*Proclama della Regina Janna, figla del
Duca di Suffolch.*" At the bottom of the page the
catch-word is written, but there is no more. The
remaining four pages of the paper are blank. The
proclamation was probably continued on other
sheets made up into the same gathering, which
are lost.

How comes this document here? The next
paper in the volume is another copy of this same
Italian translation of the proclamation, written in
an Italian hand on coarse paper, which has been
folded and sealed, and much soiled in transmission.
From the fragments of the seal I cannot make out
the device. This was obviously sent from Pole,
and a fair copy was made for use in Rome. Since
the Description of the Ordinations was copied at
the same time, it is an irresistible conclusion that
this also was sent by Pole in the same set of
despatches. When was it sent?

A copy of Jane's proclamation can hardly have
been sent except during the early months of Mary's
reign. The description of the ordinations was sent
at the same time.[1] From this an important con-

---

[1] I followed without question the assumption that the Description
was sent to Rome by Pole But whence? In August, 1553, he was
at Maguzzano ; towards the end of September he moved to Trent ;
on October 19th he was at Dillingen ; he reached Brussels in January ;
he then visited France, returning to Flanders ; not until November,

180 A ROMAN DIARY AND OTHER DOCUMENTS

clusion will follow. Pole had received his Legatine
faculties by Bull from Julius III in August, 1553.
These were found insufficient, because they enabled
him to deal with such bishops and clergy only as
had been ordained before the beginning of the
schism. Accordingly, he asked for extended powers,
which were given him by a Brief dated March 8th,
1554. This Brief contained a phrase which has
much puzzled inquirers. The Pope authorizes Pole
to exercise a dispensing and reconciling power in
the case of persons who have been ordained "*non
servata forma ecclesiae consueta.*" It has often been
conjectured that these words may contain an
allusion to the Edwardine Ordinal.[1] The con-

1554, did he land in England. Let the following dates also be compared. On July 29th, 1553, a congregation was held at Rome on
receipt of the news of Edward's death and Mary's accession; on
August 5th Pole was appointed Legate; on August 15th he sent a
letter to Mary by the hand of Henry Penning, who was joined by
Commendone at Brussels After visiting England Commendone
hastened to Italy, leaving London on August 23rd, seeing Pole at
Maguzzano on September 7th, and then going on to Rome. In consequence of his news, a Consistory of September 15th decided that
Pole's Legation should be delayed. On October 1st Pole wrote to
the Pope from Trent that he had received letters from Penning On
October 19th Penning joined him at Dillingen and was sent on to
Rome with detailed instructions to give "a full account of the affairs
of England." See the authorities in Dixon, Vol IV, pp. 98-111, and
add the instructions to Penning, *Venetian State Papers*, Vol. V,
p. 428. It is evident that a vast amount of correspondence preceded
Pole's request for the fuller powers that were given him by the Brief
of March 8th, 1554. On further consideration it seems to me that
the despatch described above must have reached Rome during the
first weeks of Mary's reign, and not later than Commendone's return.
There is nothing to show what was the source of the Description of
the Ordinal. It may have been composed at Rome from a copy of
the Book received there. The important point is that fair copies of
the Description, probably for use in Consistory, were made at the
same time as copies of Jane's Proclamation. This indicates that the
Ordinal was under the notice of the Pope and Cardinals from the
early autumn of 1553.

[1] So De Augustinis. See *Diary*, April 22nd.

JULIUS III AND PAUL IV 181

jecture becomes a certainty when we find that
Pole had already sent to the Pope a description of this Ordinal, or of what he considered
the essential parts of it. At some time during the
early months of Mary's reign, probably when he
was actually demanding an extension of his faculties
enabling him to deal with schismatical ordinations,
Pole had sent to Rome a description of the Ordinal.
The Pope replies by authorizing him to recognize
orders which had been conferred otherwise than by
the *accustomed* form of the Church. I can see only
one possible conclusion. Julius III formally[1] approved the English Ordinal in the form in which it
was laid before him, as follows :—

FORMA ET RATIO FACIENDI ET CONSECRANDI

Episcopos, Presbyteros, et Diaconos, quae cum
prius alio in libro edita foret, nunc alicubi est reformata ; cuius substantia hic solum ponitur, et omit-
tuntur preces, psalmi, interrogationes, personarum
probationes, et alia quae conveniunt.

Iusiurandum in Regis Primatum quod ordinem
accepturi coram Praelato sedenti in Cathedra iurare
debent antequam legatur Evangelium.

Ego N. ex hac die penitus renuntio reiicio,
desero et relinquo Episcopum Romae et eius
auctoritatem, potestatem, et iurisdictionem : et
nunquam assentiar, aut cum aliquo conveniam, ut
episcopus Romae usurpet, exerceat aut habeat
aliquod genus auctoritatis, iurisdictionis et potestatis, intra hoc Regnum, aut aliam Regis nostri
dictionem ; sed huiusmodi rei obstabo omni tem-

---

[1] This word is much too strong. I should have said "implicitly."

182 A ROMAN DIARY AND OTHER DOCUMENTS

pore et omni conatu, et de hac die volens admitto,
approbo, et suscipio Regiam Maiestatem solummodo
esse supremum caput in terris ecclesiae Anglicanae ;
et omni consilio et conatu absque fallacia, fraude,
aut alia minus debita ratione volo observare, custo-
dire, asserere, et defendere omnem vim et sententiam omnium et singulorum actorum et statutorum
factorum, et faciendorum intra hoc Regnum, ad
abrogandum, eradicandum, et abolendum episcopum
Romae, et eius auctoritatem, et omnium aliorum
actorum et statutorum factorum aut faciendorum, ad
confirmandam, et corroborandam Regis potestatem,
ut supremi capitis in terris ecclesiae Anglicanae.
Et haec praestabo contra omne genus hominum
cuiuscumque status, dignitatis, gradus, aut condi-
tionis sint ; et nullo pacto faciam aut attentabo, nec
pro viribus patiar fieri aut attentari, directe vel
oblique, clanculum aut aperte, quicquam ad impedi-
mentum, obstaculum, detrimentum, abrogationem
eius quod dictum est, aut partis alicuius ex eo aliqua
ratione, colore, aut praetextu. Quod si quod iusiurandum fiat aut factum iam sit per me alicui homini
ad favendum, conservandum, defendendum Episcopum Romae, aut eius auctoritatem, iurisdictionem et
potestatem, illud ego reputo ut vanum et cassum,
ita me Deus adiuvet per Iesum Christum.

Episcopus Diaconorum capitibus manum imponens singulis dicet :

Accipe auctoritatem exequendi officium Diaconi in
ecclesia Dei tibi commissa, In nomine Patris et
Filii, et Spiritus Sancti, etc.

Postea dans unicuique illorum Novum Testamen-
tum, dicet :

Accipe auctoritatem legendi Evangelium in

JULIUS III AND PAUL IV 183

Ecclesia Dei, et illud praedicandi, cum ad id rite missus fueris, etc.

Episcopus cum Presbyteris praesentibus imponet manus capitibus singulorum, qui genuflexi dignitatem presbyteri accipient, episcopo dicente:

Accipe Spiritum Sanctum; quorum peccata remittis, remissa sunt; quorum peccata retines, retenta sunt: et sis fidelis dispensator verbi Dei, et suorum sanctorum sacramentorum. In nomine Patris et Filii et Spiritus Sancti, etc.

Deinde Episcopus singulis tradens Bibliam dicet:

Accipe auctoritatem praedicandi verbum Dei, et ministrandi sacra sacramenta in congregatione, ad quam eris vocatus.

Archiepiscopus petet Regis mandatum ad episcopum inaugurandum, et iusiurandum pro Regis primatu exigitur ut a Diacono et Presbytero; sed Episcopus insuper iurabit obedientiam Archiepiscopo his verbis:

In Nomine Domini, Amen. Ego N. Electus episcopus Ecclesiae N. profiteor et polliceor omnem debitam reverentiam, et obedientiam Archiepiscopo, et Metropolitanae ecclesiae N. et eius successoribus. Ita me Deus adiuvet per Iesum Christum.

Sed cum ordinabitur ipse Archiepiscopus, cum omnia alia fiant quemadmodum pro episcopo, hoc iusiurandum omittitur.

Archiepiscopi sedentis verba:

Frater, quoniam Sancta Scriptura, et veteres Canones iubent, ne cui cito manus imponamus aut admittamus ad gubernandam congregationem Christi, qui eam sibi redemit non minori pretio quam effusionis sanguinis sui, antequam te admittam

184 A ROMAN DIARY AND OTHER DOCUMENTS

ad hanc administrationem ad quam vocaris, ex te quaeram plerosque articulos, ut praesens congregatio habeat experimentum, et ferat testimonium, quo animo sis praeditus, ut te geras in Ecclesia Dei —sequuntur in libro interrogata, quae omittimus.

Archiepiscopus Episcopique praesentes manus imponunt capiti electi episcopi, Archiepiscopo dicente:

Accipe Spiritum Sanctum, et memineris ut excites gratiam Dei, quae est in te per manuum impositionem, non enim dedit nobis Deus spiritum timiditatis, sed potentiae, dilectionis, et sobrietatis.

Tunc Archiepiscopus dabit illi Bibliam, dicens :

Attende lectioni, exhortationi, doctrinae, ac meditare quae in hoc libro scripta sunt, ut tuus profectus, qui inde erit, manifestus sit omnibus hominibus. Attende tibi ipsi et doctrinae : persiste in his, nam si id feceris te ipsum servabis, et eos qui te audierint. Sis gregis Christi Pastor, non lupus ; pasce illum, ne devores : sustine infirmos, sana aegrotos, colliga confractos, reduc eiectos, quaere perditos. Ita sis misericors, ut ne sis nimis ; sic disciplinam exigas, ut non obliviscaris misericordiam : ut cum summus Pastor venerit, accipias incorruptibilem coronam gloriae per Iesum Christum Dominum Nostrum. Amen.

THE COUNCIL OF MAINZ,
A.D. 1549

VII

THE COUNCIL OF MAINZ, A.D. 1549

*Dissertationis Apologeticae De Hierarchia Anglicana
Supplementum; Appendix I* [1]

CONCILIUM Provinciale Moguntiae habitum
est mense Maio 1549, praesidente archiepiscopo Sebastiano von Heussenstamm. Acta Concilii
mense Septembri eiusdem anni Moguntiae vulgata
sunt, quibus accessit *Institutio ad Pietatem Christianam in Concilio Provinciali promissa.* Librum
habet Bibliotheca Casanatensis.
In Concilio promulgata est *Methodus de Doctrina
Christiana*, quae sequentia habet.

CAP. XXXV, *De Sacramento Ordinis*

Fol. IX a

In collatione Ordinum, quae cum impositione
manuum velut visibili signo traditur, doceant rite
ordinatis gratiam divinitus conferri qua ad ecclesiastica munera rite et utiliter exercenda apti et idonei
efficiantur, et qua rata sint et efficacia, quae a rite
ordinatis in Ecclesia iuxta Christi et Ecclesiae institutionem geruntur etc.

[1] See *Diary*, April 22nd, May 1st.

188   A ROMAN DIARY AND OTHER DOCUMENTS

EXCERPTA EX *Institutione ad Pietatem*

CAP. *De Forma Sacramenti Ordinis*

Fol. CCXXII b

*　　*　　*　　*　　*

Episcopus igitur in conferendis Ordinibus, ad
supradictas Domini promissiones et mandata attente
respiciens, tali verborum forma utitur, quae ad promissiones huiusmodi et mandata quam proxime
accedit, eaque proprie et diserte exprimit. Tradi-
turus enim Ordinem Sacerdotalem, Accipe, inquit,
Spiritum Sanctum, quorum remiseris peccata, remittuntur eis, et quorum retinueris, retenta sunt.[1]
Similiter in aliorum omnium Ordinum collatione ex
ipso Ordinationis ritu per instrumenti traditionem,
et verborum certam formam, functionem unicuique
Ordini ex Christi et Ecclesiae institutione competentem clare exprimit.

CAP. *De Materia seu Elemento Sacramenti
Ordinis*

Foll. CCXXIII–IV

In Ordinibus maioribus, Diaconatu et Presbyterio,
internae virtutis et gratiae accipiendae externum
signum et sensibile elementum adhibetur manuum
impositio, quam ex Apostolica traditione descendere
diserte Lucas in Actis Apostolicis testatur cap. 6,
13, 14. Ad hunc autem externum manuum impositionis ritum, in verbo Dei et orationibus exhibitum,

[1] *Vide infra* Cap. *de Presbyteris.*

THE COUNCIL OF MAINZ, A.D 1549

internam et spiritalem gratiam consequi, quae in ministerio ordinati efficaciter operetur, et ad suscepti muneris executionem reddat idoneum, aperte Paulus indicat. Noli, inquiens, negligere gratiam, quae data est tibi per prophetiam cum impositione manuum Presbyterii ; et, Ut resuscites gratiam Dei quae in te est per impositionem manuum mearum. Designat autem impositio manuum in ordinando operum Sancti Spiritus resuscitationem, siquidem in digitis diversa Spiritus Sancti dona indicantur: manus autem operationem significant. Unde innuitur, ordinatum diversis Spiritus Sancti donis impleri, quae eum ad diversas Ecclesiastici muneris functiones rite et utiliter obeundas efficacem et idoneum reddant. Ambrosius mysterium impositionis manuum sic explicat. Manus impositiones verba sunt mystica, quibus confirmatur ad opus electus, accipiens potestatem, teste conscientia sua, ut audeat vice Domini sacrificium offerre Deo. Et idem, Homo imponit manus : Deus largitur gratiam. Sacerdos imponit supplicem dexteram, et Deus benedicit potenti dextera. Episcopus initiat Ordinem, et Deus tribuat dignitatem.

Itaque sicut in Baptismo aquae infusio ritus est divinitus approbatus, aptam significationem habens, ad certificandam baptizati conscientiam de interna animae purgatione, et ablutione omnium sordium spiritualium, ita in Ordinis Sacramento manuum impositio ritus est, in scripturis approbatus, aptam significationem habens ad certificandam ordinati conscientiam de dono Dei, ad aedificationem Ecclesiae pro utili et efficaci muneris in Ecclesia gerendi executione sibi collato.

190 A ROMAN DIARY AND OTHER DOCUMENTS

Ad initiationem Sacerdotum, praeter impositionem manuum, etiam Unctio adhiberi solet : cuius usus et propter vetustatem suam, et propter mysterium aptamque significationem, omnino in Ecclesia retinendus est. Ritus erat legis veteris, ut in eo populo, ex quo Christus erat nasciturus, Reges et Sacerdotes oleo unguerentur. Hanc unctionem Christiana Religio (cum caeteras legis istius antiquae caeremonias, quae futurorum significationem continebant, superveniente veritate reliquerit) propter mysterium retinuit, multiplicemque in novo populo Unctionem exercet. Unguuntur singuli confessionem Christiani nominis in mysterio Baptismi suscipientes, ut quemadmodum Christus ab unctione nomen habet, eo quod unxerit eum Deus prae participibus suis : sic ipsi quoque accepta unctione esse uncti Dei, Christique nominis participes fieri, et eius in se gratiam habere possint. Unguuntur inchoaturi vitam Christianam, quasi athletae Domini, cuius bella adversus Diaboli phalanges et seculi huius insidias pugnaturi sunt. Unguuntur in progressu vitae ad robur et confirmationem, ut omnis divinae virtutis et gratiae perfectionem et complementum accipiant. · Unguuntur in exitu vitae, ut tunc ex infirmitate aeger animus fiducia et consolatione erigatur, ne bravium illud, quod in vitae cursu tenuerunt, in fine amittant, et ne fructu fidei suae, animarum salute, despolientur.

Praeter has unctiones Christianis omnibus communes, singulari quadam unctione initiat Sacerdotes suos Catholica Ecclesia, in signum sacrationis et excellentis potestatis, quam eis ad solvenda ligandave peccata hominum Christus tradidit, ut sint reges et rectores in populo Dei ad aedificationem Ec-

THE COUNCIL OF MAINZ, A.D. 1549

clesiae, et ut ex unctione admoneantur se gratiam
consecrandi accepisse, et charitatis opera debere
extendere ad omnes. Huius autem sacerdotalis
unctionis usum non Romana solum sed Graeca
etiam Ecclesia ab ipsis Apostolorum temporibus
tenuit, cuius meminit Theophylactus. Omnis (inquit)
cuicumque concredita est praesidentia, etiam si
indignus fuerit, donum habet ex unctione, id quod
magnum divinae misericordiae est sacramentum.
In reliquis Ordinibus pro elemento sunt instrumenta quae pro Ordinis varietate Episcopus singulis
porrigens, simul admonet eos, ut in suscepto munere
rite et diligenter ministrare sollicite curent. Ex
ipso autem instrumento quodammodo ordinandus
intelligit quae sint futurae suscepti Ordinis partes et
officia.

Oratio autem in singulis Ordinibus recitatur ab
Ordinatore, qua officia eius Ordinis commemorat et
simul Deum rogat ut in obeundis officiis ad aedificationem Ecclesiae suae ordinatis per gratiam suam
benignus et efficax assistere dignetur.

Tondentur etiam ordinandi, quem ritum ab
Apostolis introductum Rabanus commemorat, ut
tonsi formam et similitudinem Christi spinis coronati
in capite prae se ferrent, et simul per tonsuram a
plebe discernerentur. Similiter per tonsuram sicut
per unctionem regalis dignitas in Sacerdotibus
designatur. Nudatum etiam a suprema parte caput
innuit ministros Ecclesiae a se abiicere debere
quaecunque animum ad divina se erigentem depri-
mere et impedire solent.

192 A ROMAN DIARY AND OTHER DOCUMENTS

CAP. *De Presbyteris.*

Fol. CCXXX b.

*　　*　　*　　*　　*

Horum officiorum Episcopus in ordinatione futuros sacerdotes verbis admonet. Qui ordinandi estis Presbyteri (inquiens) offerre vos oportet, baptizare, praedicare, et bonis operibus ac Deo placitis undique redundare. Et insuper variis ritibus adhibitis, traditisque diversis instrumentis, quae sint eorum munera insinuat. Principio enim manus capitibus eorum imponens, gratiam absolutionis, et potestatem remittendi ac retinendi peccata eis impertitur. Quorum remiseris peccata (inquit) remittuntur eis.[1] Deinde stolam utrique humero aptans, super pectore in modum crucis extendit; innuens eos suavi iugo Domini submitti debere, et contra omnes mundi casus corda praemunire, ne aut prosperis extollantur, aut in adversis animum despondentes concidant. Et casula eos convestiens admonet ut caritatem exerceant in omnes. Post haec manus eorum inungit, ut intelligant sibi concessam esse gratiam consecrandi. Demum calicem et patenam hostia superposita offerens, potestatem tradit offerendi Deo hostiam sanctam et placabilem pro totius Ecclesiae incolumitate.

---

[1] *Supra*, p. 188. De his in *Supplemento*, p 22, ita disputavi. "Notatu dignum est Concilium non modo impositionem manuum pro materia sacramentali posuisse, sed etiam formam constituisse in verbis : *Accipe Spiritum Sanctum, quorum remiseris peccata etc.*, quae verba non ut in Pontificali Romano in fine Missae sed *principio*, id est, ni fallor, in principio ordinationis dicta fuisse assertum est. (*Cap. de Presbyteris*). Utrimque videtur eadem dispositio ac in ritu Anglicano. Id melius exponere potuissem si Pontificale eis temporibus Moguntiae usurpatum sub oculis habuissem, sed ne Palatina quidem Bibliotheca exemplar continet. Quaestio deliberatu digna est utrum auctores ritus Anglicani aliquid ex libris Moguntinis mutuaverint, an mera sit coincidentia temporis."

THE PAMPHLET "DE RE ANGLICANA" AND ITS CRITICS

o

VIII

THE PAMPHLET "DE RE ANGLICANA" AND ITS CRITICS

I

DE RE ANGLICANA[1]

ECCLESIAM Anglicanam inde a saeculo XVI duo opinionum influxus agitant, alter in doctrinam Sacramentalem intendens, quem Catholicum vocare liceat, alter e fonte Puritano manans. Reformatio sub Henrico VIII incepta nihil contra fidem Catholicam effecit. Quaedam, fateor, facinorosa, quaedam adhuc ploranda evenerunt; a communione Ecclesiae Romanae recessum est, vita religiosa extirpata; in his autem quae ad doctrinam spectant, nihil mutatum. Nec tamen etiam tunc deerant qui novas res in hac parte molirentur, inter quos et episcopi rari erant, quorum princeps Cranmer. Hi igitur, mortuo Henrico, cum parvulus Eduardus partium suarum asseclis in tutelam traditus esset, civili potestate innixi multa tum circa doctrinam tum in cultu divino innovabant. Opinionibus enim Zuinglianis aliquatenus infecti extraneos haereticos, qui eas disseminarent, Petrum Martyrem, Bucerum, aliosque in Angliam vocarunt, quorum et fautores ac discipulos in Ecclesia promovebant. Attamen

[1] See *Diary*, May 5th.

196 A ROMAN DIARY AND OTHER DOCUMENTS

episcopi, qui animo et sententia Catholici erant,
sedes suas retinuerunt, novisque rebus quantum
possent sese accommodarunt. Nonnulli autem ex
his detrusi sunt, nec dubium est partes novatorum
in reformationem ulteriorem atque exitiabilem progressuras fuisse, nisi prae morte Eduardi immatura
tanta consilia subito collapsa essent.

Maria igitur regnum excipiente nonnulli episcopi
destituti sunt, inter quos Cranmer ; ceteri manebant.
Multi etiam, qui novis rebus faverant, omnia ad
nutum reginae facere properabant. Quae mutata
erant, ad normam antiquam reducta sunt ; in communionem Ecclesiae Romanae reditum est. Totus
fere clerus se submisit ; pauci admodum e patria
transfugerunt, nonnulli tam clerici quam laici poenis
haereseos afflicti sunt ; ceteri opiniones suas silentio
comprimebant.

Mortua post quinque annos Maria, regnum Elizabetha excepit. Consiliarios qui sub Maria rempublicam direxerant plerumque retinuit ; attamen res
novas cautius movebat. Peste ingravescente archiepiscopus Cantuariensis multique episcopi mortui
sunt. In sedem Cantuariensem suffectus est
Matthaeus Parker, qui Maria regnante vitam pri-
vatam degerat, vir prudens atque ab omni violentia
aversus. Cultus ac religionis facies quae tempore
Eduardi erat, quibusdam in sensum magis catholicum mutatis, reducta est. Episcopi fere omnes,
cum haec fieri nollent, civili potestate destituti sunt,
qui tamen partes suas nequaquam ad resistendum
moverunt. Pauci e clero novis rebus sese accom-
modare recusarunt, plerique spe fortasse meliorum
quieti manebant. Universa Ecclesia Anglicana
eisdem legibus eodem cultu constanter utebatur.

"DE RE ANGLICANA" AND ITS CRITICS 197

Certe post aliquot annos, cum Pius V per Bullam *Regnans in Excelsis* Elizabetham eiusque fautores excommunicasset, ei qui auctoritati Pontificiae maxime faverent ab hac Ecclesiae Anglicanae unitate recesserunt. De quibus nihil amplius dicam : ipsius Ecclesiae Anglicanae fortunam ac statum describo. Primis igitur Elizabethae annis exules, qui Maria regnante transfugerant, ab Helvetia vel Germania opinionibus Calvinianis vel amplius imbuti redierunt. Ex his partes Puritanae originem habuerunt. Exinde magna erat intra Ecclesiam Anglicanam controversia, quae usque hodie aliquo modo subsistit. Universi enim eisdem ritibus usi, eisdem fidei doctrinis adstricti, de caerimoniis, de regimine pastorali, de potestatis clavium exercitio, denique de gratiae doctrinis acriter disputabant. Partes Puritanae, partes quas Catholicas vocamus, non alio modo in Ecclesiae Anglicanae unitate sese tenebant, quam olim in regno Francico consistebant partes ultramontanae et gallicanae. Diu atque incerto eventu dimicabatur, donec anno 1662, post bellum scilicet intestinum pace instaurata, acriores ex Puritanis tandem expulsi sunt. Ex his proveniunt *Dissidentes*, qui extra ecclesiam conventibus constitutis disciplinam Calvinianam adhuc professi in indifferentismum plerique abierunt.

At in Ecclesia Anglicana partes Puritanae, quamvis attenuatae atque in dies a primordiis suis Calvinianis magis remotae, perstiterunt. Ecclesia autem partium Catholicarum consiliis gubernata plurimos annos magna cum eruditionis laude floruit. Quis enim Beveregium non novit? Qui tamen in clero Anglico vix primam palmam reportavit. Sed neque minore pietatis quam eruditionis honore stetit

198 A ROMAN DIARY AND OTHER DOCUMENTS

res nostra. Ecclesia Anglicana e tot periculis elapsa ab aliis ecclesiis nationalibus in unitate catholica comprehensis nihil distulit nisi quod communione sacrorum cum Sancta Sede careret. Nec tamen insularitate sua nimium gaudebant nostri, sed cum aliis Ecclesiis tum commercium litterarum instituerunt, tum unionem perfectiorem ambierunt. Saeculo octavo decimo ineunte quaedam in hac parte conabantur quae prospero eventu consequi potuissent nisi exteris compagibus impediti fuissent. Isto enim saeculo Ecclesia Anglicana eadem subiit quae reliquam Christianitatem affligebant. Zelum evanuit, caritas frigescebat, vita et mores clericorum relictis flagrantibus vitiis ad saecularem normam redigebantur ; et quod aliis malis fonti et origini fuit, ecclesia civili potestati magis in dies subigebatur. Quae cum paene intolerabilia fierent, subito post annum 1830 divina providentia surgebant aliqui, sacerdotes plerumque in Academia Oxoniensi demorantes, qui ad nova certamina fideles evocarent. Principio autem vitae sanctimoniam clero inculcabant, ad poenitentiam agendam, ad munera diligentius obeunda impellebant. Deinde ad externum Ecclesiae statum versi iugum civilis potestatis aut excutiendum aut certe sublevandum docuerunt, sacras Synodos et salutares disciplinae regulas resuscitandas vindicabant. Postremo ad dogmata spectabant, sanctorum patrum scripta diligentissime excoluerunt atque Anglice vulganda curaverunt, quibus novae atque haereticae opiniones, e scholis Calvinianis plerumque derivatae, penitus expellerentur.

Eodem fere tempore in Academia Cantabrigiensi quaestiones de cultu divino renovando pari studio agitatae sunt. De architectura, de musica eccle-

"DE RE ANGLICANA" AND ITS CRITICS

siastica, de ornamentis, de rubrica observanda res
erat. In primis autem de missae sollemniis fre-
quentius celebrandis sollicite deliberatum est. Fervor
incredibilis totam ecclesiam invasit. *Tractariani*,
quos ex usu tractatuum popularium praecipuos
Oxonienses vocabant, sensum Catholicum, qui
diutius frigebat, excitarunt. Tandem cum Ecclesiam
Anglicanam insulari libertate potius impeditam
quam defensam esse perciperent, ad alias ecclesias
magno cum unitatis desiderio versi causas et funda-
menta schismatis investigare inceperunt. Quocirca
decreta ac definitiones Concilii Tridentini summo
studio tractabant, ut cum eis formulas ac definitiones
Anglicanas non adeo dissonas esse monstrarent ut
ineluctabilis inde dissensio eveniret.

Ceterum partes Puritanae his rebus perterritae
contra motum catholicum strenue reluctabantur, et
talibus adversariis ipsae impares cum civilis potestatis fautoribus socia arma iunxerunt. Episcopi non
pauci his vires et nomen addiderunt, ceteri timidi et
principibus civitatis ex longo usu addicti, necnon
saecularibus curis impediti, veritatem et veritatis
defensores minime adiuvarunt; vix unus inter
vindices apostolicae traditionis exstitit. Ergo
nonnulli, de re Anglicana prorsus desperantes,
relictis armis in pacem Ecclesiae Romanae transfugerunt; alii a fide defecerunt. Nec tamen qui
restabant a conatu destiterunt, Keble, Pusey, du-
centi alii, quamvis defectu amicorum graviter afflicti,
Ecclesiae renovandae causam spe invicta sustine-
bant. Nec spes fefellit. Si quis Ecclesiam Anglicanam, qualis nunc exstat, lustraverit, eorum
labores videbit. Quod impossibile videbatur, id
auxiliante divina gratia efficere statuerunt. Haud

200 A ROMAN DIARY AND OTHER DOCUMENTS

ignari malorum ex ipsa humilitate fiduciam con-
ceperunt : *Laetati sumus pro diebus, quibus nos
humiliasti; annis quibus vidimus mala. Respice
in servos tuos, et in opera tua : et dirige filios eorum.
Et sit splendor Domini Dei nostri super nos, et
opera manuum nostrarum dirige super nos.*
Tota enim facies Ecclesiae his quinquaginta annis
renovata est. Doctrina Catholica ubique praedicatur. De praeceptis Novae Legis, de auxiliis
gratiae, de usu Sacramentorum populus instruitur.
Pro frigidis ac ieiunis ingenii Calvinistici institu-
tionibus conciones fide et caritate plenae audiuntur.
De sanctorum meritis, de consiliis perfectionis non
amplius siletur. Ubi rarius Eucharistia olim celebrabatur, nunc iugiter sacrificium offertur ; ubi
pauci Mensam Domini adibant, nunc frequens
populus digna cum adoratione de cibo caelesti participat. Munera pastoralia sacerdotes nunc aliter
praestant, nec facile invenitur qui adeo negligat :
nec modo ex paucorum zelo id pendet, sed ex sententia etiam saecularium parochus ad meliora
sequenda obligatur. Multa quae adversae partes
induxerant, aut penitus evanuerunt, aut in novos
usus conversa manent ; scholas dominicales, hymnos
populares a Puritanis in sensum Catholicum repor-
tavimus. Multa quoque ex aliis ecclesiis grati
mutuavimus, secessus seu exercitia spiritualia tam
pro clero quam pro laicis, missiones in civitatibus
et in pagis, stationes quadragesimales, hoc genus
omne, iam nobis propria sunt. Officium Divinum
pro usu nostro, semel tantum in mense recitato
Psalterio, levius est onus, sed in pluribus dioecesibus
totum Psalterium, sacerdotibus aliis alios psalmos legentibus, ex constitutione episcopi quotidie recitatur.

"DE RE ANGLICANA" AND ITS CRITICS

Ad alia pergamus. Statum religiosum qui usque a saeculo sexto decimo penitus obsoleverat anni recentes nova cum devotione reduxerunt. Societas S. Ioannis Evangelistae, anno 1866 fundata, cui domus materna apud Cowley in agro Oxoniensi sita est, grandem ecclesiam conventualem nuperrime extruxit; domus quoque in India, in Africa Meridionali, in America nunc habet. Monialium inclusarum nonnulli conventus erecti sunt; religiosarum votis paupertatis castitatis et obedientiae adstrictarum, quae in variis caritatis operibus vitam degunt, tanta est multitudo, ut iam plures religioni devotae sint quam quae tempore reformationis in Anglia exstarent. Plures insuper societates sacerdotum saecularium vitam communem degentium ab episcopis dioecesanis fundatae sunt, qui plerumque in Missionibus versantur.[1]

Haec sunt indicia renovatae Ecclesiae. Non omnia quidem ex sententia fieri dico. Nemo prudens negat multa restare quae reformatione egeant, multa quae pro pudore sileantur; nec quae iam facta vidit, aliud esse quam faciendorum arrhabonem prae se fert. Ita tamen de his gaudere nobis liceat. In hunc statum non sine multo labore pervenimus. Fructus videmus, labores vix in memoria retinemus. Attamen memoria digni sunt; siquidem de praeteritis cogitanti magna futurarum rerum fiducia erit. Cum duobus hostibus dimicatum est; cum civili potestate quae Ecclesiam in vinculis comprimere voluit, cum partibus Puritanis quae renovationi Catholicae strenuissime se opponebant. Partes Puritanae victae sunt, nec tamen evanuerunt. Adhuc restant, sed neque aequa potentia nec eadem

[1] Vide Appendicem.

202 A ROMAN DIARY AND OTHER DOCUMENTS

voluntas. Episcopi quatuor vel quinque eo intendunt, ceteri sententia Catholici sunt. Contra excessus potestatis civilis dimicantes veram potius quam speciosam victoriam ita rettulimus, ut libertate maiore quam quae appareat utamur. Anno 1856 tandem effectum est ut Synodi Provinciales, quibus annos plus centum silentium impositum esset, sessiones haberent. Definitiones de fide et doctrina, quas Concilium Regium proponere ausum est, primo quidem aliquorum animos perturbabant, nunc prae contemptu negliguntur. Cum autem potestas civilis rebus ad cultum spectantibus se ingerere conaretur, totis viribus aperte resistebatur. De rubrica sensu Catholico observanda quaestio erat. Id praecipue metuentes partes Puritanae, cum res suas in dies collabi sentirent, ad iudicia recurrebant, et cum curiae ecclesiasticae sensum Catholicum defendissent, Concilium Regium appellabant. Huius iudicio sensus Catholicus condemnatus est ; cui cum maior pars cleri obtemperare recusasset, nova lege in Parliamento facta (anno 1874) *Ritualistas*, quos vocabant, principes civitatis aggressi sunt. Inde magnus tumultus oritur. Nonnulli sacerdotes ab ecclesiis eiecti, quinque, quibus nomina Tooth, Dale, Enraght, Green, Bell-Cox, in carcere donec se submitterent detenti sunt; quibus omnibus aut per errorem iudicii aut lapsu temporis nulla facta submissione liberatis, tandem ab his tumultibus ecclesia quievit ; nunc vix credibile videtur talia esse facta. Processu contra Episcopum Lincolniensem de eisdem rebus instituto, Archiepiscopus Cantuariensis, edictis civilium tribunalium neglectis, rem propria sua auctoritate in sensu Catholico determinavit. (Anno 1890).

Cum igitur domi res ita se habeant, externis

"DE RE ANGLICANA" AND ITS CRITICS 203

iam magis vacamus, et de unitate cum aliis Ecclesiis renovanda arrectis animis deliberatur. Sunt qui ad Graecos et Russos praecipue convertantur. Cum Patriarcha Hierosolymitano, cum Metropolita Kievensi, denique cum sancta Russorum Synodo, Archiepiscopus Cantuariensis fraternum litterarum et legationum commercium instituit. Multi in sanctam Ecclesiam Romanam, tanquam matrem unde nobis lumen Evangelii primum refulsit, oculos magno cum desiderio intendunt. Nuperrime in Congressu Ecclesiastico Norwici habito Archiepiscopus Eboracensis de impedimentis unitatis ex nostra parte amovendis magna cum bonorum laude concionatus est. Illustrissimus noster vicecomes de Halifax, qui eadem strenuissime pro laicali statu movet, in eodem Congressu omnibus fere plaudentibus orationem de unitate instauranda habuit. Quem multi alii secuti sunt. Nec mirum. Nam quo magis in nostram Catholici cultus et doctrinae haereditatem intramus, eo ardentius in perfectam cum aliis Catholicis unitatem et communionem anhelamus.

Non quidem novus est atque inauditus ille animi motus. Namque inde a principio dissensionis quae saeculo sexto decimo Ecclesiam Occidentalem tam diro schismate laceravit, hunc miserrimum Christianitatis statum omnes boni inter nostros deplorabant, meliora deprecabantur. Unica Christi Ecclesia visibili caritatis vinculo contineatur oportere quis dubitat? Non nos certe dubitamus, neque a maioribus nostris id dubitandum recepimus. Imo hoc vinculum caritatis temporibus funestis dissolutum reficere cuiusque boni Christiani esse semper nobis est traditum. Ergo ut priora omittam, ipsi

204 A ROMAN DIARY AND OTHER DOCUMENTS

Tractariani eadem fere moliebantur. Quo tempore Nicolaus Wiseman, qui postea Cardinalis, tunc Vicarius Apostolicus pro Anglia fuit, magnam unitatis instaurandae expectationem habuit. Ille conversionem Angliae ad fidem et praxim Catholicam imprimis exoptans, non nisi per Ecclesiae Anglicanae ministerium hanc efficiendam putabat. Methodus diversitatum explicandarum, quam Tractariani sequebantur, ei quoque placuit. Eorum quae Oxonienses iam tunc effecerant non ignarus, populum rudem et cultus Catholici paene oblitum ad meliora praeparari videbat, instruendum sperabat; cum toto Ecclesiae corpore potius quam cum singulis et privatis agere cupiebat.[1] Cum autem singuli ex Tractarianis in Ecclesiam Romanam, ut dixi, refugissent, ceteri pro tempore debilitati omnes vires ad causam domesticam defendendam intenderunt. Nec tamen maiorum obliti sunt. Pusey post aliquot annos in eandem exspectationem cum fervida spe et caritate rediit. Anno 1865 *Eirenicon*[2] suum edidit, in quo de unitate visibili per Ecclesiam Anglicanam instauranda disseruit. Multa de diversitatibus cultus ac doctrinae addidit; talia non ad fidem spectare, formulas Anglicanas cum Romanis dissonas potius videri quam esse, potestatem R. Pontificis non esse obstaculum inevitabile, et similia. Haec tanti viri epistola incredibilem fervorem excitavit. Libri et dissertationes e prelo indesinenter fluebant. Sodalitas pro precibus in hunc finem fundendis instituta Anglicanos, Graecos, ac Romanae Ecclesiae subditos vinculo caritatis permultos

---

[1] Vide, *A Letter on Catholic Unity*, London, 1841, cuius versio gallica habetur in *Revue Anglo-Romaine*, Vol. II, p 193, 2 Maii 1896.

[2] An Eirenicon, in a Letter to the Author of *The Christian Year*. Oxford, Parker, 1865

"DE RE ANGLICANA" AND ITS CRITICS 205

coniunxit. Ex ea re primus fuit exspectationis repulsus; namque ad Sacrum Officium de hac sodalitate relato, cum quaedam de ecclesia ex *tribus commuinonibus* condenda infeliciter in constitutione sodalitatis fuissent expressa, prohibitum est ne in eius operibus participaretur (an. 1867). Frigidum et parum benevolum id multis visum est. Nec tamen opus fervere desiit. Alia epistola, quae Eirenici pars secunda habetur, ad rev. doct. J. H. Newman anno 1869 scripta, Pusey aliqua, quae de cultu B. Virginis in priori dixerat, lenius explicare conatus est. Tandem in tertia parte eodem anno ad eundem scripta, unitatem sana ratione perfici posse ostendit. "Eisdem" inquit, "patribus nati fieri non potest quin tandem nos invicem intellegere debeamus. Singulari tuo amori et magnanimi caritati haec commendam vix necesse est. Ceteris qui ex tua communione sint, per te haec tantum dicam; neque in hoc neque in priore libello me quicquam ex eis quae vos de fide credatis tangere voluisse. Nihil sane cupiebam nisi ut pro pace solida, sana, diuturna, si per me id stare posset, contenderem. Tempora funestissima et dies tribulationis in terris exspectamus. Fides confirmatur, sed infidelitas simul perficitur. Quid vero ad hanc reprimendam fieri non possit, dummodo qui unum Dominum unamque Fidem confitentur, uno quoque animo sint, dum Christianitas vinculo caritatis unita, Sancti Spiritus influxu nullis rixis vel corporis lacerationibus impedito, ad omnes in Illius amorem reducendos exeat, quem omnes amare, cui servire atque obedire cupimus. Unum tantum lapidem offensionis amovisse non parvus erit fructus per totum vitae cursum laboranti. Ille autem solus

206 A ROMAN DIARY AND OTHER DOCUMENTS

Auctor pacis et amator potest cor patrum ad filios et cor filiorum ad patres convertere. *Domine opus tuum, in medio annorum vivifica illud. In medio annorum notum facies : cum iratus fueris, misericordiae recordaberis.*"[1]

Post Concilium Vaticanum spes ista paene evanuit. Pusey nil amplius edidit. Nonnulli, qui huic exspectationi nimis fortasse innixi erant, nunc nimis deiecti a fide defecerunt. Anni sequebantur interno tumultu turbati. Nunc pacem domi consecuti, foras quoque pacem inquirimus. Neque impossibile id nobis videtur, qui tanta beneficia a Deo accepimus, tantum opus in Ecclesia confectum iam vidimus. Quem antecessores nostri magnum et insuperabilem montem putabant, in planum fieri posse nos non dubitamus.

Hinc novus animorum motus, qui tamen non novus sed renovatus. Quaestionem de Ordinationibus Anglicanis iniimus, non quidem in ea totum dissensionis radicem contineri putantes, sed in eo confisi quod hinc via ad animos conciliandos pateat. Proinde nostri huic multum instant ; ordinum suorum et sacramentorum veritatem summa fiducia tenent, et studio singulari defendunt. Qui de his dubitaverit quomodo cum eo communionis vel voluntatem concipere poterunt ? Ergo ne eis scandalum fiat, quaestionem ex hac parte aggrediamur necesse est. Magno igitur gaudio nostris erat audiisse R. Pontificem sponte in his rebus versari. De eius voluntate dubitare, qui epistolam *Ad Anglos* legit, omnino non potest.

Ut Ecclesia Romana hoc opus in finem dirigat spes est et exspectatio totius Christianitatis.

T. A. LACEY.

[1] *Is Healthful Reunion impossible ? A second Letter to the Very Rev. J. H. Newman, D.D* Oxford, Parker, 1870.

"DE RE ANGLICANA" AND ITS CRITICS 207

Appendix

Quaedam de actuali Ecclesiae Anglicanae statu, ex opere *The Church Year Book* intitulato collecta, in conspectu hic ponere liceat.

I. STATUS GENERALIS.

	In Anglia	*Alibi*
Provinciae .	2	12
Dioeceses ..	35	165
Parochiae .	13800	*circ.* 6300

II COMMUNITATES CLERICORUM.

Societas S. Joannis Evangelistae.	Domus principalis apud Cowley, quae pars est Civitatis Oxoniensis. In Missionibus et Exercitiis spiritualibus patres et conversi, votis perpetuis adstricti, plerumque versantur Domus habent apud Boston in America, apud Capetown in Africa Meridionali, Bombaiae et Poonae in India.
Communitas Resurrectionis.	Domus apud Radley. Fratres in Studiis sacris versantur
Domus Puseiana.	Societas clericorum saecularium vitam communem degentium, in sacris studiis apud Oxonienses versatorum.
Domus Oxoniensis.	Societas clericorum saecularium qui vitam communem degentes opera missionaria Londinii in regione a pauperrimis habitata exercent.
Missio Oxoniensis ad Calcutta.	Societas eiusdem generis pro Indis cultioribus ad fidem convertendis.
Societas S. Pauli.	Communitas regularium curae spirituali Nautarum addicta, olim in India fundata, nuper in Angliam inducta
Missionarii Glocestrenses.	Collegium Sacerdotum Missionariorum pro Dioecesi Glocestrensi.
Missionarii S. Andreae.	Collegium Sacerdotum Missionariorum pro Dioecesi Sarisburiensi.

208 A ROMAN DIARY AND OTHER DOCUMENTS

III. COMMUNITATES RELIGIOSARUM VOTIS ADSTRICTARUM.

Nomina Communitatum	*Domus principalis*	*Opera principalia*
"Devonport Sisters."	Ascot.	Diversa Cura infirmorum et orphanorum. Domus ad minus duo.
Communitas S. Mariae Virginis	Wantage.	Cura feminarum paenitentium Instructio primaria et superior. Opera misericordiae externa Plurimae domus tam in Anglia quam in Coloniis, etc.
Communitas S. Joannis Baptistae	Clewer.	Cura feminarum paenitentium, orphanorum, infirmorum, et convalescentium Instructio in omnibus gradibus Plurimae domus
"Sorores Pauperum" alias Societas Omnium Sanctorum.	Londinii.	Cura infirmorum et opera misericordiae externa. Domus in Anglia, in America, in Africa, in India, etc.
Societas S. Margaretae.	East Grinstead.	Cura pauperum infirmorum in domibus propriis, et alia ut supra. Plurimae domus.
Societas S. Raphaelis	Bristol.	Regulam Filiarum Charitatis a S. Vincentio datam maxima ex parte observant Domum Magilae in dioec. Zanzibarensi habent
"Sorores Bethaniae"	Londinii.	Exercitia spiritualia pro feminis Domum habent in Assyria pro feminis instruendis.
Societas S. Petri.	Horbury.	Cura feminarum paenitentium. Domus quattuor.
Societas Omnium Sanctorum.	Ditchingham.	Cura feminarum paenitentium. Domum in America septentrionali pro aboriginibus habent.
Societas S. Petri.	Kilburn	Cura infirmorum, et potissimum incurabilium. Domus septem ad minus.
Societas S. Thomae Martyris	Oxonii	Instructio, et cura orphanorum.
Societas Sanctae et Individuae Trinitatis.	Oxonii.	Oratio perpetua pro fide propaganda. Instructio puellarum. Domum Cantabrigiae habent.
Communitas SS. Mariae Virginis et Scholasticae.	Malling.	Regulam S. Benedicti observant.

"DE RE ANGLICANA" AND ITS CRITICS 209

IV OPERA PASTORALIA

Sodalitates	Missiones	Episcopi
Missiones Foraneae.	Society for the Propagation of the Gospel S. P. G. Church Missionary Society C. M. S. Central African Mission Et aliae.	In Africa Occidentali. 6 In ,, Meridionali. 9 In ,, Orientali. 4 In India. 10 Apud Sinas. 6 In Iaponia. 4 In America Septentrionali, pro aboriginibus. 10 In Guiana. 1
Missiones in Parochiis.	Anno 1895, ad minus 220 habitae sunt in Anglia.	
Secessus.	Anno 1895 habiti sunt in Anglia, ad minus, { pro clero 40 pro laicis 56.	
Seminaria.	In Anglia, maior pars cleri in Universitatibus educatur Seminaria 9 sunt Dioecesana, 7 Generalia, 5 pro Missionibus Foraneis In Coloniis et in Americae Civitatibus Unitis plurima sunt.	

V. ELEEMOSYNAE FIDELIUM.

In Anglia Episcopi et Ecclesiae Cathedrales fundos antiquissimos habent ; parochi pro decimis compositiones a terrarum dominis plerumque accipiunt. Harum pecuniarum summa est singulis annis circiter 155,000,000 librarum Italicarum. Quae hic sequuntur, e voluntaria fidelium liberalitate in Anglia tantum addita, in libris Italicis computantur.

Pro Missionibus Foraneis	Pro Clero et Cultu	Pro Ecclesiarum Fabricis	Pro Scholis aedificandis	Pro Scholis sustinendis
Anno 1894 L. 15,500,000	Anno 1894 L. 49,500,000	Singulis annis 1860–84 L. 38,000,000	Annis 1870–94 L 202,000,000	Anno 1894 L. 16,800,000

P

II

RISPOSTA ALL'OPUSCOLO

"De Re Anglicana"

In un Opuscolo intitolato "De Re Anglicana" recentemente dato alla luce da uno scrittore Anglicano, vi sono moltissimi errori che possono facilmente ingannare il lettore. Abbiamo perciò creduto necessario di provvedere con una nostra risposta che servirà a correggere e commentare questa pubblicazione. Divideremo il nostro lavoro in due parti : Nella prima parte riporteremo successivamente gli errori contenuti in alcuni paragrafi, accennando le pagine. Nella seconda parte diremo brevemente della situazione religiosa in Inghilterra e della speranza di una riunione.

PARTE PRIMA

ERRORI PRINCIPALI CONTENUTI NELL'OPUSCOLO "DE RE ANGLICANA"

ORIGINE E NATURA DELLO SCISMA
SOTTO ENRICO VIII

"*Reformatio sub Henrico VIII incepta nihil contra fidem* CATHOLICAM effecit. QUÆDAM fateor, facinorosa quædam adhuc ploranda evenerunt ; a communione Ecclesiæ Romanæ recessum est, vita religiosa extirpata ; in his autem quæ ad doctrinam spectant *nihil mutatum.* Nec tamen etiam tunc deerant qui novas res in hac parte molirentur, inter quos et episcopi *rari* erant, quorum princeps Cranmer" (p. 1, *p. ad init.*).

1° L'Autore come Anglicano nega che il Primato di giurisdizione del Romano Pontefice faccia parte della dottrina cattolica.

"DE RE ANGLICANA" AND ITS CRITICS 211

2° Dove dice "*quœdam*," dovrebbe dire invece "*multa nimis.*" Perchè sotto Enrico VIII sebbene fosse conservata la Liturgia cattolica, nondimeno furono constituiti nelle sede principali Vescovi notoriamente eretici e fautori accaniti de protestantesimo. Cromwell semplice laico e dopo il Sovrano la persona più potente del regno, Vicario generale della Corona per le cose spirituali e che negava apertamente il sacramento dell'Ordine, fu messo a capo del governo ecclesiastico. Egli si unì a Cranmer ed a'suoi seguaci in tal guisa che i predicatori della dottrina riformata furono mandati da essi in tutta l'Inghilterra propagando la loro eresia. 3° "*Rari.*" Erano invece parecchi: Cranmer (di Canterbury), Holbeach (di Lincoln), Goodrich (di Ely), Ridley (di Rochester), Barlow (di Menevia), e Shaxton (di Salisbury), tutti riformatori ben conosciuti. Altri otto si mostrarono più o meno indifferenti, diciamo "opportunisti."

VESCOVI SOTTO EDOARDO

"Attamen episcopi, qui animo et sententia CATHOLICI erant, sedes suas RETINUERUNT, novisque rebus quantum possent sese accommodarunt. NONNULLI autem ex his detrusi sunt (p 1 in fine).

1° In nessuna maniera possono chiamarsi cattolici quelli che ritennero le loro sedi sotto Edoardo. Alcuni fra gli "opportunisti" servili e finti conservarono le loro sedi e le loro rendite, e questi non ebbero una sola parola di protesta mentre si rovesciavano empiamente gli altari nelle chiese per ordine del Re e di Cranmer, e si oltraggiavano i dommi cattolici dichiarandoli blasfematori.

212   A ROMAN DIARY AND OTHER DOCUMENTS

2° "*Nonnulli*." Invece tutti i Vescovi che in qualche maniera conservavano un sentimento cattolico od un resto di venerazione per i dommi cattolici furono cacciati dalle loro sedi sotto Edoardo. Cosi Gardiner (di Winchester), Bonner (di Londra), Heath (di Worcester), Tunstall (di Durham), Voysey (di Exeter), Day (di Chichester) furono tutti destituiti, parecchi carcerati ed a loro posto sostituiti eretici ben conosciuti. In questa maniera Cranmer ed i fautori della sua eresia ottennero facilissimamente la preponderanza.

VESCOVI SOTTO MARIA

"Maria igitur regnum excipiente NONNULLI episcopi destituti sunt, inter quos Cranmer ; CETERI manebant" (p. 2, in princip).

Queste parole NONNULLI e CETERI non possono ammettersi. Di 23 vescovi che si trovavano al posto alla morte di Edoardo, non alcuni, ma la maggior parte ossia 13 furono immediatamente destituiti.

Furono destituiti 13 Vescovi eretici ; e furono restituiti quelli che sotto Edoardo erano stati destituiti, ossia 6. Furono riabilitati 6 altri dopo fatta la penitenza e l'abjura nelle mani del Card. Legato.[1] I nuovi Vescovi *costituiti* dal Legato furono 14.

SOTTO ELISABETTA

"Consiliarios qui sub Maria rempublicam direxerant PLERUM-QUE (Elisabetha) retinuit" (p. 2 verso la metà)

Abbiamo qui un'asserzione erronea. Difatti *immediatamente* dopo la sua venuta al trono Elisabetta

---

[1] Di questi vescovi riabilitati dal Card. Polo nessuno era stato consecrato secondo l'Ordinale anglicano.

"DE RE ANGLICANA" AND ITS CRITICS 213

che dalla gioventù favoriva l'eresia si diede a promuovere ardentemente ma con prudenza la causa della riforma. Chiamò al suo consiglio quelli che favorivano la nuova dottrina e in guisa tale che nel mese stesso di sua incoronazione si preparava già con accuratezza nel consiglio regio un insieme di leggi contro la fede cattolica ed il papato. Abbiamo ancora le minute di questo consiglio negli archivi del regno. Le leggi principali di questa natura stabilite nel suo primo parlamento furono le seguenti :

1º *Una legge che toglieva le annate e le decime che si pagavano alla Sede Apostolica per darle alla Regina.*

2º *Una legge che aboliva assolutamente la giurisdizione del Romano Pontefice e riconosceva la Regina come governatrice suprema della chiesa anglicana.*

3º *Una legge che abrogava la liturgia cattolica e introduceva di nuovo la 2ª liturgia di Edoardo VI, ossia quella più protestante, con pochissime mutazioni.*[1]

Queste leggi furono approvate malgrado la protesta di tutti i vescovi e del clero cattolico. In questa maniera fin dal primo anno del suo regno Elisabetta distrusse la chiesa cattolica in Inghilterra e stabilì su base sicura e nel miglior modo che poteva la religione protestante. Si deve notare che l'intenzione eretica della regina e de' suoi consiglieri si deduce evidentemente dal fatto che nell'abolizione della fede cattolica non cercarono di ritornare neanche allo stato di cose esistente sotto Enrico VIII dopo che era già stata esclusa la giurisdizione del Romano

---

[1] Queste mutazioni sono riportate nella nostra esposizione " *De ordinibus Anglicanis* " pag. 32.

214 A ROMAN DIARY AND OTHER DOCUMENTS

Pontefice. Nè si contentarono di restituire la religione riformata quale fu introdotta sotto Edoardo VI quando si manteneva almeno un residuo della credenza cattolica. Ma espressamente stabilirono colle loro leggi la *seconda* liturgia, ossia la protestante all'accesso, che massimamente piaceva ai riformatori e dalla quale fu cancellato ogni vestigio del sacerdozio cattolico e del sacrifizio. Con alcune poche mutazioni vollero restituire questa liturgia come regola pubblica di fede e di preghiera. Si aggiunga che il Parker arcivescovo di Canterbury e tutti i nuovi vescovi ed il clero dopo avere destituito i cattolici sottoscrissero volentieri all'articolo XXIX che negava la presenza reale, ed all'art. XXXI che dichiarava che i sacrifizi delle messe erano favole blasfematorie ed imposture pericolose. Gli storici più segnalati d'Inghilterra, quantunque anglicani (Nicolao Pocock ed altri), comunemente ammettono senza esitazione che i vescovi ed il clero costituito sotto Elisabetta tennero ed insegnarono quasi universalmente per un secolo intiero la dottrina sacramentale di Zwinglio e di Calvino. Il chiarissimo Card. Newman (lett. a W. Hutton) stabilisce la medesima conclusione dopo un esame accuratissimo dei fatti. Sarebbe forse difficile di ritrovare in tutta la storia ecclesiastica una mutazione o meglio una rivoluzione dottrinale più completa e più radicalmente attuata, di quella portata a termine da Elisabetta in Inghilterra l'anno 1559.

"DE RE ANGLICANA" AND ITS CRITICS 215

IL CLERO SOTTO ELISABETTA

" PAUCI e clero novis rebus sese accomodare recusarunt, plerique spe fortasse meliorum quieti manebant. Universa Ecclesia Anglicana EISDEM LEGIBUS EODEM CULTU constanter utebatur " (p. 4, verso la metà).

1° È inesatto il dire che pochi si rifiutarono (*pauci recusarunt*). Infatti tutti i vescovi, con una sola eccezione, resistettero pubblicamente e colla massima energia. Senza dubbio la maggior parte del clero defezionò ; ma secondo le investigazioni più recenti il numero de' chierici che si rifiutò ad accomodarsi alle novità fu assai maggiore di quello che comunemente si suppone ; certamente superò i due mila. Si è trovato adesso per esempio, e lo asseriscono il Pocock ed altri, che moltissimi lasciarono i loro benefizi ed in questa maniera non comparvero mai avanti agl' inquisitori della regina.

2° Se colle parole " UNIVERSA ECCLESIA ANGLICANA *eisdem legibus eodemque cultu* CONSTANTER UTEBATUR" si vuol fare intendere che le leggi, ed i principii del culto introdotti da Elisabetta furon quelli che esistevano ai tempi cattolici, è assolutamente falso. Perchè : 1.° alla fede cattolica furono sostituiti GLI ARTICOLI DI RELIGIONE che insegnavano chiaramente le eresie della riforma. 2.° Alla liturgia cattolica fu sostituita la liturgia Eduardiana dalla quale tutto ciò che accenna alla presenza reale al sacrifizio ed al sacerdozio cattolico è stato a bello studio cancellato.

3° Invece del primato della Sede Apostolica il Re

216 A ROMAN DIARY AND OTHER DOCUMENTS

e la Regina vennero dichiarati governatori supremi della Chiesa in terra. Un cambiamento più completo e più radicale dommatico, liturgico ed organico si può appena concepire.

I CATTOLICI SOTTO ELISABETTA

" Certe post aliquot annos, cum Pius V per Bullam *Regnans in Excelsis* Elizabetham ejusque fautores excommunicasset, ei qui auctoritati Pontificiæ maxime faverent ab hac Ecclesiæ Anglicanæ unitate RECESSERUNT " (p. 4 verso la fine).

Al contrario, quelli che erano massimamente favorevoli all' autorità pontificia, ossia i cattolici, non ebbero mai comunione colla setta anglicana e quindi da essa non potevano ritirarsi. Tant' e vero che non accomodaronsi alle eresie anglicane, che molti in tutta Inghilterra soffrirono la perdita dei beni e preferirono la carcere piuttosto che trovarsi presenti anche materialmente al rito anglicano. E infatti Elisabetta non trovò mezzo più vantaggioso per obligare i cattolici a frequentare le chiese anglicane dell'imporre multe ripetute all' eccesso. I nostri archivi attestano ancora oggi la resistenza dei cattolici fedeli col registrare che le multe pagate salirono alla somma di 1,000,000 di sterline (25,000,000 di lire it.). Questo dirà in eterno come lo dice pure il sangue dei nostri martiri che non mancò il piccolo gregge di fedeli che non volle macchiarsi dell' eresia anglicana.

DELLA DUPLICE SCUOLA ANGLICANA

SOTTO ELISABETTA

E DEL COSÌ DETTO CATTOLICISMO

" Ex his partes PURITANÆ originem habuerunt. Exinde magna erat intra Ecclesiam Anglicanam controversia, quæ usque hodie aliquo modo subsistit. Universi enim eisdem ritibus usi, eisdem fidei doctrinis adstricti, de cæremoniis de regimine pastorali, de potestate clavium exercitio, denique de doctrinis gratiæ acriter disputabant. Partes Puritanæ, partes QUAS CATHOLICAS VOCAMUS, non alio modo in Ecclesiæ Anglicanæ unitate sese tenebant quam olim in regno Francico consistebant partes ultramontanæ et Gallicanæ " (p. 4 in fine).

Qui si insinua un errore degno di speciale osservazione. Si fa supporre non solo che i Ritualisti si possano chiamar *cattolici*, ma che questi Ritualisti, che oggi vogliono il nome di cattolici, hanno in qualche modo esistito dai primi anni del regno di Elisabetta fino ad oggi. Ciò è storicamente falso. Basterà accennare alcuni fatti. La controversia fra i Puritani e gli Anglicani si raggirava intorno al regime episcopale, alla liturgia ed alla predestinazione. Ma nè allora, nè per un intiero secolo dopo Elisabetta possiamo trovare alcun vestigio di quelle dottrine che i Ritualisti anglicani vogliono additare come *cattoliche*. Molti Anglicani di quel secolo resistettero ai Puritani per difendere il regime episcopale almeno come più conveniente. Difesero anche la liturgia Eduardiana contro le orazioni libere e spontanee dei Calvinisti, ed il potere della scomunica e dell'assoluzione in foro esterno, almeno in senso cosi detto DECLARATORIO. Ma fra i moltissimi VESCOVI, SCRITTORI E PREDICATORI ANGLICANI di quel secolo si puo nominare appena UN SOLO CHE CREDESSE

218 A ROMAN DIARY AND OTHER DOCUMENTS

ALLA PRESENZA REALE IN SENSO OBJETTIVO, AL SACRIFIZIO DELLA MESSA O AL SACERDOZIO IN SENSO CATTOLICO[1] Tutti invece rigettarono pubblicamente queste dottrine colla medesima ostilità degli stessi Puritani, e le hanno combattute con veemenza nelle loro prediche e nei loro scritti. Sono forse questi che i Ritualisti moderni vogliono additare come predecessori cattolici? Neanche dopo un secolo ai tempi dell'Arcivescovo Laud possiamo trovare un solo che ammette il sacerdozio o il sacramento e sacrifizio dell'Eucaristia in senso cattolico. Vi sono alcuni, "*rari nantes in gurgite vasto*" che usano cautamente qualche espressioni cattoliche, come del resto fanno anche altri eretici. Ma se esaminiamo i loro scritti, ci accorgiamo subito che quelle espressioni si usavano in senso evidentemente eretico e contrario alla fede cattolica. Perciò prima dell' apparire dei Trattariani (anno 1830) si troverà uno appena degli Anglicani che credesse al sacerdozio, al sacrifizio o alla presenza reale in senso cattolico. Anche oggi ciò che insegna costantemente la maggior parte degli stessi Ritualisti sopra questi punti di dottrina, e cio che vanno predicando costantemente, difficilmente si concilia coll' insegnamento cattolico.

[1] Alcuni ammettevano la presenza reale "*per gratiam in anima communicantis*," e cio non negavano Cranmer e Calvino. Altri ammettevano che l'Eucaristia è sacrifizio ma nel senso di un sacrifizio "*laudis et gratiarum actionis* o "*panis et vini materialis.*"

"DE RE ANGLICANA" AND ITS CRITICS 219

DELLA DOTTRINA ANGLICANA

"Ecclesia Anglicana e tot periculis elapsa ab aliis ecclesiis nationalibus in unitate Catholica comprehensis nihil distulit nisi quod communione sacrorum cum Sancta Sede careret" (p 5 verso la metà).

Asserzione falsissima È ben noto, e il popolo inglese con tutti i suoi storici più segnalati lo asserisce con noi che per tre secoli e fino al 1830 non vi era una sola chiesa parrocchiale o cattedrale in tutta Inghilterra nella quale non si predicasse pubblicamente e costantemente la dottrina protestante, o nella quale non si rigettasse con oltraggio e scherno il domma cattolico del sacrifizio della messa e della presenza reale. Anche oggi la immensa maggioranza del popolo e molti vescovi anglicani rigettano le dottrine dei Ritualisti e non vogliono sentire parlare dei dommi sopraccennati, neppure in questo senso modificato. I Ritualisti rivendicano il nome di *Cattolici* precisamente dal fatto che essi s'immaginano credere fedelmente a quei dommi principali della fede cattolica che sonno comuni alla chiesa orientale ed occidentale : vale a dire al sacerdozio, che ha il potere di assolvere e di ritenere i peccati, alla presenza reale e al vero sacrifizio eucaristico identico al sacrifizio della croce. Ora se vogliamo prendere il nome di *Cattolici* secondo questo criterio è assolutamente certo che fra gli Anglicani non avvene uno fra venti anzi fra cinquanta che possa arrogarsi questo nome. È un fatto notorio, e mille volte asserito in mille maniere ogni giorno dal popolo inglese, che tutti gli Anglicani rigettano energicamente non solo il primato del Romano Pontefice, ma anche l'interpretazione cattolica dei dommi sopraccennati. È dunque un errore

220 A ROMAN DIARY AND OTHER DOCUMENTS

ed una vera derisione di volere considerare questi
Ritualisti come "LA CHIESA ANGLICANA."
Ciò sarebbe prendere erroneamente una parte esigua
per il tutto. Noi godiamo certamente e ringraziamo
il Signore che finalmente una parte dei nostri con-
cittadini accetta questi nostri dommi in un senso
che si avvicina a poco a poco al senso cattolico.
Ma la verità esige da noi impedire che all'estero si
prenda l'enorme equivoco di credere che questa
decima parte degli Anglicani costituisca il ceto
Anglicano.

DELLA TENTATA CONCILIAZIONE TRA LE FORMOLE
ANGLICANE ED I DECRETI DEL CONCILIO DI TRENTO

"Quocirca decreta ac definitiones Concilii Tridentini summo studio
tractabant (Tractariani) ut cum eis formulas ac definitiones Anglicanas non adeo dissonas esse monstrarent ut ineluctabilis inde dissensio eveniret" (p. 6 verso la metà).

L'Autore principale di questa tentata conciliazione
tra i decreti di Trento e gli articoli di religione
Anglicana fu il chiarissimo J. H. Newman (poi
Cardinale di S. R. Chiesa) il quale prima della sua
conversione alla fede cattolica fu il Capo tanto
lodato dei così detti Trattariani. Colla grazia di Dio
egli riconobbe la futilità di questo tentativo ed entrò
nel seno della Chiesa seguito poi da molti suoi
discepoli.[1] Come cattolico il Newman spiegò, dopo
alcuni anni, la impossibilità di tale conciliazione e
nella sua lettera al Rev. Hutton, nella quale espone
anche chiaramente la sua sentenza contro gli ordini
Anglicani, a vedere con argomenti irrefragabili come
tutti i vescovi e teologi per tre secoli dopo Elisa-

[1] Da quel tempo ad oggi si contano più di 500 Ministri Anglicani
convertiti alla Chiesa Cattolica.

"DE RE ANGLICANA" AND ITS CRITICS 221

betta negavano assolutamente la successione apostolica e gli altri dommi di Trento. Nessuno meglio di Newman conosceva l'Anglicanismo. Nessuno erasi mostrato più divoto a quella setta fin dalla prima fanciullezza. Nella mente, nei scritti e nella vita di questo dottissimo ed illustrissimo Cardinale abbiamo la migliore interpretazione pratica del *movimento di Oxford* e dell'opera dei Trattariani. E prova all'evidenza la futilità dell'Anglicanismo per quanto si voglia travestire con apparenze cattoliche.

STATO PRESENTE DELL'ANGLICANISMO

"Tota enim facies Ecclesiæ his quinquaginta annis renovata est. DOCTRINA CATHOLICA UBIQUE PRÆDICATUR. De præceptis novæ legis, de auxiliis gratiæ, de usu Sacramentorum populus instruitur" (p. 7. *ad init*)

Un'altro asserzione falsissima. Nessuno di noi certamente vorrà negare che l'Anglicanismo abbia cambiato molte cose negli ultimi 50 anni. Lo diciamo volentieri e ne daremo la spiegazione. Ma per asserire che la dottrina cattolica è dapertutto predicata bisogna aver perduto il senno. L'espressione "*Doctrina Catholica*" si prende qui in senso Ritualistico, ossia per significare alcune dottrine e pratiche dei Ritualisti che scimmiottano più o meno la Chiesa Cattolica. Essi prendono le nostre dottrine e le nostre pratiche cambiandole secondo il loro intento, ammettendo alcune, rigettando altre, a norma del loro giudizio privato, chiamandole poi "*la Dottrina Cattolica*." Giova però notare che anche in questo senso accomodato la dottrina così detta *cattolica* si ammette solamente da una piccola sezione della setta Anglicana, e non la troviamo in

222 A ROMAN DIARY AND OTHER DOCUMENTS

una chiesa sopra dieci. Ora se l'espressione *Dottrina cattolica* si prende nel suo vero senso, ossia per significare ciò che insegna la Chiesa Romana, in ciò che riguarda alla costituzione della chiesa, questa dottrina non esiste fra gli Anglicani; se si tratta della transustanziazione se ne trova appena appena qualche traccia; trattandosi dell'Eucaristia o del sacrifizio della Messa secondo la definizione del Concilio di Trento rarissime volte s'incontra; e questa dottrina non è predicata nè creduta nelle chiese Anglicane.

FREQUENZA DELL EUCARISTIA FRA GLI ANGLICANI.

"De sanctorum meritis, de consiliis perfectionis non amplius siletur. Ubi rarius Eucharistia olim celebrabatur, nunc JUGITER sacrificium offertur, ubi pauci Mensam Domini adibant, nunc FREQUENS POPULUS digna cum ADORATIONE de cibo cælesti participat" (p 7, *circ. med.*).

1° Non si può citare un solo vescovo Anglicano che permetta in qualsiasi modo la invocazione dei Santi. Non vi è una chiesa pubblica dove sia approvato questo culto. Qualche volta lo troveremo, è vero, malgrado le proteste della massa degli Anglicani e dei Vescovi, ma sarà in una chiesa sopra mille.

2° Senza dubbio l'Eucaristia si celebra con più frequenza adesso che cinquanta anni fa. Allora non si celebrava ordinariamente più di *tre o quattro volte all'anno* in ciascuna chiesa parrocchiale. Oggi in regola ordinaria si celebra una volta al mese. In alcune poche chiese si fa ogni domenica. Rarissime volte poi e quasi mai si celebra l'Eucaristia tutti i giorni nella chiesa parrocchiale.

"DE RE ANGLICANA" AND ITS CRITICS 223

3° Non si può dire che il popolo Anglicano frequenti l'Eucaristia. Si dica piuttosto se ne priva un po' di prima. Secondo la relazione più recente ufficialmente pubblicata dagli stessi Anglicani nel loro ANNUARIO fra 16 milioni di seguaci non si contano che 2 milioni che si comunicano.

4° L'Adorazione dell'Eucaristia è proibita espressamente nella rubrica del Libro di Preghiera Comune e negli Articoli di Religione. Nè fra gli Anglicani che si comunicano vi è uno fra cento che intenda minimamente di adorare il Sacramento. La prassi di adorare l'Eucaristia trovasi soltanto in pochissime chiese o cappelle della così detta Scuola Ritualista.

DEI MEZZI CATTOLICI ADOPERATI DAGLI ANGLICANI.

" Multa quoque ex aliis ecclesiis grati MUTUAVIMUS, secessus seu exercitia spiritualia tam pro clero quam pro laicis, missiones in civitatibus et in pagis, stationes quadragesimales, hoc genus omne, iam NOBIS propria sunt" (p 7 verso la metà).

Qui ammette giustamente l'Autore che i Ritualisti moderni hanno cercato di combattere la Chiesa cattolica in Inghilterra rivolgendo contro di esse le sue proprie armi. Ma quando dice " *nobis propria sunt* " non parla affato l'Autore per tutto il ceto Anglicano ma solamente per la scuola alla quale appartiene. L'immensa maggioranza degli Anglicani rifugge da simili mezzi e non se ne interessa. Però alcune poche persone sincere e divote trovano in questo il mezzo di giungere a Dio ed alla verità e questo ci dà consolazione e speranza di grazia più abbondante.

A ROMAN DIARY AND OTHER DOCUMENTS

DELL'UFFICIO DIVINO FRA GLI ANGLICANI

"OFFICIUM DIVINUM pro usu nostro, semel tantum in mense recitato Psalterio levius est onus, sed in pluribus diœcesibus totum Psalterium, sacerdotibus ALIIS ALIOS psalmos legentibus, ex CONSTITUTIONE episcopi quotidie recitatur" (p. 7 verso la fine).

1° L'Ufficio recitato dagli Anglicani è completamente diverso dall'Ufficio Divino della Chiesa Cattolica. L'Ufficio Anglicano non è altro che un complesso di salmi e di lezioni della Sacra Scrittura sostituito da Cranmer e dagli altri Riformatori al Breviario, dal quale però è stata esclusa con massima cura ogni invocazione ai Santi. Nè il recitarlo, per quanto breve sia, è prescritto sotto pena di peccato. Dal clero è ritenuto come semplice consiglio di divozione e si lascia in disparte dalla maggioranza.

2° La prassi di recitare il Salterio "*Aliis alios psalmos legentibus*" è evidentemente un peso lievissimo, giacchè distribuito il Psalterio fra 150 Ministri, non rimane altro che un salmo a ciascuno da recitare. Ma anche questa prassi neppure è imposta dall'Autorità nè trae seco obbligo alcuno. Perchè i vescovi Anglicani non hanno, secondo le leggi dello Stato, potere alcuno di emanare costituzioni che obblighino il Clero. Un obbligo di tal genere solo può venire da una legge Canonica la quale presuppone il consenso della Regina, come gli stessi Vescovi Anglicani riconoscono di non avere tal potere.

"DE RE ANGLICANA" AND ITS CRITICS 225

DELLO STATO RELIGIOSO TRA GLI ANGLICANI

" Statum religiosum qui usque a sæculo XVI penitus obsoleverat anni recentes nova cum devotione reduxerunt " (p. 7 verso la fine)

1° Non è vero che lo stato religioso fra gli Anglicani dal secolo XVI in poi *obsoleverat* solamente ; per tre secoli fu condannato e oltraggiato dai Riformatori, dai Vescovi e dai Teologi Anglicani.

2° Dopo il Puseismo ed il MOVIMENTO DI OXFORD prevalse il desiderio di adottare quanto apparteneva alla chiesa orientale ed occidentale, e fra i Puseisti ed i Ritualisti furono fondate alcune case di monache o meglio di donne in abito monacale. È tanto vero che questa rinnovazione dello STATO RELIGIOSO non proveniva dalla chiesa Anglicana propriamente detta che al principio s'incontrarono difficoltà immense per la resistenza dei Vescovi e della maggioranza del popolo. Dopo poi alcuni uomini, senza approvazione alcuna della Chiesa Anglicana, si riunirono in società per fare vita comune. Ma anche oggi questo tentativo si restringe al solo gruppo dei Ritualisti, e la maggioranza degli Anglicani non riconosce tali religiosi.

3° Le Monache Anglicane sono pochissime di numero : i Religiosi sono anche meno. Molte poi fra le monache non sono legate da voti. Ma tutte insieme non passano le 800. In quanto agli uomini, eccezione fatta forse della società detta di S. Giovanni Evangelista presso Cowley, se ne trovano appena che in qualche modo si possono chiamare comunità religiose. Gli stessi Anglicani

Q

226 A ROMAN DIARY AND OTHER DOCUMENTS

nei loro fogli confessano che queste società per gli uomini sono rarissime, mantenendosi difficilmente e perseverando quasi mai. Così fra quelle accennate nell'Appendice all'opuscolo DE RE ANGLICANA vi sono parecchie che sono semplici confraternite e che non hanno affatto la vita religiosa. Se si sommassero tutti questi uomini datisi allo stato religioso, non sono più di 100 ; e tanto ci viene assicurato da persone convertite alla fede e che hanno bene conosciuto queste società. Fra i così detti religiosi vi sono però parecchi sinceri e di molto zelo ai quali di gran cuore auguriamo il lume della vera fede.

IL "DOPPIO NEMICO DELL'ANGLICANISMO."

"CUM DUOBUS HOSTIBUS DIMICATUM est·[1] cum civili potestate quæ Ecclesiam in vinculis comprimere voluit ; cum partibus *Puritanis* quæ renovationi Catholicæ strenuissime se opponebant Partes *Puritanæ* victæ sunt, nec tamen evanuerunt" (p. 8, verso la metà)

Qui è necessario notare che il nome di Puritani si usa per significare tutti gli Anglicani del vecchio tipo e che sono ostili ai Ritualisti ed al Neo-Anglicanismo dei Trattariani. Questi del resto costituiscono la maggioranza del clero e del popolo inglese. I Puritani non costituiscono una setta separata : sono Anglicani protestanti e ugualmente membri della chiesa Anglicana alla pari dei Ritualisti; anzi si possono dire con più verità membri di questa

[1] Questa espressione è comunissima fra gli Anglicani in Inghilterra e si ripete in tutte le prediche e in tutti i giornali. Ma i due nemici della chiesa Anglicana qui accennati sono i *Puritani* ed i *Romanisti;* perchè chiamano Romanisti noi cattolici a motivo della nostra obbedienza al Romano Pontefice Ma l'Autore Anglicano scrivendo in Roma preferisce in modo di parlare meglio adattato alle circostanze.

"DE RE ANGLICANA" AND ITS CRITICS 227

Chiesa, perchè ne formano la parte principale e conservano fedelmente il vero Anglicanismo dei primi tre secoli. I Ritualisti li disprezzano, specialmente trovandosi a Roma, ma sono in perfetta communione con essi. Così p. es. Lord Halifax, che si può chiamare Capo e Protettore dei Ritualisti, ed il Vescovo Anglicano di Liverpool, che ritiene il Papa per Anticristo, communicano amichevolmente in sacris come membri della medesima chiesa. E temeraria l'asserzione che i Puritani sono sopraffatti. Non si vince così facilmente la maggioranza del popolo inglese. Si tollera il Ritualismo, perchè l'indifferenza religiosa ed il liberalismo rifugge dai mezzi coercitivi ; ma da ciò male si potrebbe dedurre la conclusione che il Ritualismo avrà mai la preponderanza religiosa in Inghilterra. Al contrario trae seco una parte ben piccola del populo.[1]

DEI VESCOVI ANGLICANI.

"Episcopi *quatuor* vel quinque eo intendunt. Ceteri sententia Catholici sunt."

1° L'asserzione è assolutamente erronea. In fatti si enumerano qui quattro o cinque Vescovi che sono Puritani e che si oppongono più energicamente ai Ritualisti. Sono i Vescovi di Liverpool, di Worcester, Exeter, e Sodor. Ma moltissimi altri Vescovi Anglicani mentre mostrarsi più tolleranti non approvano affatto il Ritualismo.

2° Gli altri, "*ceteri*," non si possono affatto chiamare cattolici. Perchè prendendo anche il nome

---

[1] L'Arcidiacono di Londra, W. Sinclair, ha potuto asserire recentemente che il numero dei Ritualisti in Inghilterra non supera i 35,000, ossia 1 sopra 430 Inglesi

228 A ROMAN DIARY AND OTHER DOCUMENTS

di *cattolico* nel senso dei Ritualisti, ossia per significare chiunque creda al sacerdozio, al sacrifizio della messa ed alla presenza reale, si potrà citare appena uno fra i Vescovi Anglicani che ammetta questi dommi. Come mai dunque chiamarli "*sententia catholici*"? Tre solamente fra 40 Vescovi mostrano qualche favore per le dottrine dei Ritualisti e sono il Vescovo di Lincoln, l'Arc. di York ed il Vescovo di Salisbury. Ma anche questi tre negano il domma della transustanziazione. Concedono il sacrifizio della messa nel senso commemorativo. Insegnano la presenza reale dell'Eucaristia nel senso luterano, supponendo che rimanga la materia del pane e del vino e proponendo con espressioni eretiche una presenza spirituale che male si puo definire. Lasciamo ad altri il determinare se questi posson chiamarsi cattòlici.[1]

[1] In quanto agli altri punti tutti rigettano unanimemente la dottrina cattolica sulla costituzione della Chiesa e del Romano Pontefice. Il vescovo di Lincoln, Primicerio fra i Ritualisti, ha voluto recentemente esprimere *pubblicamente la sua sentenza* colle parole del disgraziato Dollinger che l'autorità del Romano Pontefice non si potrà mai conciliare colla Sacra Scrittura e col dovere civile Fra quelli poi che rigettano l'autorità del Romano Pontefice come contraria al Verbo Incarnato, all'insegnamento dei Padri ed alla storia della Chiesa occupa facilmente il primo posto l'Arcivescovo di York. (V. il suo discorso al congresso ecclesiastico del 1895) Finalmente è tanto vero che il Vescovo di Salisbury non favorisce il cattolicismo che rigetta la giurisdizione del Romano Pontefice ne' suoi scritti e ne' suoi discorsi. Ogni anno poi offre il suo appoggio alla Società fondata per propagare il protestantesimo in Italia sotto la direzione del Conte Campello, della qual società è riconosciuto Patrono

PROCESSO DEL VESCOVO DI LINCOLN ED APPELLO DELL'ANGLICANISMO ALLA CORONA

" Contra excessus potestatis civilis dimicantes veram potius quam speciosam victoriam ita rettulimus, ut libertate maiore quam quae appareat utamur. . . . Processu contra Episcopum Lincolniensem de eisdem rebus instituto, Archiepiscopus Cantuariensis, edictis civilium tribunalium neglectis, rem PROPRIA sua auctoritate in sensu CATHOLICO determinavit " (p. 9., in princip.).

1° Una resistenza al potere civile o qualsiasi opposizione per parte dei vescovi Anglicani è cosa inaudita. Sono creati dal potere civile ed obbediscono sommessamente al loro creatore. Tutto ciò che si dice qui di resistenza e carcere, si riduce a cinque o sei Ritualisti del clero inferiore.

2° Il potere civile tiene oggi il governo supremo della Chiesa non meno che pel passato. Nessun vescovo può essere consecrato senza il consenso ed il mandato della Regina. Il vescovo novellamente consecrato presta in ginocchio giuramento nelle mani della Regina, dichiarando di ricevere da essa soltanto OGNI GIURISDIZIONE PER LE COSE SPIRITUALI. Il potere civile costituisce o divide le diocesi e le parocchie, e coll'autorità della Regina si sottopongono le anime da una ad un'altra giurisdizione. La licenza della Corona è necessaria per convocare un sinodo. Un Arcivescovo od un Vescovo non può pubblicare una legge senza previa approvazione della Regina. Non si può cambiare una parolla della Liturgia senza il permesso del potere civile e del Parlamento. Questa supremazia della Corona è in pieno suo vigore, come lo ha dichiarato ingenuamente pochi mesi or sono il principale giornale Anglicano " IL

230 A ROMAN DIARY AND OTHER DOCUMENTS

GUARDIAN." Del resto ciò è ammesso e difeso strenuamente dai vescovi Anglicani, e citano l'esempio di Costantino e degli imperatori orientali. È vana la speranza che il popolo inglese alleggerisca questo giogo, che† lo aggravierebbe maggiormente.

3° Il processo del Vescovo di Lincoln ci dà un argomento di questa servitù. È falso che l'Arcivescovo di Canterbury abbia dato la sentenza di sua propria autorità. L'Arcivescovo invece dichiarò pubblicamente nel processo, che non l'avrebbe neanche cominciato se il potere civile, per mezzo del consiglio privato della Regina, non l'avesse assicurato della sua giurisdizione e promesso di confermare la sentenza. Altrimenti egli sarebbesi astenuto da ogni atto giuridico.

4° Ma vi è un errore più grave ancora in asserire che l'Arcivescovo sentenziò in senso cattolico. Al contrario l'Arcivescovo pronunziò la sentenza in senso assolutamente protestante e secondo il principio fondamentale dei Riformatori. Perchè dichiarò che il Vescovo di Lincoln celebrando l'Eucaristia dovesse contenersi in maniera che tutti potessero ben vedere ogni suo atto alla Mensa, e ciò per mantenere espressamente il principio fondamentale di Lutero, di Calvino e di Cranmer che i sacramenti conferiscono la grazia non *ex opere operato*, ma come segni esterni della passione che eccitano la fede nel cuore degli astanti. Quindi nel processo medesimo l'Arcivescovo protestò che la sua sentenza in questa materia era assolutamente conforme ai principii della Riforma protestante. Per conseguenza non sentenziò nè di sua propria autorità nè in senso cattolico.

NUMERO DEGLI ANGLICANI

Nell'elenco dato dall'Autore si asserisce che gli Anglicani hanno:

2 *provincie ecclesiastiche in Inghilterra, ed altrove* . . . 12

35 *diocesi in Inghilterra, ed altrove* 165

Questa statistica può facilmente ingannare chi non conosce il vero stato e numero degli Anglicani. Si deve sapere che il numero degli Anglicani in Inghilterra ed altrove non supera i 25000000, di quali 16 in Inghilterra, 7 nell' impero Britannico, oltre 2 milioni circa negli Stati Uniti. Così per 16 milioni in Inghilterra hanno 35 Diocesi, e per 9 milioni altrove ne hanno 115.[1] Così il numero dei Vescovi supera la proporzione del popolo. Si deve notare inoltre che l'Anglicanismo non è affatto la religione dominante nell'impero Britannico. In Inghilterra non conta guari più della metà del popolo. In Iscozia, in Irlanda, nel Canadà, in Australia e nelle Indie la minoranza solamente appartiene alla setta Anglicana. Negli Stati Uniti poi è una minoranza ben piccola e non supera la quinta parte dei cattolici. Quindi non si potrebbe concepire illusione maggiore che quella di supporre che il ritorno della nazione Inglese e delle altre nazioni dell' impero alla fede, dipenda solamente o neanche principalmente da una qualche unione in massa degli Anglicani.

Questi sono alcuni degli errori che abbondano nell' opuscolo.

[1] I dissidenti poi usciti dal seno della Chiesa per legge stabilita e divisi in più di 250 sette, contano 12000000 di seguaci.

232 A ROMAN DIARY AND OTHER DOCUMENTS

PARTE SECONDA

DELLA SPERANZA DI UNA RIUNIONE

"Hinc novus animorum motus, qui tamen non novus sed renovatus. Quæstionem de Ordinationibus Anglicanis inimus, non quidem in ea totum dissensionis radicem contineri putantes, sed in eo confisi quod hinc via ad animos conciliandos pateat. Proinde nostri huic multum istant · ordinem suorum et sacramentorum veritatem summa fiducia tenent et studio singulari defendunt. *Qui de his dubitaverit, quomodo cum eo communionis vel voluntatem concipere poterunt?*" (p 12).

DELL' INTENZIONE DEGLI ANGLICANI

Nell' ultima frase qui sopra si rivela la mente degli Anglicani. Cercano essi veramente la verità e l'unione? Se davvero lo desiderano, come mai non possono neanche concepire un desiderio di communione con Roma, senza la previa ricognizione dei loro ordini? Chi cerca con animo sincero il regno di Dio, la prima domanda che si fa è questa: Che cosa debbo fare per salvarmi? Cristo ha veramente istituito una sola e vera Chiesa, arca di salute? Questa Chiesa è proprio quella governata dai successori di Pietro? È necessario per la salute eterna sottomettersi al Romano Pontefice? Questo sono le questioni che spontaneamente sorgono nella mente degli Anglicani sinceri, le quali sono modificate dalla validità o nullità degli Ordini Anglicani. Gli altri poi non si curano di prendere in considerazione questi dubbi, parlando di unione, senza il patto che la validità degli ordini loro sia dalla S. Sede ammessa. Parlando così non apparisce chiaro che sono spinti da altri motivi? Quali sono essi?

"DE RE ANGLICANA" AND ITS CRITICS 233

A tutti noi che viviamo in Inghilterra e conosciamo la situazione religiosa, questi motivi sono manifesti ; ne daremo una breve exposizione.

1º Fino all' anno 1830 non vi era in Inghilterra che la Vecchia Scuola dell' Anglicanismo. Questa non desiderava altro che una chiesa insulare, nazionale ed al tutto conforme alle dottrine della Riforma. Non cercava nè si curava delle pratiche e delle dottrine estranee, mentre poi in Inghilterra combatteva strenuamente i dommi cattolici. Anche ai nostri giorni la maggioranza del popolo prende questo atteggiamento.

2º Dopo il 1830 sorse il *Puseismo* o *Neoanglicanismo* introdotto dai Trattariani e dai Ritualisti. Questi animati da spirito assai diverso e da altre intenzioni, cambiarono in molte cose l' aspetto e lo scopo dell' Anglicanismo. Fra di essi un buon numero di dotti e sinceri, leggendo le opere de' SS. Padri e viaggiando in paesi cattolici giunsero a riconoscere la bellezza, la dignità, l'antichità, e la verità di molti dommi e pratiche della chiesa cattolica. Non volevano tuttavia sottomettersi al Romano Pontefice, nè abbandonare la Chiesa Anglicana.

3º In conseguenza di ciò seguirono altre vie; cercarono di rinnovare a poco a poco il culto e le dottrine della chiesa Anglicana a somiglianza della chiesa di oriente e di occidente ; mantenendo però sempre immutata la loro indipendenza dalla Sede Romana, i loro diritti e la loro libertà ottenuta per mezzo della Riforma, e rigettando come una usurpazione la giurisdizione del Romano Pontefice. A questo scopo non si stancavano di proclamare, come fanno tuttora, che la Chiesa Anglicana è un ramo della

234 A ROMAN DIARY AND OTHER DOCUMENTS

chiesa cattolica e che fa parte vera ed integrale della chiesa di Cristo e che si identifica con quella degli Apostoli. Quindi tanti sforzi per arrogarsi tutto ciò che trovano nella chiesa cattolica in materia di culto, di pratiche e mezzi di divozione, di parati sacri e dell' ornamentazione delle chiese. In questo modo hanno potuto ingannare il popolo e trattenere le anime sincere che si avvicinavano alla vera Chiesa, dicendo : " Non vi è bisogno di abbandonare il nostro ceto per cercare questo o quello dai Romanisti. Tutte queste cose le potete godere in seno alla chiesa Anglicana. Noi abbiamo tutto ciò che hanno loro ; anzi da noi potrete avere quanto credete trovare nella chiesa Papistica e meglio ancora, eccezione fatta della giurisdizione papale, che è una usurpazione e fonte detestabila di novità e di superstizione."

4° Questa nuova situazione vien ben delineata colle parole recenti di un vescovo cattolico d'Inghilterra. " Dal tempo della Riforma il Demonio ha combattuto costantemente per mezzo dell'eresia la fede cattolica in Inghilterra, LA OSTEGGIO APERTAMENTE E VIOLENTEMENTE. Non avendo ottenuto un pieno intento ha mutato da quell'anno in poi la sua tattica, e combatte la Chiesa cattolica IMITANDOLA ed usando contro di essa un travisamento delle sue dottrine, ed usurpando le sue pratiche trascina le anime semplici. Questa tattica è più temibile dell'altra, benchè colla grazia di Dio speriamo di sventarla."

5° In questi ultimi tempi il Neoanglicanismo o Ritualismo che più che mai e con ogni studio vuole arrogarsi il nome di cattolicismo, fa ogni sforzo per escludere dall'Inghilterra la così detta

"DE RE ANGLICANA" AND ITS CRITICS 235

usurpazione del Romano Pontefice.[1] Oggi si ha la speranza e l'ambizione, mille volte espressa dagli Anglicani nei loro scritti e nelle loro prediche, di estendere in tal modo la chiesa Anglicana nell' impero Britannico, rappresentandola come parte integrale della Chiesa cattolica, che possa addivenire l'emula della chiesa Greca e Romana ; anzi di esse più pura, più ricca e più dotta.

In questa guisa la Chiesa anglicana rimarrà libera ed indipendente, conserverà in pace tutti i diritti conquistati dalla Riforma colle sue molteplici eresie, e senza sottomettersi all'obbedienza del Romano Pontefice, avrà agli occhi di tutti la gloria ed il prestigio del nome cattolico. Fra quelli che vagheggiano questo piano vi sono alcuni che ammettono la precedenza o un Primato di onore del Romano Pontefice e tutto al più *de jure ecclesiastico.*

6° Chi non vede che per riuscire in questa loro speranza ed ambizione, è cosa essenziale l'ottenere la ricognizione degli ordini Anglicani? Senza di ciò la chiesa orientale ed occidentale non potrà mai ammettere gli Anglicani alla sua vera comunione. Ne hanno anche bisogno per potere meglio combattere le sette da loro dissidenti. Perciò desiderano tanto ottenere dalla S. Sede una qualsiasi ricognizione degli ordini loro.

7° Con questo scopo gli Anglicani fanno concepire una vaga speranza di quella riunione tanto desiderata dal cuore paterno del S. Padre, affermando che la ricognizione degli ordini ne spianerebbe la via. Se questa concessione, supponendola

---

[1] L'Arcivescovo di York (che è Anglicano) in una lettera recentissima ha dichiarato che "LA CHIESA ANGLICANA MENTRE ADDIVIENE DI GIORNO IN GIORNO PIU CATTOLICA DIVIENE IN PARI TEMPO PIU ANTIROMANA E ANTIPAPALE."

236 A ROMAN DIARY AND OTHER DOCUMENTS

possibile, addivenisse realtà, gli Anglicani certamente avrebbero mille ragioni dommatiche per non unirsi a noi. Così l'Anglicanismo otterrebbe il suo intento e la speranza di una unione in senso cattolico sarebbe più che mai svanita.

8° Ma si domanda se veramente nella chiesa Anglicana vi sia un movimento o una disposizione negli animi per l'unione colla Sede Romana. Rispondiamo : Se il Romano Pontefice consentisse ad abrogare i decreti del concilio di Trento e Vaticano, ovvero a spiegarli in senso nuovo e non cattolico ; o se dichiarasse che il semplice Primato di onore o fondato " DE JURE ECCLESIASTICO " basta al suo ministero, o in altri termini, se il Pontefice si facesse Anglicano, non vi è dubbio che molti fra i Neoanglicani si unirebbero alla Chiesa Romana. Ma se il Pontefice Romano come custode infallibile della verità cattolica si rifiuta a fare simili concessioni, eccezione fatta di quelle anime sincere, ogni giorno più numerose, che entrano nel seno della chiesa, nessuno fra i Vescovi Anglicani, pochi del Clero, e pochissimi del laicato cercano l'unione in senso cattolico. Questa è una abberrazione inconcepibile, dicono essi, coll'Arciv. di Canterbury.

9° Chi non vede che la medesima conclusione si deduce dalla lettera del celebre Gladstone all'Arciv. di York. In essa, benchè compilata con una moltitudine di parole, l'Autore ha costantemente in presenza la Chiesa Anglicana indipendente come parte uguale e integrale della Chiesa di Cristo al pari della Greca e della Romana. Invita il Romano Pontefice ad unirsi a questa triplice federazione, perchè queste tre Chiese difendono contro gl'infedeli i dommi della Trinità, dell'Incarnazione e della suc-

"DE RE ANGLICANA" AND ITS CRITICS 237

cessione apostolica. Vuol persuadere il Pontefice a riconoscere una certa uguaglianza fra queste Chiese, e per giungere a questo sogno, usa il linguaggio di una deferente adulazione per ottenere la ricognizione degli ordini Anglicani. Il celebre capo del liberalismo inglese ha cercato di distruggere l'opera del Concilio Vaticano sotto Pio IX, ed oggi sotto Leone XIII vorrebbe renderla affatto inutile.

10° Quindi possiamo asserire che, lasciando in disparte le buone disposizioni delle anime sincere, questo nuovo tentativo non è altro che un assalto insidioso contro la Chiesa Romana. Tutto il clero e tutto il popolo cattolico in Inghilterra lo attesta, e gli stessi Inglesi non cattolici non lo nascondono. Così il gran giornale inglese il *Times*, che rappresenta più di qualunque altro la mente del popolo inglese, scriveva il 1 Giugno 1896 che se il Romano Pontefice annuiva alle pretensioni del sig. Gladstone ammetterebbe che la chiesa Anglicana è parte vera ed integrale della Chiesa di Cristo e si metterebbe in contraddizione co'suoi antecessori. Ecco le parole del giornale : " Il Sig. Gladstone non dice che dobbiamo riconoscere il Papa come Capo supremo della Chiesa. È il Papa che asserisce che ciò costituisce la prova *" stantis aut cadentis ecclesiæ "* e che egli ci accoglierà nell' ovile solo se noi gli diamo soddisfazione in questo punto. Possiamo essere sicuri che se il Papa è persuaso che una sua ricognizione degli Ordini Anglicani preparerà la via ad una ricognizione da parte nostra del sue pretese, la via in qualche modo sarà spianata. Ma se questa ricognizione nostra non accade,[1] se il

---

[1] Ossia la ricognizione del Romano Pontefice come Capo Supremo della Chiesa.

238 A ROMAN DIARY AND OTHER DOCUMENTS

Clero ed il laicato Anglicano persiste nella sua indipendenza *la ricognizione degli Ordini anglicani servirà ad indebolire piuttosto che fortificare la posizione del Papa e della sua Chiesa. Equivarrebbe ad una confessione che la chiesa d'Inghilterra è ed è sempre stata un ramo vero e vivente della Chiesa cattolica, e che il suo clero possiede quei poteri soprannaturali che il Card. Vaughan ha rivendicato come cosa esclusivamente della Chiesa sua. Ciò non può essere l'intenzione del Papa, ma è quasi certo, che questa sarebbe la conseguenza.* È abbastanza probabile che una sezione del partito della Chiesa Alta sarebbe disposta ad accettare pienamente le proposte del Papa. Ma una parte maggiore e più assennata non lo farebbe affatto. Tutto al più una ricognizione degl' Ordini Anglicani per parte del Papa servirebbe *a confermarli nella persuasione della verità e della sicurezza della loro posizione,* lasciendo gli altri come sono." (*Times,* 1 Giugno 1896.)

Se ci si domandasse se la situazione attuale in Inghilterra ci dà speranza di un ritorno al seno della Chiesa, rispondiamo che questa speranza colla grazia di Dio è grande assai.

1° In tutta Inghilterra le conversioni sono numerose. Questo numero già grande di convertiti crescerà senza dubbio facendosi più evidente che la Chiesa Cattolica Romana è la sola in Inghilterra che abbia diritto alle prerogative e al nome di *cattolica.*

2° Il Neoanglicanismo o Ritualismo benchè costituisca una piccola minoranza della setta Anglicana porta almeno questo vantaggio, che a suo malgrado modifica le disposizioni di alcuni, e facendo conoscere alcune dottrine e pratiche cattoliche spianano la via a molti per conoscere ed entrare nella

Chiesa Cattolica. In una sola diocesi si sono convertiti in questa maniera più di mille all'anno. Siamo persuasi che continuando quest'opera, molti si persuaderanno sempre più della verità e bellezza della fede cattolica e dell' inutilità di cercarla fuori della Cattedra di Pietro. Si libereranno dalle reti del pseudo-cattolicismo, e il nemico di Dio sarà respinto colle sue stesse armi.

CONCLUSIONE

1° Da tutto ciò si deduce che la Chiesa Cattolica in Inghilterra trova indirettamente un considerevole aiuto nell'opera dei Ritualisti in quanto che aiutano e dispongono meglio l'animo degl'Inglesi, e ciò dà buone speranze di messe più abbondante.

2° Per raggiungere questo fine salvando la verità e la giustizia, è assolutamente necessario astenersi da tutto ciòche può dare anche apparentemente approvazione e forza alla setta *pseudo-cattolica*, o che possa confermare in qualsiasi modo la sua autorità. Altrimenti non solo verrà offuscata la verità dommatica e storica, ma il popolo inglese sarà ingannato riguardo alla vera Chiesa Cattolica, e il ritorno dell'Inghilterra alla fede diventerà impossibile o sarà ritardato indefinitivamente.

Questa è la nostra testimonianza sulla situazione della Chiesa nella nostra patria e coscenziosamente la diamo per amore di Cristo, sottomettendola umilmente alla considerazione del suo Vicario in terra.

Roma, Festa di S. Guglielmo Arciv. di York
8 *Giugno* 1896.

J. C.ᶜᵒ MOYES, s.t.d.
F. A. GASQUET, o.s.b., s.t.d.

III

THE *RISPOSTA* EXAMINED

(From the *Guardian* of October 7th, 1896)

READERS of the *Guardian* have no doubt been interested in the translation of the extraordinary memoir presented to the Holy Office by Dom Gasquet and Canon Moyes.[1] I am told that some would be further interested in an account of the "*opuscolo*" entitled *De Re Anglicana*, to which it was a reply.

When Father Puller and I were in Rome last May we were urged by some friends to write a brief account of the present state of the Church of England, and especially of the nature of the parties within the Church which trace their origin to the fierce controversies of the Reformation period. We were very unwilling to do this. It was difficult— nay, impossible—to write impartially ; it was distasteful to write anything like a panegyric upon ourselves. Yet there seemed to be a need of something. One of the Cardinals to whom the question of the English ordinations was to be submitted frankly admitted that he knew nothing whatever about the English Church, and would welcome information. "There are plenty of men," we were told, "ready to say all that can be said

---

[1] A fragmentary translation of the First Part, and a more continuous version of the Second Part, had appeared in the preceding number of the *Guardian*. I understand that a complete translation, both of *De Re Anglicana* and of the *Risposta*, was afterwards published in the *Tablet*.

"DE RE ANGLICANA" AND ITS CRITICS

against you; there are none to present the other aspect of the case unless you do it yourselves."

We yielded to these instances, and wrote a brief pamphlet. I was alone responsible for the form of it, but I think I may say that Father Puller concurred in all that was said; the better part of the matter, indeed, was supplied by his unrivalled knowledge of the facts. The statement was obviously an *ex parte* one; it pretended to be nothing else. But I am not afraid to claim that it was composed with careful moderation and candid truthfulness. It was not published; it was printed for private circulation, and it consisted of matter so familiar to every instructed Englishman that there would be no point in circulating it in England. But it has been so savagely attacked as untruthful and treacherous that some people may be interested to see what it contains, and as there are some few copies in hand I have sent them to the British Museum, to Sion College, to the University Libraries, and at this conjuncture to the reception-room of the Church Congress, where anyone who cares to do so may consult them.

The method of the *Risposta* was to print successive extracts from the pamphlet, and to append a reply. I give a few specimens of these replies.

Speaking of the state of religion under Henry VIII, I had said :—

"Nec tamen etiam tunc deerant qui novas res in hac parte molirentur, inter quos et episcopi rari erant, quorum princeps Cranmer."

Commenting on the word *rari*, my critics reply:—

"There were, on the contrary, many : Cranmer

242 A ROMAN DIARY AND OTHER DOCUMENTS

(of Canterbury), Holbeach (of Lincoln), Goodrich (of Ely), Ridley (of Rochester), Barlow (of Menevia), and Shaxton (of Salisbury), all well-known reformers."

Thus, in order to combat my statement, they include among the well-known reformers Goodrich and that poor time-server, Shaxton, who both conformed without hesitation under Mary, and Ridley, who was not raised to the episcopate until six months after Henry's death.

Under Edward VI, I said, many partisans of the foreign Reformation were promoted to places in the Church :—

"Attamen episcopi, qui animo et sententia Catholici erant, sedes suas retinuerunt, novisque rebus quantum possent sese accommodarunt. Nonnulli autem ex his detrusi sunt, nec dubium est partes novatorum in reformationem ulteriorem atque exitiabilem progressuras fuisse, nisi prae morte Eduardi immatura tanta consilia subito collapsa essent."

That is surely a sufficiently guarded statement. Now for the reply :—

"In no way could those who retained their sees under Edward be called Catholic."

The comment on the word *nonnulli* is :—

"On the contrary, all the Bishops who in some way retained a Catholic feeling or a remnant of veneration for the Catholic dogmas were driven from their sees under Edward. Thus Gardiner (of Winchester), Bonner (of London), Heath (of Worcester), Tunstall (of Durham), Voysey (of Exeter),

"DE RE ANGLICANA" AND ITS CRITICS 243

Day (of Chichester) were all deprived, many were imprisoned, and in their places well-known hereticks were substituted. In this way Cranmer and the fautors of his heresy easily obtained the preponderance."

Thus history is written in the latitude of Rome. Would either author have put his name to such statements if intended for circulation in England? The Bishops who retained their sees under Edward can in no way, they say, be called Catholics. Yet of these Goodrich, Sampson, Kitchin, Thirlby, King, Chambers, Salcot, Wharton, and Aldrich, who held their sees and administered their dioceses throughout Edward's reign, continued to do so without question under Mary. Of these, moreover, Wharton was at once promoted to another see, and Thirlby was chosen as the most suitable ecclesiastic for ambassador to the Papal Court. Such are the men who are described as having retained no trace of Catholic sentiment or of respect for Catholic dogmas.

Another subtle touch in the description may be noted. Six Bishops are named as having been deprived under Edward; they are mentioned as examples, and we are further told that "many were imprisoned." Would any one suppose from this account that these six were the only Bishops in any way disturbed by the Government of Edward VI, and that only five of them were imprisoned? What meaning could the writers intend to convey but that a clean sweep was made of a large number of Catholic-minded Bishops, into whose place numerous ardent reformers were promoted?

244 A ROMAN DIARY AND OTHER DOCUMENTS

In the same vein they reply to my next sentence —"Maria igitur regnum excipiente nonnulli Episcopi destituti sunt, inter quos Cranmer; ceteri manebant." They complain of the words *nonnulli* and *ceteri*. I will at once admit that the word *nonnulli* was not well chosen, and might be misleading, since out of the twenty-three Bishops then holding sees thirteen, or a clear majority, were removed. It is hard to see why the word *ceteri* should be attacked, since whether many or few were deprived, it is still true that the rest remained. But I would observe that these critics, who are severe on me for describing thirteen as *nonnulli*, had themselves, immediately before, described the five Bishops imprisoned under Edward as *many*. They then proceed to wrap up and disguise the inconvenient fact that the rest continued unchallenged in their sees :—

"Those who had been deprived under Edward were restored, that is six. Six others were rehabilitated after doing penance and abjuring before the Cardinal Legate. The new Bishops constituted by the Legate were fourteen."

Does this accurately convey the fact that all the twelve first spoken of were reconciled and rehabilitated by the Legate in exactly the same way, that three more—Goodrich, Sampson, and Chambers— went on unchallenged under Mary, though they died before the reconciliation with Rome was complete, and that another—Kitchin—went on all through Mary's reign apparently without any formal rehabilitation ?

These statements are ingeniously made ; they deal with trivial details, and they cannot be checked

"DE RE ANGLICANA" AND ITS CRITICS 245

unless by one who is familiar with the history of the time and armed with the necessary lists. Why were they made in this fashion? Was it pure ignorance or blundering? Possibly Canon Moyes might have been capable of that. But Dom Gasquet is the author of a book upon the period which is conspicuously careful and accurate. In his *Edward VI and the Book of Common Prayer* he has frequent occasion to speak of these various Bishops and to distinguish their various attitudes. He recognizes the influence of what he calls the Catholic party among the Bishops, and the power they had of checking and delaying the policy of Cranmer. Why does he in this *Risposta* tell so different a tale?

An explanation at once suggests itself. During the controversy about the Edwardine Ordinal great stress has been laid upon the fact that it was brought into use by the authority of Bishops who did not by any means belong to Cranmer's school. The effect of this argument had to be removed, or it would be impossible to condemn the Ordinal on the score of intention. Therefore a false colour must be spread over the history of the time. The Edwardine Bishops must be represented as one and all ardent reformers. The accession of Mary must be shown as making a clean sweep of them all. It was no doubt safe to do this in the strict privacy of the Holy Office at Rome. I ask again, would either writer have put his name to such statements for public circulation in England?

They continue with some bold denials of fact. I said that Elizabeth on her accession, "Consiliarios qui sub Maria rempublicam direxerant plerumque

246 A ROMAN DIARY AND OTHER DOCUMENTS

retinuit : attamen res novas cautius movebat." My
critics fasten on the word *plerumque* and say, " Here
we have an erroneous assertion." They are great
on adverbs and adjectives of quantity. In this
case I might have given figures. Elizabeth retained eleven of the members of Mary's Council,
the total number, I believe, being seventeen or
eighteen. Is this majority improperly described by
the word *plerumque ?* The critics fired off a charge
of falsehood—that is easily done when no reply is
expected—but they were too prudent to quote
figures in their support.

It was necessary again to accentuate the change
made by the new reign. So we are told that
Elizabeth and her advisers " were not content with
restoring the reformed religion as it was introduced
under Edward VI, when at least a remnant of
Catholic belief was retained." This is very wantonness of argument. We have just been told that
not a single Bishop who retained his see under
Edward had the least tincture of Catholic feeling,
or the smallest remnant of veneration for Catholic
dogmas. That was said when the business was to
depress the Edwardine times. But now the settlement of Elizabeth is to be blackened ; and so, to
deepen the shadow, it is compared with the less
gloomy time of Edward, when some remnant of
Catholic belief was retained.

I made the familiar statement that after the issue
of the Bull of Excommunication in 1570, " Ei qui
auctoritati Pontificiae maxime faverent ab hac
Ecclesiae Anglicanae unitate recesserunt." To
this it is replied that even before 1570 all the
" Catholics " in England had " suffered the loss of

"RE RE ANGLICANA" AND ITS CRITICS 247

their goods and preferred imprisonment rather than be present, even materially, at the Anglican rite." Then, with an appeal to "our archives," we are told that the fines for recusancy amounted to a million sterling; that is, be it noted, before the year 1570. These writers are probably acquainted with Parson and his *Reasons Why Catholiques Refuse to Goe to Church*, in which, so late as 1580, he lamented that many Catholics continued to frequent the Anglican service. But it would have been very awkward to admit this fact at Rome last summer.

Elsewhere they find in my description of the parties within the English Church a marvellous insinuation that there have been "ritualists" ever since the first years of Elizabeth. "This," they naively say, "is historically false." But then it turns out that by "ritualists" they mean all who have the slightest shadow of belief in the priesthood or the sacraments. It is not, of course, to be supposed that even they are at all orthodox. "That which they constantly preach can with difficulty be reconciled with Catholic teaching." And even so they form only a tiny fraction of the English Church. "The Archdeacon of London, W. Sinclair, was able recently to assert that the number of ritualists in England does not exceed 35,000, or one in 430 English." I do not know whether the Archdeacon has ever said anything that could be twisted into this; he may possibly have said that there were about thirty-five thousand members of the English Church Union.

Upon the present state of the English Church the writers are very bold. The Eucharist, we learn,

248 A ROMAN DIARY AND OTHER DOCUMENTS

is *ordinarily* celebrated once a month. "In *some few* churches it takes place every Sunday." Suggestive adjectives of quantity again! But if five Bishops were *many* under Edward VI it is not surprising that several thousand churches are *some few* under Victoria. The writers were not speaking by guess-work, for the very next sentence shows that they have referred to the *Church Year-book*.

The climax of misrepresentation and malignancy is perhaps reached in the comment on the following sentence :—

"Multa quoque ex aliis ecclesiis grati mutuavimus, secessus seu exercitia spiritualia tam pro clero quam pro laicis, missiones in civitatibus et in pagis, stationes quadragesimales, hoc genus omne, iam nobis propria sunt."

I wrote this sentence very carefully and deliberately, wishing to express what we owe to the Churches of the Roman communion. But my *grati* could no more disarm rancour than the truth could silence contradiction. Here is the comment :—

"Here the author admits with justice that the modern ritualists have sought *to combat the Catholic Church in England by turning against her her own arms.* But when he says, *Nobis propria sunt,* the author does not really speak for the whole Anglican body, but only for the school to which he belongs. The immense majority of Anglicans are averse to such methods, and take no interest in them."

And what are these methods? Retreats and Quiet Days, parochial Missions, Lenten courses. These things are peculiar to the "Ritualists," in

"DE RE ANGLICANA" AND ITS CRITICS 249

which school my critics kindly place me. The immense majority of Anglicans take no interest in Missions; regard with aversion Quiet Days and Lenten sermons. *Risum teneatis amici.*[1] This is the kind of information that was served up for the Congregation of the Holy Office when about to enter on the study of the English ordinations. It is dated the 8th of June. That was the day that Father Puller and I left Rome. On the same day, we were told, the papers concerning the question of English orders were sent to the Cardinals to whom the matter was referred.

[1] It will be observed that in this article I examined only the statements and suggestions made in the First Part of the *Risposta*. The argument of the Second Part with its sustained imputation of bad faith, directed not so much against my pamphlet as against all those with whom I was acting, could be rebutted only by steady perseverance in the course impugned. It even had a certain value as corroborating our assertion that it was useless to talk about reunion without first removing all doubts about the validity of the English ordinations. The writers, for example, underlined my words, "*Qui de his dubitaverit, quomodo cum eo communionis vel voluntatem concipere poterunt?*" It is difficult to understand how the Pope could after this write to Cardinal Richard of certain Englishmen, "qui veritatem rei de ordinationibus suis exquisere a Nobis sincero animo videbantur." (Quoted by Brandi, *Roma e Canterbury*, p. 53). We had tried with the utmost sincerity to make it plain that we were not seeking instruction: we had no doubts on the matter.

THE SOURCES OF THE BULL
APOSTOLICAE CURAE

IX

THE SOURCES OF THE BULL
APOSTOLICAE CURAE

I

EXAMINATION OF THE BULL

(From the *Contemporary Review* of December, 1896)

THE papal condemnation of the English ordinations has been received with a general murmur
of complacency. Most men hastened to say that
they had expected nothing else ; some went further
and declared, in a superior manner, that all who
were looking for anything else had been living in a
fool's paradise. Those who accepted the decision
as final, and those who tossed it aside as of no
account, vied with each other in asserting that it
came as a matter of course, inevitable as the seasons;
they differed only in attributing the result severally
to the infallible accuracy or to the invincible
obstinacy of the Roman Church. A small minority
confessed their surprise or disappointment. They
had looked for something else ; not, perhaps, for a
decision purely favourable, but at least for a modification of the practice hitherto prevailing, for an
expression of doubt which would leave the question
open for the future. Was this expectation the result

254 A ROMAN DIARY AND OTHER DOCUMENTS

merely of a sanguine temperament? Was it begotten of an overstrung wish?

In the early summer I was at Rome with Fr. Puller and M. Portal. As every one knows, the Pope had appointed a Commission of Inquiry to examine the question of English Orders. Two members of the Commission had expressly invited us to help them with our special knowledge of the facts. When the work of the Commission was finished we stayed in Rome for some weeks longer, in obedience to a suggestion from a very high quarter, to give further information where it was needed and desired. All this time there was undoubtedly in Rome a general expectation of something new. The Pope himself, by appointing the Commission of his own motion, had made the question acute and practical. The reunion of the separated Churches was known to be his dearest wish, and he was understood to be specially interested in England. But Englishmen urged, with singular unanimity, that a full recognition of their Orders was a condition without which they could not even think of reunion. It was natural to suppose that in ordering an inquiry the Pope was at least hoping to remove a hindrance. Two of the Commissioners had published opinions favourable to the recognition. A third was known to have written privately on the question at the Pope's request; his conclusions would probably have remained unknown had not Cardinal Vaughan, in a moment of indiscretion, revealed to a chance assembly at an English seminary the fact that he had pronounced emphatically for the validity. This was heard of at Rome, and all knew that Duchesne, Gasparri, and

SOURCES OF BULL *APOSTOLICAE CURAE* 255

de Augustinis, the most distinguished historian, canonist, and theologian of the Commission, were in some sort united in defence of English Orders. An entirely adverse decision seemed impossible. Men talked not so much about the difficulty of making a new departure, but rather about the difficulties which stood in the way of complete recognition. A very eminent ecclesiastic spoke to me of one such difficulty; it was hardly possible, he said, to recognize English Orders without defining the essentials of a valid ordination, and the Roman Church had always avoided such a definition. The practice of three hundred years, indeed, of itself cried out against a sudden reversal; yet a change of some sort seemed inevitable. " These are very extraordinary people," said a certain Cardinal, after reading an account of the English Church; " of course, we cannot acknowledge their Orders all at once, but something will have to be done." For three hundred years English clergymen submitting to the Roman Church had always been reordained. That fact alone threw a doubt upon their Orders, which would not easily be solved. But if our friends were doubtful, some of those who were at the opposite pole of friendship were equally harassed by uncertainty. One evening in May a well-known prelate of English birth was sitting in Cardinal Rampolla's antechamber, talking to a French Dominican lately returned from the East. " There is a big question here," he said, "about Anglican Orders. Very strange! The *High Church* claim to have valid Orders. Two French priests are supporting them—the Abbé Duchesne and the Abbé Portal. There has been a Commission of Inquiry

256 A ROMAN DIARY AND OTHER DOCUMENTS

and the matter is now going to the Holy Office. There will not be much change—*I think.*" A bystander, who could not help overhearing the remarks, noted them down, being interested in the reserve.

An Italian priest of our acquaintance who had been intimately concerned in the question, had a farewell audience of the Pope. Speaking of English affairs he said, "These Anglicans are at the door." "And I will throw it wide open," exclaimed the Pope, with enthusiasm. Our friend left Rome convinced that, whatever was the outcome of the inquiry, Leo XIII would refuse to promulge an adverse decision. If the controversy could not be closed in a favourable sense it would at least be left open.

There were indeed other voices. A not unfriendly observer, who had the best of opportunities for knowing what would come, told us that he looked for an absolute condemnation. "It is impossible, utterly impossible," cried one of our friends impulsively. "C'est toujours l'impossible qui arrive," was the oracular reply. It was known that strenuous efforts were being made to procure such a result. During the month that followed the closing of the Commission various opinions were expressed about the next step. The Pope would send the matter to the Holy Office; he would appoint a special committee of Cardinals to consider it; he would deal with it himself in person. If it went to the Holy Office, we were told, there was nothing to hope for but at best a tacit continuation of the existing practice. Most of the Cardinals whom we saw professed entire ignorance of the Holy Father's intentions. A sharp struggle in the innermost councils of the Curia was anticipated. A very

SOURCES OF BULL *APOSTOLICAE CURAE* 257

highly placed Cardinal, in bidding us farewell, said impressively, " Remember that you have some very strong friends in Rome."

At length we heard that all the documents and arguments were to be sent to certain Cardinals on June 8, with a direction to study them carefully for a month at least. That was the very day we left Rome, and we were unable to find out whether the question was referred to the Holy Office or no. We learn from the Bull that such was the case. We do not learn, nor could we expect to learn, anything about the discussion which ensued. The disputes of the Sacred Congregation are not made public ; we are never likely to know what part was played by the strong friends of whose support we were assured. What we do know is the result. The Cardinals of the Holy Office decided unanimously against the validity of English Orders.

How is the result to be accounted for ? Why was the general expectation so completely falsified ? It is an obvious thing to say that we see here the result of a candid and exhaustive investigation. The trend of opinion was in favour of the validity ; the wishes of the Pope himself were supposed to look that way. But the truth prevailed ; careful inquiry showed the falsity of the favourable opinion ; the highest wishes and the hopes that gathered round them were inevitably swept aside. It is a clear and simple argument, very comforting to those who played an active part against us in the controversy. But a slight examination of the Bull will awaken some doubts about the conclusion.

In the first place, the Bull does not bear those marks of careful and exhaustive study which might

s

258 A ROMAN DIARY AND OTHER DOCUMENTS

be expected. The historical argument contains extraordinary blunders, surely out of place in the finished work of experts. Some of these, which have no important bearing on my present subject, were exposed as soon as the Bull appeared. Another I shall deal with below. The theological argument is very nebulous. Its defenders are not sure of its meaning. As every one knows, the English ordinations are declared invalid on account of defective form and intention. A French writer has shown that the defect of intention is inferred from the use of a defective form.[1] But English critics of the Bull have shown that what is lacking in our form is lacking also in other forms which are recognized as valid by the Roman Church ; indeed, in the ancient Roman form itself. Father Bernard Vaughan replies hotly that the fault is attributed not to the form in itself, but to the employment of the form in a new and defective sense.[2] That is to say, the defect of form results from a defective intention. The two arguments combined will make an excellent circle. Read apart, they leave us wondering what the Bull does mean.[3] Is this the result of thorough and exhaustive study ? Again, we read in the Bull some old and venerable arguments which have done duty in the controversy for generations. I do not complain of that ; the use of old arguments is legitimate, as long as they are thought to retain any force against old positions. But the defence of the English Ordinal has lately proceeded on new lines.

[1] *Revue Anglo-Romaine.* Tom. iii. p. 598.
[2] *Tablet,* Oct. 31, p. 706.
[3] Father Brandi (*Condanna delle Ord. Angl.,* p. 72) missed my point here, supposing me to have found this vicious circle in the Bull itself. It was in the interpreters of the Bull.

SOURCES OF BULL *APOSTOLICAE CURAE* 259

Mgr. Gasparri, following the lead of his colleague, M. Boudinhon, startled us a year ago by grounding the vadidity of our ordinations upon the use of certain prayers, the importance of which we had overlooked. To the P. de Augustinis rumour attributed an even more startling and original defence. In the argument of the Bull we might expect to see these new defences attacked and pulverized. We find one of them barely alluded to, the other entirely ignored. Is this the outcome of a laborious investigation?

But, in the second place, the Bull itself testifies to its own origin. The decision of the Cardinals is described in significant terms : " *Ii ad unum consensere, propositam causam iim pridem ab Apostolica sede plene fuisse et cognitam et iudicatam . eius autem denuo instituta actaque quaestione, emersisse quanto illa iustitiae sapientiaeque pondere totam rem absolvisset.*" It was not a new decision at all ; the Cardinals found that the Holy See had already long since decided the question ; the new inquiry served only to illustrate the justice and wisdom then displayed. We learn also from the Bull what was the precedent here referred to. It was the decision of the year 1704, given by Clement XI in the Gordon case. This, we are told, has always been regarded by the Roman Court as a final settlement ; nothing but ignorance of its true nature has enabled any Catholic writer to treat the question of English Orders as an open one.[1]

---

[1] Adeo ut, quoties deinceps in re simili decernendum fuit, toties idem Clementis XI communicatum sit decretum Quæ cum ita sint, non videt nemo controversiam temporibus nostris exsuscitam, Apostolicæ Sedis iudicio definitam multo antea fuisse documentisque Illis haud satis quam oportuerat cognitis, fortasse factum ut scriptor aliquis catholicus disputationem de ea libere habere non dubitarit.

260 A ROMAN DIARY AND OTHER DOCUMENTS

A natural question rises to the mind. If these circumstances were known to the authorities at Rome, why was any investigation ordered? If nothing but ignorance of these facts could render possible a free discussion of the subject, why should not that ignorance have been dispelled by simply publishing the truth? Why this apparatus of a Commission of Inquiry? Was it a farce? Respect for the personal character of Leo XIII forbids us to attribute to him so stupid a pleasantry. The appointment of the Commission must have had some serious object. What was it? It can hardly have been to inquire into the facts of the Gordon case. They were all on record. The Commissioners were assuredly not called to Rome to inform the Pope what his predecessor Clement XI had done. Were they invited to sit in judgment on his decision? That seems an impossible subversion of parts. Why, again, was there so general an expectation of a new departure? Was this confined to those who were ignorant of the Gordon case? We found it in the minds of some who could not possibly share this ignorance. What then? Did they expect a Papal decision to be overthrown?

Here is a budget of questions. I have not a string of answers ready to hand, but I will call attention to some circumstances which may possibly throw a little light upon the difficulty. I am very imperfectly informed, and yet, at the same time, I have to be on my guard against a breach of confidence. It will easily be understood that our opportunities of acquiring knowledge at Rome were strictly limited, and at the same time some things came in our way which we are not altogether free to disclose

SOURCES OF BULL *APOSTOLICAE CURAE* 261

Soon after the opening of the Commission we learnt that the chief rock ahead was the Gordon decision. We were not a little surprised. The existing practice was known to be grounded on that case, but small value was commonly attached to the precedent. What was known of it was due to Le Quien, who, in his reply to Le Courayer, published certain documents in the case obtained from the Holy Office. From these it appeared that John Gordon, Bishop of Galloway, ordained according to the English rite, who had gone into exile with James II, petitioned the Holy See to declare his Orders invalid, in order that he might be reordained. In his petition he set out reasons for the invalidity, including a relation of the Nag's Head fable, a preposterous account of the English Forms of Ordination, and a very inadequate complaint against the intention of the English bishops. The matter was referred to the Holy Office, and the Orders which Gordon had received were declared invalid. The decree, as given by Le Quien, was apparently based upon the statements of the petition. It was therefore supposed to be infected by the vice of its origin. It had a certain validity, as ruling the practice ; but theological or argumentative value it had none. The question could be reopened, as one upon which there had been no real adjudication.

Pressing these considerations, we were told that Le Quien's account was erroneous or defective. The Holy Office did not proceed merely upon the statements of Gordon's petition. The English rites were carefully examined. A Consultor named Genetti, a man of some mark in his time, was even

262 A ROMAN DIARY AND OTHER DOCUMENTS

sent to England to pursue inquiries. As a result of these investigations, the Sacred Congregation decided that Gordon was invalidly ordained. We tried to obtain further information. We asked if we might be allowed to examine the documents in the case. We were told that the archives of the Holy Office were absolutely inaccessible. We gathered a few hints of what was going on in the Commission. It was said that Cardinal Mazzclla, who presided over the sittings, forbade any attempt to go behind the Gordon decision. The Commission, he said, was under the Holy Office, the commissioners were consultors of the Congregation, and could not revise the decree of their superiors. They might investigate the history of the controversy; they might analyse the constituents of the English rite; but they could not debate the validity of the form, which had already been judged invalid. This we pieced together from scattered hints. We caught a suggestion, also, that the form had been pronounced invalid because it did not consist in a prayer. This implied that in the year 1704 the Holy Office was so far penetrated by the teaching of Morinus as to rule, contrary to the then prevailing opinion of the schools, that the form of ordination must essentially be a prayer. This was hardly credible; and the less so as we knew that only a month later a body of consultors of the same Congregation, in their puzzling response on Abyssinian Orders, inclined to the view that *Accipe Spiritum Sanctum* was a sufficient form for priestly ordination.[1]

What we heard of this matter justified the

This subject is discussed in *De Hierarchia Anglicana*, App. vi.

SOURCES OF BULL *APOSTOLICAE CURAE* 263

opinion freely expressed at Rome, that if our question went to the Holy Office it was useless to look for any change of the existing practice. The Cardinals individually might be well disposed, but acting in the Congregation they were bound by their own precedents; they might refuse to put out any fresh condemnation, but they would not innovate. We know from the Bull that the question did go to the Holy Office, and the result more than fulfils the prediction. The Gordon decision is quoted as conclusive. Our information about the ground of that decision is also verified in part. It was based exclusively upon a defect of form and intention. But we are not told in what the defect of form consisted. Is there a definition in the documents? If so, one could wish that it had been published. We are afforded some negative information. We are told that the condemnation of Gordon's Orders did not rest upon the omission from the English rite of the *Tradition of the Instruments*. But even this is not asserted directly, as might be expected. We are asked to infer it. If that had been the case, we are told, the Holy Office would, according to custom (*de more*), have required not an absolute but a *conditional* reordination. In this passage, if I am not mistaken, we have another example of extraordinary blundering in the conduct of the argument.

The classical authority for the custom referred to is a passage in that wonderful medley, the treatise *De Synodo Diœcesana* of Benedict XIV. The origin of the practice of conditional reordination in such a case is there referred to a certain resolution

264 A ROMAN DIARY AND OTHER DOCUMENTS

of the Sacred Congregation of the Council. The Tradition of the Instruments had been accidentally omitted in the ordination of a priest, and the Congregation was consulted as to what should be done. The prevailing opinion seems to have been that the omitted ceremony should be supplied. A decretal of Gregory IX was quoted in support of this, and also a passage from Natalis Alexander. In deference, however, to the opinion of certain theologians who held that the Tradition of the Instruments must not be treated separately, but should cohere with other parts of the rite, the Sacred Congregation, for greater caution, ordered the whole ordination to be conditionally repeated.[1] Such is the origin of the practice. And what is the date of this resolution? It was adopted, says Benedict XIV, "*priusquam huic operi extremam manum admoveremus.*" There can be no doubt that by these words he indicates a date after his book was begun, and before it was finished. Now he tells us in the Preface that he began it after his promotion to the See of Bologna and finished it after his election as Pope. He was promoted to Bologna in 1731, and was raised to the apostolic throne in in 1740. Between these dates, then, falls the resolution in question. But that being so, how can it be said that in 1704 custom would have required conditional reordination in case the Tradition of the Instruments were omitted? The custom was not yet established.[2]

---

[1] *De Synodo Diœcesana.* Lib. viii. cap x. §§ 1, 12, and 13.

[2] Father Brandi, in the *Civiltà Cattolica* of January 2nd following, and Father Ryder, in a long correspondence maintained in the columns of the *Guardian* during the next three months, made out a very good case for the probability that the Holy Office in 1704 would have

SOURCES OF BULL *APOSTOLICAE CURAE* 265

This explanation must have slipped into the Bull by an extraordinary oversight. Taken in connexion with other blunders, it shows, in spite of all appearances to the contrary, how incomplete was the preparation of the materials upon which the decision was based. But to return to the point, this inference failing us, we are thrown back into entire ignorance of the specific defect alleged in the Gordon case. Cannot this ignorance be dispelled? Is it too much to hope that even yet we may have the judgment of the Holy Office published in full by authority?

How important this may be I will now try to show. Why is the Gordon precedent regarded as binding? One can easily understand that a mere Committee of Consultors was forbidden to go behind it. The Sacred Congregation itself was naturally unwilling to reverse it. But was the Roman Pontiff himself bound? All the steps that he had taken indicated a real wish to reopen the question. He cannot have appointed the Commission merely to report on a foregone conclusion. He conveyed to his intimates the idea that he was bent on a new departure. If he had followed his bent, if there had been a real investigation, the result might perhaps have been a condemnation of English Orders; but the decision would have been conceived in a different form; it would assuredly not have dealt so loosely with the terms of the problem; it would not have ignored the newer conditions of the controversy. As it is, there

---

acted in the way indicated ; but I do not think they established the fact that there was at that time anything *praescriptum de more*, as asserted in the Bull.

266 A ROMAN DIARY AND OTHER DOCUMENTS

is no pretence of a really new decision. The old one is confirmed, and is treated as in itself conclusive. The Pope has failed to reopen the question, as he desired. What was the hindrance?

The answer is obscurely indicated in the Bull. Readers of the authorized translation were puzzled by the careful dating of the decree given in the Gordon case, *feria quinta*. The date is significant. Matters of ordinary moment are dealt with by the Holy Office in their ordinary sessions; but graver matters are reserved for an extraordinary session, presided over by the Pope in person. This extraordinary session is always held on Thursday, *feria quinta*. A decree of the Sacred Congregation thus dated has therefore an additional solemnity. It is pronounced by the Pope in person, and none but the Pope can vary it. But can even the Pope vary it? A small but influential school of Roman theologians holds that he cannot. It is well known what diverse interpretations of the definition of infallibility are current in the Roman schools. There are extremists, and there are minimizers. By some of the former it is held that all decrees given by the Pope in the Holy Office, *feria quinta*, come under the definition. They are therefore, so far as they deal with faith and morals, irreformable. Not even the Pope himself may call in question the decrees of his predecessors thus pronounced. The Gordon decision would come under this rule.

Is this the way in which the Pope was bound? Is he constrained by the opinion of a small school of theologians? To the average Englishman such an idea may seem strange; he conceives the Pope as

SOURCES OF BULL *APOSTOLICAE CURAE* 267

an absolute spiritual monarch, and wonders why he should not break through such trammels. But it is a fixed principle of the Roman Curia, and a principle founded in grave reasons, never to act in a manner that would directly contravene any theological opinion seriously maintained in the schools and tolerated by the Church. This *tutiorism*, as it is called—this principle of always following the safer course—finds its chief scope in regulating the practice of the Church with regard to the sacraments; but it is obviously applicable also to such delicate questions as those which turn upon the definition of infallibility. No decision of the Holy See can safely be impugned which, in the opinion of any serious theologians, is infallible and irreformable. The Pope himself could not revise it, unless he should first formally reprobate and extinguish the opinion which bars his way. But the formal reprobation of an opinion maintained by grave theologians is the most extreme exercise of the Papal authority; it is a thing to be done only under pressure of urgent necessity.

If, then, I am not misinformed, the Pope found himself practically debarred from reopening any question touching faith and morals decided in the Gordon case. There may have been a debate, a struggle, over the value to be assigned to the opinion which stood in the way. There may have been argument about the scope of the Gordon decision itself, and its relation to faith or morals. It must have had some relation to facts as well. To ask what constitutes the essential form in the English rite is to raise a question of fact. And hence arises the importance of knowing accurately

268 A ROMAN DIARY AND OTHER DOCUMENTS

the terms of the decision. It pronounced the form
of the English rite invalid. But what was regarded
as the form? The majority of theologians would
say that some one prayer or other formula must
constitute the essential form. Others would find it
in a combination of the various elements which the
rite contains. Taking the former view, theologians
of acknowledged eminence have pointed out several
prayers in the Ordinal which, in their judgment,
are sufficient. But others, again, have fastened
upon some element of the rite as the essential form
which could not be defended as adequate. There is,
for example, a sort of blessing, which follows the examination of the candidates. This was regarded by
Billuart as the form, and he pronounced it insufficient ; a judgment in which every theologian would
probably concur. Whence did he derive his idea?
Is it possible that this was the form which the Holy
Office declared defective? If so, the decision, so
far as it concerns the faith, was one with which no
English theologian will quarrel. We should reply
that there was an error with regard to the facts.
But in that case the decision is not, in the view of
any theologian, irreformable. The most extreme
interpretation of the Vatican definition will not
make the Pope infallible in matters of fact. In the
recent Bull we find a similar inaccuracy. Here,
again, the Pope has taken as the essential form of
the English rite a phrase which, at all events apart
from its context, no English divine acknowledges
to be such. This he declares insufficient. We
have no quarrel with him on that account. Some
of us may contend that the words, " Receive the
Holy Ghost," taken by themselves, would be a

SOURCES OF BULL *APOSTOLICAE CURAE* 269

sufficient form ; but the contention is purely academic, and has no bearing on the validity of English Orders. We have other objections, and graver, to the reasons on which the declaration is grounded ; but whether they be good or bad, their application to the question at issue is vitiated by the error in matter of fact. It is not impossible that in the Gordon case, if all the documents were published, a like state of things would be disclosed. A theological proposition, which we should not be able or should not care to dispute, may have been erroneously applied to the facts of the English ordinations.

On these grounds I urge the importance of a disclosure of all that can be known about the Gordon case. I hope that my motives in pressing this will not be misconstrued. They are the same as those which stirred all with whom I was acting in our visit to Rome, and in the movement which led to that visit. With a single eye to a future, and perhaps far distant, reunion of Christendom, we laboured to find a course by which the Church of Rome might retreat from a false position with the least possible loss of dignity, with the least possible dislocation of traditional policy. We have reason to believe that our labours were looked upon with no disfavour by the highest authorities. In spite of that, we have met with a grievous disappointment. " I do not know that I shall ever recover from this blow," writes one of our friends over sea. But, in recovering from the first sense of defeat, our plain duty is thoroughly to search out the causes of the disappointment. I make this essay in that direction. If it be true that we stumbled

270 A ROMAN DIARY AND OTHER DOCUMENTS

upon a decision of the Holy See which, on the tutiorist principle, is covered by the definition of infallibility, our difficulty is narrowed down to a clear issue If the Gordon decision stands in the way because of a theological opinion regarding it as irreformable, then the question of English Orders can be effectively reopened only on one of three conditions : Either the definition of infallibility must be abandoned, or the restraining opinion must be reprobated, or the decision itself must be shown faulty in matter of fact. The first alternative would, no doubt, commend itself to most Englishmen, but it is not for present discussion ; the second also raises difficulties which we are not yet called upon to face ; the third is dependent upon evidence that may possibly be forthcoming.

The recent Bull itself adds little or nothing, I believe, to the difficulty. It stands or falls with the Gordon decision. The reasoned argument which it contains can easily be set aside. I note one point, the importance of which I am unable to gauge. The Pope tells us that he summoned the Cardinals of the Holy Office before him, *feria quinta*, and they gave their judgment. But he did not there and then confirm it.[1] He took time to consider, and eventually gave his decision in the form of a Bull. Has he thus avoided a pronouncement which, in the opinion of some theologians, would be irreformable ? Those who would fain share the hopes which some of us entertain, need not be discouraged by the air of finality, the atmosphere

---

[1] Verumtamen optimum factu duximus supersedere sententiæ, quo et melius perpenderemus conveniretne expediretque eandem rem auctoritate nostra rursus declarari, et uberiorem divini luminis copiam supplices imploraremus.

SOURCES OF BULL *APOSTOLICAE CURAE* 271

as of the Medes and Persians, which is cast about the decision by the use of the curial language. Minds that are unfamiliar with that remarkable dialect may be awestruck by the solemn condemnation of all who shall challenge the Bull as obreptious or subreptitious. But these are, of course, only the common forms of the Chancery. It is pretty safe to assume that in the Bull itself there is nothing to prevent a reopening of the question.

It is manifest that without such reopening the reunion of Christendom remains impossible. The Church of England has not a shadow of doubt concerning her own Orders, and cannot tolerate the expression of doubt by others. Until they are fully acknowledged there can be no union. But the Church of England is not a negligible quantity in Christendom. She is not like the separate Churches of the East, venerable for their antiquity, more venerable for their stedfastness through centuries of repression and persecution, but insignificant in numbers, stationary or retrograde in point of influence. It was said to me by a Roman friend who is deeply versed in the problem, that Rome, England, and Russia are the three great factors in the reunion of Christendom, and that a union of any two of these, excluding the third, would only aggravate the evil of disunion. Therefore, every one who would labour for union must labour also for the favourable solution of the question of the ordinations.

I do not pretend that this is the only or the greatest difficulty. There remain great questions, going down to the roots of Christian practice, if not of Christian belief, the solution of which would

272 A ROMAN DIARY AND OTHER DOCUMENTS

overtax any mere human wisdom. No man can hope for reunion who does not believe in the divine origin and the divine ordering of the Church. But to them who believe in this there is no word impossible. They watch for opportunities. They welcome every expression of hope, coming from whatever side. On the morning of the day we left Rome we were waiting in Cardinal Rampolla's antechamber, when there came out from the inner room a number of Cardinals, who had been attending a congregation. One of them spied us, came up, and seizing a hand of each, cried aloud : "Vous partez donc aujourd'hui ; trop tôt, trop tôt! Mais nous nous reverrons ; nous arrangerons nos différends ; nous nous reverrons." It was done so publicly that I need not reserve his name. I do not expect to see Cardinal Segna again ; but as long as I live I shall remember his kindness, and I have an unshaken faith in the fulfilment of the rest of his prophecy.

II

THE GORDON DECISION

(From the *Guardian* of December 9, 1896)

In an article written for the current number of the *Contemporary Review* I discussed the relations of the Bull *Apostolicae Curae* to the Gordon decision of 1704, and expressed a hope that some at least of the documents in this case might be published. My wish was anticipated. The article was hardly through the press when I received the *Civiltà*

SOURCES OF BULL *APOSTOLICAE CURAE* 273

Cattolica of November 11th, containing the text of the decree. It is as follows :—

" Feria v diei 17 Aprilis, 1704, in solita congregatione S.R. et universalis Inquisitionis habita in Palatio S. Petri Coram SSmo. Dno. Nro. Clemente Papa xi.

" Delata instantia Joannis Clementis Gordon Episcopi Anglicani, ad Catholicam fidem conversi, et quibusdam scripturis seu iuribus alias collectis pro simili casu, quamvis olim non fuerit decisus, vel saltem hac de re nihil fuisset decretum, cum voto DD. consultorum, qua petebat, ut non obstante consecratione episcopali obtenta ab episcopis sectae Anglicanae, et ritu solito illius pseudoepiscoporum, sibi concederetur facultas transeundi ad ordinem Presbyteratus ritu catholico suscipiendum, cum sua consecratio ad Episcopatum nulla sit, tum propter deficientiam successionis episcoporum in Anglia et Scotia, qui illum consecraverunt, tum propter alia motiva, quibus nulla redditur dicta illius consecratio.

" SSmus., auditis votis emorum Cardinalium, decrevit quod Ioannes Clemens Gordon ex integro et absolute ordinetur ad omnes ordines et praecipue Presbyteratus, et quatenus non fuerit confirmatus, prius Sacramentum Confirmationis suscipiat."

Such is the text of the decree, extracted by the writer in the *Civiltà Cattolica* from the archives of the Holy Office. It differs considerably from that given by Gasparri in his pamphlet, *De la valeur des Ordinations Anglicanes*, p. 16, who also prefixes the petition presented by Gordon, as if it formed an

T

274 A ROMAN DIARY AND OTHER DOCUMENTS

integral part of the decree itself. In the text as now published the arguments and statements of the petition are briefly summarized. A more important, though far less extensive, variation is the addition of the words "et quibusdam scripturis . . . consultorum," which are curiously interjected in the sentence "Delata instantia . . . qua petebat." There is nothing corresponding to this in the text given by Gasparri, which merely has "Lecto supradicto memoriali [*i.e.*, Gordon's petition] Sanctissimus D.N. Papa praedictus auditis votis, etc." The decree, as so read, implied that the decision was based solely on the statements made by Gordon himself, which included the most fanciful rendering of the Nag's Head Fable, and an extraordinary statement that the essential form in the English rite was : "Accipe potestatem praedicandi verbum Dei, et administrandi sancta eius sacramenta." This being so, the value of the decree itself was naturally put no higher than that of the reasons on which it was based. But, as I have explained elsewhere, we had already learnt that the decision was not based exclusively, or even mainly, on Gordon's petition ; there was an independent inquiry. This statement was confirmed by what we read in the recent Bull. It is confirmed afresh by the newly published text of the decree. There were brought into the case *quaedam scripturae seu iura alias collecta pro simili casu.*

The information, however, which I had gathered from various sources, and which I have published in the *Contemporary*, appears to be inexact in one particular. There is no trace of any independent inquiry at the time when the Gordon case actually

SOURCES OF BULL *APOSTOLICAE CURAE* 275

came on.[1] The new elements *alias collecta* had been already gathered for use in dealing with a previous case, when, however, no formal decision had been given. This was the case, alluded to in the recent Bull, which came before the Holy Office in 1684. As described by the writer in the *Civiltà*, this case concerned "a young Calvinist heretic, who, passing from France into England, was there ordained to the diaconate and then to the presbyterate, by the pseudo-bishop of London, according to the use of that sect. The young man, returning to France and embracing the Catholic religion, wished to marry. He accordingly asked whether the orders he had received were valid, and so constituted an impediment to his marriage." The consultors of the Holy Office resolved as follows :—" Feria II. die 13 Augusti 1685 DD. CC. mature discusso dubio unanimi voto responderunt pro invaliditate praedictae ordinationis. An autem expediat ad hanc declarationem in praesenti casu devenire EE. PP., oraculo reliquerunt." The Cardinals of the Congregation judged it inopportune to pronounce on the case at that juncture, and so the decision was *Dilata.*

The *vota* and the Acts of this case, our informant says, were the *scripturae et iura* imported into the Gordon case. It was not in 1704, but in 1684, that investigations were made by Genetti and others, the results of which were brought to bear

---

[1] Replying to me in the second edition of his *Condanna delle Ord. Agl* (p. 40), Fr. Brandi, the writer of the article in the *Civiltà*, corrected this by a reference to the words "duobus vel tribus novis votis," quoted below. But I do not gather that any fresh information was forthcoming ; the new *vota* were perhaps opinions newly passed upon the old materials,

276 A ROMAN DIARY AND OTHER DOCUMENTS

upon Gordon's petition. I gather from the *Civiltà* that no fresh materials of any kind, except the petition itself, were brought into the case in 1704[1]; but, as the Pope says in the recent Bull, "Eadem acta repetita et ponderata sunt." Of these *Acta* the writer gives us some glimpses, provokingly brief and incomplete. He tells us that the stories about Parker's consecration are positively excluded from among the reasons of the decision, because it is repeatedly asserted that "in so grave a matter a resolution of such consequence could not be grounded on a fact disputed between Catholics and Protestants," and the "definite (*adeguata*) decision ought to be connected not with the facts of Parker's case, which depended upon a very confused (*assai imbrogliata*) story . . . but upon the defect of intention, and of the words used by the Anglican heretics in priestly ordination." This, however, is a very different thing from saying that the fables in question had no influence upon the judgment of the Consultors or of the Congregation. Such language is perfectly consistent with a personal belief in the truth of the stories. Still quoting, as I gather, from a report of the proceedings of 1684, presented to the commission of 1704, the writer adds that "the principal subject of discussion was the examination of the Edwardine form, which was in use for more than a hundred years, and of the same form, as changed under Charles II in 1662," and that in the course of this examination the forms employed by the Easterns, whether Catholic or heretic, were brought into comparison. In 1704, he continues, quoting now in Latin :—

---

[1] But see the note on the preceding page.

SOURCES OF BULL *APOSTOLICAE CURAE* 277

"Duobus vel tribus novis *votis* fuit denuo *demonstrata* nullitas istarum ordinationum, *potissimum* ex insufficientia formae."

This sort of information is interesting, but all is very vague and unsatisfying. If we are told so much, why are we not told more? What was actually regarded as the essential form, the insufficiency of which was fatal to the English ordinations? The writer keeps to the same studied vagueness when he approaches the question of the Tradition of the Instruments. The documents which he has before him prove, he says, that "*if the question was touched*"—a curiously conditional sort of statement —"this was done, not to prove an essential defect in itself, but only to show that, along with the lack of this, there lacked entirely all determination of the words employed in the *form*, and all designation of the *power* which it was intended to confer." When a statement of this kind is made we are compelled, in the absence of fuller information, to read between the lines. We may err in doing so, but if we err we may be corrected by the production of further evidence.

What, then, does the information before us amount to? That can be very simply summarized. The Ordinal was examined; the essential form was found to be indeterminate, and insufficient

The crucial question remains unanswered. What was taken to be the essential form? Until this question is answered it remains impossible to estimate the value of the decision. Is there anything in the information given from which we may infer an answer? Something issues from a close and careful study.

278 A ROMAN DIARY AND OTHER DOCUMENTS

I note in the first place that Gordon himself in his petition made a certain identification of the form. "Nulla enim materia utuntur, nisi forte traditione Bibliorum, nulla forma legitima; imo formam Catholicorum abiecere et commutavere in hanc : *Accipe potestatem praedicandi verbum Dei, et administrandi sancta eius sacramenta :* quae essentialiter differt a formis orthodoxis."

It is clear, then, what Gordon took to be the essential form. He says nothing about the prayers or the *Accipe Spiritum Sanctum.* There can be no question, either, what he took to be the form of presbyteral ordination according to the Roman rite. It was *Accipe potestatem offerre sacrificium,* etc., which alone could by any stretch of language be said to have been *changed* into *Accipe potestatem praedicandi,* etc. It is also noticeable that he makes no allusion to the imposition of hands as the matter. But does this represent merely the personal opinion of Gordon? Estcourt has well remarked that a petition such as his would not be drawn up by the party himself. It was a formal document, and would certainly be drafted by an official familiar with the practice of the Roman Court. The *motivum,* even if it included some matter supplied by the petitioner, would follow the opinions dominant at Rome. It is, then, at least probable that the opinion about the English form, set forth in the petition, was prevalent in the official world of Rome. But a full investigation of the English Ordinal had taken place twenty years earlier. Was this opinion the outcome of that investigation? It seems highly probable. One expression used in the petition adds to the probability. The English

SOURCES OF BULL *APOSTOLICAE CURAE* 279

form, thus understood, differs, it is said, *a formis orthodoxis*. It is contrasted, not with the Roman form alone, but with all others recognized in the Church. But in 1684, as we have seen, the English Ordinal was brought into comparison with the Eastern rites: an opinion which describes the English form specifically as differing essentially from all orthodox forms, obviously suggests a reference to that investigation.

Again, the insufficiency of the form seems, according to our information, to have been somehow connected with the lack of the Tradition of the Instruments. This indicates obscurely, but not doubtfully, that the form under consideration was one corresponding to the *Accipe potestatem*, etc., of the Roman rite; and this, as I have said, could be none other but that put forward by Gordon: "Take thou authority to preach the Word of God, and to minister the holy sacraments in the congregation, where thou shalt be lawfully appointed thereunto." If this was the form before the investigators there is no wonder that they found it lacking in determination, and in the proper designation of the power of the priesthood which it was intended to confer.

Reading thus between the lines of the information given us, I seem to find that the Holy Office in 1684 and 1704 took as the essential form in the English rite neither any one of the prayers, nor the formula *Receive the Holy Ghost*, etc., nor the blessing *Almighty God Who hath given you this will*, etc. (which was taken as the form by Billuart), but the formula *Take thou authority to preach*, etc. If this be the form which was judged insufficient,

280　A ROMAN DIARY AND OTHER DOCUMENTS

we have the great advantage of being in perfect accord with the Sacred Congregation, and we may simply set aside the consequent condemnation of the English ordinations as based on an error of fact.[1]

The inference is not intrinsically improbable. The opinion was still dominant in the Roman schools that the essential matter of presbyteral ordination was the Tradition of the Instruments, with or without the imposition of hands, and the essential form the words *Accipe potestatem offerre,* etc. Such was the opinion of de Lugo, who was reckoned the greatest of modern theologians; it reigned almost without dispute in the Sorbonne; the Thomists were pledged to it. Morinus, it is

---

[1] Father Brandi (*op. cit.* p. 47) replied expressly under this head by referring to "la forma esaminata al tempo di Paolo IV," i.e. the form set out in the Description of the Ordinal reproduced above, pp. 181–4. The same rite, he adds, with the modifications made in 1662, was examined afresh in 1684–5. No doubt; but the sixteenth century Description sets out *Accipe auctoritatem praedicandi, etc.,* side by side with *Accipe Spiritum Sanctum, etc*, and does not in any way indicate which of them is to be regarded as the "forma essentialis." So too are set out the two forms used in the consecration of a bishop, *Accipe Spiritum Sanctum, etc.,* and *Attende lectioni, etc.* There is nothing here to show which was considered the essential form in 1684–5, and so my question remains unanswered "Abbiamo voluto ciò notare," says Father Brandi, "affine di soddisfare al dubbio proposto dal Signor Lacey nel *Guardian.*" He must credit me with a rare simplicity. For the opinion of Duchesne and others who had access to the documents, see above pp. 48, 100, 128, and 135. Their judgment that the Congregation regarded *Accipe Spiritum Sanctum* as the essential form is not lightly to be set aside, but was it anything more than a probable inference from doubtful evidence? I myself had the privilege of perusing the materials collected by Canon Moyes from the dossier of the case; but I did not fully realise their importance, and made no notes of them. It seems probable that Father Brandi has produced all that is relevant, and this leaves the conclusion doubtful.

SOURCES OF BULL *APOSTOLICAE CURAE* 281

true, had shown conclusively that all Eastern ordinations, and all the more ancient ordinations of the West, had been validly conferred by prayer and imposition of hands; but the immediate result of his work was only to strengthen the opinion of those who held that the form and matter were different for the East and for the West. Some years after the Gordon case was decided, Hardouin still held this opinion as almost axiomatic, while disfiguring it in his own fashion with a fantastic theory of a double divine appointment. Benedict XIV was, I believe, the first theologian who seriously shook its credit; and even he did this while actually recording a decision of the Congregation of the Council which required its recognition, in the specific form put forward by de Lugo, as at least probable. Even if the Congregation of the Holy Office in 1684–1704 was enlightened beyond the measure of the time—a very unlikely supposition — and put aside the Tradition of the Instruments as not essential, it remains probable in the highest degree that they regarded *Accipe potestatem offerre* as the essential form of presbyteral ordination in the Latin rite, and finding a formula *Accipe potestatem* etc. in the English rite, took that as a matter of course to be the essential form.

The inference, then, is not intrinsically improbable, and it seems to follow from the information which is given us. If it be erroneous, let the error be shown. The archives of the Holy Office either contain the necessary evidence or they do not. If it is there, let us have it. The Roman authorities presumably wish to convince us. Evidence alone will have that effect. If nothing

282 A ROMAN DIARY AND OTHER DOCUMENTS

more is produced we shall be disposed to assume either that the archives contain nothing to the purpose, or that what they contain would rather confirm us in our opinion than convince us of error.[1]

[1] The purport of the concluding sentence may not be very clear. Its form was certainly affected by the habit of thought then dominating me, which is described above in the Introduction ; but even at the time the possible "error" of which I was thinking was nothing else but a mistake about the actual details of the decision in Gordon's case.

THE THEOLOGY OF THE BULL
APOSTOLICAE CURAE

X

THE THEOLOGY OF THE BULL
APOSTOLICAE CURAE

(A paper read at Sion College, on Tuesday, November
10th, 1896)

IT is natural to ask how we should regard the
Papal Bull on English Orders. You may
lightly answer that we should regard it with perfect
indifference, that the Bishop of Rome and his
opinions and judgments are nothing to us, that we
may pass them by with silent contempt. But I
think such an answer will not give you permanent
satisfaction. It will occur to you that Christians are
all members one of another, that, however much we
may be sundered by controversy and by differences
of practice, we are all members of the one Body of
Christ, and the interests that we have in common
are far more and far greater than those which
divide us. Among these common interests there is
none greater than the defence of the truth ; and
among Christian truths there are few more important than the truth of the sacred ministry—that
ministry of reconciliation which the Lord Jesus
Christ intrusted to the Apostles for the perfecting
of the saints, for the edifying of the Body of Christ.
This ministry is spread throughout the Church, and

285

286 A ROMAN DIARY AND OTHER DOCUMENTS

upon the testimony of the whole Church we rely for our understanding of its nature and attributes. The fundamental doctrines of the faith are attested by the common teaching of all parts of the Church, so that no teaching which is denied or even ignored by a considerable part of the Church can be recognized with certainty as being true to the original type. In the same way the reality of the sacred ministry is attested by its existence in all parts of the Church alike. Any serious divergence, therefore, between different parts of the Church endangers the hold of all upon the truth. We in England know only too well what mischief is done by disputes about the reality of a ministry confessedly new and constituted by men who have separated themselves from the Church. Much greater is the confusion when the ministry which one part of the Church claims to have received by direct succession from the Apostles is denounced by another part of the Church as a mere empty shadow.

That is how the matter stands. The English Church claims the possession and use of a sacred ministry, a holy priesthood, which is common to the whole Church, which is, therefore, identical with that of the Roman Church. Futile distinctions have at times been drawn by men whose dislike of everything Roman has warped their judgment; but the testimony of the Church as a whole is unmistakable. In the Preface to the Ordinal is expressed the intention of retaining and continuing the orders which were conferred before the Reformation, and none will question their identity with those of the Roman Church. Priests ordained by the Roman rite have always, in spite of the

THEOLOGY OF BULL *APOSTOLICAE CURAE* 287

fierce protests of the early Puritans, been recognized in practice as sharing the same ministry with us. The late Primate in his last message to the English people restated this obvious truth. The Orders of the English Church are identical with those of the Roman Church. But the head of the Roman Church declares them to be null.

Such a declaration was mischievous enough when it was supposed to deal only with a matter of fact. Until lately the authorities of the Roman Church apparently held that in the English Church real Orders were not in fact conferred, but no reasons for the denial were publicly given. Individual theologians might suggest reasons, but they had no authority. Others, again, were able to combat the denial by showing that there were no reasons at all on which to ground it. This is now changed. The Bull not only declares English Orders null, but gives a reason. And the reason given is that the forms used in conferring them are worthless; they were deliberately chosen to express an altogether inadequate conception of the sacred ministry. This is a far more mischievous declaration than the former. It is one thing to say that a part of the Christian Church, through some untoward accident, lacks a valid ministry; it is a far more serious thing to say that a part of the Church has deliberately wrecked the Christian priesthood. In saying this you break up the testimony of the whole Church to the truth of the sacred ministry. If the charge be true, you must face that consequence unflinchingly. If the charge be false, then you are responsible for the confusion of thought which ensues. To accuse a man falsely of heresy is not only an injustice to

288 A ROMAN DIARY AND OTHER DOCUMENTS

him, it imperils the truth which he has actually taught.

We know the charge against the English Church to be false. We can see the harm that will come from it. We may hold the Roman Church responsible. But we are not on that account without further interest in the matter. We may be unshaken ourselves; but we have not ourselves only to think of. Perhaps we are satisfied that the Roman Church will suffer most. Are we to congratulate ourselves on this? I would remind you of the wise and noble words spoken on this head by the Bishop of Rochester at the late Church Congress. If the Roman Church suffers the whole Church suffers, and we suffer who are members of that one Body.

I shall not on this occasion take up the cudgels in defence of the English ordinations. A question of even greater importance is stirred by the recent Bull. It is not only a personal matter for us English Churchmen. There is a truth at stake. What is Holy Order? I will call it a sacrament, if you will not misunderstand me. I will call it, with Hooker a χάρισμα or gift of the Holy Spirit, and its effect a certain mark or character indelibly impressed upon the recipient. I will say, with Jeremy Taylor, that in ordination is conferred a twofold grace of sanctification, by which, on the one hand, the recipient is separated for the work of the ministry, and, on the other, he is rendered capable of worthily fulfilling his vocation. I will say with the whole Church that this grace is given by an outward sign, by public prayer with imposition of hands. When we have said this, the question whether ordination

THEOLOGY OF BULL *APOSTOLICAE CURAE* 289

ought to be called a sacrament is a mere question of words. If the grace of the ministry is a gift of the Holy Ghost, conferred by a sacramental sign, what are the powers of the Church in this regard? The Church can but act ministerially. The Church, in the person of a bishop, can give or withhold the grace of the ministry by imparting to a man or refusing him the external sign. But when once the grace has been given the Church cannot take back the gift. It is as with baptism. The Church may give a man baptism, or for a good cause may refuse it. But once he is baptized the Church cannot undo his baptism. Neither, on the other hand, if he has not been properly baptized, can the Church by any sort of decree produce in him the effect of baptism.[1] The Church can only inquire into the facts of the case, and when the facts are known declare that as a matter of fact the man is or is not baptized. A priest, as representing the Church, does this whenever a child is brought to him after being privately baptized. He holds a formal inquiry, takes evidence, and declares the result. It is the same with ordination. The Church can inquire whether a man has been properly ordained or no, and may be able to decide the fact upon the evidence. But no decision can alter the facts. A defective ordination cannot be made good, a valid

---

[1] Yet the practice κατ' οἰκονομίαν of the Eastern Church is not to be ignored. The wise decretal of Innocent III *de presbytero non baptizato* is another matter " Respondemus presbyterum, quem sine unda baptismatis extremum diem clausisse significasti, quia in sanctae matris Ecclesiae fide et Christi nominis confessione perseveraverit, ab originali peccato solutum, et caelestis patriae gaudium esse adeptum, asserimus incunctanter" *Lib III Decr. tit* 43, *cap* 2 Denzinger, *Enchiridion*, No 343.

U

290 A ROMAN DIARY AND OTHER DOCUMENTS

ordination cannot be annulled, by any subsequent decree.

The question of the validity of baptism is usually a simple one, though difficult cases do sometimes occur. It is simple because the principal conditions of a true baptism were ordained by our Lord himself, and so are undoubtedly required. He taught the necessity of baptism by water, and he taught his Church to baptize *In the name of the Father, and of the Son, and of the Holy Ghost.* In the language of theologians he thus appointed specifically the *matter* and the *form* of baptism. If this matter and this form were not used we decide at once that there was no true Christian baptism.[1]

For ordination, on the other hand, there is no clear evidence that our Lord himself appointed any specific matter or form. We may think it probable that he did so, and since probability is the chief guide of life we shall be careful to act on this view ; we should not dare to ordain a man without using that matter and form which our Lord may have appointed. But there is no certainty of this, and therefore a decision about the validity of an ordination is far less simple than one concerning baptism. You can never say curtly and definitely— "Certain things are absolutely required by the teaching of Christ for a valid ordination. This man was ordained without those requisites. Therefore his ordination is null and void."

What, then, can the Church decide in such a

---

[1] But see Nicholas I, *Responsa ad Consulta Bulgarorum,* cap. 104 : "Hi profecto si in nomine sanctae Trinitatis vel tantum in Christi nomine, sicut in Actibus Apostolorum legimus, baptizati sunt (unum quippe idemque est, ut sanctus exponit Ambrosius), constat eos non esse denuo baptizandos."

THEOLOGY OF BULL *APOSTOLICAE CURAE* 291

case? It can be ruled with perfect certainty that a given ordination is good and valid. If it be found on inquiry that a man has been ordained in a way which the Church ordinarily accounts sufficient, it is clearly impossible to go behind the facts. He may at once be pronounced validly ordained. But if the ordination has been effected in a manner unusual or not fully recognized, it is not so simple a matter. Such an ordination cannot claim immediate acceptance ; but neither can it be at once declared null. The form employed may be a valid one, though unusual. An inquiry is called for. On what lines should it proceed? What sort of decision can be looked for ?

Two separate questions will present themselves. What are the essential elements of a valid ordination ? And were those elements duly observed in the supposed case ? The former question raises a very great difficulty. The essentials of a valid ordination have never been defined. We know that certain forms are sufficient, but we do not know whether they are necessary, or whether other forms might not be substituted. Can the Church define what is necessary, so as to rule out all ordinations that lack any part of it ?

There is a difference of opinion among theologians which bears upon this question. Some believe that, although there is no record of such appointment in the Gospels, yet our Lord did really appoint a proper matter and form of ordination, and taught the Apostles to use it. Others believe that he left to his Church the power to appoint the matter and form. It is hard to say

292 A ROMAN DIARY AND OTHER DOCUMENTS

which of these two opinions has the greater weight of authority on its side.

Take the former hypothesis. Then the essentials of a valid ordination are what our Lord appointed. The Church has only to find out what these are ; every ordination which has them will be valid, every ordination which lacks them will be void. But how are they to be found ? How can we recover any teaching of our Lord which has not been recorded ? We may study the practice of the Apostles. What their Lord taught them to do they certainly did. If he commanded them to ordain men to the sacred ministry in a certain way, they would undoubtedly do it in that way and no other. But we find the Apostles ordaining by imposition of hands, with prayer. The same mode of ordaining was continued in the Church and remained in use without variation or addition for several hundred years. So far as Christian antiquity has been explored no other kind of ordination is found.[1] In the greater part of the Eastern Church there is nothing else to this day, and in the Western Church, while many additions have been made to the rites of ordination, the old elements remain side by side with the new. There is no ordination without prayer and imposition of hands. If then our Lord prescribed any mode of ordaining, it must have been this. But further, it may be asked what sort of prayer was required ? It is clear that no fixed form was appointed, since there is great variety among those which the Church has used.

---

[1] I had not forgotten my own studies in the consecration of bishops with imposition of the Gospel text (*supra*, pp 7, 16), but was only stating an hypothesis which I myself rejected.

THEOLOGY OF BULL *APOSTOLICAE CURAE* 293

Is there no limit then? May any prayer be used? Can holy orders be conferred, for example, by the recitation of the Lord's Prayer, with imposition of hands? Again we look to the practice of the Church. We find that in all the prayers that have been used, widely as they differ, there is a common element. This common element may be very briefly expressed. There is a prayer for the ordinand that he may receive the grace necessary for the worthy accomplishment of the duties of the order to which he is called. This we find in all the prayers, and therefore we may suppose it necessary. We may presume that our Lord commanded such a prayer to be used. But, after all, this is only a presumption, and it is based on imperfect evidence. We do not possess all the prayers which were ever used in the Church for conferring Orders. Should more of them come to light, we may possibly find these lacking some part of what we have thought universal and essential. The possibility has been recently illustrated. A distinguished French theologian, M. Boudinhon, in view of the controversy about English Orders, lately undertook the very task that I am describing. He compared all the known prayers of ordination recognized as valid by the Roman Church. He found that all contained an express mention of the order to be conferred. He therefore took this to be essential. Soon after he had published the result of his studies, I pointed out to him that he had left out of count the ordination prayers contained in the Canons of Hippolytus, which were in use at Rome during the third century. Of these the prayer for a deacon has no mention of the diaconate. M. Boudinhon

294 A ROMAN DIARY AND OTHER DOCUMENTS

at once admitted that his conclusion must be modified ; the mention of the order could not be required as essential.[1]

The weakness of the method pursued by M. Boudinhon is evident. He was building on imperfect evidence ; and it is hard to see how the evidence can ever be completed. You can never get beyond a presumption that certain things were prescribed by our Lord as essential to a valid ordination. You may take it for certain that the ordinations used in the Church do really contain what the Lord commanded; but you cannot be sure that any particular element in them was so required. Something which is common to them all may nevertheless have been added by human authority. On the hypothesis of a matter and form appointed by Christ himself, it is safe to declare an ordination valid because it conforms to the usage of the Church ; but any judgment must be highly precarious which condemns an ordination as void for lack of something which may not after all be essential.

---

[1] Achelis, p 66 I would not now assert the Roman character of these Canons In his *Condanna delle Ordinazioni Anglicane* (p 53), Father Brandi pointed out that the word *servitium* in Achelis' rendering may represent an orginal διακονίαν. This critic handled both M. Boudinhon and me rather severely, and not unjustly, for arguing from a Latin translation made by a German from an Arabic version of a lost Greek original. I kiss the rod ; but I do not know why my castigator himself underlined the words *Diaconus* and *Diaconatus* in this same doubtful translation They occur in the text of the Canon , we were concerned, of course, only with the wording of the Prayer of Ordination which the Canon contains. The incident retains its interest as illustrating the precariousness of an argument drawn from a necessarily imperfect collation of the rites used in the Church. Indeed, Father Brandi's criticism enhances its interest ; for here is confessedly a form of ordination probably used in the Church, the exact wording of which cannot be recovered See also *Introduction*, pp 14-17.

THEOLOGY OF BULL *APOSTOLICAE CURAE* 295

Let us pass to the second hypothesis. We are now to suppose that our blessed Lord intrusted to his Church the power of appointing the matter and form by which the grace of the ministry was to be conferred. We stand here on surer ground, for if this power was given to the Church it seems clear that the Apostles exercised it when they performed their first ordination with prayer and the imposition of hands. These they made the essentials of ordination. Then it would seem that any ordination conferred in this manner, with suitable prayer and imposition of hands, must be accepted as valid. But a further question arises. Can the Church, after appointing the essential elements of ordination, change them and appoint others in their stead? It seems a not unnatural conclusion. We can hardly suppose the powers of the Church to have been exhausted by the first exercise of them. Some theologians have maintained that a change of this kind has in fact been made. In the Eastern Church, they say, the priesthood is still conferred, as in the beginning, by prayer and the imposition of hands ; but in the Western Church there has been substituted the Porrection of Instruments with the accompanying words, "Accipe potestatem offerendi sacrificium, etc." The truth is that St. Thomas Aquinas and his followers did indeed take this for the essential matter and form of priestly ordination ; but they probably supposed it to have been in use from the beginning. With a better knowledge of Christian antiquity the scholars of a later age detected their historical mistake, but the great authority of St. Thomas delayed the rejection of his theological opinion, and therefore

296 A ROMAN DIARY AND OTHER DOCUMENTS

an actual change of the matter and form was insisted upon. This raises a heavy crop of difficulties. By what authority can such a change be made? Clearly it need not be made by the whole Church, or for the whole Church at once. What then? May any individual Bishop change the usual matter and form, and substitute another at his discretion? Or what sort of intermediate authority is required? Again, if a new matter and form has been introduced by competent authority, will that deprive the old matter and form of their efficacy, so that Orders conferred by them will be no longer valid? The most learned of the Popes, Benedict XIV, cuts these knots in a summary and, I think, a satisfactory manner :—" Even if such power has been given to the Church," he says, " it is a pure and arbitrary assumption to say that she has used it. Where and when, in what age, in what Council, or by what Pontiff, has any such change been made?"[1] A change of this moment could only be made by a formal legislative act of the Church; and no such act can be shown.[2] Some would refer to the decree *Exultate*, in which Eugenius IV defined the porrection of the instruments and the accompanying words as the essential matter and form of priestly ordination. But in no way can this definition be regarded as having legislative force, above all for the Western Church. It was

---

[1] *De Syn. Dioec*, lib. viii. cap x, § 10

[2] What is of importance is not the question whether the Church, or a part of the Church, has power to introduce a new mode of ordination, but whether it is possible to invalidate a mode previously in use. On the hypothesis under discussion, the former question seems to demand an affirmative answer; the latter question may be answered theoretically in the affirmative, but there is no ground for supposing such a power to have been exercised in practice.

THEOLOGY OF BULL *APOSTOLICAE CURAE* 297

addressed to the case of the Armenians who were seeking reconciliation with the Roman see; and Armenians are not Westerns. It was not meant to bring in a new custom, for it is a definition, according to the Pope's mind, of what is and always has been the matter and form of Holy Order. Modern theologians of the Roman schools, who almost all repudiate this definition, labour to avoid the appearance of contradicting a Papal decision. They speak of the decree as dealing only with the accessories of ordination, or as merely describing the actual Latin rite.[1] There seems no ground whatever for attributing to it legislative force. Nor is there anything else of the kind. No formal change of the matter and form of ordination can be traced. The original institution therefore stands. Imposition of hands and prayer formally constitute the rite of ordination. The contents of the prayer are not fixed, for the prayers used in the Church are known to have varied widely. On the hypothesis which I am now considering the Church might indeed impose a certain form, and make it necessary for the future. But such a step must be taken in the most formal and public manner, and it could in no case affect the validity of Orders conferred in the past. We are thus brought almost to the same position in which the former hypothesis landed us. It is safe to declare ordinations valid which conform to the usual pattern. It is highly precarious to declare an ordination void on the ground of something wanting in the prayers which accompany the imposition of hands.

I have examined these two hypotheses at length,

[1] Benedict XIV, *ibid.* § 8   Gasparri, *De Sacr. Ord*, n 1007

298 A ROMAN DIARY AND OTHER DOCUMENTS

because there is sometimes a danger of sliding imperceptibly from one to the other, and the natural result is much confusion of thought. The essentials of ordination depend either upon the institution of Christ, or upon the appointment of the Church. In either case the practical result for our purpose is much the same. In the former case it is perhaps impossible to arrive at an exhaustive definition of the essentials. In the latter case this is possible, but it has never been done. In the Roman Church, and in all the Churches that bow to Rome, this fact has usually been recognized. In the Council of Trent care was taken to avoid anything which might seem to be such a definition.[1] In practice the Roman Church allows the validity of ordinations conferred by all manner of rites, if only with prayer and the imposition of hands. In consequence of a succession of movements towards reunion, mostly abortive, the Roman Church has had occasion to accept or reject Orders conferred by almost every known rite used in any part of the Church, orthodox or heretical ; and in every case save one such Orders have been acknowledged as good. The one exception, I need not tell you, is that of the English Church. In no single case have the ordinations thus accepted any resemblance to those of the Roman Church as finally developed during the middle ages. In no single case, as the great French scholar Morinus testified, could any matter and form be found in them, save the imposition of hands and prayer ; and the Orders so conferred have been recognized as good. The prayers thus used

---

[1] The subject was treated in the *Church Quarterly Review*, Vol. V. See also Denny, *Anglican Orders and Jurisdiction*, p. 193

THEOLOGY OF BULL *APOSTOLICAE CURAE* 299

are very diverse, some expressing with great fulness the characteristic powers of the various orders, others conceived in the most general terms ; some alluding more or less clearly to the power of offering the eucharistic sacrifice, others ignoring it altogether. I have already mentioned M. Boudinhon's comparative study of these forms. Carefully separating what is common to all, and so presumably essential, he finds that it amounts to this—

"Deus qui . . . respice propitius super hunc famulum tuum, quem ad diaconatum (*vel* presbyteratum, *vel* episcopatum, *seu* summum sacerdotium) vocare dignatus es ; da ei gratiam tuam, ut munera huius ordinis digne et utiliter adimplere valeat."[1]

With him agrees entirely Mgr. Gasparri, who notes also that many of the rites thus recognized are those of heretical Churches, probably dating from a time when their authors had already broken away from the unity of the Church. Thus the ordinations of the Nestorians, of the Armenians, and of other branches of the Monophysites, and even of the barbarous Church of Abyssinia, have been recognized as good, without any inquiry into their origin[2] It was enough that they were effected by a rite analogous to those used in the Catholic Church.

It was put to me by a distinguished person when I was in Rome that there was a practical difficulty

---

[1] *De la validité des Ord. Angl*, p 50   As I have said, he afterwards modified this, no longer regarding the actual *naming* of the order necessary.

[2] Gasparri, *De la valeur des Ord. Angl.*, p. 42

300 A ROMAN DIARY AND OTHER DOCUMENTS

in the way of recognizing English Orders, because
that could not be done without defining the essentials of ordination, a definition from which the
Roman Church had always shrunk. I pointed out
in reply that there was no such need, since the
English Ordinal certainly contained those elements
at least which are common to the various Eastern
ordinations recognized at Rome. My remark was
received with polite incredulity by one who, however eminent in his own way, probably knew little
of the English Ordinal and less of the Oriental rites.
His attitude, however, is instructive. If it was
impossible to recognize English Orders without
defining the essentials, still more was it impossible
without such a definition to condemn them as void.
You cannot say that a rite lacks essentials unless
you first determine what the essentials are. And if
it does not lack essentials it is valid.

You will, perhaps, take me up here with a demurrer.
Is it, then, impossible for the Church ever to pronounce any ordination invalid? Must everything
be accepted which its authors put forward as a rite
of ordination? I answer that it would be extremely
precarious to declare absolutely invalid the Orders
conferred by any bishop, even by a rite of his own
appointment, and that the Roman Church has never
done this except in dealing with England. But
short of this the authorities of the Church can do
much. It is one thing to have genuine Orders, or
Orders which may possibly be genuine; it is quite
another thing to have the right to exercise them.
It may be difficult or impossible to declare a man's
Orders absolutely void; it is easy, and it may be
right, to forbid him to use them. If they are doubtful,

THEOLOGY OF BULL *APOSTOLICAE CURAE* 301

this ought to be done ; but where there is room for doubt there is room for conditional reordination. The internal practice of the Roman Church follows this rule. On the ground that some theologians have raised a doubt whether the porrection of instruments be not in the Western Church essential to a valid ordination, the Roman Church requires conditional reordination, if by accident that ceremony has been omitted. On the same principle any particular Church might lawfully exclude from its altars a priest ordained in another Church, and might insist on a conditional reordination before admitting him.[1] If the Roman Church were to consider our English ordinations doubtful, and to rule that no English priest should be admitted to officiate at Roman altars without conditional reordination, I do not know that we should be at all concerned, and I am sure that no confusion would be imported into the science of theology.

The recent condemnation of English Orders does impart confusion into the science of theology. In this respect it concerns us. Practically we may ignore it ; but from the scientific point of view we are almost as much interested as the Roman theologians themselves. Theological science is not the property of this or that Church ; it is the property of all Christians. Where we differ there is controversial theology ; where we agree there is the far wider and more important sphere of dogmatic theo-

---

[1] I would not say this now. A bishop may certainly, subject to established rights of appeal, forbid a priest ordained elsewhere to exercise the sacred ministry within his diocese ; but to make reordination one of the terms of admission seems to be an offence against the fundamental unity of the Episcopate analogous to those of which St. Cyprian complained in his controversy with Stephen of Rome.

logy. Now for some time past the theology of Holy Orders has been passing from the controversial sphere to the dogmatic. I do not mean that all open questions were in the way of being closed, but that on all sides there was a growing agreement on certain great principles; and one of these principles was that Holy Orders were validly conferred by imposition of hands with a prayer for the ordinand, conceived in however wide and general terms. The recent condemnation of English Orders cuts sharply across this tendency. Our belief will not be affected by it, but we can hardly venture to say as much of Roman theologians; and whatever the effect on individuals may be, you must remember that the only solid basis for theology, so far as it goes beyond the express letter of Holy Scripture, is the general agreement of all parts of the Church. There is more than one source of such agreement. It may be sustained by tradition; it may be arrived at by patient study; it is reached sometimes through vehement controversy. When it is attained, we can teach as from a sure standing place.

And how is such agreement frustrated by the recent Bull? This pronouncement cuts across the current of theology; it is out of harmony with the practice of the Roman Church itself. You will say that it only confirms the practice of three hundred years. Yes, the practice as regards England. But the reasons alleged for the decision render the practice of the Roman Church as regards the Oriental Churches utterly irrational. You will know to what I refer. It has been proved to demonstration that in the English rite are found all the elements which are common to those Eastern ordinations

THEOLOGY OF BULL *APOSTOLICAE CURAE* 303

which the Roman Church acknowledges for good.[1] They are sufficient there, but here they are held insufficient. The Roman Church, departing from its traditional caution, ventures, at least by implication, on a definition of the essential form. The English form, says the Bull—we will not ask for the moment what constitutes that form, for I am now criticizing the theology of the Bull and not defending our Ordinal—the English form is insufficient, because its words "minime sane significant definite ordinem sacerdotis vel eius gratiam et potestatem, quae praecipue est potestas *consecrandi et offerendi verum corpus et sanguinem Domini.*" That is to say, no form can be valid which does not definitely signify the sacerdotal or sacrificial powers which are attached to the presbyterate. Now it has been abundantly shown that both the ancient Roman rite, and some of the Eastern rites allowed by the Roman Church, have not the slightest allusion to these powers.[2] What follows? Shall we draw the absurd conclusion that the Pope condemns as null and void the Orders of his predecessors during nine hundred years ; that he condemns as theologically invalid the Orders of Easterns which in practice he acknowledges for

---

[1] See the analyses in Gasparri, *De la Valeur*, etc , and Boudinhon, *De la Validité*, etc.

[2] It has often been said that to argue thus is to ignore the *vel* in the passage quoted ; all recognized forms mention *either* the presbyterate *or* the power of sacrificing. But the *prayers* of the English Ordinal expressly mention the presbyterate, and of these prayers it is said immediately below . "detractum esse quidquid in ritu catholico dignitatem et officia sacerdotii perspicue designat. Non ea igitur forma esse apta et sufficiens sacramento potest quae id nempe reticet quod deberet proprium significare." That is to say, mention of the presbyterate is not sufficient.

304 A ROMAN DIARY AND OTHER DOCUMENTS

good? There is only one possible evasion of this conclusion. We may suppose the Pope to mean that when once the expression of these powers has been introduced in any part of the Church, it becomes in some way essential; and so, since the English Church once employed it and then gave it up, something that was become essential was abandoned. If this be his meaning he is still hopelessly at cross purposes with all recent theology, and we may leave him to battle with Benedict XIV, who will ask him how, when, where, by whom, these things were made essential.

Again, one of the prayers which we use in the consecration of a bishop is treated as an insufficient form, on the ground that it makes no mention of the *summum sacerdotium :* and of this expression also there is no trace in other rites approved by the Roman Church. Elsewhere it is said that in the whole Ordinal " nulla est aperta mentio sacrificii, consecrationis, sacerdotii, potestatisque consecrandi et sacrificii offerendi." I pass by the astounding assertion that in the English Ordinal there is no mention of the *priesthood ;* it is more germane to my present purpose to note that in other rites as well none of these things are mentioned. Nay, the Roman form itself, says Gasparri—meaning, of course, the ancient prayer which he regards as being the essential form of the existing Roman rite—" the Roman form for the presbyterate says nothing of the power of consecrating and of sacrificing." [1] Yet again, that prayer of the English Ordinal which, as M. Boudinhon says, corresponds precisely to the common form obtained by abstrac-

---

[1] *De la valeur*, etc , p 40.

THEOLOGY OF BULL *APOSTOLICAE CURAE* 305

tion from a comparison of all the forms in use—the prayer beginning *Almighty God, the giver of all good things*—is ruled out on the ground of some vague doubts about the supposed opinions of the authors of the Ordinal; as if their opinions could affect the meaning of words contained in a public formulary.

This treatment of the English Ordinal is in sharp contrast with the teaching and practice of the Roman Church in dealing with the Eastern Churches, orthodox or heretical. Expressions are here treated as essential, the absence of which in Eastern rites is not regarded as fatal. The forms of those rites are accepted simply for what they say; here the words are not to be taken in their natural sense, but in a sense doubtfully attributed to their authors. Everywhere else a form sufficient in itself is taken as sufficiently claiming an orthodox meaning; here we are told that a certain form is on extrinsical grounds to be rejected "etiamsi forte haberi ea posset tanquam sufficiens in ritu aliquo Catholico quem Ecclesia probasset." The question forces itself: If the form were not sufficient, how could the Church approve it; if it were sufficient, how could the Church refuse approbation?

In this way the Bull imports confusion into the theology of Holy Order. It is not the first time that a Pope has wrought such confusion by a rash assertion. The Roman Church, so staunch a witness to certain truths, has a bad record in this matter. In the ninth century infinite trouble was caused by Popes who declared the ordinations of their predecessor, Formosus, null and void, merely because he had not been canonically

x

306 A ROMAN DIARY AND OTHER DOCUMENTS

elected. Other Popes, again, declared them valid. Contradiction followed contradiction. Men were reordained, and again excommunicated because of their reordination. It was long before the stream of ecclesiastical tradition ran clear.

Again, Eugenius IV in the fifteenth century defined the porrection of the instruments as the matter of priestly ordination. He did but utter the contemporary teaching of the schools; but it is one thing for an opinion to pass current in the schools, it is another for a Pope to propound it in a formal decree. The *Decretum pro Armenis* seems to have slept for a time, but it was revived in the middle of the sixteenth century. Pole seems to have published it in his Legatine Council for England. It dominated for another century the schools of theology. As a consequence the ordinations of the Uniat Greeks were challenged, and would probably have been condemned, had not the French Oratorian Morinus come to the rescue and by his profound erudition shattered the authority of Eugenius.

The stream of theology again ran clear; prayer and imposition of hands were all but universally recognized as the only essentials of ordination, and comparative study was narrowing down the requisites of the prayer. Now comes this ill-considered utterance. Ill considered it is. Do not be misled by the show of erudition and careful investigation which ushered it in. It does not represent the learning of those who were called in council— of an historian like Duchesne, of a theologian like De Augustinis, of a canonist like Gasparri. It ignores their arguments, hardly deigning to pay them the compliment of an answer.

THEOLOGY OF BULL *APOSTOLICAE CURAE* 307

It must do mischief—mischief practical and scientific. It confuses the plain lines of theology. It hinders the holy work of the reunion of Christians. But will the mischief abide? History forbids us to believe it. The like mischief done in the past by the like means had its day and then was healed. The condemnation of English Orders will go the way of the condemnation of the ordinations of Formosus; the Bull *Apostolicae curae* will go the way of the decree *Exultate*.[1] Its arguments already shattered, its blunders exposed, it will one day lose also the extrinsic authority which attaches to a Papal utterance.

[1] That very eclectic theologian, Dr. C A. Briggs of the Union Seminary at New York, writes in his *Church Unity* (p. 121), "Pope Pius X assured me in a private interview that this decision of his predecessor as to Anglican Orders cannot be brought under the category of infallible decisions" I understand, however, that the accuracy of his memory has been challenged See also, below, the section on *Gregory IX and Greek Ordinations*

THE INTERPRETATION OF
THE ENGLISH ORDINAL

XI

THE INTERPRETATION OF THE ENGLISH ORDINAL

(A Paper written for the Church Historical Society iu the year 1898.)

THERE is an old debate as to the meaning of the English Ordinal. It speaks of *bishops* and *priests*. But in what sense are these words to be accepted? It is urged, on the one hand, that they are familiar words in constant use for centuries, and must bear in the Ordinal the sense which they had acquired by ecclesiastical usage. It is contended, on the other hand, that a new departure was made by the reformers, who used the old words indeed, but in a sense of their own, either altogether novel, or at least foreign to the sense of the preceding age and looking back to the early days of Apostolic Christianity ; *priest* is only a derivative by phonetic decay of *presbyter*, and this word means etymologically an elder, in which sense alone, and not in any sacerdotal sense, the reformers used it. This judgment is delivered in the most diverse quarters. Leo XIII, in his Bull on Anglican Orders, declares that the words *bishop* and *priest* in the Ordinal are *nomina sine re ;* ardent Protestants agree enthusiastically that priesthood in the Roman

311

312 A ROMAN DIARY AND OTHER DOCUMENTS

sense is unknown to the English Ordinal and to the English Church.

In the *Month* of March, 1898, there is an article dealing with this question. The writer looks to the origin of the Ordinal, and asks what light is thrown upon its meaning by the circumstances of its introduction. Father Sydney Smith is a courteous antagonist, one who always tries to understand his adversary, and labours still more to avoid misrepresenting him. In the article to which I refer he has missed in one particular the point of an argument commonly advanced on our side; for the rest he fairly joins issue.

His contention is that "Cranmer and his adherents were the true authors of the Ordinal"; and that "the Ordinal received its meaning from the minds of its compilers.[1]" The conclusion apparently intended, though unexpressed, is that the purpose of the compilers was to exclude the idea of the true priesthood of the Church, and that consequently the forms of the Ordinal do not signify that priesthood, and cannot convey it.[2]

There is a twofold answer to this contention. In the first place, we do not know with certainty who were the authors or compilers of the Ordinal, and therefore we cannot draw any conclusions from their real or supposed opinions. Secondly, the compilers were incapable of imposing any meaning of their own upon the Ordinal; its true sense was determined by other and less personal forces.

It is true enough that in a sense Cranmer and his adherents were the authors of the Ordinal. It was

---

[1] *Month*, pp. 231, 235.

[2] This argument is explicitly developed by Brandi, *Roma e Canterbury*, p 36.

INTERPRETATION OF THE ENGLISH ORDINAL 313

at their instance that new rites of Ordination were introduced. But this is obviously a loose way of talking, and from a consideration of this kind we cannot draw any conclusion as to the sense of the new rites. In a period of reform or revolution those who bring about a change are not unfrequently disappointed with the result of their efforts. The promoters of the English Ordinal were possibly in this case. They may have had the most mischievous purpose in agitating for a new rite, and yet in obtaining it may have missed their aim. There is a further looseness of thought in speaking of " Cranmer and his adherents." The phrase suggests an organized party under a recognized leader, with a definite policy and avowed intentions. In 1550 there was no such thing. But further, among those who moved for the new Ordinal, there were some who were in no sense adherents of Cranmer. Father Sydney Smith enumerates the bishops who voted in the House of Lords for and against the proposal :—
" Cranmer, Goodrich, Barlow, Ridley, Ferrar, Wharton, Sampson, Skyp, voted for the Bill; Tunstall, Heath, Day, Thirlby, Aldrich, voted against it. Of these, the first five who voted for the Bill were unmitigated Calvinists. Wharton and Sampson were Opportunists; Skyp was the only one on that side entitled to be called schismatic only, and not heretic as well." [1]

Here is more loose writing. It is an anachronism to speak of "Calvinists" at all at so early a date. But let us interpret the term generously, and take it to mean such as sympathized with the Helvetic reformers. Is the assertion then accurate? Barlow

[1] *Month*, p 232.

314 A ROMAN DIARY AND OTHER DOCUMENTS

is a puzzling person. He was Lutheran in early life. He afterwards wrote fiercely against both Lutherans and Oecolampadians. He then became bishop and pursued a wavering course. Hooper claimed him as a Sacramentarian, on the ground of some private conversation.[1] He was charged with heresy after Mary's accession, but he made his peace, resigned his bishopric, and republished his book against the Reformers. He afterwards went abroad, and was concerned in the disputes of the exiles at Frankfort; but here he seems to have been connected rather with Lutherans than with the Reformed.[2] It is rash to call him an "unmitigated Calvinist." Goodrich also was claimed by Hooper, but Mary left him undisturbed, and his Register at Ely shows him vigorous in prosecuting heretics. If he was in any sense a Calvinist, it was of a mitigated type. The title of Opportunist, which Father Sydney Smith fixes on Wharton and Sampson, would suit Goodrich and Barlow quite as well. But even Cranmer and Ridley, though they eventually went very far in agreement with the Helvetic reformers, were only beginning that phase of their development in the early months of 1550. To call them at this period "unmitigated Calvinists" is to fly in the face of history.[3] Of Ferrar's opinions very

---

[1] *Original Letters*, I. p 76.

[2] See his curious *Dialoge*, published in 1531 and again in 1553, and in particular the Preface of 1553. It has been reprinted with an introduction by the Rev. J. R. Lunn, 1897. In 1559 Melanchthon commended him to Elizabeth, and the Markgraf of Brandenburg described him as "attached to the Confession of Augsburg" *State Papers, For.* Elizabeth, 1558-9, pp 109, 154.

[3] Two years later, Martin Micronius was complaining to Bullinger of Ridley's "worldly policy" and opposition to reform *Orig. Lett* II, p. 580.

INTERPRETATION OF THE ENGLISH ORDINAL 315

little is known. Such were the men whom Father Sydney Smith speaks of as "Cranmer's solid phalanx of five." On the same side were three others, of whom it is allowed that one at least was no heretic. But why are Wharton and Sampson suspect? Both retained their sees unchallenged under Mary; Wharton was at once promoted to Hereford. Of the eight bishops who voted for the new Ordinal, four were orthodox enough for Mary and her advisers. If these are rightly to be called the authors of the rite, what is meant by attributing the authorship exclusively to Cranmer and his adherents?

But Father Sydney Smith slips from the word "authors" to the word "compilers." The vote in Parliament merely determined in general that there should be a new Ordinal. The drafting of the rite was committed to six prelates and six other learned men. These are the compilers from whose minds the Ordinal, he says, received its meaning. Who then were they? We are met with the difficulty that little is known about them. Internal evidence, as well as the overwhelming balance of probability, makes it practically certain that Cranmer was one of them. We know that Heath was another. Who the other ten were is unknown. How then can we infer from their unknown minds the true meaning of the Ordinal? Conjecture has been busy, which, however, is nothing more than conjecture. It has been suggested—and Father Sydney Smith leans to the suggestion—that the same men were appointed who fifteen months before had deliberated on the Book of Common Prayer. But these were thirteen in number, not twelve, and Heath was not among

316 A ROMAN DIARY AND OTHER DOCUMENTS

them. The conjecture is, therefore, a doubtful one.[1] But if the actual persons are unknown, can we safely conjecture anything as to the composition of the committee in general? A study of the practice of the time leaves no room for doubt that all parties were represented. " But in any case," says Father Sydney Smith, "as they were appointed by the Council in which Somerset's and Cranmer's opinions ruled, they must have been predominantly Calvinist in their sentiments."[2] Looseness of statement dogs him on this occasion, for Somerset had fallen from power three months previously, and certainly had no voice in the appointment. That the majority of the committee belonged to the reforming party is likely enough, but we know that care was taken, on all such occasions, to include a fair number of the more conservative bishops.[3] To the twelve men thus appointed the text of the new Ordinal was submitted, and within a week eleven of them subscribed it as approved. Among these, we have reason to believe, were men of unquestioned orthodoxy. If then "the Ordinal received its meaning from the minds of its compilers," we have to reckon with these orthodox members of the committee. We need not suppose that they had their own way

[1] It is supported by Canon Dixon, who supposes Heath to have been substituted for Day, and Cranmer to be added, as president, to the twelve. *Hist.*, vol. ii. p. 493, and vol. iii. p. 195.

[2] *Month*, p. 233.

[3] The "Windsor Commission," which drew up the *Order of Communion* and the Book of Common Prayer, included seven bishops, of whom Cranmer, Ridley and Holbeach were of the reforming party, Thirlby, Skyp and Day were conservative, while Goodrich may, perhaps, be called indifferent. In April, 1549, a commission to inquire against heretics was appointed on exactly the same lines. The bishops were Cranmer, Ridley and Holbeach, Thirlby, Heath and Day, with Goodrich. *Rymer*, xv. 181.

INTERPRETATION OF THE ENGLISH ORDINAL 317

in all things, but at least the Ordinal does not stand for anything to which they could not subscribe.[1] It cannot, then, be taken as excluding the idea of the Catholic priesthood. Whatever Cranmer's own proclivities were, he had his colleagues to consider In this connexion Father Sydney Smith makes a bold assertion. "The text," he says, "to which they assented is hardly more than an English translation of an ordination rite composed by Bucer."[2] But of what does Bucer's rite consist? It begins with the hymn *Veni Sancte Spiritus.* Then follow three psalms, and two lessons from the New Testament. The "principal Ordainer" then reads an exhortation to the ordinands, and a prayer for the outpouring of the Holy Ghost upon them, and proceeds to the imposition of hands with a benediction resembling nothing that was ever used in the Church. There is no *Veni Creator*, no Litany; there is no use of what were then regarded as the crucial words, *Accipe Spiritum Sanctum.* There is only a single rite; three orders of ministers are nominally recognized, but all alike are called *presbyters*, and the form of ordination is the same for all. A curiously distorted imagination is needed to see in the English Ordinal "hardly more than a translation" of this.[3] It may be that something was

---

[1] On Heath's refusal to subscribe, see below, p 324.

[2] *Month*, p 233 Bucer's proposed rite of ordination is included in his treatise *De ordinatione legitima ministrorum revocanda*, which is printed in his *Scripta Anglicana*, pp 238–259. Basel, 1577.

[3] The elements common to Bucer's rite and the Ordinal are as follows His three Psalms, 40, 132, 135, are those appointed in the Ordinal for the "Introit to the Communion" His lessons appear among those appointed in the Ordinal for Epistle and Gospel. His exhortation is practically the same as that in our ordination of priests. His prayer before the imposition of hands is a longer, and in some

318 A ROMAN DIARY AND OTHER DOCUMENTS

borrowed from Bucer by the compilers of the Ordinal; but if so, their divergence from him is the more significant. Either Cranmer himself and his adherents did not agree with him, or else, agreeing with him in theory, they found it necessary to conciliate their colleagues by differing widely from him in practice. The more we suppose Cranmer to have agreed with Bucer, the greater weight we must assign to the influence of his orthodox colleagues, and the more we must take their opinions into account as determining the sense of the Ordinal.

But all this is in the region of pure conjecture, or of doubtful inference. We can find here no stable ground on which to build an argument. I think I have proved my first point. Cranmer and his adherents were in no sense the sole authors of the Ordinal; as for its compilers, since we do not know who they were, we cannot infer its meaning from their real or supposed opinions.

I contend, further, that the compilers, whoever they may have been, were incapable of imposing their own meaning upon the Ordinal. They were not, in the strict sense, authors. They were not composing a theological treatise originating with themselves. Their action was purely ministerial, and if the words which they wrote need any external interpretation, it must be sought not from them, but from those for whom they were acting. We cannot

---

respects a superior recension of the prayer *Almighty God and Heavenly Father* in the same rite. On the other hand his formula for use at the imposition of hands runs thus "Manus Dei omnipotentis, Patris, et Filii, et Spiritus Sancti, sit super vos, protegat et gubernet vos, ut eatis, et fructum vestro ministerio quam plurimum afferatis, isque maneat in vitam aeternam,"

INTERPRETATION OF THE ENGLISH ORDINAL 319

determine the sense of the Ordinal by investigating the opinions of its compilers. A judge, when called upon to interpret an Act of Parliament, might as well summon the draftsman and interrogate him as to his opinions on the subject-matter of the Act. We may carry the analogy further. The private opinions of the Members of Parliament who vote for a Bill, or even of the ministers in charge of it, will not affect the interpretation of the resulting Act. Mr. Balfour is known to be in favour of female suffrage, but that would not affect the interpretation of a doubtful passage in a Registration Act carried through Parliament under his leadership. Father Sydney Smith seems to rely on a criterion of this kind. He complains that we wish the language of the Ordinal to be interpreted by the views of those who opposed it in Parliament, "rather than by those of Cranmer's solid phalanx of five who were on the victorious side." He has an elaborate sneer at this:—
"Some day, perhaps, our judges may rule that Acts of Parliament, though carried by the votes of the Government in the teeth of fierce opposition, should be interpreted always in a sense consistent with the views of the Opposition; but until this new ruling is made, it is surely more according to established precedents that we should interpret the Edwardian Ordinal by the opinions of Cranmer than by those of Heath and Tunstall."[1]

He could hardly have chosen a more unfortunate illustration. The sense of a Statute is not determined in this fashion. It may very well happen that an Act, when interpreted by the judges, will disappoint the

[1] *Month*, p. 233.

320 A ROMAN DIARY AND OTHER DOCUMENTS

intention of its promoters and will serve the ends of those who were in opposition. For an instance, we have only to look at the Education Act of 1870. It was warmly supported by Churchmen: it was fiercely opposed by Dissenters. According to Father Sydney Smith it ought always to be interpreted in a sense favourable to Churchmen. We may wish he were right in this instance; but the instance only shows how egregiously he is wrong. It illustrates the hollowness of his contention that we are bound to interpret the Ordinal by the opinions or the intention of Cranmer.

But further, it is here that Father Sydney Smith, as I have said, misses the point of an argument advanced on our side. No one has ever suggested anything so absurd as that the Ordinal should be interpreted by the opinions of Heath and Tunstall or of the rest who voted with them in the minority. The argument is that account should be taken, not only of those who voted for a new rite, still less of those only who went all lengths with Cranmer, but of the English episcopate as a whole. The fact has been continually pressed that although there was some opposition when the change was first mooted, yet the new Ordinal was at once adopted and brought into use by the English episcopate.[1] Father Sydney Smith demurs to the use of any such phrase. "It seems to mean," he says, "that Convocation passed the measure; and yet it is morally certain that Convocation never had any say at all in the Ordinal of 1550."[2] But surely

[1] The final adoption of the Ordinal dates from 1559, for which see above, p. 124. But here we are considering its meaning as a ritual composition, and for that we must go back to its origin

[2] *Month,* p. 231.

INTERPRETATION OF THE ENGLISH ORDINAL 321

Father Sydney Smith is aware that bishops can act otherwise than synodically. When, indeed, had they ever acted synodically in dealing with such matters? In the whole history of Ecclesiastical Councils down to the year 1662 there cannot be found a single synodical act regulating the rites and ceremonies of Ordination. All those employed in various parts of the Church were grounded on usage; theoretically they were based on the authority of the bishops using them. Certain English bishops, exercising the same authority, adopted the new Ordinal. We must not indeed forget that it was enjoined by an Act of Parliament; we must allow that in all probability most of them disliked the new rite exceedingly, adopting it only under pressure from without; we know that they got rid of it with alacrity, as soon as the external pressure was withdrawn; but we are concerned with their public action, not with their motives, and as a matter of fact they did adopt the Ordinal and bring it into use. It was they who gave to the Ordinal its ecclesiastical sanction.

Who were the men who did this? We stand at the beginning of the year 1550. There were at that time twenty-four bishops in actual possession of their sees; for Gloucester and Norwich had just become vacant, while Gardiner of Winchester and Bonner of London were in prison. Of these twenty-four, *six* have been accused, rightly or wrongly, of heresy about the Sacraments.[1] Of the remaining eighteen it may suit Father Sydney

---

[1] Cranmer, Ridley, Ferrar, Barlow, Holbeach, and Goodrich. But of these six, Holbeach and Goodrich were not accused during their lifetime, and Barlow, though accused, was acquitted.

Y

322 A ROMAN DIARY AND OTHER DOCUMENTS

Smith to call some "Opportunists," but they were never accused of heresy, and five of them he himself describes as "notable for their firm adherence to the Catholic doctrine."[1] Such was the episcopate which accepted the Ordinal and brought it into use. It is not known how many of these bishops actually used the new rite. Many of the records have perished, and Mr. Frere has shown that ordinations were in a great measure confined to some few convenient centres.[2] But we know that some of them used it, and among these were King of Oxford, whose orthodoxy has never been impeached, and Thirlby and Aldrich, who are among those "notable for their firm adherence to the Catholic doctrine."[3] Of more importance it is to observe that the Ordinal was brought into general use without protest and without question. Doubtless it was unwelcome; yet the opponents of the reform could only muster five bishops to vote against it in the House of Lords. Once it was carried, all opposition ceased. The majority of the bishops must have adopted the Ordinal in a Catholic sense.

Did they do this only as individuals? Did the sense vary with the user? Did the Ordinal bear an orthodox sense when Aldrich used it in the diocese of Carlisle, an heretical sense when Ridley ordained in London? The suggestion is not, perhaps, entirely absurd: let us consider it.

The Church of England is not of course a single

---

[1] *Month*, p. 232.

[2] *The Marian Reaction*, pp. 101-3.

[3] For King and Thirlby, see Frere, *ibid.* pp. 95, 105, 193. Aldrich was one of the consecrators of Harley in May, 1553. Stubbs, *Reg. Sacr. Angl.* p. 81 (first edition).

INTERPRETATION OF THE ENGLISH ORDINAL 323

corporate body, but it has a certain unity and homogeneity. To the Church of England as a whole the Ordinal was propounded, and by the Church of England as a whole it was adopted. It was a public document of the Church of England. Now it is a fixed rule for the interpretation of public documents that they are to be understood, not in any esoteric sense which the words may bear, but in the sense in which the words are generally used by the community.

I have said that the sense of the Ordinal must be sought not from the compilers, but from those for whom they acted ministerially. For whom did they act? They acted for the Church of England as a whole. The sense of the Ordinal, then, is the general sense of the Church of England as then existing. Those who introduced it necessarily put upon it that general sense, not any private esoteric meaning of their own. The Ordinal contained familiar words, and they were taken in the familiar sense. When a bishop ordained a priest in the autumn of 1549, and again ordained a priest in the spring of 1550, using on the second occasion a new rite introduced with the express intent that the order of priesthood "should be *continued*, and reverently used, and esteemed, in this Church of England,"[1] we are bound to suppose that these two acts were taken in the same sense by the bishop, by the subject of the ordination, and by the Church at large. We should require overwhelming evidence to prove the contrary, and evidence there is none. Nay, there is evidence on our side. The Venetian Daniele Barbaro, who was in England as

[1] Preface to the Ordinal of 1550.

324 A ROMAN DIARY AND OTHER DOCUMENTS

Envoy of the Republic, wrote of the new rite for conferring holy orders, " Nor do they differ from those of the Roman Catholic religion save that in England they take oath to renounce the doctrine and authority of the Pope."[1] It is strange to observe with what persistent silence those who attack the Ordinal pass over this testimony of Barbaro.

But we shall be reminded that Heath refused to sign the Ordinal. He was one of the twelve commissioners appointed to issue it, and he refused to put his name to the book. Here then is at least one bishop who protested. Father Sydney Smith makes the most of his witness :—" He absolutely refused to subscribe it on grounds of conscience, and preferred rather to be imprisoned and eventually deprived of his see. One would have thought that by such action he showed sufficiently his dissent from the doctrine of the new rite, and yet, just because he was weak enough to promise his passive obedience, which as a matter of fact he was never in a position to render, he is claimed, as we have seen, as one of the compilers whose opinions, even in preference to those of Cranmer, the rite he refused to sign must be held to express."[2]

This is skilful advocacy, which it is not difficult, however, to knock to pieces. In the first place, there is nothing whatever in the record about "grounds of conscience" for Heath's original

---

[1] Rawdon Brown, *Venetian State Papers*, vol v p 349. Daniele Barbaro became Patriarch of Aquileia in 1550

[2] *Month*, p. 233. The details of Heath's case will be found in Pocock's *Burnet*, vol. iii. pp 339–40, and Dasent's *Acts of the Privy Council*, vol iii. p 360 Also in *Estcourt*, App. x pp. xxix–xxxi. See also *Dixon*, vol. iii pp. 196, 322.

INTERPRETATION OF THE ENGLISH ORDINAL 325

refusal to subscribe, nor is there any evidence of "dissent from the doctrine of the new rite." On the contrary, it is recorded in the minutes of the Privy Council that on February 28 he was ordered to sign the book, "specially for that he cannot deny but all that is contained in the book is good and godly." That throws no light on his private opinion, but it shows that he had not based his refusal on the grounds supposed. On March 4 he was committed to the Fleet for refusing to subscribe. Eighteen months afterwards he was brought again before the Council and ordered to sign the book on pain of deprivation of his bishopric; and like a man of spirit, "hearing that commandment, he resolutely answered he could not find in his conscience to do it." In the second place, it was not merely on this account that he faced his deprivation. During his eighteen months' imprisonment events had marched apace, and he knew well that if he yielded this point there were others that he could not yield. "There be many other things," he said, "whereunto he would not consent, if he were demanded, as to take down altars and set up tables." In the third place, it was not only "*passive* obedience" that he promised. By promising obedience he meant that he would use the book. "He would obey it, but not subscribe it." Why should this be put down to weakness, when he was so sturdy on the less important point of subscribing? We cannot suppose that Heath, who was ready to suffer for his principles, would have consented to "obey" the book, if he had dissented from its doctrine. He disliked it, perhaps, intensely, but the evidence shows that

326 A ROMAN DIARY AND OTHER DOCUMENTS

he received it in a Catholic sense. We claim this witness for our side.

One other argument may be glanced at, which Father Sydney Smith is too good a theologian to use, though others may. The same bishops who adopted the Ordinal afterwards rejected it, and in some cases reordained the men whom they had themselves promoted with its rites.[1] How then could they believe in it? The answer is not far to seek. There is no evidence to show why these men were reordained. Various grounds for such a course are familiar to theologians. One out of many is the invalidity of the rite used in the first ordination. The bishops who reordained men in 1554 may conceivably have thought the rite which they had formerly used an invalid one; but there is no evidence to show that such was their opinion. Nor, if there were evidence, would it concern the present issue. We are not considering here the validity of the rite; we are considering the meaning of its terms. When King of Oxford in 1554 reordained men whom he had ordained by the English rite in 1552, he may possibly have come to the conclusion that he had been using an invalid rite, but we are perfectly certain that he meant precisely the same thing on both occasions.

Our claim, then, is that in the interpretation of the Ordinal we are bound to follow the general sense of the Church of England, as it was in 1550. We are not concerned with the sense of the English Church, or the consent of English theologians, in 1580 or in 1850. We are concerned with the year of origin. It is worse than useless to bring into

---

[1] See Frere, *The Marian Reaction*, pp. 118–121.

INTERPRETATION OF THE ENGLISH ORDINAL 327

evidence, either on the one side or on the other, opinions that have been current since or are current now. They cannot affect the meaning of a document which was propounded to the Church and accepted by the Church at that specific time. The words of the Ordinal mean what they meant in 1550; and in 1550 they bore the meaning which was attached to them by the general sense of the English Church. What was that meaning? Can there be any doubt? The Church of England was then using a service book which spoke of "Mass" and "Altar."[1] Every member of the Church had been brought up in the old doctrines of the priesthood and the sacrifice. Helvetic and Lutheran opinions had been within four years ruthlessly persecuted by all in authority. Persecution had ceased, but the old doctrinal standards were as yet untouched. Some few men of mark in the Church were venturing to question the received belief, but they did so, in public at least, with caution.[2] In the Church at

---

[1] In March, 1550, Hooper wrote to Bullinger about the Prayerbook: "I am so much offended with that book, and that not without abundant reason, that if it be not corrected, I neither will nor can communicate with the Church in the administration of the Supper" *Orig. Lett.* I, p. 79. He overcame his scruples afterwards, but things were then moving rapidly towards the correction that he desired.

[2] The testimony of the witnesses at Gardiner's trial in 1551, as to what was then the authorized and current teaching of the Church and realm of England, is of great interest. It may be seen condensed in Dixon, *Hist.*, Vol. III. pp 110, 268. The general effect is that none of the old teaching was even impugned until Peter Martyr began his lectures at Oxford in the year 1549. The *Necessary Doctrine* or "King's Book" of 1543 was still the legal standard of teaching Hooper wrote in the above quoted letter that he feared Ridley's promotion to London might cause some change in his conduct. "I can scarcely express to you," he says, "under what difficulties and dangers we are labouring and struggling that the idol of the mass may be thrown out" He had been lecturing on St John's Gospel, and says, "I incurred great odium, and not less danger, from

328 A ROMAN DIARY AND OTHER DOCUMENTS

large, among clergy and laity alike, innovation was hardly begun. To such a public as this was propounded a rite for the ordination of " Bishops " and " Priests." There was only one sense in which it could be received.

In Cardinal Vaughan's *Vindication* of the Papal Bull concerning Anglican Orders there is an admirable sentence which I quote with great pleasure in this connexion. It has often been pointed out in controversy that the older Roman rite of ordination does not contain any reference to the sacrifice, nor even the specific term *sacerdos*. It has only the ambiguous *presbyter*. The Cardinal replies to this : " Words take their meaning from the communities in which they are used. Now in the Catholic Church the terms 'priest' and 'bishop' have always had a sacrificial meaning."[1] Precisely so ; words take their meaning from the communities in which they are used, and at the time when the Ordinal was introduced, whatever may have been the case at other times, in this community of the Church of England the words " bishop " and " priest " bore the specific meaning which they had borne for ages in the Catholic Church.

---

the sixth chapter." Of the new Ordinal in particular he wrote " I have sent it to Master Butler, that you may know their fraud and artifices, by which they promote the kingdom of antichrist, especially in the form of the oath." In the following June he writes that Cranmer "is not so decided as I could wish, and dares not, I fear, assert his opinion in all respects." *Orig Lett.* I, pp 79, 80, 81, 89.

[1] *Vindication*, p. 47.

GREGORY IX
AND GREEK ORDINATIONS

XII

GREGORY IX
AND GREEK ORDINATIONS

*(A Paper Written for the Church Historical Society
in the year 1898.)*

MUCH has been said about the unalterable
character of Papal decisions regarding the
sacraments. Some of these have been ambigu-
ously expressed, and have lent themselves readily
to varied explanations. Others there are which
appear on the surface clear and definite, but the
apparent force of which has been attenuated, or
even reversed, by the advancing knowledge of
theologians. There is one of the thirteenth century which has never, I believe, exercised the in-
genuity of commentators.

In the year 1231 the Archbishop of Bari was
troubled in mind about the Greeks, who were probably numerous in his Apulian province. They used
a form in baptism which seemed to him of doubtful
validity. He was not sure about their confirmation,
administered with the holy chrism by simple priests.
They used a kind of corporal, blessed by a bishop,
in place of a portable altar-stone, when saying
Mass in places unprovided with a duly consecrated
altar. Worst of all, there were some who, after so
doubtful a baptism, had procured for themselves

331

332 A ROMAN DIARY AND OTHER DOCUMENTS

holy orders, and were professing to exercise the priesthood. In his perplexity the Archbishop appealed to the reigning Pontiff, Gregory IX. The Pope replied to him, resolving his doubts, in a letter which deserves to be quoted entire. I borrow the text from M. Auvray's edition of the *Registers of Gregory IX* :—

"Consultationi tue breviter respondemus quod Greci qui sub hac forma verborum : *baptizetur talis in nomine Patris, et Filii, et Spiritus Sancti,* baptizati ab aliquo extiterunt, non sunt, cum non fuerint secundum formam evangelicam, baptizati, et ideo tam illos quam de cetero baptizandos sub hac forma : *ego te baptizo in nomine Patris et Filii et Spiritus Sancti,* precipimus baptizari. Eos autem qui extra tempora constituta sacros ordines receperunt, caracterem non est dubium recepisse, quos pro transgressione huiusmodi prius eis penitentia imposita competenti, sustinere poteris in susceptis ordinibus ministrare, attentius provisurus ut id de cetero fieri in tua provincia non permittas. Crismati vero, ut verbis tuis utamur, a simplici sacerdote confirmationis munus minime receperunt ; quia de solis apostolis legitur, quorum sunt episcopi successores, quod per manus impositionem Spiritum Sanctum dabant, et ideo tam illi quam confirmandi de cetero a solis episcopis consignentur. Illis quoque qui pro altari viatico utuntur panno lineo, a Greco episcopo benedicto, studeas firmiter inhibere ne in panno huiusmodi celebrare presumant ; sed id de cetero faciant, vel in altari itinerario, vel in altari maiori, secundum ritum Ecclesiae consecrato. Ad hec quia nonnulli, ut asseris, taliter baptizati se fecerunt et ad maiores et minores ordines pro-

GREGORY IX AND GREEK ORDINATIONS 333

moveri, nos, quod tutius est sequentes, eos primo secundum formam superius tibi traditam baptizatos per singulos ordines precipimus ordinari. "Dat. Reate. II. idus novembris, pontificatus nostri anno quinto."[1]

The letter is very clear, though it contains some things not easily accounted for. In the first place, the Greek baptisms are broadly declared invalid. Their *form* is defective. It is not, however, certain that Gregory IX knew what he was doing in this matter. His words, carefully weighed, suggest that he was unaware that the form which he condemns was invariably used by all the Greeks. He would seem to have thought it a mere occasional aberration. But, wherever it was used, he rules absolutely that no baptism was effected. He expresses no doubt; he leaves nothing vague. He does not merely charge the Greeks generally with using a defective form, or merely assert that no valid form is contained in their rite. He quotes the form used; he quotes it accurately, and he dogmatically declares it invalid. He lays it down as a dogmatic fact that such as are baptized in this form are not baptized at all.

---

[1] *Les Registres de Grégoire IX*, tome I, n 740 Published in the *Bibliothèque des écoles françaises d'Athènes et Rome*. An incomplete account of this epistle is given by Raynaldus in his continuation of Baronius. Under the year 1231 he records that the Archbishop of Bari consulted the Pope on three questions. the validity of holy orders conferred at forbidden times; the validity of confirmation conferred by a simple priest with the holy chrism; and the use of *antimensia* He quotes at length the parts of the letter dealing with these three questions, but passes over in silence the first sentence and the last, in which the Greek baptisms and ordinations are dealt with, adding the date immediately after the words, *secundum ritum Ecclesiae consecrato*, as if the letter there ended (Raynaldi, *Annales*, anno 1231, cap. 30.)

334 A ROMAN DIARY AND OTHER DOCUMENTS

Can we determine the ground on which he so decided? About forty years afterwards St. Thomas discussed in the *Summa* this same question. He argues (P. iii. qu. 66, art. 5) that the minister ought to be mentioned (*significari*) in the form of baptism. There are two causes of baptism—the principal, which is the Holy Trinity, and the instrumental, which is the minister—and both ought to be mentioned. The minister is mentioned in the words *Ego te baptizo.* He allows, however, the sufficiency of the Greek form, on the ground that "quia exprimitur actus exercitus per ministrum cum invocatione Trinitatis, verum perficitur sacramentum." This defence of the Greek form was adopted almost verbally by Eugenius IV at Florence in the *Decretum pro Armenis* :—" Quoniam cum principalis causa ex qua baptismus virtutem habet sit Sancta Trinitas, instrumentalis autem sit minister qui tradit exterius sacramentum, si exprimitur actus qui per ipsum exercetur ministrum, cum Sanctae Trinitatis invocatione, perficitur sacramentum."

St. Thomas, in requiring mention of the minister, was following the traditional teaching of the schools ; but by his time, the baptism of the Greeks being in practice allowed as good, a certain modification was necessarily imported. Forty years previously Gregory IX, insisting perhaps more rigidly on this requirement, ruled out all Greek baptisms as invalid. He wrote, indeed, as if he supposed the form *Ego te baptizo* to be actually prescribed in the Gospel.

Was the Pope indeed ignorant of the Greek use, or did he purposely ignore it in pursuance of a

GREGORY IX AND GREEK ORDINATIONS 335

policy of repression? He goes on to condemn the practice of conferring holy orders at other than the appointed times, without seeming to be aware that he is insisting on a purely Western custom. In the same way he condemns the use of *antimensia*, the specially consecrated linen cloths with which the Greeks have immemorially supplied the lack of a consecrated altar. So, too, he treats the Greek mode of confirmation as if it were an altogether unheard-of novelty.[1] Lastly, he deals with Greek ordinations. Here, again, he assumes that what we know to have been universal was only individual and eccentric. *Some*, he says, have been advanced to holy or lesser orders after a baptism of the kind which he has condemned. Even this statement is founded on the bare assertion of the Archbishop of Bari. Such men, the Pope says, are to be first baptized properly and then ordained afresh. His definition of dogmatic fact invalidates in reality all Greek ordinations whatever. He appears, indeed, to base his decision on tutiorist grounds. If we could read his words—*quod tutius est sequentes*—in the sense which they would bear in a seventeenth-century document, it would follow that he expressed only a doubt as to the validity of these ordinations, which would involve, according to later usage, a conditional reordination. But to read these refine-

---

[1] Here, again, it is interesting to compare what is said by Eugenius IV. He echoes the very words of Gregory IX—"De solis apostolis legitur, quorum vices tenent episcopi, quod per manus impositionem Spiritum Sanctum dabant;" but by an ingenious turn the Eastern custom is rendered tolerable —"Legitur tamen aliquando *per apostolicae sedis dispensationem* ex rationabili et urgente admodum causa simplicem sacerdotem chrismate per episcopum confecto hoc administrasse confirmationis sacramentum." The Oriental use depends upon a presumed Papal dispensation.

336 A ROMAN DIARY AND OTHER DOCUMENTS

ments into a thirteenth-century document would be a gross anachronism; and further, it would involve the intolerable consequence that a man who was certainly unbaptized might possibly be validly ordained. Gregory IX, whether he meant it or not, whether he knew it or not, laid down a dogmatic definition which excludes the possibility of valid ordinations in the Greek Church.

As history shows, this position was not sustained by the Popes who succeeded him. Yet Gregory IX was no ordinary Pontiff. He was one of the greatest in the great constructive period of the Papacy. How came he to give such a decision? How came it to be so speedily ignored? If we had only his prohibition of ordinations apart from the appointed seasons and of the use of *antimensia*, we might see in his letter merely a determination not to allow Greek customs to get a foothold in the West. He bids the Archbishop take care not to permit anything of the kind for the future *in his province*. But the rest of his decision touches graver matters. He is dealing precisely with those three sacraments which confer character; and he denies to the Greeks the real character alike of baptism, of confirmation, and of holy orders. Why this? In the year 1231 the Greek Church was barely emerging from the lowest depth of depression. A Latin emperor was still seated on the throne of Constantinople; it was still open to a Pope to dream of latinizing the Eastern Church. At the same time, in Southern Italy, Frederick II was using Greeks and Saracens alike in his bitter contest with the Papacy. Greeks were in special ill odour at Rome, and their ecclesiastical standing

GREGORY IX AND GREEK ORDINATIONS 337

was of the weakest. But it would be unjust to attribute to Gregory IX a motive of mere policy. We need not suppose him free from prejudice. Prejudice may help to account for the tone of his letter ; but, as regards the substance, we have no reason to doubt that he honestly decided according to his knowledge of the truth that was in him. But in practice the decision was speedily reversed. Events and opinions marched apace. Within thirty years the Latin dynasty of Constantinople was ended. The Emperor Michael Palaeologus was only too ready to fortify his uncertain throne by the friendship of the Pope. The Swabian danger had passed away, and the Popes on their side were ready to listen to overtures from the Greeks. The rapid growth of systematic theology furnished explanations which tended to remove the differences dividing Christians, and the first of many abortive schemes of reunion was attempted. In 1274 Gregory X received the Greeks into communion. From that time forward it was practically impossible to impugn their sacraments.

The decision of Gregory IX was thus robbed of all lasting effect. It would be interesting to speculate on what would have followed if this letter, instead of slumbering in the Papal archives, had been published to the world, and so had contributed to the formation of practice and opinion. A small part of it—the part relating to the time for ordination—was incorporated by Raymond of Peñaforte in the Decretals.[1] If the whole of the letter, or the part of it

---

[1] Lib. i. tit 11, *de temp ordin.* c. 16. This was quite regular. He followed the ordinary method of the compilers of such codes, extracting from various decretal letters of the Popes such sentences only as bore upon the subjects to be treated. If it be asked why he did not

z

338 A ROMAN DIARY AND OTHER DOCUMENTS

relating to baptism, had in the same way been made public, it would certainly have been quoted by St. Thomas in his article on the form of baptism, where he does actually quote a decretal of Alexander III of similar tendency. In that case he could not have defended the validity of Greek baptisms. They would have been put aside as unquestionably invalid. Where, then, would have been the Greeks at Lyons, at Vienne, at Florence? Their presence there may have done little good, but it did at least keep alive the idea of union, the conception of a Christendom which was not wholly Latin. If the validity of Greek sacraments had been formally denied, the chasm between East and West would have been made broader and more impassable, the Western idea of the Church would have become still narrower than it actually was. Christendom was spared this further evil, because a decretal epistle of Gregory IX lay forgotten in the registers of the Vatican.

use, in dealing with baptism, the important decision upon the form of baptism given in this letter, the answer is that he had ready to his hand a decision given by an earlier Pope, the decretal of Alexander III mentioned in the text, which seemed effectually to cover the same ground. He cites this as follows (Lib. III tit. 42. *de bapt.* c. 1). "Si quis puerum ter in aqua immerserit in nomine Patris, et Filii, et Spiritus Sancti, amen, et non dixerit : *ego te baptizo in nomine Patris, et Filii, et Spiritus Sancti, amen,* non est puer baptizatus." Equally with Gregory IX, Alexander III regarded the words *ego te baptizo* as essential ; but, as he did not specifically declare the Greek form invalid, his decretal did not bar the way to an explanation which allowed the validity of Greek baptisms. Yet there can be little doubt that the compiler and his contemporaries would have taken it in the most rigorous sense. The only modification allowed by the Gloss of Bernard of Parma (died 1263) is the omission of the word *ego*, "quia plenum generat sensum haec vox *baptizo*, sine hoc pronomine *ego.*" St. Thomas (*loc. cit.*), quoting the decretal, says that the "actus baptismi" is expressed "vel per modum nostrum vel per modum Graecorum."

ated use only.
APPENDICES

APPENDIX I

Sanctissimi Domini nostri Leonis, divina Providentia Papae XIII Litterae Apostolicae de Ordinationibus Anglicanis.

LEO EPISCOPVS, Servus Servorum Dei, ad Perpetuam rei Memoriam.

APOSTOLICAE curae et caritatis, qua *pastorem magnum ovium, Dominum nostrum Iesum Christum*,[1] referre pro munere et imitari, aspirante eius gratia, studemus, non exiguam partem pernobili Anglorum nationi tribuimus Voluntatis in ipsam Nostrae testis in primis est epistola, quam superiore anno propriam dedimus *ad Anglos regnum Christi in fidei unitate quaerentes* · eiusdem quippe gentis et veterem cum Ecclesia matre coniunctionem commemorando revocavimus, et felicem reconciliationem, excitata in animis orandi Dei sollertia, contendimus maturare. Rursusque haud ita pridem, quum communibus universe litteris de unitate Ecclesiae fusius agere visum est, non ultimo loco respeximus Angliam ; spe praelucente, posse documenta Nostra tum catholicis firmitatem tum dissidentibus salutare lumen afferre Atque illud fateri libet, quod aeque gentis humanitatem ac multorum sollicitudinem salutis aeternae commendat, id est quam benevole Anglis probata sit instantia Nostra et dicendi libertas, nullo quidem acta humanae rationis impulsu. Nunc autem eâdem Nos mente eodemque animo deliberatum habemus studia convertere ad quamdam non minoris momenti causam, quae cum ea ipsa re votisque Nostris cohaeret.

[1] Heb. XIII. 20.

342 A ROMAN DIARY AND OTHER DOCUMENTS

Quod enim apud Anglos, aliquanto postquam ab unitatis christianae centro abscessum est, novus plane ritus ordinibus sacris conferendis, sub rege Eduardo VI, fuit publice inductus; defecisse idcirco verum Ordinis sacramentum, quale Christus instituit, simulque hierarchicam successionem, iam tenuit communis sententia, quam non semel Ecclesiae acta et constans disciplina firmarunt. Attamen recentiore memoria hisque maxime annis invaluit controversia, sacraene Ordinationes ritu eduardiano peractae, natura sacramenti effectuque polleant; faventibus, affirmate vel dubitanter, non modo scriptoribus anglicanis nonnullis, sed paucis etiam catholicis praesertim non anglis. Alteros quippe movebat praestantia sacerdotii christiani, exoptantes ut duplici eius in corpus Christi potestate ne carerent sui; movebat alteros consilium expediendi quodam modo illis reditus ad unitatem : utrisque vero hoc persuasum esse videbatur, iam studiis in eo genere cum aetate provectis, novisque litterarum monumentis ex oblivione erutis, retractari auctoritate Nostra causam non inopportunum fore. Nos autem ea consilia atque optata minime negligentes, maximeque voci obsequentes apostolicae caritatis, censuimus nihil non experiri quod videretur quoquo modo conducere ad animarum vel avertenda damna vel utilitates fovendas.

Placuit igitur de retractanda causa benignissime indulgere : ita sane, ut per summam novae disquisitionis sollertiam, omnis in posterum vel species quidem dubitandi esset remota. Quapropter certo numero viris doctrina et eruditione praestantibus, quorum compertae erant dissimiles in ipsa causa opiniones, negotium dedimus ut momenta sententiae suae scriptis mandarent : eos deinde ad Nos accitos iussimus communicare inter se scripta, et quidquid eo amplius ad rem cognitu esset dignum, indagare atque expendere. Consultumque a Nobis est, ut ipsi diplomata opportuna omni possent copia in tabulariis vaticanis sive nota recognoscere sive inexplorata educere ; itemque ut prompta haberent quaecumque eiusdem generis acta apud sacrum Consilium, quod *Suprema* vocatur, asservarentur, neque minus quaecumque ad hoc tempus

APPENDIX I 343

doctiores viri in utramque partem evulgassent. Huiusmodi adiumentis instructos, voluimus eos in singulares
congressiones convenire ; quae ad duodecim sunt habitae,
praeside uno ex S. R. E. Cardinalibus a Nobismetipsis
designato, data singulis facultate disputandi libera. Denique earumdem congressionum acta, una cum ceteris
documentis, Venerabilibus Fratribus Nostris Cardinalibus
ex eodem Consilio iussimus exhiberi omnia ; qui meditatâ
causa eâque coram Nobis deinde agitata, suam quisque
sententiam dicerent.

Hoc ducendae rei ordine praestituto, ad intimam tamen
aestimationem causae aequum erat non ante aggredi,
quam id perstudiose quaesitum apparuisset, quo loco ea
iam esset secundum Apostolicae Sedis praescriptiones
institutamque consuetudinem ; cuius consuetudinis et
initia et vim magni profecto intererat reputare. Quocirca
in primis perpensa sunt documenta praecipua quibus Deces-
sores Nostri, rogatu reginae Mariae, singulares curas ad
reconciliationem ecclesiae Anglicae contulerunt. Nam
Iulius III Cardinalem Reginaldum Polum, natione Ang-
lum, multiplici laude eximium, Legatum a latere ad id
opus destinavit, *tamquam pacis et dilectionis Angelum
suum*, eique mandata seu facultates extra ordinem
normasque agendi tradidit [1]; quas deinde Paulus IV confirmavit et declaravit. In quo ut recte colligatur quidnam
in se commemorata documenta habeant ponderis, sic
oportet fundamenti instar statuere, eorum propositum
nequaquam a re abstractum fuisse, sed rei omnino
inhaerens ac peculiare. Quum enim facultates Legato
apostolico ab iis Pontificibus tributae, Angliam dumtaxat
religionisque in ea statum respicerent ; normae item
agendi ab eisdem eidem Legato quaerenti impertitae,
minime quidem esse poterant ad illa generatim decernenda
sine quibus sacrae ordinationes non valeant, sed debebant
attinere proprie ad providendum de ordinibus sacris in eo
regno, prout temporum monebant rerumque conditiones
expositae. Hoc ipsum, praeter quam quod ex natura et

[1] Id factum augusto mense MDLIII per litteras sub plumbo, *Si ullo
unquam tempore* et *Post nuntium Nobis*, atque alias.

344 A ROMAN DIARY AND OTHER DOCUMENTS

modo eorumdem documentorum perspicuum est, inde
pariter liquet, quod alienum prorsus fuisset, ita velle de iis
quae sacramento Ordinis conficiendo necesse sunt, pro-
pemodum commonefieri Legatum, eumque virum cuius
doctrina etiam in Concilio Tridentino eluxerat.

Ista probe tenentibus non difficulter patebit quare in
litteris Iulii III, ad Legatum apostolicum perscriptis die
VIII martii MDLIV, distincta sit mentio, de iis primum qui
rite et legitime promoti, in suis ordinibus essent retinendi,
tum de iis qui *non promoti ad sacros ordines*, possent, *si
digni et idonei reperti fuissent, promoveri.* Nam certe
definiteque notatur, ut reapse erat, duplex hominum
classis : hinc eorum qui sacram ordinationem vere susce-
pissent, quippe id vel ante Henrici secessionem, vel si
post eam et per ministros errore dissidiove implicitos, ritu
tamen catholico consueto ; inde aliorum qui initiati essent
secundum Ordinale eduardianum, qui propterea possent
promoveri, quia ordinationem accepissent irritam. Neque
aliud sane Pontificis consilium fuisse, praeclare confirmat
epistola eiusdem Legati (die XXIX ianuarii MDLV) facultates suas episcopo Norwicensi demandantis. Id amplius
est potissime considerandum quod eae ipsae Iulii III
litterae afferunt, de facultatibus pontificiis libere utendis,
etiam in eorum bonum quibus munus consecrationis
minus rite et non servata forma Ecclesiae consueta im-
pensum fuit : qua quidem locutione ii certe designabantur
qui consecrati eduardiano ritu, praeter eam namque et
catholicam formam alia nulla erat eo tempore in Anglia.

Haec autem apertiora fient commemorando legationem
quam Philippus et Maria reges, suadente Cardinali Polo,
Romam ad Pontificem februario mense MDLV miserunt.
Regii oratores, viri tres *admodum insignes et omni virtute
praediti*, in quibus Thomas Thirlby, episcopus Eliensis, sic
habebant propositum, Pontificem de conditione rei religiosae in eo regno notitia ampliore edocere, ab ipsoque
in primis petere ut ea quae Legatus ad eiusdem regni
cum Ecclesia reconciliationem curaverat atque effecerat,
haberet rata et confirmaret. eius rei causâ omnia ad
Pontificem allata sunt testimonia scripta quae oportebat,

APPENDIX I 345

partesque Ordinalis novi proxime ad rem facientes. Iam
vero Paulus IV, legatione magnifice admissa, eisque
testimoniis per certos aliquot Cardinales *diligenter dis-
cussis*, et *habita deliberatione matura*, litteras *Praeclara
carissimi* sub plumbo dedit die XX iunii eodem anno. In
his quum comprobatio plena et robur additum sit rebus a
Polo gestis, de ordinationibus sic est praescriptum · . . .
*qui ad ordines ecclesiasticos . . . ab alio quam ab episcopo
rite et recte ordinato promoti fuerunt, eosdem ordines . . . de
novo suscipere teneantur.* Quinam autem essent episcopi
tales, *non rite recteque ordinati,* satis iam indicaverant
superiora documenta, facultatesque in eam rem a Legato
adhibitae. ii nimirum qui ad episcopatum, sicut alii ad
alios ordines, promoti essent, *non servata forma Ecclesiae
consueta,* vel non servata *Ecclesiae forma et intentione,*
prout Legatus ipse ad episcopum Norwicensem scribebat.
Hi autem non alii profecto erant nisi qui promoti secundum novam ritualem formam, cui quoque examinandae
delecti Cardinales attentam operam dederant. Neque
praetermittendus est locus ex eisdem Pontificis litteris,
omnino rei congruens, ubi cum aliis beneficio dispensationis egentibus numerantur qui *tam ordines quam
beneficia ecclesiastica nulliter et de facto obtinuerant. Nulliter*
enim obtinuisse ordines idem est atque irrito actu nullo-
que effectu, videlicet *invalide,* ut ipsa monet eius vocis
notatio et consuetudo sermonis ; praesertim quum idem
pari modo affirmetur de ordinibus quod de *beneficiis
ecclesiasticis,* quae ex certis sacrorum canonum institutis
manifesto erant nulla, eo quia cum vitio infirmante collata.
Huc accedit quod, ambigentibus nonnullis quinam revera
episcopi, *rite et recte ordinati,* dici et haberi possent ad
mentem Pontificis, hic non multo post, die XXX octobris,
alias subiecit litteras in modum Brevis : atque, *Nos,*
inquit, *haesitationem huiusmodi tollere et serenitati conscientiae eorum qui schismate durante ad ordines promoti
fuerant, mentem et intentionem quam in eisdem litteris
Nostris habuimus clarius exprimendo, opportune consulere
volentes, declaramus eos tantum episcopos et archiepiscopos
qui non in forma Ecclesiae ordinati et consecrati fuerunt*

346 A ROMAN DIARY AND OTHER DOCUMENTS

rite et recte ordinatos dici non posse. Quae declaratio, nisi apposite ad rem Angliae praesentem, id est ad Ordinale eduardianum, spectare debuisset, nihil certe confecerat Pontifex novis litteris, quo vel *haesitatationem tolleret* vel *serenitati conscientiae consuleret.* Ceterum Apostolicae Sedis documenta et mandata non aliter Legatus intellexit, atque ita eis rite religioseque obtemperavit : idque pariter factum a regina Maria et a ceteris qui cum ea dederunt operam ut religio et instituta catholica in pristinum statum restituerentur.

Auctoritates quas excitavimus Iulii III et Pauli IV aperte ostendunt initia eius disciplinae quae tenore constanti, iam tribus amplius saeculis, custodita est, ut ordinationes ritu eduardiano, haberentur infectae et nullae ; cui disciplinae amplissime suffragantur testimonia multa earumdem ordinationum quae, in hac etiam Urbe, saepius absoluteque iteratae sunt ritu catholico. In huius igitur disciplinae observantia vis inest opportuna proposito. Nam si cui forte quidquam dubitationis resideat in quamnam vere sententiam ea Pontificum diplomata sint accipienda, recte illud valet : *Consuetudo optima legum interpres.* Quoniam vero firmum semper ratumque in Ecclesia manserit, Ordinis sacramentum nefas esse iterari, fieri nullo modo poterat ut talem consuetudinem Apostolica Sedes tacita pateretur ac toleraret. Atqui eam non toleravit solum, sed probavit etiam et sanxit ipsa, quotiescumque in eadem re peculiare aliquod factum incidit iudicandum. Duo eiusmodi facta in medium proferimus, ex multis quae ad Supremam sunt subinde delata : alterum (an. MDCLXXXIV) cuiusdam Calvinistae Galli, alterum (an. MDCCIV) Ioannis Clementis Gordon ; utriusque secundum rituale eduardianum suos adepti ordines. In primo, post exquisitam rei investigationem, Consultores non pauci responsa sua, quae appellant vota, de scripto ediderunt, ceterique cum eis in unam conspirarunt sententiam, *pro invaliditate ordinationis :* tantum quidem ratione habita opportunitatis, placuit Cardinalibus respondere, *Dilata.* Eadem vero acta repetita et ponderata sunt in facto altero : quaesita

APPENDIX I 347

sunt praeterea nova Consultorum vota, rogatique doctores egregii e Sorbonicis ac Duacenis, neque praesidium ullum perspicacioris prudentiae praetermissum est ad rem penitus pernoscendam, Atque hoc animadvertisse oportet quod, tametsi tum ipse Gordon cuius negotium erat, tum aliquot Consultores inter causas *nullitatis* vindicandae, etiam adduxissent illam prout putabatur ordinationem Parkerii, in sententia tamen ferenda omnino seposita est ea causa, ut documenta produnt integrae fidei, neque alia ratio est reputata nisi *defectus formae et intentionis*. Qua de forma quo plenius esset certiusque iudicium, cautum fuerat ut exemplar Ordinalis anglicani suppeteret ; atque etiam cum eo singulae collatae sunt formae ordinandi, ex variis orientalium et occidentalium ritibus conquisitae. Tum Clemens XI, Cardinalium ad quos pertinebat consentientibus suffragiis, ipsemet feria V, die XVII aprilis MDCCIV, *decrevit*. ".. Ioannes Clemens Gordon *ex integro et absolute* ordinetur ad omnes ordines etiam sacros et praecipue presbyteratus, et quatenus non fuerit confirmatus, prius sacramentum Confirmationis suscipiat." Quae sententia, id sane considerare refert, ne a defectu quidem *traditionis instrumentorum* quidquam momenti duxit : tunc enim praescriptum de more esset ut ordinatio *sub conditione* instauraretur. Eo autem pluris refert considerare, eamdem Pontificis sententiam spectare universe ad omnes Anglicanorum ordinationes. Licet enim factum attigerit peculiare, non tamen ex peculiari quapiam ratione profecta est, verum ex *vitio formae*, quo quidem vitio ordinationes illae aeque afficiuntur omnes : adeo ut, quoties deinceps in re simili decernendum fuit, toties idem Clementis XI communicatum sit decretum.

Quae quum ita sint, non videt nemo controversiam temporibus nostris exsuscitatam, Apostolicae Sedis iudicio definitam multo antea fuisse : documentisque illis haud satis quam oportuerat cognitis, fortasse factum ut scriptor aliquis catholicus disputationem de ea libere habere non dubitarit. Quoniam vero, ut principio, monuimus, nihil Nobis antiquius optatiusque est quam ut hominibus recte animatis maximâ possimus indulgentia et caritate pro-

348 A ROMAN DIARY AND OTHER DOCUMENTS

desse, ideo iussimus in Ordinale anglicanum, quod caput est totius causae, rursus quam studiosissime inquiri.

In ritu cuiuslibet sacramenti conficiendi et administrandi iure discernunt inter partem *caeremonialem* et partem *essentialem*, quae *materia et forma* appellari consuevit. Omnesque norunt, sacramenta novae legis, utpote signa sensibilia atque gratiae invisibilis efficientia, debere gratiam et significare quam efficiunt et efficere quam significant. Quae significatio, etsi in toto ritu essentiali, in materia scilicet et forma, haberi debet, praecipue tamen ad formam pertinet; quum materia sit pars per se non determinata et quae per illam determinetur. Idque in sacramento Ordinis manifestius apparet, cuius conferendi materia, quatenus hoc loco se dat considerandam, est manuum impositio; quae quidem nihil definitum per se significat, et aeque ad quosdam Ordines, aeque ad Confirmationem ursurpatur. Iamvero verba quae ad proximam usque aetatem habentur passim ab Anglicanis tamquam forma propria ordinationis presbyteralis, videlicet, *Accipe Spiritum Sanctum*, minime sane significant definite ordinem sacerdotii vel eius gratiam et potestatem, quae praecipue est potestas *consecrandi et offerendi verum corpus et sanguinem Domini*,[1] eo sacrificio, quod non est *nuda commemoratio sacrificii in Cruce peracti*.[2] Forma huiusmodi aucta quidem est postea iis verbis, *ad officium et opus presbyteri*: sed hoc potius convincit, Anglicanos vidisse ipsos primam eam formam fuisse mancam neque idoneam rei. Eadem vero adiectio, si forte quidem legitimam significationem apponere formae posset, serius est inducta, elapso iam saeculo post receptum Ordinale eduardianum, quum propterea, Hierarchiâ extincta, potestas ordinandi iam nulla esset. Nequidquam porro auxilium causae novissime arcessitum est ab aliis eiusdem Ordinalis precibus. Nam, ut cetera praetereantur quae eas demonstrent minus proposito sufficientes in ritu anglicano, unum hoc argumentum sit instar omnium, de ipsis consulto detractum esse quidquid in ritu catholico digni-

---

[1] Trid. Sess. XXIII, *de sacr. Ord. can*, 1.
[2] *Ib* Sess. XXII, *de sacrif Missae, can*, 3.

APPENDIX I 349

tatem et officia sacerdotii perspicue designat. Non ea igitur forma esse apta et sufficiens sacramento potest, quae id nempe reticet quod deberet proprium significare. De consecratione episcopali similiter est. Nam formulae, *Accipe Spiritum Sanctum*, non modo serius adnexa sunt verba, *ad officium et opus episcopi*, sed etiam de iisdem, ut mox dicemus, iudicandum aliter est quam in ritu catholico. Neque rei proficit quidquam advocasse praefationis precem, *Omnipotens Deus;* quum ea pariter deminuta sit verbis quae *summum sacerdotium* declarent. Sane nihil huc attinet explorare, utrum episcopatus complementum sit sacerdotii, an ordo ab illo distinctus : aut collatus, ut aiunt, *per saltum*, scilicet homini non sacerdoti, utrum effectum habeat necne. At is procul dubio, ex institutione Christi, ad sacramentum Ordinis verissime pertinet, atque est praecellenti gradu sacerdotium, quod nimirum et voce sanctorum Patrum et rituali nostra consuetudine *summum sacerdotium, sacri ministerii summa* nuncupatur. Inde fit ut, quoniam sacramentum Ordinis verumque Christi sacerdotium a ritu anglicano penitus extrusum est, atque adeo in consecratione episcopali eiusdem ritus nullo modo sacerdotium confertur, nullo item modo episcopatus vere ac iure possit conferri : eoque id magis quia in primis episcopatus muniis illud scilicet est, ministros ordinandi in sanctam Eucharistiam et sacrificium.

Ad rectam vero plenamque Ordinalis anglicani aestimationem, praeter ista per aliquas eius partes notata, nihil profecto tam valet quam si probe aestimetur quibus adiunctis rerum conditum sit et publice constitutum. Longum est singula persequi, neque est necessarium : eius namque aetatis memoria satis diserte loquitur, cuius animi essent in Ecclesiam catholicam auctores Ordinalis, quos adsciverint fautores ab heterodoxis sectis, quo demum consilia sua referrent. Nimis enimvero scientes quae necessitudo inter fidem et cultum, inter *legem credendi et legem supplicandi* intercedat, liturgiae ordinem, specie quidem redintegrandae eius formae primaevae, ad errores Novatorum multis modis deformarunt. Quamobrem toto

350 A ROMAN DIARY AND OTHER DOCUMENTS

Ordinali non modo nulla est aperta mentio sacrificii, consecrationis, sacerdotii, potestatisque consecrandi et sacrificii offerendi ; sed immo omnia huiusmodi rerum vestigia, quae superessent in precationibus ritus catholici non plane reiectis, sublata et deleta sunt de industria, quod paulo supra attigimus. Ita per se apparet nativa Ordinalis indoles ac spiritus, uti loquuntur. Hinc vero ab origine ducto vitio, si valere ad usum ordinationum minime potuit, nequaquam decursu aetatum, quum tale ipsum permanserit, futurum fuit ut valeret. Atque ii egerunt frustra qui inde a temporibus Caroli I conati sunt admittere aliquid sacrificii et sacerdotii, nonnullâ dein ad Ordinale facta accessione : frustraque similiter contendit pars ea Anglicanorum non ita magna, recentiore tempore coalita, quae arbitratur posse idem Ordinale ad sanam rectamque sententiam intelligi et deduci. Vana, inquimus, fuere et sunt huiusmodi conata : idque hac etiam de causa, quod, si qua quidem verba, in Ordinali anglicano ut nunc est, porrigant se in ambiguum, ea tamen sumere sensum eumdem nequeunt quem habent in ritu catholico. Nam semel novato ritu, ut vidimus, quo nempe negetur vel adulteretur sacramentum Ordinis, et a quo quaevis notio repudiata sit consecrationis et sacrificii ; iam minime constat formula, *Accipe Spiritum Sanctum*, qui Spiritus, cum gratia nimirum sacramenti, in animam infunditur ; minimeque constant verba illa, *ad officium et opus presbyteri* vel *episcopi* ac similia, quae restant nomina sine re quam instituit Christus. Huius vim argumenti perspectam ipsi habent plerique Anglicani, observantiores Ordinalis interpretes; quam non dissimulanter eis obiiciunt qui nove ipsum interpretantes, Ordinibus inde collatis pretium virtutemque non suam spe vana affingunt. Eodem porro argumento vel uno illud etiam corruit, opinantium posse in legitimam Ordinis formam sufficere precationem, *Omnipotens Deus, bonorum omnium largitor*, quae sub initium est ritualis actionis; etiamsi forte haberi ea posset tamquam sufficiens in ritu aliquo catholico quem Ecclesia probasset.

Cum hoc igitur intimo *formae defectu* coniunctus est

APPENDIX I 351

defectus intentionis, quam aeque necessario postulat, ut sit, sacramentum. De mente vel intentione, utpote quae per se quiddam est interius, Ecclesia non iudicat : at quatenus extra proditur, iudicare de ea debet. Iamvero quum quis ad sacramentum conficiendum et conferendum materiam formamque debitam serio ac rite adhibuit, eo ipso censetur id nimirum facere intendisse quod facit Ecclesia. Quo sane principio innititur doctrina quae tenet esse vere sacramentum vel illud, quod ministerio hominis haeretici aut non baptizati, dummodo ritu catholico, conferatur. Contra, si ritus immutetur, eo manifesto consilio ut alius inducatur ab Ecclesia non receptus, utque id repellatur quod facit Ecclesia et quod ex institutione Christi ad naturam attinet sacramenti, tunc palam est, non solum necessarium sacramento intentionem deesse, sed intentionem immo haberi sacramento adversam et repugnantem.

Isthaec omnia diu multumque reputavimus apud Nos et cum Venerabilibus Fratribus Nostris in Suprema iudicibus ; quorum etiam Coetum singulariter coram Nobis advocare placuit feria v, die XVI iulii proximi, in commemoratione Mariae D. N. Carmelitidis. Iique ad unum consensere, propositam causam iam pridem ab Apostolica Sede plene fuisse et cognitam et iudicatam : eius autem denuo instituta actâque quaestione, emersisse illustrius quanto illa iustitiae sapientiaeque pondere, totam rem absolvisset. Verumtamen optimum factu duximus supersedere sententiae, quo et melius perpenderemus conveniret ne expediretque eamdem rem auctoritate Nostra rursus declarari, et uberiorem divini luminis copiam supplices imploraremus. Tum considerantibus Nobis ut idem caput disciplinae, etsi iure iam definitum, a quibusdam revocatum sit in controversiam, quacumque demum causa sit revocatum ; ex eoque pronum fore ut perniciosus error gignatur non paucis qui putent se ibi Ordinis sacramentum et fructus reperire ubi minime sunt, visum est in Domino sententiam Nostram edicere.

Itaque omnibus Pontificum Decessorum in hac ipsa causa decretis usquequaque assentientes, eaque plenissime

352 A ROMAN DIARY AND OTHER DOCUMENTS

confirmantes ac veluti renovantes auctoritate Nostra, motu
proprio certa scientia pronunciamus et declaramus, Ordinationes ritu anglicano actas, irritas prorsus fuisse et esse
omninoque nullas.

Hoc restat, ut quo ingressi sumus *Pastoris magni*
nomine et animo veritatem tam gravis rei certissimam
commonstrare, eodem adhortemur eos qui Ordinum atque
Hierarchiae beneficia sincera voluntate optent et re-
quirant. Usque adhuc fortasse, virtutis christianae
intendentes ardorem, religiosius consulentes divinas Litteras, pias duplicantes preces, incerti tamen haeserunt et
anxii ad vocem Christi iamdiu intime admonentis. Probe
iam vident quo se bonus ille invitet ac velit. Ad unicum
eius ovile si redeant, tum vero et quaesita beneficia
assecuturi sunt et consequentia salutis praesidia, quorum
administram fecit ipse Ecclesiam, quasi redemptionis suae
custodem perpetuam et procuratricem in gentibus. Tum
vero *haurient aquas in gaudio de fontibus Salvatoris*,
sacramentis eius mirificis : unde fideles animae in amicitiam
Dei, remissis vere peccatis, restituuntur, caelesti pane
aluntur et roborantur, adiumentisque maximis affluunt ad
vitae adeptionem aeternae. Quorum bonorum revera
sitientes, utinam *Deus pacis, Deus totius consolationis* faciat
compotes atque expleat perbenignus. Hortationem vero
Nostram et vota eos maiorem in modum spectare volumus,
qui religionis ministri in communitatibus suis habentur.
Homines ex ipso officio praecedentes doctrina et auctoritate, quibus profecto cordi est divina gloria et animorum
salus, velint alacres vocanti Deo parere in primis et
obsequi, praeclarumque de se edere exemplum. Singulari
certe laetitia eos Ecclesia mater excipiet omnique com-
plectetur bonitate et providentia, quippe quos per arduas
rerum difficultates virtus animi generosior ad sinum suum
reduxerit. Ex hac vero virtute dici vix potest quae ipsos
laus maneat in coetibus fratrum per catholicum orbem,
quae aliquando spes et fiducia ante Christum iudicem,
quae ab illo praemia in regno caelesti ! Nos quidem,
quantum omni ope licuerit, eorum cum Ecclesia reconciliationem fovere non desistemus ; ex qua et singuli et

APPENDIX I 353

ordines, id quod vehementer cupimus, multum capere possunt ad imitandum. Interea veritatis gratiaeque divinae patentem cursum ut secundare contendant fideliter, per viscera misericordiae Dei nostri rogamus omnes et obsecramus. Praesentes vero litteras et quaecumque in ipsis habentur nullo unquam tempore de subreptionis aut obreptionis sive intentionis Nostrae vitio aliove quovis defectu notari vel impugnari posse ; sed semper validas et in suo robore fore et esse, atque ab omnibus cuiusvis gradus et praeeminentiae inviolabiliter in iudicio et extra observari debere decernimus : irritum quoque et inane si secus super his a quoquam, quavis auctoritate vel praetextu, scienter vel ignoranter contigerit attentari declarantes, contrariis non obstantibus quibuscumque.

Volumus autem ut harum litterarum exemplis, etiam impressis, manu tamen notarii subscriptis et per constitutum in ecclesiastica dignitate virum sigillo munitis, eadem habeatur fides quae Nostrae voluntatis significationi his praesentibus ostensis haberetur.

Datum Romae apud Sanctum Petrum anno Incarnationis Dominicae millesimo octingentesimo nonagesimo sexto, idibus Septembribus, Pontificatus Nostri anno decimo nono.

A. CARD. BIANCHI,   C CARD. DE RVGGIERO.
Pro-Datarius.

Visa

DE CVRIA. I. DE AQVILA E VICECOMITIBVS.

Loco  *Plumbi.*

Reg. in Secret. Brevium.

           I. CVGNONI.

2 A

APPENDIX II

RESPONSIO ARCHIEPISCOPORUM ANGLIAE AD LITTERAS
APOSTOLICAS LEONIS PAPAE XIII DE ORDINA-
TIONIBUS ANGLICANIS.

UNIVERSIS ECCLESIAE CATHOLICAE EPISCOPIS IN-
SCRIPTA.

Da pacem, Domine, in diebus nostris !

BREVIARIUM EPISTULAE

I. Controversia haec quomodo a litteris Papae Leonis
(Idibus Septembribus anni 1896 datis) orta sit.

II. Propositum nostrum in hac responsione conscribenda.

III. Controversiae de materia et forma ordinis et de ordinationibus nostris non novae sunt. Sed mens Pontificum
Romanorum de his rebus semper incerta fuit.

IV. Leo Papa in hac controversia ineunda multa bene
resecuit.

V. De praxi Curiae Romanae solum et de forma et intentione ecclesiae nostrae disputat Leo.

VI. De praxi, Reginaldo Polo legato. Reconciliatio ante
adventum Poli paene absoluta est, et nulli presbyteri ob
defectum ordinis destituti. Unus forsan et alter sub eo
reordinati. Porro probatur Polum propagasse principia
Eugenii IV a Leone XIII reiecta. Sed praxis cum
opinione vix consensit.

VII. De praxi in causa Iohannis Gordon, quae ex quatuor
rationibus infirmatur. Documenta nova publici iuris
fieri debent.

VIII. De materia, forma et intentione in ordinibus conferendis,
partim cum Papa consentimus, sed de intentione
"quatenus extra proditur," non quae coniecturaco lli-
gatur ex usu libertatis in Ordinalibus reformandis quae
unicuique ecclesiae competit.

APPENDIX II 355

IX. Doctrinae scholasticae de materia et forma sacramentorum non nimium insistendum est : solum enim Baptisma omnino certas habet

X. Quod ex ritu Confirmationis plenius ostenditur.

XI. Doctrina Tridentina de sacrificio Eucharistico et Canon missae cum Liturgia nostra comparantur.

XII. Respondetur argumentis de formis necessariis in presbyteris et episcopis faciendis, collatione formarum quae Romae saeculis III et VI in usu erant.

XIII. Episcopos nihil refert "summos sacerdotes" dici, neque etiam "sacerdotes" in consecratione dici necesse est, cum ordinatio episcoporum *per saltum* tempore exoleverit.

XIV. Respondetur argumentis duobus a Papa maxime, ut videtur, approbatis, quorum primum est de verbis in forma A.D 1662 additis ; et priori loco de sufficientia formae anni 1550 in consecratione episcopi.

XV. Similiter de forma eiusdem anni in ordinatione presbyterorum. Ostenditur hanc solis sacerdotibus convenire. Addita fuerunt alia verba ob Presbyterianorum opiniones, oratione *Omnipotens Deus* in alium locum remota. Haec mutatio animadversione digna est cum ipse Papa de sufficientia formae anni 1662 haesitet, et videatur agnoscere ordinationis partes moraliter coniunctas unam actionem efficere.

XVI. Secundo argumento respondetur de cerimoniis et orationibus a Patribus nostris resectis.

XVII. Tertio argumento respondetur de intentione Ecclesiae nostrae, quae constat praecipue ex praefatione Ordinalis et orationibus "Eucharisticis."

XVIII. Tota ratio mutationum a nobis factarum explicatur a proposito Patrum nostrorum revertendi ad Dominum et ad Apostolos. Cerimoniae et orationes resectae recentiores fuerunt vel non necessariae, vel Liturgiae, lingua vulgari recitandae, non idoneae.

XIX. Dominus noster et Apostoli in his rebus fidissimi duces. Virtus formulae nostrae in sacerdotio conferendo ex collatione Ordinalis cum Pontificali asseritur.

356 A ROMAN DIARY AND OTHER DOCUMENTS

XX. Decretum Papae non nostros tantum ordines subvertit sed etiam Orientalium necnon suorum. Nos aequo studio pacem et unitatem colimus et multa ab eo bene dicta agnoscimus. Rogamus ut quid Christus voluerit in ministerio Evangelico constituendo patienter expendatur. Conclusio

Appendix. De causa Johannis Gordon · cuius petitio mendax ordinationis presbyterorum formam tantum respexit. Summarium, decreto S. Officii praefixum, collationem Ordinalis nostri neglegentissime factam ostendit et consecrationem episcopi solum tangit De consuetudine anni 1704 circa omissionem traditionis instrumentorum et de responsione consultorum S. Officii de Aethiopum ordinationibus.

Universis Ecclesiae Catholicae Episcopis Archiepiscopi Angliae salutem.

I. Saepius officio nostro accidit ut, cum de communi salute velimus scribere, oriatur occasio de quaestione aliqua controversa disserendi, quae in aliud tempus abici non possit. Hoc certe recenter evenit cum, mense Septembri proxime praeterito, litterae typis mandatae et publici iuris iam factae, subito ex Roma perlatae essent, quae totum nostrum statum ecclesiasticum subvertere conarentur. His quidem litteris, ut par erat, animos nostros diligenter advertebamus cum carissimus frater noster Edwardus, tunc Archiepiscopus Cantuariensis et totius Angliae Primas et Metropolitanus, Deo ita volente, morte inopina praereptus est. Qui rem nobis tractandam, quam ipse sine dubio summa cum doctrina et theologica gratia tractaturus erat, ultimis suis verbis scriptis legavit. Placuit ergo nobis Archiepiscopis et Primatibus Angliae hanc epistulam conscribendam curare, ut tum venerabili fratri nostro Leoni Papae XIII, cuius nomine litterae istae proferuntur, tum ceteris episcopis Ecclesiae Christianae per totum orbem propagatae, veritas rei innotesceret.

II. Grave quidem hoc munus est et quod non sine aliquo vehementis animi affectu peragi possit. Sed cum nos a

APPENDIX II 357

principe Pastorum ad partem muneris sui tremendi in Ecclesia Catholica sustinendam vere ordinatos esse firmiter credamus, iudicio litterarum istarum nihil commovemur. Opus ergo, quod nobis necessario incumbit, "in spiritu lenitatis" adgredimur; et maioris momenti ducimus ut doctrina nostra de sacris ordinibus et ceteris ad eos pertinentibus ad futuram rei memoriam palam fiat, quam ut victoriam ex alia ecclesia Christi in controversia reportemus. Controversiae tamen forma his litteris dari necesse est, ne quis dicat nos argumentorum ex alia parte prolatorum aciem evitasse.

III. Controversia vetus erat, sed non acerba, de forma et materia ordinum sacrorum, quae ex natura rei exorta est, cum nihil de ea traditum a Domino aut ab Apostolis Eius inveniatur, nisi exemplum notissimum orandi cum manuum impositione. De hac etiam re parum pronuntiaverunt Concilia Provincialia, nihil certum et absolutum Oecumenica et generalia.

Neque etiam Concilium Tridentinum, cui Patres nostri non interfuerunt, rem directe tangit. Quae obiter dixit de impositione manuum (*sess* XIV *de extrema unctione cap.* III) et exactius de vi verborum "Accipe Spiritum Sanctum," quae pro forma ordinis accipere videtur (*sess.* XXIII *de sacramento ordinis, canone* IV), nobis satis placent, et certe nulla cum offensione audiuntur.

Controversia recentior et acerbior de validitate ordinationum Anglicanarum fuit, cui controversiae theologi Romani cum ardore se immiscuerunt, et varia nobis plerumque crimina et defectus imputaverunt. Sunt et alii ex eis, neque ii minime prudentes, qui defensionem nostram generosius susceperint. Pontificum autem Romanorum sententia rationibus plene instructa nunquam antea prodiit, nec, cum praxis reordinandi sacerdotes nostros, quamvis non sine exceptione, manifeste obtineret, propter quos defectus reordinarentur rescire poteramus. Notae erant de Formoso lites indignae et de haereticis schismaticis et simoniacis ordinationibus vacillationes longae. Praesto erant Innocenti III de unctione necessario supplenda epistula et Eugenii IV Decretum ad

358 A ROMAN DIARY AND OTHER DOCUMENTS

Armenos; monumenta historica saeculi XVI, sed magna ex parte usque hodie incognita; iudicia varia Pontificum recentiorum Clementis XI et Benedicti XIV, sed Clementis quidem verbis generalibus concepta et ea ratione incerta. Aderat etiam Pontificale Romanum, de tempore in tempus reformatum, sed, quale nunc exstat, tam confuse compositum ut mentes inquirentium magis turbaret quam adiuvaret. Si quis enim ritum *de ordinatione presbyteri* spectet, videt manus impositionem propriam a formae prolatione seiungi. Nescit etiam si ille qui in rubricis "ordinatus" dicitur, revera iam ordinatus sit, an potestas quae ad finem officii detur per verba "Accipe Spiritum sanctum, quorum remiseris peccata remittuntur eis, et quorum retinueris retenta sunt" cum impositione manuum Pontificis, necessaria sit pars sacerdotii (ut Concilium Tridentinum[1] videtur docere) an non necessaria. Similiter etiam, si quis ritum *de consecratione electi in episcopum* perlegat, in orationibus et benedictionibus pro viro consecrando nusquam eum "episcopum" dici inveniet nec "episcopatum" de eo praedicari[2] Quod ad orationes attinet occurrit prima vice nomen episcopatus in missa "infra actionem."

Ex his igitur documentis plane inter se variantibus et indefinitis nemo vel prudentissimus expiscari poterat quid secundum Pontifices Romanos sacris ordinibus revera essentiale et necessarium foret.

IV. Frater ergo ille noster venerabilissimus litteris Idibus Septembribus datis, quae verbis *Apostolicae curae* incipiunt, hanc quaestionem modo adhuc inusitato adgressus est, quamquam argumenta ab eo prolata satis antiqua sunt. Neque negare volumus eum in hac controversia ineunda commoditati Ecclesiae et veritati rerum consuluisse cum notionem vanissimam, sed theologorum

---

III. [1] *Sess.* XXIII *de sacr. ord. canone* 1 ubi potestas aliqua consecrandi et offerendi, in sacerdotio postulatur una cum potestate peccata remittendi et retinendi. Cf *ib cap.* 1. De his vide plura infra cap. xv et xix.

III [2] "Cathedra episcopalis" post unctionem in benedictione memoratur

APPENDIX II 359

scholae post S. Thomam Aquinatem usque ad Benedictum XIV et etiam usque hodie late acceptam, de traditionis instrumentorum necessitate proiecerit. Idem quoque alios errores et fallacias bene neglexit, quos et pro parte nostra in hac responsione neglecturi, sumus, et speramus theologos ex parte Romana, exemplo eius adductos, in posterum esse neglecturos.

V. Totius itaque iudicii eius cardo in duobus punctis vertitur, scilicet in praxi curiae Romanae et in forma ritus Anglicani, cui subiacet quaestio tertia, sed a secunda non facile separanda, de intentione nostrae ecclesiae. De illa statim respondebimus, quamvis nostro iudicio minoris momenti sit.

VI. De praxi curiae et legati Romani saeculo XVI, quamvis multa scripserit, credimus Papam nobiscum revera esse incertum. Videmus enim nihil eum habere quod documentis huc usque bene cognitis addi possit, et ex exemplari minus perfecto litteras Pauli IV *Praeclara carissimi* citare et ex eo disputare. Ubi sunt, exempli gratia, facultates Polo post Augusti diem V 1553 et ante Martii diem VIII 1554 concessae, quas Julius III, litteris hoc die datis, "libere utendas" circa ordines minus rite aut non servata consueta forma susceptos confirmat, non autem clare definit? Nam sine illis facultatibus "normae agendi" a Polo observandae parum notae sunt. Distinctio enim de "promotis" et "non promotis" a Papa memorata (§ 3), quae in utrisque litteris fit, non statum cleri Edwardiani attinere videtur, sed illorum qui sine ulla ordinatione praetensa beneficia tenerent, ut saepe eo tempore fiebat. Quis vero penitus cognovit vel quod in hac re factum sit vel quibus ex rationibus factum? Partem scimus: partem nescimus. A nostra tamen parte probari potest opus reconciliationis istius sub Maria regina (a Iulii die VI 1553 ad XVII diem Novembris 1558) auctoritate regia et episcopali, ante adventum Poli, maxima ex parte consummatum fuisse.

In quo conficiendo multa inconstantia et inaequalitas apparet. Et cum multi sacerdotes Edwardiani, propter

360 A ROMAN DIARY AND OTHER DOCUMENTS

varias causas et praesertim ob coniugium initum inveniantur deprivati, ob defectum ordinis, quantum scimus, nulli· Aliqui propria voluntate reordinati sunt. Aliqui unctionem susceperunt in supplementum ordinis iam collati, quae cerimonia tunc temporis magni momenti a quibusdam ex episcopis nostris habebatur.[1] Aliqui, et fortasse plures numero, in beneficiis suis sine reordinatione permanserunt, immo aliquando ad nova promoti sunt. Polus autem mense demum Novembri anno 1554 in Angliam ex exilio reversus est, et mensibus sequentibus quindecim reconciliationem ad finem perduxit. Principium vero operis eius videtur fuisse ut statum rerum ante adventum suum existentem agnosceret, et omnes vires ad dominatum Papae restituendum converteret. In quo unus et forsan alter (plures enim adhuc non inventi sunt) sub Polo reordinati sunt, annis Sc. 1554 et 1557; quo tamen anno hi duo cursum reordinationis inceperint, incertum est. Certe, post Poli adventum, paucissimi reordinati sunt. Alii forsan supplementum aliquid ordinis, qualecunque illud fuerit, acceperunt, sed hoc in Registris nostris non apparet.

Sed si multi sub Reginaldo Polo, legato Romano, reordinati essent, nihil mirandum fuisset, cum ille in constitutionibus suis legatinis duodecim, ad calcem constitutionis secundae, Eugenii IV Decretum lege Armenis subiunxerit, "quia" ut ait "in iis quae ad doctrinam capitis ecclesiae et sacramentorum pertinent hic (*i.e*, in Anglia) maxime erratum est."[2] Et hoc non ut archiepiscopus

VI [1] Vide Jacobum Pilkington *Expositionem super prophetam Aggeum* ii. 10–14, quae anno 1560 edita fuit (*Works* Parker Society p. 163). "Proximis temporibus papisticis episcopi nostri illi sancti eos omnes qui sine tali unctione ministri facti fuissent ad se vocabant et benedictione papali benedicebant et ungebant, et illico res absoluta est pro vivis et defunctis sacrificare poterant : sed eis coniuges ducere nullo modo licebat" etc. Cf Innocentium III *ep*. vii 3 (1204).

VI. [2] Vide Labb et Cossart *Concilia* tom xiv p 1740, Paris. 1672, et tom. xiii p. 538 ad A D. 1439. Confer etiam *Concilia Mag. Britanniae* ed. Wilkins tom. iv p 121 col 2 qui liber paulum differt et verba Decreti Eugeniani omittit Constat Eugenii verba ex Aquinatis *Expositione in articulos fidei et sacramenta ecclesiae* plerumque esse desumta (*Op*. tom. viii pp 45–9 Venet 1776).

APPENDIX II 361

noster sed ut legatus Papae fecit. Anno enim 1556 ineunte hae constitutiones promulgatae sunt. Presbyter
autem Polus ordinatus tandem fuit die XX mensis Martii
eiusdem anni ; et proximo die, quo archiepiscopus noster
legitimus Cranmerus vivus combustus est, missam prima
vice cantavit ; die vero XXII archiepiscopus consecratus est.
Decreti autem Eugenii IV, a Polo repetiti, verba hic
citamus, cum plane ostendant quam lubricum et infirmum
fuerit in hac re Romanae ecclesiae iudicium. Porro cum
Leo papa doctrinam Poli in hac re collaudet, et scribat
alienum prorsus fuisse Legatum a Papis commonefieri "de
eis quae sacramento ordinis conficiendo necesse sunt,"
decreti Eugeniani penitus oblivisci videtur, quod in alia
parte litterarum suarum tacite repudiavit. (Cf. § 3 et § 5.)
"Sextum sacramentum est ordinis : cuius materia est illud,
per cuius traditionem confertur ordo : sicut presbyteratus
traditur per calicis cum vino, et patinae cum pane porrec-
tionem : diaconatus vero per libri evangeliorum dationem :
subdiaconatus vero per calicis vacui cum patina vacua
superposita traditionem· et similiter de aliis, per rerum ad
ministeria sua pertinentium assignationem. Forma sacerdotii talis est : *Accipe potestatem offerendi sacrificium in
ecclesia pro vivis et mortuis. In nomine Patris, et Filii, et
Spiritus Sancti* Et sic de aliorum ordinum formis prout
in Pontificali Romano late continetur. Ordinarius minister
huius Sacramenti est episcopus : effectus, augmentum
gratiae, ut quis sit idoneus minister." Hic ne verbo quidem
attinguntur impositio manuum et invocatio Spiritus Sancti
in ordinandos. Eugenius tamen, ut ex explicatione ceter-
orum sacramentorum patet, non de rebus ab Armenis
supplendis, ut Romani interdum dictitant, sed de rebus
sacramentorum administrationi penitus necessariis, Aquinatis vestigia diligenter secutus, Ecclesiam quasi magistri
loco erudit. Ita quoque in priori parte decreti eiusdem
scribit: "Haec omnia sacramenta tribus perficiuntur, videlicet rebus tamquam materia, verbis tamquam forma, et
persona ministri conferentis sacramentum cum intentione
faciendi quod facit ecclesia : *quorum si aliquod desit, non
perficitur sacramentum*" (*Conc.* XVI p 1738)

362 A ROMAN DIARY AND OTHER DOCUMENTS

In ecclesia autem nostra a mense Martio 1550, usque ad diem 1 Novembris 1552, cum traditio instrumentorum aliqua maneret (sc calicis cum pane in presbyteris, et baculi pastoralis in episcopis, et Bibliorum in utrisque), formae tamen eidem coniunctae, in eas paene quae nunc in usu sunt, iam mutatae erant. Anno autem 1552 etiam traditio calicis et baculi omissa est, Bibliorum tantum restabat. Decessit vero Edwardus rex Iulii die VI 1553. Itaque, secundum hoc decretum, presbyteri illi omnes reordinandi erant. Sed opinio cum praxi vix consensit. Neque ipse Paulus IV, cum in brevi *Regimini universalis* de episcopis "rite et recte ordinatis" caveat, quidquam de forma ordinationis presbyterorum exigit. (Vide infra Appendicem ad finem)

VII. Fundamentum secundum, sed vix firmius, sententiae papalis de praxi curiae apparet esse iudicium Clementis XI de causa Johannis Gordon, episcopi quondam Gallovidiensis, latum feria quinta die XVII Aprilis anni 1704 in Congregatione generali Inquisitionis, vel, ut dici solet, S Officii.

De qua causa hic breviter respondemus, cum propter tenebras S Officio circumfusas, et in litteris Papae parum dissipatas, dilucide tractari non possit. Quod plenius dici possit in Appendicem reiecimus. Quatuor autem sunt praecipue rationes propter quas haec causa infirmo et imbecillo fundamento iudicii eius videatur. Imprimis, cum ipse Gordon proprio motu oraret ut ordines Romano ritu susciperet, causa ex altera parte non audita est. Secundo, petitio eius fabulam istam cauponariam pro fundamento habuit, et mendaciis de ritu nostro vitiata fuit. Tertio, nova documenta "integrae fidei" a Papa citata adhuc ambagibus involuta sunt, et ipse de eorum tenore et sententia, quasi incertus, disputat.[1] Quarto, decretum S. O, si illud cum iudicio Papae concordare reputemus, vix conciliari potest cum responsione consultorum eiusdem

---

VII. [1] Confer *Apostolicae curae* sec. 5 "Quae sententia, id sane considerare refert, ne a defectu quidem *traditionis instrumentorum* quidquam momenti duxit tunc enim praescriptum de more esset ut ordinatio *sub conditione* instauraretur" e. q. s Quae argumentandi ratio longe abest a citatione documenti perspicacis Vide Appendicem.

APPENDIX II 363

S. O. de Aethiopum ordinationibus, quae ante dies fere octo dicitur data, et a theologis Romanis usque ad annum 1893 pro documento auctoritate praedito saepius edita fuit. Proferenda sunt ergo omnia ista documenta si res ex aequo iudicanda sit. In fine notandum est Gordon nunquam ultra ordines minores in ecclesia Romana processisse. Satis enim fecit tantum ut pensione ex quibusdam beneficiis aleretur.[1]

VIII. Bene certe fecit Papa qui in his sententiis tam infirmis non adquieverit, sed rem de novo retractandam censuerit; quamvis hoc specie potius quam re factum videatur. Cum enim causa ab eo ad S. Officium delata fuerit, constat illud, traditionibus suis constrictum, vix potuisse a iudicio in causa Gordoniana lato, quamvis male fundato, dissentire. Porro cum rem ipsam attingit et Concilii Tridentini vestigiis insistit, nihil a fundamento iudicii eius sententia nostra abhorret. Materiam ordinationis recte dicit impositionem manuum. De forma iudicium eius non tam clare enuntiatur; sed credimus eum velle dicere formam esse orationem vel benedictionem ministerio tradendo idoneam, quae nostra etiam sententia est. Neque Papam deserimus cum suadet intentionem ecclesiae in sacris ordinibus conferendis, "quatenus extra proditur," recte investigandam esse. Cum enim mentem interiorem sacerdotis vix quisquam adsequi possit, ut ab ea validitatem sacramenti pendere fas non sit dicere, voluntas certe ecclesiae et facilius exquiri potest, et vera et sufficiens esse debet. Quae quidem intentio ab ecclesia nostra generaliter proditur cum promissionem ab ordinando exigat, ut doctrinam sacramenta et disciplinam Christi recte ministrare velit, et eum, qui huic promisso infidum se monstraverit, iure puniendum doceat. Et in Liturgia continuo oramus pro Episcopis et Parochis "ut tam vita quam doctrina sua verum vivumque (Dei) verbum annuntient, et sancta (Eius) sacramenta recte et rite ministrent."

VII. [1] Vide Le Quien *Nullité des Ord. Anglicanes, Paris* 1725, II. pp. 312 et 315.

364 A ROMAN DIARY AND OTHER DOCUMENTS

Sed intentio Ecclesiae "quatenus extra proditur" exquirenda est, ex formulis scilicet publicis et sententiis definitis quae rei summam recta via tangant, non ex omissionibus et reformationibus per occasionem factis, secundum libertatem quae unicuique Provinciae et genti competit, nisi si quid forte omittatur quod in verbo Dei aut statutis universae Ecclesiae cognitis et certis ordinatum fuerit. Si enim consuetudinem medii aevi et saeculorum recentiorum pro norma quis adsumat, videte, fratres, quam contra libertatem Evangelii agat et veram regni Christiani indolem. Et, si hunc modum in validitate sacramentorum iudicanda sequimur, omnia in incertum trahimus, nisi solum Baptisma, quod, secundum iudicium universae Ecclesiae, materiam et formam a Domino ordinatas habere videatur.

IX. Agnoscimus ergo cum Papa ordinum sacrorum materiam esse impositionem manuum : agnoscimus formam esse orationem vel benedictionem ministerio tradendo idoneam : agnoscimus intentionem ecclesiae, quatenus extra proditur, investigandam esse, ut perspiciamus si cum mente Domini et Apostolorum, et Ecclesiae universae statutis, concordet. Non tamen apud nos tantum valet doctrina illa, a scholasticis post tempus Gulielmi Autissiodorensis (A D. 1215) toties decantata, quod unicuique ex sacramentis Ecclesiae forma una et materia omnibus numeris definita esse debeat Neque eam credimus apud Romanos de fide esse. Periculum enim erroris maximum inducit si quis Papa vel Doctor, qui multum apud suos valeat, hanc vel illam formam aut materiam, neque in verbo Dei neque a Patribus Catholicis aut Conciliis definitam, pro necessaria agnoscendam hominibus persuadeat

Unicum est enim, ut diximus, sacramentum Baptisma, quod et forma et materia penitus certum est. Et hoc naturam rei sequitur. Cum enim Baptisma Christi omnibus ostium Ecclesiae sit, et ab omnibus Christianis, si necessitas urgeat, ministrari possit, condiciones validi Baptismatis omnibus notae esse debent. Quod autem ad Eucharistiam attinet (si quaestiones de azymis et sale,

APPENDIX II 365

de aqua, et ceteras huiusmodi ut minores seponas)
materiam satis certam habet · de forma eius plena et
essentiali usque hodie disceptatur. Confirmationis vero
materia non adeo certa est ; et nos quidem Christianos de
ea diverse sentientes invicem damnandos nullo modo
censemus. Forma autem Confirmationis incerta est et
prorsus generalis, oratio scilicet vel benedictio plus minus
congrua, quae in singulis ecclesiis fuerit usitata. Et sic
de aliis.

X. Sed hic locus de Confirmatione paulo latius tractari
debet : multum enim lucis in quaestionem a Papa propositam infert. Scribit enim de impositione manuum
quod materia sit quae "aeque ad Confirmationem usur-
patur." Confirmationis ergo materia, Papa iudice, impositio manuum videtur esse, ut a traditione Apostolica
nos etiam accepimus. Sed Romana ecclesia, pro impositione manuum unicuique conferenda, extensionem
manuum super turbam parvulorum aut simpliciter " versus
confirmandos," multa per saecula, corrupta consuetudine
adhibuit.¹ Orientales (cum Eugenio IV) chrisma materiam
esse docent, et impositione manuum in hoc ritu nulla
utuntur. Si ergo doctrina de materia et forma sacramentorum certa admittenda esset, Romani parum recte
multis retro saeculis Confirmationem ministraverunt, Graeci
nullam habent Et plures quidem ex illis corruptionem a
Patribus illorum factam re confitentur, impositione manuum
cum chrismatione iuncta, ut rescivimus, multis in locis, et
rubrica in Pontificalibus quibusdam de hac re addita. Et
quaerere licet an Orientales, qui ad Romanos convertantur,
iterum Confirmatione egeant? an confitentur Romani eos
aequum ius in materia immutanda usurpasse, sicut ipsi in
corrumpenda ?

Quodcumque responderit Papa, satis clarum est illi doc-

X. ¹ In Sacramentario " Gelasiano" dicto (saec forsan vii) adhuc
legimus *Ad consignandum imponit eis manum in his verbis* · sequitur
oratio de septiformi dono Spiritus. Et in ordinibus " Sancti Amandi"
dictis, qui saeculi forsan viii sunt, cap iv pontifex tangit *capita ipsorum de manu* In " Gregoriano" autem *levata manu sua super
capita omnium dicit*, etc. In Pontificali vero vulgato . *Tunc extensis
versus confirmandos manibus dicit*, etc.

366 A ROMAN DIARY AND OTHER DOCUMENTS

trinae de forma et materia definita non ubique pressius insistendum ; omnia enim sacramenta Ecclesiae, excepto baptismate, idcirco in dubitationem trahi posse.

XI. Quaerimus ergo qua ex auctoritate formam definitam in sacris ordinibus tradendis Papa invenerit? Testimonium nullum ab eo adlatum vidimus nisi locos duo e Concilii Tridentini placitis (*sess.* XXIII *de Sacramento ordinis, canone* I, et *sess.* XXII *de sacrificio missae, canone* III), quae post Ordinale nostrum compositum promulgata sunt, ex quibus colligit praecipuam sacerdotii Christiani gratiam et potestatem esse consecrationem et oblationem corporis et sanguinis Domini. Auctoritas plane eius Concilii apud gentem nostram nunquam accepta est, et ab eo multa vera cum falsis, multa incerta cum certis, commixta invenimus. Quoad locos autem a Papa citatos respondemus, nos de S. Eucharistiae consecratione maxima cum reverentia curare, et solis sacerdotibus rite ordinatis et nullis aliis Ecclesiae ministris permittere. Eucharistiae etiam sacrificium vere docemus, nec sacrificii crucis "nudam esse commemorationem" credimus, ut Concilio illo citato nobis videtur imputari. Satis tamen credimus in liturgia nostra qua in S. Eucharistia celebranda utimur,—corda habentes ad Dominum, et munera, quae antea oblata sunt, iam consecrantes ut nobis corpus et sanguis fiant Domini nostri Jesu Christi,—sacrificium quod ibidem fit ita significare. Memoriam scilicet perpetuam pretiosae mortis Christi qui ipse est Advocatus noster apud Patrem et propitiatio pro peccatis nostris, usque ad Adventum Eius secundum praeceptum Eius observamus. Primo enim sacrificium laudis et gratiarum offerimus; tum vero sacrificium Crucis Patri proponimus et repraesentamus, et per illud remissionem peccatorum et omnia alia Dominicae passionis beneficia pro tota et universa Ecclesia impetramus ; sacrificium denique nostrum ipsorum Creatori omnium offerimus, quod per oblationes creaturarum Ipsius iam significavimus. Quam actionem totam, in qua plebs cum sacerdote partem suam necessario sumit, sacrificium Eucharisticum solemus nominare.

APPENDIX II 367

Porro cum nos satis stricte admoneat Papa de necessitudine quae "inter fidem et cultum, inter *legem credendi et legem supplicandi* intercedat," aequum videtur ut animum et vestrum et nostrum ad liturgiam Romanam propius vertamus. Et cum ipsum "Canonem Missae" diligenter inspiciamus, quid de notione sacrificii ibidem prodita luculenter apparet? Cum formulis nostris Eucharisticis satis consentit, vix aut ne vix quidem cum Concilii Tridentini placitis. Vel potius dici debet a Concilio illo duos sacrificii explicandi modos simul proferri, unum qui cum scientia liturgica et prudentia Christiana concinat, alterum qui theologiae populari et periculosae de propitiatione Eucharistica addictus sit. In Canone autem Missae sacrificium, quod offertur, quatuor modis describitur. Primo loco est "sacrificium laudis,"[1] quae notio totam actionem permeat, et quodammodo sustinet, et in unum quasi corpus coniungit. Secundo est oblatio facta a servis Dei et cuncta familia Eius, de qua oblatione petitur "ut nobis corpus et sanguis fiat" Filii sui Domini nostri. Tertio est oblatio Maiestati Eius de suis "donis ac datis" (id est de frugibus segetum et arborum, ut recte explicat Innocentius III[2], quamvis verba Domini de eis iam dicta sint a sacerdote), qui Panis sanctus vitae aeternae et Calix salutis perpetuae nominantur. Quarto loco et ultimo (*Supra quae propitio*) sacrificium, tribus modis oblatum, et, secundum sententiam Romanam, iam plene consecratum, cum sacrificiis patriarcharum Abel et Abrahae, et cum eo quod obtulit Melchisedech, comparatur. Quod cum "sanctum sacrificium, immaculata hostia" dicatur, non solum ratione offerentis sed etiam oblatorum com-

---

XI. [1] "Sacrificium laudis" id est Eucharisticum vel pacificum (*Anglice* "thank-offering" vel "peace-offering") quod in hac re ab aliis sacrificiis differt, cum in illo, homo, qui offert, cum Deo partem oblationis ex ritu sumat. Nomen ex veteri versione Latina est (vide Pentateuchum Lugdunensem), quod ab Hieronymo "pro gratiarum actione oblatio" vel "hostia gratiarum" redditur, *Levit.* vii. 12, 13 Unde in liturgia nostra ambo coniunguntur. "this our sacrifice of praise and thanksgiving."

XI. [2] *De sacro altaris mysterio* v cap. 2.

368 A ROMAN DIARY AND OTHER DOCUMENTS

parari videtur.[1] Deinde rogat ecclesia ut haec perferantur per manus sancti Angeli ad sublime altare Dei. Denique occurrit, post secundam seriem nominum sanctorum, orationis particula (*Per quem haec omnia*) quae ad benedicendas fruges aptior videtur, quam sacrificio eucharistico idonea.

Ex praecedentibus ergo plane constat *legem credendi* a Concilio Tridentino propositam aliquantum ultra limites *legis supplicandi* progressam esse. Res certe mysterii plena est et quae mentes hominum facile ad cogitationes altas et profundas, valido amoris et pietatis affectu, adtrahat Sed, cum summa reverentia tractari debeat, et caritatis Christianae vinculum non disputationum subtilium occasio habenda sit, definitiones curiosae de modo sacrificii et de ratione qua coniunguntur sacrificium aeterni sacerdotis et sacrificium Ecclesiae, quae aliquo certe modo unum sunt, nostro iudicio, vitandae sunt potius quam promovendae.

XII. Quare ergo forma et intentio nostra in presbyteris et episcopis faciendis impugnatur?

Scribit quidem Papa, si ea quae minoris momenti sunt negligamus, "ordinem sacerdotii vel eius gratiam et potestatem, quae praecipue est potestas *consecrandi et offerendi verum Corpus et Sanguinem Domini*, eo sacrificio quod non est *nuda commemoratio sacrificii* in cruce peracti" in presbytero ordinando debere significari. De episcopi consecrandi forma quid voluerit non adeo clarum est, sed videtur, secundum setentiam illius, quovis modo "summum sacerdotium" oportere de eo praedicari.

XI. [1] Haec oratio interpretes satis torsit. Conferendi sunt e g. Innocentius III *de sacro altaris myst* v 3, Bellarminus *de sacr. Euch.* (*de missa*) lib. vi 24, Romsée *Sensus literalis rituum missae* art. xxx. Vetustior eius forma apparet in [Pseudo-Ambrosii] libro *de Sacramentis* iv 6 § 27 ubi partes eius inverso ordine leguntur. Scribitur etiam "per manus Angelorum tuorum." Tempore Leonis I Canoni Romano iam addita videtur, si vera sint quae in *Vita* eius referuntur, de verbis "sanctum sacrificium, immaculatam hostiam," ab illo subiunctis. Cf. *serm.* iv 3, ubi de Melchisedech dicitur "illius sacramenti immolans sacrificium, quod Redemtor noster in suo corpore et sanguine consecravit."

APPENDIX II 369

Utrumque tamen mirum est, cum in antiquissima formula Romae saeculo tertio post Christum ineunte, ut videtur, usitata, (cum eadem plane forma et pro episcopo et pro presbytero, excepto nomine, adhibeatur) nihil omnino dictum sit de "summo sacerdotio" aut de "sacerdotio," neque de sacrificio corporis et sanguinis Christi. "Orationes et oblationes quas (Deo) offeret die noctuque" solum commemorantur, et potestas ad remittenda peccata tangitur.[1]

In Sacramentario autem veteri Romano, quod saeculo VI forsan tribui potest, pro presbyteris solum orationes tres adhibentur Duae sunt breviores sc. *Oremus, dilectissimi* et *Exaudi nos*, et tertia longior, praefationi Eucharisticae similis, quae vera Benedictio est, et cum impositione manuum olim coniuncta, quae incipit *Domine sancte pater omnipotens, aeterne Deus, honorum omnium*, etc. Quae orationes a saeculo sexto ad nonum, et forsan ultra, sine ullis aliis cerimoniis, totum ritum presbyteri ordinandi in ecclesia Romana continebant. Hae orationes, parum immutatae, in Pontificali Ramano retinentur, et quasi nucleum formulae *de ordinatione Presbyteri* efficiunt, quamvis impositio manuum, longiori formae olim coniuncta, in principium actionis transierit, et ad finem missae rursus data sit. In Benedictione autem "sacerdotium" de presbyteris non praedicatur, nec quidquam in orationum serie illa de sacrificandi potestate aut de peccatis remittendis dicitur. "Gratia" etiam "sacerdotalis," quae in Pontificalibus plurimis in oratione secunda invocatur, in quibusdam et nostris et extraneis[2] simpliciter "gratia spiritualis" est. Sed haec forma sine dubio valida est.

Similia dici possunt de forma episcopi consecrandi. Orationes et Benedictio in Pontificali hodierno restant, parum mutatae. Incipiunt vero *Exaudi Domine supplicum preces* (nunc *Adesto*), *Propitiare Domine* et *Deus honorum*

XII. [1] Vide *Canones Hippolyti* ab Hans Achelis editos t. VI voluminum dictorum *Texte und Untersuchungen* Gebhardti et Harnack Lips. 1891, pp 39–62.

XII. [2] Vide e.g E. Martene *de ant ecc. rit.* t. II p 429, 493, Rotom. 1700.

2 B

370 A ROMAN DIARY AND OTHER DOCUMENTS

omnium. Secunda "cornu gratiae sacerdotalis," tertia "summum sacerdotium" memorat, sed nihil aliud quod ad propositum Papae confirmandum proferri potest. Cetera omnia quae in Pontificali habentur, ex usu temporum recentiorum, et praesertim ex ritibus Gallicanis, derivantur[1] Et hoc etiam dicendum est de potestate peccata remittendi, quae a Concilio Tridentino una cum " potestate aliqua consecrandi et offerendi" (not. III[1]) et aequa cum significantia, memoratur. Nusquam apparet usque ad saec. XI in ordinatione presbyteri: nusquam in forma antiqua Romana de consecratione episcopi. Apparet tantum in longa interpolatione Gallicana ad benedictionem episcopi *Sint speciosi munere tuo pedes eius* usque ad *ut fructum de profectu omnum consequatur.*

Sed Papa qui ad Concilium Tridentinum provocat ab eodem iudicari debet. Aut ergo hae formulae Romanae nullae erant propter defectus de sacrificio et de peccatis remittendis, aut auctoritas Concilii illius nulla est ad hanc quaestionem de necessaria forma ordinis decidendam.

Alia etiam forma antiqua[2] consecrandi episcopi, apud

XII. [1] Sacramentarium vetus Romanum ex tribus potissimum libris colligi potest, quod ad orationes attinet, "Leoniano" sc., "Gelasiano" et "Gregoriano" dictis. Primus tamen solus Romanus est sine ullo alio colore Gelasianus in Galliam invectus saec. VIII ineunte, et Gregorianus sub Carolo Magno, ab Hadriano Papa, circa A.D 780 transmissus—ambo ritus et orationes Gallicanos Romanis immixtos habent. "Ordines" etiam tres pro ritibus conferendi sunt, sc. Mabillonii VIII et IX et ordines "Sancti Amandi" dicti, qui a viro erudito L Duchesne in Appendice libri *Origines du culte chrétien* anno 1889 Parisiis prima vice typis mandati sunt. Qui omnes eandem simplicitatem ostendunt.

XII [2] Haec forma e g in *Leofrici Exoniensis Missali* occurit (pag. 217 ed F E. Warren, Oxon., 1883), in Pontificali quodam Gemmeticensi (Martene *de ant eccl. rit.* t ii p. 367) et in Sarisburiensi (vide Maskell *Monumenta Ritualia Eccl. Angl.* ed. 2 Oxon. 1882 vol. ii p 282). Verba de mysteriis celebrandis et *Admonitio ad sacerdotes* (ib p. 246) pro exemplo patribus nostris videntur fuisse in ordinatione presbyteri Haec forma, cum formulis *Canonum Hippolyti* et *Constitutionum Apostolicarum* necessitudine quadam coniuncta, antiquitatem satis magnam redolet, et, verbis de summo sacerdotio exceptis, aeque ad presbyterum ordinandum idonea videtur. Sunt qui credant eam esse Romanam et ab Augustino Cantuariensi in nostrum usum derivatam fuisse.

APPENDIX II   371

nos quidem et alibi saeculo XI usitata, hic citari potest, quae parem simplicitatem exhibeat. Incipit *Pater sancte omnipotens Deus qui per Dominum* et pro consecrandis orat, "ut antiquitus instituta possint sacramentorum mysteria celebrare. Per te in summum, ad quod assumuntur, sacerdotium consecrentur," sed nihil de sacrificio, nihil de peccatis remittendis loquitur.

XIII. De episcoporum titulo simpliciter et statim respondemus, nomen "summi sacerdotis," nullo modo necessarium esse, ad hoc officium in forma consecrationis describendum. Ecclesia enim Africana etiam a primatibus suis hoc nomen manifesto repudiavit:[1] "pontificalis" autem "gloria," quae interdum in Sacramentariis invenitur, gentilem vel iudaicam dignitatem potius quam ecclesiasticum ordinem refert. Nobis nomen episcopi sufficit, quod officium eorum designet qui, Apostolis remotis, cum praecipui in Ecclesia pastores permanserint, ordinandi et confirmandi ius exercerent et, una cum presbyteris pluribus, unam "parochiam," vel ut nunc dicitur dioecesin, regerent. Quorum ordini Papa se ipsum, in principio epistulae suae, secundum morem maiorum recte adnumerat. Sacerdotes sine dubio sunt episcopi, ut sunt presbyteri, et eo nomine saeculis antiquioribus magis quam presbyteri gaudebant; et quarto vel quinto demum saeculo presbyteri, saltem apud Latinos, sacerdotes pleno iure dici consuescebant. Sed ideo episcopos nostris temporibus in forma consecrationis "summos sacerdotes" dici oportere non sequitur. Aliter forsan erat de "sacerdotio" episcoporum saeculis antiquioribus, certe usque ad nonum et fortasse usque ad undecimum, cum homo adhuc diaconus, *per saltum*, quod dicitur, saepe episcopus sine presbyteratu fieret.[2] Iis ergo

XIII. [1] Vide *Conc. Carth* III (A D 397) *canonem* 26. "Ut primae sedis episcopus non appelletur princeps sacerdotum, aut summus sacerdos, aut aliquid huiusmodi, sed tantum primae sedis episcopus" Huic autem concilio interfuisse creditur S. Augustinus Hipponensis. Locus de hoc nomine a Baronio etc. citatus Augustini certe non est.

XIII. [2] De hac re confer Mabillonii *commentarium praevium in ordinem Romanum* capp xvi et xviii (Migne *Pat. Lat.* tom 78 pp. 912-3, et 919-20) et Martene *de ant. eccl. rit.* lib. I cap. viii, art. iii,

372 A ROMAN DIARY AND OTHER DOCUMENTS

temporibus certe idoneum si non necessarium fuit sacerdotium de eo praedicari, ut in oratione quae adhuc in Pontificali adhibetur, scilicet de cornu gratiae sacerdotalis. Sed cum haec consuetudo *per saltum* consecrandi longo tempore exoleverit (quamvis nullo forsan statuto prohibita), et episcopus aliquo saltem tempore sacerdos exstiterit in presbyteratu, sacerdotium denuo conferri nunc non est necessarium, nec (si iudicium nostrum ingenue fateamur) rectissimum et optimum. Nec, cum secundum Concilium Tridentinum (*sess* V. *de Ref c.* II et *sess.* XXIV *de Ref. c.* IV) "praecipuum episcoporum munus" sit praedicatio evangelii, a Romanis hoc exigendum est. Ideo neque "summum sacerdotium" neque "sacerdotium" ullum novum de episcopis praedicari est necesse.

Nos tamen, cum in Ordinali nostro de summis sacerdotibus et pontificibus sileamus, usum horum nominum in aliis documentis publicis non refugimus. Exempla enim proferri possunt ex *libro precum publicarum* etc anno 1560 latine edito, ex epistula duodecim episcoporum pro Grindallo archiepiscopo A D. 1580, et ex mandato archiepiscopi nostri Whitgift suffraganeo suo episcopo Dovoriensi dato A.D. 1583.[1]

sec. 9, 10, t II p 278 sq, et ordinem Mabillonii VIII (=Martene I) qui in codicibus saec. IX invenitur, ubi patet nihil discriminis factum fuisse in forma si consecrandus diaconus tantum foret Canon enim Sardicensis XIII in Occidente parum servabatur, ut, inter alia, ex versione Dionysii Exigui patet, qui verba canonis ἐὰν μὴ καὶ ἀναγνώστου καὶ διακόνου καὶ πρεσβυτέρου ὑπηρεσίαν ἐκτελέσῃ sic reddit "nisi ante et lectoris munere et officio diaconi *aut* presbyteri fuerit perfunctus" Exempla afferuntur Johannis diaconi, S Galli discipuli (Walafridus Strabo in *vita S. Galli* c 23-25, A D 625), Constantini anti-papae (A.D 767), et paparum Pauli I (A D 757), Valentini (A.D. 827), et Nicolai I (A.D 858) Hunc morem inter alia Latinis obiciebat Photius Constantinopolitanus Rem non negabat Nicolaus, sed de promotione Patriarchae ex laico Graecos arguebat, *Ep.* lxx ap Labb. et Cossart. *Concil* VIII p 471 B Ordinatio etiam diaconi in Episcopum *per saltum* intellegitur in rituali Syrorum Nestorianorum apud Morinum *de sacr. ord.* parte II p 388, ed Antverp 1695 = Denzinger *Ritus Orientalium* t. II p 238 (1864)

XIII. [1] Vide orationem pro clero et populo post Letaniam et *Conc Mag Brit.* IV. pp. 293 et 304. Secundo loco Grindallus a confratribus suis vocatur "eximius Christi praesul et summus in Ecclesia Anglicana sacerdos Dei."

APPENDIX II 373

XIV. Duobus autem argumentis contra formam nostram prolatis, quae praecipue Papae placent, paulo latius respondebimus. Piimum quidem est nos post centum fere annos (AD 1662) post verba "Accipe Spiritum sanctum" quaedam addidisse quae *officium et opus episcopi* vel *sacerdotis* (cf. infra cap. XV et not. 1 et 3) designarent. Et innuit verba illa Domini nostri, sine verbis postea additis, non per se satis fuisse sed manca et non idonea. Sed in Pontificali Romano, cum consecretur Episcopus per impositionem manuum consecratoris et assistentium Episcoporum forma sola est "Accipe Spiritum sanctum." In Pontificalibus autem recentioribus nostris Spiritus sanctus invocabatur per Hymnum "Veni Creator," Exoniensi excepto in quo forma Romana additur Sequebatur oratio de cornu gratiae sacerdotalis. Sed, ut diximus, in nulla oratione, ante consecrationem perfectam, apparet in Pontificali nomen episcopi vel episcopatus; ita ut videantur Patres nostri anno 1550 et postea, si in forma erraverint, ut innuit Papa, omisso nomine episcopi, una cum ecclesia Romana hodierna errasse Sed illo tempore continuo apud nos sequebantur verba S. Pauli quibus credebatur memorare consecrationem S. Timothei in episcopum Ephesium, et manifesto in hunc sensum usurpata. Sunt vero "Et memento ut resuscites gratiam Dei quae est in te per impositionem manuum Non enim dedit nobis Deus spiritum timoris sed virtutis et dilectionis et sobrietatis" (2 *Tim.* i 6, 7). Et recordari potestis, fratres, haec verba sola a Concilio Tridentino citari, ut probet ordinem conferre gratiam (*sess.* XXIII *de sacr ord. cap.* III). Haec ergo forma, vel simplex ut in Pontificali, vel duplex ut apud nos, abunde sufficit ad creandum episcopum, si intentio vera manifestetur, quae patet per alias orationes et suffragia (quae officium, opus et ministerium episcopi diserte commemorant), per examen et similia. Non dicimus vero verba "Accipe Spiritum sanctum" necessaria esse, sed sufficientia Non enim in Pontificalibus nostris antiquioribus apparent neque in Romanis, neque omnino in Orientalibus. Sed cum Concilio Tridentino libenter con-

374 A ROMAN DIARY AND OTHER DOCUMENTS

fitemur, ea verba non frustra dici ab episcopis,[1] vel in consecratione episcopi, vel in ordinatione presbyteri, cum verba Domini sint ad Discipulos, ex quibus omnia officia nostra et potestates fluxerint, et tam sacrae rei apta et idonea. In Diaconatu non tam idonea sunt, itaque a nobis in ea ordinatione non adhibentur.

XV. Forma quoque presbyteri faciendi apud nos anno 1550 et postea aeque idonea fuit Oratione enim Eucharistica finita, quae ad institutionem Domini nostri mentes nostras revocat, sequebatur impositio manuum ab Episcopo cum sacerdotibus assistentibus facta cui coniuncta est forma imperativa ex Pontificali desumta, sed eadem plenior et gravior. (Cf. cap. XIX.) Post verba enim "Accipe Spiritum sanctum" continuo sequebantur, ut in Pontificali Romano hodierno, quod mirum in modum silet Papa, "quorum remiseris peccata remittuntur eis; et quorum retinueris retenta sunt;" et statim a Patribus nostris ex Evangelio (S. Luc. xii 42) et S. Paulo (1 ad Cor. iv 1) bene addita "et sis fidelis Dispensator verbi Dei et sanctorum sacramentorum eius; in nomine Patris et Filii et Spiritus Sancti. Amen." Quae forma nulli alii ministro ecclesiae nisi sacerdoti congruit, qui et potestatem clavium (quae vocatur) habeat et verbum et mysteria Dei populo solus pleno iure dispenset, sive in presbyteratu maneat, sive in episcopatum ad maiora munera promotus fuerit. Deinde sequebatur, ut nunc sequitur, collatio potestatis praedicandi et ministrandi sacramenta, ubi quis ad haec constitutus fuerit minister, cum traditione Bibliorum sacrorum, quae nostro iudicio instrumenta praecipua ministerii sacri sunt, et cetera in se (iuxta ordinis gradum proprium) comprehendunt. Et ob causam Gordonianam forsan non inutile fuerit explicare, has formas non verbis tantum sed re differre. Prima enim, quae cum impositione manuum coniungitur, "Accipe Spiritum sanctum" cum verbis sequentibus, dat facultates et potestates sacerdotii generales, et, ut dici solet, characterem imprimit Secunda autem, cum traditione Bibliorum, dat auctoritatem ut ille

XIV. [1] Vide Conc 7rid. sess xxiii de sacr. ord can iv.

APPENDIX II 375

qui ordinatus sit Deo publice ministret et potestatem exerceat super fideles qui unicuique in parochia sua vel cura animarum committendi sunt Quae mandata simul iuncta omnia necessaria sacerdotio Christiano comprehendunt et, nostro iudicio, clarius ostendunt quam in sacramentariis et pontificalibus factum est. Neque enim nomen ipsum "sacerdotis" et similia declinamus aut in *Libro precum publicarum seu ministerii ecclesiasticae administrationis sacramentorum, etc.* sub Elizabetha Regina A.D. 1560 latine edito, aut in aliis documentis publicis latina lingua conceptis.[1] Et hoc non sine significatione factum videtur, cum in versionibus Biblicis nostris, saeculo XVI editis, verbum ἱερεὺς id est "sacerdos" per "Priest" reddatur (quod in Ordinali Anglicano semper usitatur, et saepissime in officio Eucharistico et alibi); πρεσβύτερος autem i e. "Presbyter" vertitur "Elder" id est "Senior."

Cum ergo verba *ad officium et opus episcopi* vel *sacerdotis* (ut nos Latine reddere solemus "the office and work of a priest") anno 1662, addita essent, non videtur Romanae controversiae gratia factum, sed ad erudiendas Presbyterianorum mentes, qui in nostro libro fundamentum suis opinionibus quaerebant. Historicis bene notum est eo tempore certamen Ecclesiae Anglicanae cum eis viris et aliis novatoribus, rege occiso et regis filio expulso et ecclesiastico statu everso, multo acerbius fuisse quam cum Romanis. Addita sunt vero verba non ut formam sensu liturgico perficerent. Mutationes enim illae longius nos a Pontificalibus trahebant non propius adducebant. Scopus ergo additamenti erat ut differentia ordinis manifestaretur. Addita sunt etiam eodem tempore alia eiusdem generis contra novatores, velut in Letania precationes contra "rebellionem" et contra "schisma," oratio pro Magna Curia Parlamenti et pro stabilitate pacis internae et religionis, et orationes quatuor temporibus dicendae.

XV. [1] E g in articulis religionis anni 1562, in canonibus anni 1571 et alibi. vide *Conc Mag. Brit.* tom iv. pp. 236, 263, 429. Similiter in versione graeca libri nostri, anno 1665 Cantabrigiae edita Ἱερωσύνη et ἱερεὺς in ordinali et in officio Eucharistico et alibi leguntur. In quibusdam versionibus latinis "presbyter" potius reperitur.

376 A ROMAN DIARY AND OTHER DOCUMENTS

Quae Papam latere forsan non mirandum est; sed haec omnia difficultatem monstrant libri nostri interpretandi ex separatione gentium et ecclesiarum ortam.[1]

Sed forma saeculi XVI per se non modo sufficiens sed abunde sufficiens erat. Oratio enim *Omnipotens Deus, omnium bonorum dator*, quae pro vocatis "in officium sacerdotii" Deum apprecatur ut Ipsi fideliter in hoc officio deserviant, pars formae tunc temporis erat et ab episcopo immediate ante examen dicebatur.[2] Nunc vero, cum verba nova eandem sententiam diserte exprimant in alium locum remota est et pro collecta diei sumitur.

Hanc etiam mutationem Papam fugisse non miramur: sed res animadversione digna est. Observamus enim eum in hac parte litterarum aliquantulum cunctari, cum innuat formam anni 1662 forsan in se sufficientem aestimari debere, si modo centum fere annis antiquior fuisset (§ 7). Opinionem etiam eorum theologorum videtur amplecti, qui formam non in oratione vel benedictione una, vel precativa quam dicunt vel imperativa, sed in serie tota formularum vinculo quodam morali coniunctarum, constare credant. Pergit enim disputare de auxilio causae nostrae "novissime," ut credit, "accessito ab aliis eiusdem Ordinalis precibus." Quae provocatio nostra nullo modo nova est, sed facta fuit saeculo XVII cum iam argumentatio

---

XV. [1] Vide G. Burnet *Hist Ref.* II p. 144 (1680) et *Vindication of Ordinations of Ch of Eng.* p 71 (1677); H. Prideaux *Eccl Tracts* pp. 15, 36, 69–72 etc. (1687) ed. 2, 1715, cf. eiusdem epistulam ap. Cardwell *Conferences* p 387-8 n., ed. 3 Oxon 1849.

XV. [2] Operae pretium est hanc orationem annorum 1550 et 1552 hic referre, cum verba illa *ad officium et opus presbyteri* vel *sacerdotis* tam magni Romae aestimentur.

"Omnipotens Deus, omnium bonorum dator, qui per Spiritum sanctum tuum varios ministrorum ordines in Ecclesia tua constituisti; Respice propitius hos famulos tuos in officium sacerdotii iam vocatos, et eos doctrinae tuae veritate et innocentia vitae ita adimple, ut tam ore quam bono exemplo tibi in hoc officio fideliter deserviant, ad gloriam tui Nominis et ad Congregationis profectum Per merita." Haec oratio notionem "benedictionis" *Deus honorum omnium* breviter exprimit Sunt qui credant "bonorum" variam lectionem esse pro "honorum."

APPENDIX II 377

Romana de verbis additis primum innotesceret.[1] Neque
illum ab opinione Johannis Cardinalis de Lugo credimus
dissentire qui docet totam ordinationem unam actionem
efficere, nec referre si materia et forma ab invicem
seiunctae sint (ut in Pontificali fit) si ea quae intercedant
moraliter coniungantur.[2]

XVI. Argumentum autem praecipuum et firmissimum
illud Papae videri credimus quod non de verbis in forma
nostra additis, sed de cerimoniis et orationibus in cetera
actione peragenda a nobis sublatis, nos incuset. Scribit
enim (§ 7) "Nam ut cetera praetereantur quae eas (preces)
demonstrent in ritu Anglicano minus sufficientes proposito,
unum hoc argumentum sit instar omnium, de ipsis consulto
detractum esse quidquid in ritu catholico dignitatem et
officia sacerdotii perspicue designat Non ea igitur forma
esse apta et sufficiens sacramento potest, quae id nempe
reticet quod deberet proprium significare." Et infra addit
quae partim falsa sunt, partim lectores in errorem facillime
abductura, et Patribus nostris et nobis iniqua :—" Toto
Ordinali non modo nulla est aperta mentio sacrificii,
consecrationis, sacerdotii, potestatisque consecrandi et sacrificii offerendi : sed immo omnia huiusmodi rerum vestigia
. . . sublata et deleta sunt de industria" (§ 8). Et alio
loco, magna (piget dicere) cum rerum ignorantia, scribit de
parte "ea Anglicanorum, non ita magna, recentiore tempore coalita, quae arbitratur posse idem Ordinale ad sanam
rectamque sententiam intelligi et deduci." Deinde a nobis
negari et adulterari sacramentum ordinis affirmat, nos
repudiare (in Ordinali scilicet) omnem notionem consecrationis et sacrificii, et dicit officia presbyteri et episcopi
restare "nomina sine re quam instituit Christus." His

XV [1] Vide Gilb Burnet *Vindication* pp. 8, 71, qui scribit haec
additamenta Ordinationi non essentialia esse sed explicationes tantum esse eorum "quae antea per alias harum formularum partes
satis clara fuerant," et Humf Prideaux *Eccl Tracts* p. 117 qui
orationem *Omnipotens Deus* exscribit et de ea disputat. Similia
scripserat J. Bramhall (1658) *Works* A C. L iii pp 162-9, Oxon
1844
XV. [2] *De sacramentis in gen.* disp ii sec V § 99, t. iii p. 293-4,
Paris 1892

378 A ROMAN DIARY AND OTHER DOCUMENTS

duris et inconsultis verbis respondimus iam ex parte, monendo incertam et periculosam viam ab eo iniri qui ex coniectura tantum ecclesiae nostrae actus interpretetur, et sibi ius adsumat novi decreti proponendi de ordinis forma necessaria, quod episcopos nostros legitimos, saeculo decimo sexto ecclesiam gubernantes, ob regulam illis plane incognitam, damnet. Ecclesiarum particularium libertas in ritibus reformandis non ita pro arbitrio Romae tollenda est. Nam, ut infra partim monstrabimus, "ritus catholicus" nullo modo unus est, sed multum inter se variant ritus etiam a Romanis approbati.

Sed tacet intentionem ecclesiae nostrae ex praefatione Ordinalis nostri notissimam, tacet principium a Patribus nostris semper propositum quod actus eorum sine interpretatione inimica explicat.

XVII. Intentio certe ecclesiae nostrae, non partis recenter coalitae, ex titulo Ordinalis et praefatione eidem praefixa abunde patet. Titulus quidem anno 1552 erat "Ordo et ritus faciendi et consecrandi Episcopos Presbyteros et Diaconos." Praefatio autem, quae statim sequitur, sic incipit :—"Manifestum est omnibus, Sacram Scripturam et veteres auctores diligenter perlegentibus, exstitisse in Ecclesia Christi ex Apostolorum temporibus hosce ministrorum ordines, Episcopos, Presbyteros et Diaconos. Quae quidem munera ita magni semper aestimabantur, ut nemo auderet privata sua auctoritate ullo eorum fungi, nisi qui iam vocatus esset, probatus, examinatus, et eidem sustinendo par esset satis cognitus: et praeterea per preces publicas cum impositione manuum ad id approbatus et admissus. Igitur eo fine ut isti Ordines in Ecclesia Anglicana conserventur et reverentia debita usurpentur et aestimentur : necessarium est neminem (nisi qui iam Episcopus, Presbyter aut Diaconus sit) ullo eorum fungi, nisi qui secundum ritum sequentem ad id vocatus, probatus, examinatus et admissus fuerit." Infra autem dicit inter alia "quisque autem in Episcopatum consecrandus annum tricesimum complevisse debet." Et in ritu ipso "Consecratio" Episcopi saepius memoratur. Successio

APPENDIX II 379

etiam et propagatio horum officiorum a Domino per
Apostolos et ceteros ecclesiae antiquae ministros diserte
significatur in orationibus "Eucharisticis" quae praemit-
tuntur verbis *Accipe Spiritum sanctum.* Intentio igitur
Patrum nostrorum fuit haec officia a primis temporibus
derivata conservare et propagare "et reverentia debita
usurpare et aestimare," eo nimirum sensu quo ab Apostolis
recepta sunt et eo usque in usu erant. Quod a Papa
indebite siletur.

XVIII. Sed Leo papa haec omnia et similia "nomina
sine re quam instituit Christus" vocat. At contra principium fundamentale nostrorum Patrum fuit omnia ad
auctoritatem Domini in sacris Scripturis revelatam revo-
care. Cerimonias ergo ab hominibus confectas et additas
rescindebant, etiam illam notissimam codicem Evangeliorum
tenendi super caput episcopi ordinandi, dum benedictio
funditur et manus imponuntur, qua et Latinis et Orientalibus hodie communis est,[1] quamvis ecclesiae Romanae
antiquae incognita.
Una igitur materia in imprimendo charactere utebantur
nostri, sc. impositione manuum, una in tradenda potestate
publice ministrandi et facultates exercendi super gregem
unicuique commissum, sc. Bibliorum vel Evangeliorum
traditione, quam ex ritu novum episcopum inaugurandi et
similibus videntur adsumsisse, ut in Pontificali manet
Evangeliorum traditio post annulum episcopo datum.
Ceteras velut traditionem instrumentorum et ornamen-
torum, benedictionem et unctionem manuum et capitis,
cum orationibus consequentibus, recentius institutas, et in
Ordinale antiquum Romanum ex aliis plerumque gentibus
et praesertim ex Gallia acceptas, pleno iure rescindebant

XVIII. [1] Vide *Constitutiones Apost.* VIII. 4 et *Statuta Ecclesiae
antiquae* canone 2, quae Gallicana, ex provincia Arelatensi, videntur,
quamvis interdum falso nomine Concilii Carthaginensis IV circum-
ferantur. Hunc ritum ab ecclesia Romana alienum fuisse diserte
testatur auctor libri, qui in Alcuini nostri operibus editur, *de divinis
officiis* cap. xxxvii, saec. fortasse XI "non reperitur in auctoritate
veteri neque nova, neque in Romana traditione." (Migne *P.L.* tom
101 p. 1237.) Et sic Amalarius *de eccl. off.* II 14 (*P.L.* 105 p. 1092).
De usu in consecratione papae vide Mabillon. *Ord.* IX 5.

380 A ROMAN DIARY AND OTHER DOCUMENTS

Porrectio instrumentorum, ut satis notum, ex formulis ordinum minorum fluxit, et Pontificalibus ante saeculum XI incognita fuit, quo tempore a scriptoribus primum memorari videtur. Hac reformata recidebat etiam formula nova " Accipe potestatem offerre sacrificium Deo missamque (vel ut in Pontificali Romano "missasque ") celebrare tam pro vivis quam pro defunctis," etc. Oratio vero ad benedicendas manus etiam ante saec XVI ad placitum episcopi dici vel dimitti poterat Unctio Gallicana et Britannica est, non Romana. Non enim solum a libris "Leoniano " et "Gelasiano "abest, sed ab ordinibus VIII et IX Mabillonii et a " S. Amandi," qui saeculi, ut videtur, VIII–IX consuetudinem repraesentant. Porro saeculo nono Nicolaus Papa I scribit A.D. 874 ad Rudolfum Bituricensem,in Romana ecclesia nec presbyterorum nec diaconorum manus chrismate inungi.[1] Primus qui aliquid tale commemorat est Gildas Britannicus.[2] Similia etiam dici possunt de unctione capitis, quae ex imitatione consecrationis Aaronicae, ut alia plura, manifeste fluxerit, et saeculo IX vel X extra Romam, ut ex Amalario (*de eccl. off.* ii. 14) et Pontificalibus nostris colligi potest, primum apparuerit.[3]

Restat Benedictio Gallicana *Deus sanctificationum omnium auctor*, quae ex abundanti Benedictioni Romanae addita est (cap XII), et similiter a Patribus nostris reiecta est. Quae oratio verbis interpolatis manifeste corrupta, ut in Pontificali Romano habetur, doctrinae transsubstantiationis, a nobis reiectae, favere videbatur, et in se vix intellegi

XVIII. [1] Migne *Pat Lat* tom 119 p. 884, ubi numeratur epist 66. Cf. et Martene *de ant ecc rit* lib I cap VIII art IX sec 9 et 14 Haec Nicolai responsio " Praeterea sciscitaris " in Gratiani *Decreto dist* XXIII. cap 12 inseritur.

XVIII. [2] *Epistola* § 106 p 111 ed Stevenson, 1838, qui benedictionem memorat " qua initiantur sacerdotum vel ministrorum manus " Unctio manuum presbyterorum et diaconorum in Sacramentariis Anglicanis saeculorum X et XI praescribitur

XVIII. [3] Confer *Conc Trid. Sess* XXIII *de sacr ord. canone* v, quod cum videatur admittere in ordinatione unctionem "non requiri," anathematizat eos qui eam, et alias ordinis cerimonias, " contemnendas et perniciosas "dixerit

APPENDIX II 381

poterat, ita ut liturgiae in lingua vulgari dicendae, ad populi
nostri aedificationem, nullo modo idonea videretur. Eadem
tamen, qualiscunque sit, nihil de potestate sacrificandi
docet.

XIX. Quid mirum ergo si orationes illas ex liturgia,
lingua vulgari recitanda, resecarent Patres nostri ut ad
simplicitatem Evangelii redirent? In quo viam viae
a Romanis initae oppositam certe sequebantur. Romani
enim a simplicitate paene Evangelica incipientes, suorum
rituum severitatem ornamentis Gallicanis distinxerunt, et
cerimonias a Vetere Testamento traductas decursu
temporis addiderunt, ut discrimen inter populum et
sacerdotes etiam atque etiam significaretur. Quas cerimonias nullo modo "contemnendas et perniciosas," aut
suis locis et temporibus inutiles dicimus, sed non necessarias
esse profitemur. Saeculo ergo XVI cum Patres nostri
liturgiam, in usum tam plebis quam cleri ordinarent, paene
ad origines Romanas reversi sunt. Utrique enim, et Patres
eorum sancti, et nostri, quos novatores dicunt, eosdem
duces fidissimos sequebantur, Dominum et Apostolos.
Nunc vero ecclesiae hodiernae Romanae exemplum, quae
tota in offerendo sacrificio occupatur, quasi exemplar
unicum nobis proponitur. Quod a Papa tam strenue
factum est, ut scribere non dubitet de Ordinalis nostri
precibus "consulto detractum esse quidquid in ritu
catholico dignitatem et officia sacerdotii perspicue designet"
(§ 7).

At nos fidenter asserimus Ordinale nostrum, in hac
praesertim re, Pontificali Romano variis modis praestare,
cum et ea quae ex institutione Christi ad naturam sacerdotii attinent (§ 9), et effectum rituum catholicorum in
Ecclesia universa usitatorum, clarius et fidelius exprimat.
Quod ex collatione Pontificalis et Ordinalis, nostro
quidem, iudicio, ostendi potest.

Formula Romana incipit cum praesentatione ab Archi-
diacono facta et duplici adlocutione episcopi, prima ad
clerum et populum, secunda ad ordinandos—in ordinatione enim presbyteri examen nullum publice fit. Sequitur

382 A ROMAN DIARY AND OTHER DOCUMENTS

impositio manuum episcopi, et deinde presbyterorum assistentium, sine ullis verbis effecta ; de quo ritu perplexo Cardinalis de Lugo iudicium citavimus (cap. xv). Deinde dicuntur orationes tres antiquae, duae breves et Benedictio longior (cap XII), quae ab episcopo "extensis manibus ante pectus" iam dicitur. Haec, quae in antiquis libris "Consecratio" dicitur, ab auctoribus probatis,[1] post Morinum, vera ordinationis Romanae forma creditur, et cum impositione manuum olim sine dubio coniungebatur : nunc vero, ut in Confirmatione fit (cap. x), extensio manuum pro impositione adhibetur, nec tamen ipsa necessaria creditur. Certe, si ordinationes Romanae antiquae valent, hac oratione dicta ordinatio presbyterorum etiam nunc in ista ecclesia perfecta est. Illa enim forma quae semel pro aliquo sacramento Ecclesiae suffecerit, et adhuc intacta et integra retineatur, eadem mente retenta credi debet ; nec sine sacrilegio quodam asseri potest eam virtutem suam perdidisse, cum alia post eam tacite addita sint. Propositum vero partis recentioris formulae Romanae non id certe fuit ut partem antiquiorem vi propria evacuaret ; sed non inepte credi potest hoc fuisse, ut sacerdotes iam ordinati primo ad sacrificium offerendum variis ritibus et cerimoniis praepararentur, deinde ut potestatem offerendi diserte traditam acciperent, tertio ut iidem in missa celebranda ius sacerdotii usurparent, denique ut alia potestate sacerdotali, peccata scilicet remittendi, publice ornarentur. Quae sententia ex verbis Pontificalium veterum confirmatur, ut e.g. in Pontificali Sarisburiensi legitur "Benedic et sanctifica has manus *sacerdotum tuorum.*" Haec igitur omnia quae post antiquam illam formam sequuntur, sicut verba nostra anno 1662 addita, simpliciter non necessaria sunt. Potestates enim istae vel implicite et ex usu tradi possunt, ut apud antiquos fiebat, vel statim et diserte ; sed ad ordinationis efficaciam modus traditionis nullo modo pertinet.

Quae cum partim perspexissent patres nostri, et viderent

XIX. [1] Vide Martene *de ant. eccl. rit.* I cap VIII art. IX § 18 t. ii p. 320 ed. Rotom. 1700, et Gasparri *Tract. Can. de s. ord.* § 1059 Paris 1893

APPENDIX II 383

doctrinam scholasticam circa transsubstantiationem panis et vini, et recentiorem de sacrificio crucis in missa (ut credebatur) repetito, populari sensu cum quibusdam ex sequentibus cerimoniis et orationibus coniungi, apud se quaerebant quomodo ritus ille totus non modo integrior et purior, sed perfectior et nobilior evaderet. Et cum eo tempore de antiquitate orationum primarum nullo modo constaret, sed doctorum sententiae formis imperativis omnem virtutem tribuerent, animos suos ad has potius quam ad illas advertebant.

In quem finem primo simplicitatem persequebantur, et totius ritus partes ad unum quasi culmen dirigebant, ita ut nemo dubitare posset quo momento gratia et potestas sacerdotii daretur. Ea est enim simplicitatis vis ut animos hominum magis ad divina evehat quam series longa cerimoniarum, quamvis rectissima voluntate coniunctarum. Orationibus ergo praemissis, quae et officium sacerdotii et successionem a ministerio Apostolorum declarabant, impositionem manuum cum verbis Domini nostri iungebant. Et in hac re exemplum Ecclesiae Apostolicae consulto[1] secuti sunt, quae primo " ad orationem se convertebat," deinde manus imponebat et ministros suos dimittebat, non Romanae, quae impositionem manuum primo adhibet. Secundo, cum de variis sacerdotii officiis secum reputarent, videbant Pontificale vulgatum circa duas res defici. Cum enim in adlocutione episcopi haec officia recenserentur " sacerdotem oportet offerre, benedicere, praeesse, praedicare et baptizare" vel similia, et in forma antiqua pro presbyteris de "ratione dispensationis sibi creditae reddenda" dictum esset, in ceteris tamen formis nihil nisi de sacrificio offerendo et de peccatis remittendis dicebatur, et eae potestatum collationes longius ab invicem seiungebantur. Videbant etiam pastoralis officii munera parum habere loci in Pontificali, quamvis de illis Evangelium plenissime eloquatur. In ipsa ergo praeclara adlocutione ab episcopo pronuntianda, et in examine dignissimo quod

---

XIX [1] Vide adlocutionem Archiepiscopi ad populum in consecratione Episcopi, et Act. xiii 3. Cf. vi 6 et xiv 22.

384 A ROMAN DIARY AND OTHER DOCUMENTS

sequitur, officium pastorale, quod est praesertim Nuntii, Speculatoris et Dispensatoris Domini, sacerdotibus nostris praecipue proponebant : quae nisi quis legerit et perpenderit, et cum sacris Scripturis comparaverit, Ordinalis nostri virtutem plane non novit Quod vero ad sacramenta attinet, in formis imperativis recensendis Domini nostri verbis primum locum dabant, non ex reverentia tantum sed quia eo tempore haec verba pro forma necessaria vulgo crederentur. Deinde omnia " sacramentorum mysteria antiquitus instituta" (ut sacramentarii nostri veteris verbis utamur ; vide cap. XII[4]) sacerdotibus nostris commendabant, non unius tantum partem, aliis posthabitis, extollebant. Denique formam, quae characterem imprimit, cum forma quae iurisdictionem confert, una collocabant.

Et in his et similibus, quae longum esset recensere, exemplum Domini nostri et Apostolorum sine dubio sequebantur. Non enim solum dixisse memoratur Dominus " Hoc facite in meam commemorationem" et " Euntes ergo docete omnes gentes baptizantes eos,"—ut rite ministranda sacramenta doceret, set multa et observatione dignissima de pastorali officio, et suo, qui Pastor bonus est, et discipulorum suorum qui exemplo Illius moniti vitas suas ponere pro fratribus debent. (Confer Evangelium S. Johannis x 11–18 et 1 Ep. Joh. iii 16) Multa quoque in Evangelio tradidit de praedicatione verbi, de dispensatione servis electis commissa, de missione Apostolorum et discipulorum suo loco, de peccatorum conversione et remissione delictorum in Ecclesia, de ministerio invicem faciendo, et cetera similia. Hoc ergo modo Sapientiae divinae placebat praesertim Nuntios, Speculatores et Dispensatores suos erudire, ut mundo, post discessum Eius, testimonium darent, et plebem sanctam in Adventum suum rite praepararent. Et quod fecerat Dominus fecerunt et Apostoli. Testis S. Petrus cum Seniores, id est presbyteros et episcopos, ut Consenior obsecrat " pascite qui in vobis est gregem Dei," et " cum apparuerit Princeps pastorum, precipietis immarcessibilem coronam" (1 Pet. v 1–4). Testis

APPENDIX II

S. Paulus cum presbyteros et episcopos Ephesios admonet voce (Act. xx 18–35) et cum Epistula insigniter spirituali erudit (Eph. iv 11–13). Testis S. Gregorius Papa, cui gens Anglicana, per totum mundum iam dispersa, tantum debet, qui in libro suo *de regula Pastorali* multus est de his rebus et de moribus pastorum, sed de sacrificio offerendo paene aut omnino silet. Qui liber tanto in honore erat ut episcopis saeculo IX infra ipsam ordinationem daretur, una cum libro canonum, addita monitione ut vitas suas secundum eius praecepta regerent.[1]

Sanctus etiam Petrus, qui Pastorale officium tanto cum studio presbyteris commendat, in priori parte eiusdem epistulae totam plebem, ut sacerdotium sanctum, de spiritalibus hostiis Deo offerendis admonet (1. Pet. ii 5 et 9). Quod demonstrat illud presbyteris magis proprium esse, cum personam Dei adversus homines repraesentet (*Ps.* xxiii [xxii], Es. xl 10, 11, Jerem. xxiii 1–4, Ezech. xxxiv 11–31), hoc quodammodo cum plebe communicari. Sacerdos enim, cui dispensatio sacramentorum et praesertim Eucharistiae consecratio mandetur, nunquam solus ministrare debet, sed semper cum plebe astante et participante altari deservit.[2] Et sic prophetia

XIX. [1] Hoc testatur Hincmarus in praefatione *Opusculi LV Capitulorum* · Migne *Pat Lat* tom 126 p 292

XIX. [2] Hoc ex Liturgiis Graecis antiquis et Missali Romano constat, in quibus paene omnia plurali numero dicuntur. Confer e g. *Ordinem Missae :* " Orate fratres ut meum ac vestrum sacrificium acceptabile fiat apud Deum Patrem Omnipotentem " ; et in *Canone* " Memento Domine famulorum famularumque tuarum N et N et omnium circumstantium . [pro quibus tibi offerimus, vel] qui tibi offerunt hoc sacrificium laudis," et postea . " Hanc igitur oblationem servitutis nostrae sed et cunctae familiae tuae," etc De his lege e g. S. Petrum Damianum in libro *Dominus vobiscum* cap. viii, de verbis " pro quibus tibi offerimus etc. ". " patenter ostenditur quod a cunctis fidelibus non solum viris sed et mulieribus sacrificium illud laudis offertur, licet ab uno specialiter offerri sacerdote videatur. Quia, quod ille Deo offerendo manibus tractat, hoc multitudo fidelium intenta mentium devotione commendat "; et de " Hanc igitur ". " Quibus verbis luce clarius constat quia sacrificium, quod a sacerdote sacris altaribus superponitur, a cuncta Dei familia generaliter offeratur."

2 C

386 A ROMAN DIARY AND OTHER DOCUMENTS

Malachiae (i 11) impletur, et per oblationem Ecclesiae mundam magnum est Dei nomen in gentibus.

Respondemus ergo nos, Sacris Scripturis insistentes, in sacerdotibus constituendis dispensationem et ministerium verbi et sacramentorum, potestatem peccatorum remittendi et retinendi, et cetera pastoralis, officii munera, recte inculcare et praedicare, et omnia alia in eis resumere et recapitulare. Cuius rei et ipse Papa testis est, qui Pontificalis apicis honorem, ex triplici commendatione gregis Christi S. Petro paenitenti data, maxime deducit. At quod in se tam honorificum reputat, cur in sacerdotibus Anglicanis nihil ad dignitatem et officia sacerdotii conferre credit?

XX. In finem fratrem nostrum in Christo venerandum monitum velimus ne iniquus sit in hac sententia proferenda non solum nobis sed et aliis Christianis, et inter eos antecessoribus suis, qui aeque certe secum Spiritu sancto fruebantur. Orientales enim nobiscum ob defectum intentionis damnare videtur, qui in *Confessione orthodoxa,* circa annum 1640 edita, duas tantum sacerdotii sacramentalis potestates nominent scilicet solvendi delicta et praedicandi ; qui et in *Catechismo longiore Russico,* Mosquae anno 1839 edito, nihil de sacrificio corporis et sanguinis Christi docent, et officia tantum sacramenta ministrandi et gregem pascendi inter ea quae ad ordinem pertinent, commemorant. Porro de tribus ordinibus ita loquuntur :—" Diaconus sacramentis inservit : Presbyter sacramenta consecrat, sub episcopo : Episcopus non tantum ipse sacramenta consecrat, sed potestatem habet per manuum impositionem aliis impertiendi donum et gratiam ut illa consecrent." Nobiscum certe mysteriorum plurium ministerium sacerdotibus magis convenire, quam unius sacrificii oblationem, docent.

Et hoc quidem in forma apud Graecos nunc usitata apparet, in oratione quae incipit *Deus qui magnus es in potentia* :—" hunc quem voluisti, ut subiret gradum Presbyteri, imple dono sancti tui Spiritus, ut fiat dignus qui assistat inculpatus sanctuario tuo, praedicet Evangelium tui regni, administret verbum tuae veritatis, offerat tibi

APPENDIX II 387

dona et sacrificia spiritualia, renovet populum tuum per lavacrum regenerationis" etc (Habert *Lib. Pontif.* p. 314, ed. 1643)

Sed de Patribus suis, quorum ordinationes supra descripsimus, quid iudicaturi sint etiam atque etiam Romani videant. Si enim Patres nostros ante annos ducentos et quinquaginta invalide ordinatos novo decreto Papa pronuntiet, nihil obstat quominus omnes simili modo ordinatos ordines nullos accepisse, eodem iure, necessario decernendum sit. Et si Patres nostri, qui formis, ut dicit, annis 1550 et 1552 nullis uterentur, nullo modo eas reformare anno 1662 possent, sui quoque eidem legi subiacent. Et si Hippolytus et Victor et Leo et Gelasius et Gregorius, in ritibus suis, partim parum de sacerdotio et de summo sacerdotio, et nihil de potestate offerendi sacrificium corporis et sanguinis Christi dixerint, ecclesia ipsa Romana sacerdotium nullum obtinet, et Sacramentariorum reformatores, quocunque nomine gauderent, nihil pro ritibus sanandis efficere poterant. "Hierarchia enim" ut ait, "extincta" ob nullitatem formae, "potestas ordinandi nulla fuit." Et si Ordinale "valere ad usum ordinationum minime possit, nequaquam decursu aetatum, quum tale ipsum permanserit, futurum fuit ut valeret. Atque ii egerunt frustra, qui inde a [saeculis VI et XI] conati sunt admittere aliquid sacrificii et sacerdotii, [et de peccatis remittendis et retinendis], nonnulla dein ad ordinale facta accessione." Et sic, una cum nostris, omnes ordines suos subvertit Papa, et iudicium propriae ecclesiae infert. Eugenius quippe IV magnum periculum nullitatis ecclesiae suae intulit, cum doceret novam materiam et formam ordinis, et ne verbo quidem veras attingeret. Nemo enim scit quot ordinationes, eo docente, factae fuerint sine ulla impositione manuum aut forma idonea. Leo autem formam prioribus Romanis episcopis incognitam, et intentionem in Orientalium catechismis deficientem, postulat.

Ad summam, cum ad nos haec omnia nomine pacis et unitatis afferantur, notum omnibus esse volumus nos aequo saltem studio pacem et unitatem in Ecclesia prosequi. Quae autem frater noster Leo Papa XIII in aliis

388 A ROMAN DIARY AND OTHER DOCUMENTS

litteris de tempore in tempus scripsit aliquando verissima esse, et semper bona cum voluntate scripta, agnoscimus. Discrimen enim et disceptatio inter nos et illum ex diversa interpretatione eiusdem Evangelii oritur, quod unice verum omnes credimus et veneramur. Multa etiam in ipso amore et reverentia digna esse libenter profitemur. Sed error ille apud Romanos inveteratus capitis visibilis pro Christo invisibili substituendi, verba eius bona fructu pacis privabit. Quid Christus ergo voluerit in ministerio Evangelico constituendo nobiscum patienter, quaesumus, fratres reverendissimi, expendatis. Hoc prius facto alia sequentur tempore suo cum Deus voluerit.

Faxit Deus ut etiam ex hac controversia oriatur plenior veritatis notitia, patientia maior, et amplius pacis desiderium in Ecclesia Christi, Salvatoris mundi.

F. CANTUAR :
WILLELM : EBOR :

Data est haec epistula feria sexta die xix
mensis Februarii A.S. 1897.

APPENDIX.—DE CAUSA JOHANNIS GORDON

Johannes Gordon, de quo in capitulo VII breviter disseruimus, episcopus Gallovidiensis in Scotia meridionali anno 1688 in ecclesia Cathedrali Glasguensi sacratus est. Qui regem Jacobum II in exilium secutus, postea in ecclesiam Romanam receptus est et sub condicione denuo baptizatus est. Idem nomen Clementis Papae tunc regnantis suo praenomini addidit. Hic vir, ut notum est, ex eodem Pontifice postulavit, petitione vel memoriali quae hodie exstat,[1] ut

App. [1] Vide M Le Quien *Nullité des Ordinations Anglicanes* tom ii. App pag lxix–lxxv, Paris 1725—cui subsequitur decretum S. Officii Confer E. E. Estcourt *The question of Anglican Ordinations discussed* (Lond. 1873) App xxxvi pp. cxv sq, qui aliud summarium vel argumentum causae et aliam decreti subsequentis formam, aliqua cum cura repetita, typis mandavit. Carta regis pro consecratione (post electionem) data est 4 die Februarii, et signata 4 Septembris 1688 . summarium consecrationem die 19 Septembris habitam refert

APPENDIX II   389

ordines Romano ritu susciperet.   Cuius libelli non opus est ut omnia argumenta recenseamus   Sufficit dicere ea maxime a veritate rerum abhorrere   Fundamentum est fabula de Parkeri archiepiscopi consecratione.   De materia, forma et intentione scribit: " Nulla materia utuntur nisi forte traditione Bibliorum, nulla forma legitima : imo formam Catholicorum abiecere et commutavere in hanc : *Accipe potestatem praedicandi verbum Dei et administrandi sancta eius Sacramenta ;* quae essentialiter differt a formis orthodoxis.   Deinde quae intentio ab illis formari poterit, qui negant Christum aut primam Ecclesiam ullum incruentum instituisse sacrificium ? " Nullam ergo rationem habuit verioris materiae et formae apud nos usitatae, scilicet impositionis manuum et verborum " Accipe Spiritum sanctum" et quae tunc ut nunc anteibant et sequebantur.   Quid vero sibi vellet Gordon cum hoc facinus in se admitteret, nescimus.

Hac ergo ex petitione, quae formam ordinationis presbyterorum solum tetigit, causam Clemens XI iudicavit : et facile credebatur ab eis, qui historiam ex libro Michaelis Le Quien tantum cognovissent, secundum mentem Johannis Gordon simpliciter iudicasse.   Res tamen aliter cecidit, ut constat ex summario, quod decreto praefigitur, quod Estcourt anno demum 1873 typis mandavit, et quod miro modo in hac controversia neglectum fuit, et ex litteris Leonis Papae XIII, qui scribit :—" Qua de forma, quo plenius esset certiusque iudicium, cautum fuerat ut exemplar Ordinalis anglicani suppeteret." Summarium enim, die consecrationis et ceteris huiusmodi prius recitatis, ita pergit :—" Actio sic fere peragebatur.   *Primo,* fiebant preces secundum Liturgiam Anglicanam.   *Secundo,* habebatur concio ad populum de dignitate et officio episcopi. *Tertio,* supradicto Johanne genibus provoluto, omnes supradicti pseudo-episcopi imposuerunt manus capiti et humeris dicendo *Accipe Spiritum Sanctum ; et memento ut suscites gratiam quae in te est per manuum impositionem, non enim accepimus spiritum timoris, sed virtutis dilectionis et sobrietatis.   Quarto,* peractis pauculis precibus pro gratiarum actione, terminata fuit actio." Sequitur decreti

390 A ROMAN DIARY AND OTHER DOCUMENTS

forma, quae, priori in parte, ab illa quam suppeditat Le Quien satis differt, quamvis illi non contradicat. Exemplar autem summarii et decreti, ut ab Estcourt editur, ex S. Officio prodiit die 2 Aprilis anno 1852, et Angelum Argenti, ipsius S O. notarium, testem habuit; ita ut pro documento vero teneri possit.

Notabit prudens lector *primo* formam consecrationis episcopi hic tantum citari, cum Gordon in petitione (quamvis falso) formam ordinationis presbyterorum solum respexisset. Unde statim exoritur quaestio an S.O. Johannis Gordon dicta de ordinatione presbyterorum pro veris habuerit, necne? Si enim vera crediderit, iudicium eius, tali mendacio suffultum, nullum est: si falsa, quare nihil de ea forma accuratius tradidit? *Secundo* observabit, formam hic citatam non esse eam quae anno 1688, saltem in Anglia, in usu erat, sed priorem, annorum scilicet 1550 et 1552. Non enim habet verba anno 1662 addita *ad officium et opus episcopi in ecclesia Dei quod iam tibi committitur, etc.;* et verba ab omnibus consecratoribus prolata dicuntur. Porro tam neglegenter collata fuit forma ut *gratiam* pro *gratiam Dei*, et *non enim accepimus* pro *non enim dedit nobis Deus* (2 Tim. I. 7, secundum S. Hieronymum) substituta sint. Nec tamen, *tertio,* cum illis libris, nec cum recentiori, actionis descriptio revera concordat. Nusquam enim in Ordinalibus nostris impositio manuum "humeris" praescribitur; et multa, sicut praesentatio, examen, hymnus *Veni Creator,* silentio praetereuntur. Quod vero in summario "quarto" dicitur, nullo modo verum est. Post verba enim *Accipe Spiritum sanctum* e.q.s. sequitur traditio Bibliorum sacrorum cum forma altera imperativa *Attende lectioni, exhortationi, et doctrinae,* etc. Deinde sacra Cena celebratur. Denique annis 1550 et 1552 sequebatur tantum oratio una (*Super hunc famulum tuum, quaesumus, Pater misericors*) cui anno 1662 subiuncta est altera (*Actiones nostras*) cum benedictione (*Pax Dei quae exsuperat*). "Pauculae" vero "preces pro gratiarum actione" nusquam sunt. Porro "concio" in libris annorum 1550 et 1552 non praecipitur, sed primum in Ordinali anni 1662 apparet—quamvis probabile sit concionem fuisse. Haec

APPENDIX II 391

ergo collatio Ordinalis Anglicani, qualecunque id fuerit, saltem quatenus ex summario iudicari possit, neglegentissima fuit, et ad ordinationem presbyterorum forsan non extendit : certe, quacunque ex causa fuerit, de ea silet. Quod vero de mentione omissa traditionis Bibliorum, in consecratione Episcopi, dici debeat, nescimus. Verba " sic *fere* peragebatur " neglegentiam, in tam gravi causa culpabilem, indicare videntur. Hactenus omnia ex documentis iam cognitis descripsimus. Sed addit Papa ex scriniis, ut videtur, secretis S. Officii, quod nobis antea incognitum fuit : " ın sententia tamen ferenda omnino seposita est ea causa (*i.e.* Parkeri consecratio) ut documenta produnt integrae fidei," et statim : "neque alia ratio est reputata nisi defectus formae et intentionis." Quae sunt ergo ista "documenta integrae fidei" et quos et quales defectus, si ullos, formae et intentionis commemorant ? An defectus in consecratione episcopi sunt ? Vel in ordinatione presbyterorum ? Aut in ambabus ? Haec maximi momenti sunt, si res ex aequo iudicanda sit. Papa quidem disputat sententiam illam nihil momenti a traditionis instrumentorum defectu duxisse, et rationem subiungit " tunc enim praescriptum de more esset ut ordinatio *sub conditione* instauraretur." Quae argumentatio tum in seipsa debilis est, tum videtur demonstrare documenta ista nihil revera commemorare de genere defectus, cum id ex coniectura tantum colligatur. Et quaerere licet, an revera illo tempore mos iste obtinuerit. Exempla enim, quae ex annis 1604 et 1696 citantur, non de cerimonia omissa sunt, sed de presbyteris ad instrumenta tradenda ab episcopo ordinante delegatis (Le Quien ii pp. 388–394). Anno etiam 1708 cum Capuccinus quidam, cum porrectione patenae, sed sine hostia, casu ordinatus esset, decrevit Congregatio Concılii integram ordinationem *sub condıtione* iterandam quasi de re nova decerneret.[1] Hoc anno quaestio non fuit de

App [1] Vıde P Gasparrı *Tract. canonıc de sacr. ordinat.* sec. 1084 (tom ıı. p. 261, Parıs 1894) Sımılıs causa de altero Capuccıno, subdıacono, resoluta fuıt ab eadem Congregatıone 10 dıe Jan 1711 . vıde *Thesaurum Resolutıonum* tom. ıx parte 2, p. 165.

392 A ROMAN DIARY AND OTHER DOCUMENTS

omissione totius cerimoniae sed de parte eius tantum.
Quaestio de omissione cerimoniae integrae postea, ut
videtur, agitabatur, cum "quidam sacerdotio initiandus,
etsi omnes consuetas manuum impositiones ab Episcopo
accepisset, ad Episcopum tamen, solita Patenae cum
hostia, et Calicis cum vino instrumenta porrigentem, ad
alia tunc temporis distractus, non accessisset." Scribit
enim Benedictus XIV in libro suo de Synodo Dioecesana,
qui Romae primum anno 1748 edebatur, quod super
quaestionem illam "priusquam huic operi extremam
manum admoveremus, fuit in Sacra Congregatione Concilii disceptatum" (lib. viii. cap. x). De anno silet, sed
satis longo tempore post causam Gordonianam videtur
fuisse: et, etiam tunc, quaestio non exorta est de omissione cerimoniae istius consulto facta sed fortuita. Si ergo,
circa annum 1740, Congregatio Concilii de iteranda ordinatione huius rei gratia disceptaret et non sine longo, ut
videtur, consilio "sub conditione" iterandam rescriberet,
anno 1704 mos iste vix obtinuit.

Sed summarium et decretum S. Officii, certe secundum
interpretationem a Papa traditam, vix conciliari possunt
cum documento alio quod ex illo corpore ante dies octo
aut novem prodiisse dicitur, et in *Collectaneis* etiam S. C.
de propaganda fide anno 1893, sub numero 1170, ex parte
insigniori typis mandatum fuit. Responsionem dicimus
de Aethiopum Monophysitarum ordinationibus,[1] in qua

App. [1] Vide de ritu Aethiopum illo tempore Iobi Ludolfi *Commentarium in Hist Aethiop.* pp 323–8 Francof. ad M. 1691. Dubia
de his ordinationibus proposita et responsionem consultorum supremae Inquisitionis primus quantum scimus evulgavit, Benedicti
XIV temporibus, Philippus de Carboneano (1707-1762), ex Fratribus
minoribus, Professor Collegii urbani de propaganda fide, in *Appendicibus* ad *Theol. Moral. univ* Pauli G. Antoine, Romae anno 1752
(p. 677 sq), et alibi saepe editis, ut Ven. 1778 (III. 1, p. 172) Taurini
anno 1789 (V p 501 sq) et Avenione 1818 (V p. 409) Quod de
Appendicibus in Concinae *Theol. Mor* scribit Gasparri, *Tract. Can.
de sacr. Ord.* sec. 1057 Paris 1893, nobis non liquet. De hac causa
vide etiam E. E Estcourt, *The question of Anglican ordinations discussed* (Lond. 1873) in appendicibus xxxiii, xxxiv et xxxv, ubi formulae
ordinationum Coptorum et Aethiopum, Resolutiones S. Officii
annorum 1704 et 1860, et litterae (24 Nov., 1867) Ludovici P. J. Bel,

APPENDIX II 393

ut constat, ordinationes presbyterorum neglegentissimae approbantur, solum tactu manus et verbis *Accipe Spiritum sanctum* effectae, sine ulla alia materia et forma nisi forsan ea quae in oratione contineatur quae de sacerdotio omnino silet.[1] Hoc documentum iam videmus a quibusdam "votum consultoris merum " dici, et, quantum fieri potest, repudiari. Sed patet aliquam responsionem huiusmodi illo tempore datam fuisse : in responsione enim S.C.S.O. anni 1860 occurrunt verba " detur responsio huius S.C. Supremae Inquisitionis fer. IV 9 Apr. 1704 " Sequitur responsio a theologis Romanis edita, sed nunc repudiata. Et huius documenti sententiam anno 1875 Cardinalis Patrizi, secretarius S C.S O., pro virili parte extenuavit, P. Franzelini, postea Cardinalis, verbis usus, quamvis non omnia ab eo scripta divulgaverit.

Si haec ergo responsio vera et genuina est, quaerere licet an S. O. formam ordinationis nostrae pro presbyteris approbavit, et formam consecrationis episcopi tantum

Episcopi Agathopolitani et Vicarii Apostolici Abyssiniae, typis mandatae sunt. Vide etiam P. Gasparri *Tract. Can de sacr. Ord.* sec. 1057 et 1058, qui addit litteras Cardinalis Patrizi secretarii S.C.S. Officii ad Cardinalem Manning 30 Apr 1875 datas. Confer etiam *Revue Anglo-Romaine* tom i. pp 369-375 (1896) ex qua *Collectanea* Propagandae citamus, et A. Boudinhon in *Le Canoniste Contemporain* tom. XX pp 5-10, Paris 1897, qui quaedam alia Romae recenter edita addit. Ph. de Carboneano responsionem sub die 10 Aprilis (i e. feria v) refert, quem sequitur Manning, nec repugnat Patrizi. Responsio anni 1860 et *Collectanea* Propagandae diem 9 Aprilis memorant.

App [1] Ordinationis formam Aethiopicam pro presbytero subiungimus ab Ludolfo anno 1691 editam *Comment in Hist. Aeth.* p. 328 :—
" Deus mi, Pater Domini et Salvatoris nostri Jesu Christi, respice hunc servum tuum, et largire illi spiritum gratiae et consilium sanctitatis, ut possit regere populum tuum in integritate cordis Sicut respexisti populum electum, et mandasti Moysi, ut eligeret seniores, quos replevisti eodem spiritu quo donaveras servum tuum et famulum tuum Moysen Nunc autem, Domine mi, da isti servo tuo gratiam quae nunquam deficit conservans nobis gratiam spiritus tui et competentem portionem nostram , supplens in nobis cultum tuum in corde, ut celebremus te sincere. Per etc."
Forma ab episcopo L. P. J. Bel repetita parum differt (Estcourt p. cxiii).

394 A ROMAN DIARY AND OTHER DOCUMENTS

improbavit ? Plane nescimus : sed non adeo incredibile est.[1]

Si falsa et supposititia est, ubi gentium vera evanuit? et cur falsa tam diu et tam publice locum eius tenuit? Et quis posthac credat S O. de tali controversia, vel etiam de indole documentorum suorum, idoneum testem esse ? Has ob causas iure dicimus tenebras S. Officio circumfusas a litteris Papae Leonis parum dissipatas fuisse. Documenta penes S.O conservantur, et publici iuris fieri debent si veritati rerum consulendum sit. Ut nunc tamen res manet, nemo est qui non iudicet causam Gordonianam imbecillo et invalido firmamento esse, si quis ordines nostros ob praxim curiae Romanae nullos esse probare voluerit.

App. [1] Credit Gasparri Paulum IV ordinationes nostras pro presbyteris et diaconis approbasse *De la valeur des Ordinations Anglicanes* pp. 14, 15, 45, Paris 1895. Cf supra p 12.

APPENDIX III

LEONIS PAPAE XIII EPISTULA AD ARCHIEPISCOPOS
ANGLIAE.

Illustrissimi ac Reverendissimi Domini,—

CUM vestris litteris libellus una nobis est redditus
quem vos Constitutioni nostrae obiciendum duxistis,
quam de ordinationibus ritu Anglicano actis anno su-
periori edidimus. Singula, quae profertis, prosequi, alieni
officii est. Id tamen non videt nemo, quemadmodum
Nos quaestionem de vestris ordinationibus haud aliter
potuisse aggredi dirimendam atque ex praescriptis catholici dogmatis, ita quae vos de ipsis ordinationibus, de
sacerdotio, de S. Eucharistia et sacrificio profitemini,
longe abesse nimirum ab iis quae a Catholica et Romana
Ecclesia traduntur. Ex delata Nobis, etsi inmerito, fidei et
sacramentorum custodia detrectare officium nequaquam
potuimus, quod Nobis est adversus Deum animosque
Christi sanguine redemptos quamobrem meditata iterum
diuque causa, nihil cunctandum ulterius iudicavimus,
ordinationes ritu vestro actas irritas edicere omninoque
nullas Quamquam tamen, dum ita Nos religioni officii
responderemus, spe laetabamur non defuturos qui sententiam nostram aequo animo habituri essent in eamque
ituri, celari tamen vos nolumus doluisse etiam quod
persuasum erat, sententiam eandem moleste pluribus
ferendam esse, qui quum fide bona secus ac nos cogita-
rent, difficile adducendi essent ut veritatem addiscerent.
Praeiudicatae enim opiniones, studia partium, mentium a
pueris informatio, ipse denique consuetudinum patriarum
amor, quibus ex amplitudine gentis dignitas accedere
videatur, mirum quantam in animos vim exerceant, ut

396 A ROMAN DIARY AND OTHER DOCUMENTS

facile idcirco perviaeremus eos, quibus de re nulla foret adhuc iniecta dubitatio, in deteriorem fere partem iudicium nostrum esse accepturos. Damus namque ultro, homines ab catholica unitate seiunctos alienisque doctrinis a teneris imbutos, quamdiu veritas non apte satis aperteque proponatur, bona sinceraque fide duci posse. Scrutator autem cordium Deus unus est. Id porro solatio nos afficit maxime, studium religionis acre per Britanniam vigere ; nec modo in iis qui anglicanis ritibus favent, verum etiam in ceteris plerisque, qui aeque a Catholicis atque ab Anglicanorum communitate dissident. Saepe nobis de hac re confirmavit dilectus filius Noster Westmonasteriensis archiepiscopus ; qui multa de vestratum sinceritate rettulit tuendaeque religionis industria, operamque suspexit quae istic datur plurime in eam partem ut religiosa institutio maneat in populo, comprimatur intemperantia potus, morum continentia custodiatur, aequa plebi et opificibus levatio provideatur. Praeclaras hasce dotes moralesque virtutes et catholicas traditiones, quae in vobis adhuc vigent, a vetustate acceptas dum animo reputamus, vehementi incendimur desiderio ut eam demum repetat ecclesiae Christi unitatem, quam maximo emolumento insignique laude, diuturno saeculorum spatio, gens vestra tenuit. Quod si hae nostrae industriae, quae Christi caritatem unice spectant sempiternamque animarum salutem, optatos nondum exitus sunt habiturae, at liceat saltem ad constans precandi studium impense enixeque hortari, quo nihil necesse magis ad unitatem fovendam. Nemo quippe venit ad Christum nisi Pater traxerit eum.

Litteras non ita pridem dedimus ad catholicos universos de Spiritu Sancto exorando, videlicet ut idem Spiritus, cuius est docere omnem veritatem et caritatem Dei diffundere in cordibus, gentes omnes, easque maxime quae Christiano censentur nomine, eodem fidei et caritatis vinculo coniungat. Quidni illi etiam, qui in vobis sincere adamant divinae obsequi voluntati, hortatione nostra utantur ?

Nos quidem vestris occasionem oblatam litteris per-

APPENDIX III

libenter nanciscimur, ut vos ceterosque omnes, qui religiosae unitati student, de propensissima voluntate nostra certiores iterum faciamus. Cor plane nostrum patet ad vos, eo nempe amore impellente, quo Romani Pontifices nationem vestram nullo non tempore sunt prosequuti, quemque Nos Pontifici qui succedet, suavissimae veluti haereditati, transmissuri sumus. Interea, adprecantibus benignissima Christi Matre Maria, Petro Apostolorum Principe, Gregorio et Augustino, quorum opera lux evangelii genti vestrae est invecta, omnipotentem Deum enixe obsecramus, ut divitias in vos bonitatis Suae uberrime effundat.

Ex aedibus Vaticanis, die xx Junii MDCCCXCVII.

APPENDIX IV

BIBLIOGRAPHY

Of Books, etc., marked with an asterisk * I have no knowledge at first hand.

Reviews of Books are not included unless they present some features of special interest.

DALBUS, FERNAND [F. Portal]. Les Ordinations Anglicanes. [La Science Catholique]¹ Arras, 1893-4

GASPARRI, P. Tractatus Canonicus de Sacra Ordinatione. Vol. I, pp x-444; Vol. II, pp. 399. Paris, 1893-4

BOUDINHON, A De l'Ordre et des Ordinations (à propos d'un livre recent). [Bulletin de l'Institut Catholique de Paris, pp 178-88.] Paris, 1894

*———— Étude théologique sur les Ordinations Anglicanes. [Le Canoniste Contemporain, Juin et Juillet.] Paris, 1894

DUCHESNE, L. Les Ordinations Anglicanes; par F. Dalbus; compte rendu [Bulletin Critique, 15 Juillet.] Paris, 1894

WORDSWORTH, JOHN (Bishop of Salisbury). De Validitate Ordinum Anglicanorum Responsio ad Batavos. pp. 23. Salisbury, 1894

*———— Trois Lettres sur la position de l'Eglise Anglicane. Salisbury, 1894

CARINI, SJ., Franc. M. Monsignor Niccolò Ormaneto, Nunzio Apostolico alla Corte di Filippo II Re di Spagna, 1572-77. pp. vii-142. Rome, 1894

¹ Also *en brochure*, pp 40 Arras, 1894. Second Edition with letters from Cardinal Bourret, the Archbishop of Albi, and the Bishops of Cahors and of Salisbury. Paris, 1894.

APPENDIX IV 399

* CAMM, O.S.B., Bede. La Controverse sur les Ordinations Anglicanes. [Revue Bénédictine, Tome XI, pp. 529–40; Tome XII, pp. 123–33.] 1894–5

VAN SCHAIK, G. C., and others. De la Validité des Ordinations Anglicanes: Lettre à l'Épiscopat vieux-catholique de Hollande par la Commission chargée d'étudier cette question pp. 43 Rotterdam, 1895

*CROWE, J. Anglican Orders and the Theory of the Intention of the Minister. [Irish Ecclesiastical Record, pp. 7–17.] Dublin, 1895

DELASGE, GUSTAVE. Validité des Ordinations Anglicanes. pp. 32. Paris, 1895

DENNY, EDWARD. ⎰ De Hierarchia Anglicana Dissertatio Apologetica. Praefante R.D. Saris-
LACEY, T. A. ⎱ buriensi Epo. pp. xvi–265. London, 1895

LAURAIN, P. Le Renouvellement des Ordinations. [Le Canoniste Contemporain, 208ᵉ Livraison. pp. 193–212.] Paris, 1895

BOUDINHON, A. Ordinations Schismatiques Coptes et Ordinations Anglicanes.[1] pp 32. Paris, 1895

―――― De la validité des Ordinations Anglicanes. pp. 89. Paris, 1895

LEHMKUHL, S.J., AUG. *Intentio* und *forma* bei den Sakramenten. [Theologischpraktische Monats-Schrift, pp. 599–604.] Passau, 1895

TOURNEBIZE, S.J., F. L'Église d'Angleterre a-t-elle réellement le Sacerdoce? [Études Religieuses, Tome lxiv, pp. 400–23, 574–605]. Paris, 1895

―――― le Mouvement Religieux en Angleterre. [Études Religieuses, Tome lxv, pp 513–28.] Paris, 1895

GASPARRI, P. De la Valeur des Ordinations Anglicanes.[2] pp. 91. Paris, 1895

―――――――――――――――――――――――――

[1] Reprinted from *Le Canoniste Contemporain*
[2] Reprinted, with corrections and additions, in the *Revue Anglo-Romaine*, Vol. I, pp 481–93, and 529–57.

400 A ROMAN DIARY AND OTHER DOCUMENTS

REVUE ANGLO-ROMAINE. Tome I, pp. 812; Tome II, pp. 812; Tome III, pp. 768. Paris, 1895-6

LEO XIII. Leonis Papae XIII Epistola Apostolica ad Anglos. [Revue Anglo-Romaine, Tome I, pp. 33-40.] Paris, 1895

* MARSHALL, A. F. The Moral Aspects of the Question of Anglican Orders. [American Catholic Quarterly Review, January, 1896.]

ANONYMOUS. Les Ordinations Anglicanes, à propos d'une Brochure.[1] [Revue Anglo-Romaine, Tome I. pp. 577-92.] Paris, 1896

—— Anglican Orders. [Church Quarterly Review, Vol. 41, pp. 281-303; Vol. 42, pp. 24-51.] London, 1896

TOURNEBIZE, S.J., F. Le Mouvement vers l'Union en Angleterre. [Études Religieuses, Tome lxvii, pp. 159-70.] Paris, 1896

RAGEY, Le Père. La Crise Religieuse en Angleterre. pp. 299. Paris, 1896

MAC DEVITT, J. Are Anglican Orders Valid? pp. xv-75. Dublin, 1896

HALIFAX, Viscount. Autorité et Juridiction. [Revue Anglo-Romaine, Tome I, pp 337-9.] Paris, 1896

UCALEGON. Autorité et Juridiction. [Ibid. pp. 339-47]. Paris, 1896

BOUDINHON, A. Primauté, Schisme et Juridiction. [Ibid. pp. 348-57.] Paris, 1896

PORTAL, F. La Crise Religieuse en Angleterre. [Ibid. pp. 728-46.] Paris, 1896

PULLER, S S J.E., F. W. Les Ordinations Anglicanes et le Sacrifice de la Messe.[2] pp. 57. Paris and London, 1896

---

[1] The authorship was afterwards acknowledged by Cardinal Segna.

[2] Reprinted, with corrections and additions, from the *Revue Anglo-Romaine*.

APPENDIX IV 401

LACEY, T. A. L'imposition des mains dans la Consecration des Évêques.[1] pp. 20. Paris, 1896

—— La Doctrine de Nicholas Ridley sur l'Eucharistie. [Revue Anglo-Romaine, Vol. I, pp. 637–47.] Paris, 1896

—— De l'Unité de l'Église, d'après les Théologiens Anglicans. [Ibid, Tome II, pp. 529–38.] Paris, 1896

—— Dissertationis Apologeticae de Hierarchia Anglicana Supplementum. pp. 48. Rome, 1896

—— De Re Anglicana.[2] pp. 15. Rome, 1896

GASQUET, O.S.B., F. A. { Risposta all' opuscolo intitolato
MOYES, J. { "De Re Anglicana."[2] pp. 27. Rome, 1896

BAYFIELD ROBERTS, J. B. Primauté, Schisme, et Juridiction. [Revue Anglo-Romaine, Tome I, pp. 769–78; Tome II, pp 3–13.] Paris, 1896

BOUDINHON, A. Les Aspects Moraux de la Question des Ordres Anglicans. [Ibid., Tome II, pp. 60–74.] Paris, 1896

—— Primauté, Schisme, et Juridiction. [Ibid., pp. 97–107, 160–71] Paris, 1896

—— Nouvelles Observations sur la Question des Ordres Anglicans. [Ibid, pp 625–32, 673–82, 770–91.]

DENNY, EDWARD. L'Église Anglicane et le Ministère des Églises de la Réforme. [Ibid, pp. 481–90, 539–54] Paris, 1896

PORTAL, F. Une Conférence à Londres. [Ibid., Tome III, pp. 16–24.] Paris, 1896

* KARENT, S. La Forme sacramentelle dans les Ordinations Anglicanes. [Études Religieuses.] Paris, 1896

LEO XIII. S Smi Domini nostri Leonis divina Providentia Papae XIII Epistola Encyclica de Unitate Ecclesiae. [Revue Anglo-Romaine, Tome III, pp. 641–66.] Paris, 1896

---

[1] Reprinted, with corrections and additions, from the *Revue Anglo-Romaine*   [2] Printed for private circulation.

402 A ROMAN DIARY AND OTHER DOCUMENTS

LEO XIII. Sanctissimi Domini nostri Leonis, divina Providentia Papae XIII Litterae Apostolicae de Ordinationibus Anglicanis. [With an English translation.] pp. 49. London, 1896

SMITH, S.J., SYDNEY F. Companion to the Encyclical "Satis cognitum." pp. iv–129. London, 1896

———— Le Mouvement de Réunion en Angleterre [Études Religieuses, Tome lxix, pp. 5–33.] Paris, 1896

YORK, Archbishop of. Sermon preached at the opening of the Church Congress at Shrewsbury. Official Report, pp. 6–19. London, 1896.

VAUGHAN, Cardinal. Discours prononcé à la conférence annuelle de la *Catholic Truth Society*, tenue à Hanley le 28 Septembre.[1] [Revue Anglo-Romaine, Tome III, pp. 465–80.] Paris, 1896

BROWNE, G. F. (Bishop of Stepney). Anglican Orders; a Speech delivered at the Church House, on Thursday, Oct. 15th, 1896. pp. 48. London, 1896

PULLER, S S.J.E., F. W. The Bull *Apostolicae Curae* and the Edwardine Ordinal. pp. 64. London, 1896

BENSON, ARTHUR H. T. The Pope's Bull on Anglican Orders. pp. 79. Dublin, 1896

BAMPTON, S.J., REV. Fʳ. The Papal Bull on Anglican Orders. pp. 12. London, 1896

COMMITTEE OF THE CHURCH HISTORICAL SOCIETY. On the Encyclical *Satis Cognitum.* pp. 23. London, 1896

———— A Treatise on the Bull *Apostolicae Curae.* pp. 67. London, 1896

FRERE, W. H. What is the position of the Roman Catholic Body in England? pp. 30. London, 1896

———— The Marian Reaction in its Relation to the English Clergy. A Study of the Episcopal Registers. pp. 288. London, 1896

[1] I have not been able to obtain an English edition of this.

APPENDIX IV 403

OXENHAM, F. N. Some Considerations suggested by the Letter of Leo XIII on Anglican Orders. pp. 24. London, 1896

STORY, ROBERT HERBERT. The Pope and Anglican Orders. pp. 24. Edinburgh, 1896

SWETE, HENRY BARCLAY. On the Bull *Apostolicae Curae.* pp. 27. Cambridge, 1896

STOKES, GEORGE T The Pope on Anglican Orders ; two introductory Lectures on the religious relations between Rome and England. pp. 48. Dublin, 1896

HALL, H. E. Anglican Orders and the Papal Bull. pp. 32. London, 1896

STALEY, VERNON. Are our Clergy rightly Ordained ? pp. 20. London, 1896.

TOURNEBIZE, s J., F. Ordres Anglicans et Ministères des Églises Réformées. [Études Religieuses, Tome lxix, pp. 651–76] Paris, 1896

LACEY, T. A. The Pope and the Anglicans ; (i) The sources of the Bull. [Contemporary Review, December, pp. 793–803.] London, 1896

CATHOLICUS. The Pope and the Anglicans ; (ii) The Policy of the Bull. [Ibid , pp. 804–9.] London, 1896

BARNES, ARTHUR STAPYLTON. The Popes and the Ordinal. pp. 197 London, 1896

—————— No Sacrifice—No Priest; or, Why Anglican Orders were Condemned. pp. 24. London, 1897

* FEREY, —— Les Ordinations Anglicanes. [Revue du Monde Catholique] 1897

COLLINS, WILLIAM EDWARD. The Internal Evidence of the Letter " Apostolicae Curae " as to its own Origin and Value. pp. 31. London, 1897

RADFORD, DANIEL. The Providential Character of the recent Papal Bull. pp. 22. London, 1897

FULLER, MORRIS. The Anglican Ordinal. pp. 79. London, 1897

404 A ROMAN DIARY AND OTHER DOCUMENTS

RESPONSIO ARCHIEPISCOPORUM ANGLIAE AD LITTERAS
APOSTOLICAS LEONIS PAPAE XIII DE ORDINA-
TIONIBUS ANGLICANIS. pp 43. London, 1897
ANSWER OF THE ARCHBISHOPS OF ENGLAND TO THE
APOSTOLIC LETTER OF POPE LEO XIII ON ENGLISH
ORDINATIONS. pp. 48. London, 1897
ΆΠΑΝΤΗΣΙΣ ΤΩΝ 'ΑΡΧΙΕΠΙΣΚΟΠΩΝ 'ΑΓΓΛΙΑΣ
ΠΡΟΣ ΤΑ 'ΑΠΟΣΤΟΛΙΚΑ ΓΡΑΜΜΑΤΑ ΠΑΠΑ
ΛΕΟΝΤΟΣ ΤΟΥ ΙΓ' ΤΑ ΠΕΡΙ ΤΩΝ 'ΑΓΓΛΙΚΑΝΙ-
ΚΩΝ ΧΕΙΡΟΤΟΝΙΩΝ. pp. 55. London,1897.

BRANDI, S.J., SALVATORE M. La Condanna delle Ordinazioni Anglicane.[1] pp. 80. Rome, 1897

——— Roma e Canterbury. Esame della Risposta degli
Arcivescovi Anglicani alla Bolla *Apostolicae Curae*.[1]
pp. 71. Rome, 1897

RIVINGTON, LUKE. Tekel: or The Anglican Archbishops arraigned at the Bar of Logic, and Convicted
of 75 Flaws. pp. 47. London, 1897

ANONYMOUS. An Examination of the Arguments in the
Papal Letter on Anglican Orders; and the Pope's
Criteria applied to the Roman Ordinal. pp. 17. Phila-
delphia, 1897

LOWNDES, ARTHUR. Vindication of Anglican Orders.
Vol I, pp. xx–436; Vol. II, pp. 602–cclxxxi. New
York, 1897

RAGEY, R. P. Le Concile Anglican de Lambeth. [Le
Correspondant, 25 juillet, pp. 208–21; 10 août,
pp. 520–39.] Paris, 1897

VON HACKELBERG-LANDAU. Die Anglicanischen Weihen
und ihre neueste Apologie.[2] Graz, 1897

JEAFFRESON, HERBERT H. A Letter on the Papal Bull
Apostolicae Curae. pp. 22. London, 1897

[1] Reprinted, with additions, from the *Civiltà Cattolica*.
[2] Reprinted from the *Literar. Anzeiger fur das Katholische
Oesterreich*.

APPENDIX IV   405

ROE, HENRY. The Continuity of the Church of England
    and the Papal Encyclical *Apostolicae Curae.* pp 87.
    Quebec, 1897

* SOKOLOFF, V. Ierarkhija Anglikanskoi Episkopaljnoi
    Tzerkvi pp. 362. Moscow, 1897

—— One Chapter from an Enquiry into the Hierarchy
    of the Anglican Episcopal Church. pp. 44. London,
    1897

SMITH, J. BAINBRIDGE. Ordinals Past and Present and
    their Witness to the Validity of English Orders.
    pp. 108. London, 1898

VINDICATION OF THE BULL "APOSTOLICAE CURAE."
    By the Cardinal Archbishop and Bishops of the
    Province of Westminster. pp. 122. London, 1898

COMMITTEE OF THE CHURCH HISTORICAL SOCIETY.
    Priesthood in the English Church: a study of the
    "Vindication of the Bull *Apostolicae Curae*" pp. 70.
    London, 1898

FIRMINGER, WALTER K. The Alterations in the Ordinal
    of 1662: Why were they made? pp. 64. London,
    1898

—— Some Comments on "The Vindication of the
    Bull *Apostolicae Curae.*"[1] pp. 22. Calcutta, 1898

* SPOTTISWOODE, GEORGE A. The Holy Orders of the
    Church of England. London, 1898.

SMITH, S.J., SYDNEY F. Anglican Criticisms on the
    "Vindication." [The Month, No. 405, pp. 227-37.]
    London, 1898

LACEY, T. A. The Interpretation of the English Ordinal.
    pp. 27. London, 1898

—— Gregory IX and Greek Ordinations. pp. 16.
    London, 1898

—— The Unity of the Church, as treated by English
    Theologians. pp. 160. London, 1898

[1] Reprinted, with additions, from the *Indian Church Quarterly
Review.*

406 A ROMAN DIARY AND OTHER DOCUMENTS

BULGAKOFF, A. The Question of Anglican Orders, in respect to a " Vindication " of the Papal Decision. Translated by W. J. Birkbeck. pp. 46. London, 1899

FIDELIS. [Charles Willes Wilshere] Leo XIII an Paulus IV ? Auctore Laico. pp. 23. London and Paris, 1900

* MOYES, JAMES. Aspects of Anglicanism ; or, Some comments on certain events in the 'nineties. pp. viii— 499. London, 1906.

FIRMINGER, W. K. Some Ancient Ordination Ceremonies. [Indian Church Review, Oct., pp. 429–50.] Calcutta, 1901

WORDSWORTH, JOHN (Bishop of Salisbury). The Ministry of Grace. pp. xxiv.—486. London, 1901.

'ΑΝΔΡΟΥΤΣΟΣ, ΧΡΗΣΤΟΣ. Τὸ κῦρος τῶν Ἀγγλικῶν Χειροτονιῶν ἐξ ἐπόψεως Ὀρθοδόξου.[1] pp. 96. Constantinople, 1903.

LAWLOR, HUGH JACKSON. The Reformation and the Irish Episcopate pp. 59. London, 1906

SERLE, S. E. B. The Validity of Anglican Ordinations. pp. 16. London, 1907.

BRIGGS, CHARLES AUGUSTUS. Church Unity ; Studies of its most important problems. pp. xii—459. London, 1910.

SNEAD-COX, J. G The Life of Cardinal Vaughan, Vol. I, pp. x –483 ; Vol. II, pp. 498. London, 1910

[1] A very inaccurate English translation of this work was published in the year 1910

INDEX

INDEX

A

Abyssinian Campaign, Requiem Mass attended by the King and Members of Legislature, 79 (note)

Abyssinian Ordinations (1704), 127, 130, 262, 299, 363, 392 (note)

Accipe Spiritum Sanctum. See Forms of Ordination

Act Book of the Convent of Canterbury, 39

Agliardi, Mgr., Papal Nuncio to the Czar's Coronation, 58

Aldrich, Bishop of Carlisle, and the English Ordinal, 313, 322

Alexander III, Decretal of, 338

Alexander, Natalis, on the Tradition of the Instruments, 264

Alexander VII, likeness to Napoleon III, 36

Alexandria, Church of, Primitive customs of, 7, 16, 64, 292 (note)

Alva, Duke of, Treaty with Elizabeth, 77 (note)

Amelli, Dom, Prior of Monte Cassino—
 Letter from, 132
 Visits to, 23, 67, 68

Anglican Orders—
 Commission on, appointed by Leo XIII, 8, 9, 10, 11, 15–17, 21, 22, 23, 29, 31, 50, 51, 54, 57 (note), 59, 60–2, 81, 87, 145–46, 148–49, 254–62
 Difficulties in the way of, 8–17, 21–3, 48, 50, 61, 114, 299–300
 Members of, 8, 31
 Order of Procedure, 54
 Condemnation of, in the Bull *Apostolicae Curae*, 253–282
 By the Holy Office, 256, 257
 Ground of the Decision, 266–72
 Inconsistency of the Roman Position, 298–307
 Sources of the Bull, 253–82
 Theology of the Bull, 285–307
  confusion introduced into, 301–7

Anglican Orders—
 Memorandum on, by W. E. Gladstone, 139
 Paul IV, Bull of, implicit acceptance of, in, 171–6. *See also* Edwardine Orders, English Ordinal, Forms of Ordination, Holy Office. Pole's Mission of Reconciliation, and Reunion

Apostolicae Curae, the Bull of Leo XIII—
 Sources of the Bull, 253–82
 Theology of the Bull, 285–307

Aquinas, St. Thomas, View of the essential form in Ordination, 44, 280, 205
 Greek Baptism, 334, 337–8

Archives. *See* Holy Office

Armenian Church, recognition of Orders by Rome, 298, 299
 Decretum ad Armenos, 33, 95, 296–7, 306, 334, 335 (note), 357, 358, 360, 361

Armenian Mass at S Nicola da Tolentino, description of, 70, 74–6

Arian Baptism, Validity of, 44

Arras, Cardinal Bishop of, Letter of Bishop Quadra to, 122

Association for Promoting the Unity of Christendom, 204

Auvray, M, Registers of Gregory IX, 332, 333

B

Baptism, Sacrament of—
 Immutable formula for, 11
 Practice of the Eastern Churches, 108, 289 (note), 331–35, 338 (note)
 Unalterable when once given, 289, 290

Barbaro, Daniele (Venetian State Papers), quotation from, (30,) 32, 34, 178, 323, 324

Barlow, Bishop, case of, 21, 22, 30, 34, 38, 39, 40, 41, 42, 46, 47, 50, 51, 61, 97, 99, 101–16, 126, 153–68, 211, 313, 314
 Career of, 313, 314

2 D 2   409

410 A ROMAN DIARY AND OTHER DOCUMENTS

Barlow, Bishop—
Dialoge of, Rev. J. R. Lunn on,
30, 39, 93, 94, 314 (note)
Royal Mandate, 39, 40, 61, 64,
102, 104, 106, 107, 108, 126
Letters to the *Tablet* on, 157–68
Memorandum delivered to Cardinal Mazzella, 153–7
Text of, 108–10, 155, 156
Vote in favour of the English
Ordinal, 313, 316 (note)
Bari, Archbishop of, and Greek
Ordinations, 331, 332, 333 (note),
335, 336
Barnes, A S., reference to, 36, 47, 50
Benedict XIV, *De Synodo Diæcesana*,
263, 264
on the question of change in the
essential form of Orders, 296,
297, 304
Benedictines of San Anselmo, Mass
at 36, 37
Bibliography, 398
Biblioteca Casanatense, 34, 50
Biblioteca Nazionale, books of reference in, 34, 96
Billuart, on the Essential Form in
Orders, 268, 279
Birkbeck, W. J., reference to, 29,
57 (note)
Bishops, Consecration by imposition
of the Gospel Text, 7, 16, 292
(note)
Deprivation of, 105
Alleged instances of, 211, 212,
242–5
Edward VI and later, under,
196, 211, 212, 242–5
Power of, to ordain, limited by
their catholicity, 12, 13
Royal Mandate for Consecration
of. *See* Barlow case
Sarum Pontifical for Consecration of, 31–3, 96
See also Forms of Ordination and
the Barlow and Gordon cases.
Bliss, Mr, assistance rendered by,
73 (note), 177
Bonner, Bishop—
Deprivation of, 212, 242
Reordinations, possible, by, 57,
58
Bossierre, M de, reference to, 35, 50
Boudinhon, Abbé—
Comparison of the English
Ordinal with other Forms recognized by Rome, 14–17,
259, 293, 294, 299, 303 (note),
304, 305

Boudinhon, Abbé—
De la validité des Ord Angl.,
by, 299 (note), 303 (note)
De Hierarchia, review of, by, 5
Gasparri, Mgr., association with,
6, 14–17, 83, 259, 299
Primauté, Schisme et Juridiction, by, 84 (note)
Bouix, *Tractatus de Curia Romana,*
130
Bourret, Cardinal, Reference to, 7
Brandi, S. J. Fr., S. M
Civiltà Cattolica, articles in, 264
(note), 272–5
Condanna delle Ord. Angl., 258
(note), 275 (note), 280 (note),
294 (note)
Documents in the Gordon Decision, 272–5
Roma e Canterbury, by, 172,
249, 312 (note)
Briggs, Dr C. A., 307 (note)
Brechin, Bishop of, reference to, 68
Bright, Canon, note on an incident
with, 35 (note), 96
Brown, R., *Venetian State Papers,*
324 (note)
Bruno, Giordano, political demonstration, 55
Bucer, Martin, *De Ordinatione Legitima,* 123, 195, 317, 318
Bulach, Abbé Zorn de, visit from, 65
Bulkeley, Bishop, consecration of, 40
Bullinger, references to, 314 (note),
327 (note)
Bulls, Papal. *See* under names of
Popes

C

Calendar of Letters and State Papers
. . . preserved in the Archives of
Simancas, extracts from, 116–23
Canoniste Contemporain, Review in, 5
Canons of Hippolytus. *See* Hippolytus
Canterbury, Archbishop of, and the
question of licensed leave of absence, 92, 93
Act Book of the Convent of, 39
Convocation of (1531), 146. *See
also* Leo XIII, Reply of the
English Archbishops to
Canterbury Register. *See* Cranmer
Cardinals, Commission of. *See* Holy
Office
Carini, Padre, Pamphlet by (Monsgr.
Nicolo Ormaneto . . . Nunzio . . .
alla Corte di Filippo II), 77 (note)

INDEX

Carne, Sir Edward, Embassy to Rome, 176
Carthage, Conference of, 54
Casetta, Mgr., Patriarch of Antioch, reference to, 69
Cassino, Monte, visit to the Monastery at, 23, 67, 68
Catacomb of St. Priscilla, visit to, 34, 35, 96
Cecil, Wm, References to (Simancas Papers), 116-18, 121, 124, 125
Chabot, M., visit from, 36
Chambers, Bishop, retains his See under Edward VI and Mary, 243, 244
Chandler, Bishop, Royal Mandate for Consecration of, 159
Church Quarterly Review on Essentials of Ordination, 298
Church Year Book, statistics, 207-9, 248
Civiltà Cattolica, Fr. Brandi on the Gordon Decision, in, 264 (note), 272, 273
Claudio, San, Order of Mass at, 38
Clement XI, Decision in the Gordon case, 259, 260
Clifton, Bishop of, reference to, 103
Coleridge, *Christabel*, reference to, 145
Chalcedon, Council of, 51
Colosseum by moonlight, 72
Commission on Anglican Orders. *See* Anglican Orders
Communion, frequency of, in English Church, 222, 247, 248
Communities, Religious, in the English Church—
  Clerical, 207
  Lay, 208
Comprehensiveness of the English Church, 227
Concilio, The. See the Simancas Correspondence, 116-25
Conditional Reordination. *See* Reordination.
Contemporary Review, article in, "The Sources of the Bull *Apostolicae Curae*," 253-72, 274
Councils of the Church. *See* Chalcedon, Mainz, and Trent
Convocation of Canterbury (1531), 146
Cowley, Society of St. John the Evangelist at, 201, 207, 225
Cranmer, Archbishop—
  Attainder of, 105
  Consecration of, 29
  English Ordinal and, 29, 40, 42, 210, 211, 241-45, 312-20, 321 (note), 324, 328 (note)

Cranmer, Archbishop—
  Register of, 39, 41, 112, 113, 161-3, 167, 168
  Sense in which Paul IV condemns, 42
Crawford, F. Marion, Characters of, identified in Roman Society, 66, 67
Cromwell, Letter to Tuke, 34, 96-7, 127
Crowe, Mr, Correspondent of the *Daily Telegraph* and *Tablet*, inquiry from, 55
Crypt of St. Peter, Mass in, 24
Cyprian, St., Controversy with Stephen of Rome, 301 (note)

D

Daniel, Mgr, meeting with, 64
D'Annibale, on the *Decretum ad Armenos*, 95
Dasent, Acts of the Privy Council, 324 (note)
Day, Bishop, deprivation under Mary, 212, 243
  Vote against the English Ordinal, 313, 316 (note)
De Augustinis, Fr., interview with, 60
  Member of the Pope's Commission, 8, 31, 306
  Memorandum on Anglican Orders, 6, 42-6, 54 (note), 95, 99, 100, 115, 180 (note), 254, 255, 259
  Abstract of, 42-6
De Hierarchia Anglicana, by E. Denny and T. A. Lacey, 5, 6, 39, 64, 66, 69, 95 (note), 98, 99 (note), 115, 123 (note), 172, 187, 262
  Supplement to, 64-6, 83, 99 (note), 123, 130, 161, 164 (note), 171, 177, 187
  Council of Mainz, 187
De Re Anglicana, by T. A. Lacey, 20, 67, 69, 72, 78, 83, 133, 195
  Adverse criticism, 20, 21, 210-39, 240-9
  Printed for private circulation only, 20, 133, 241
Risposta all'Opuscolo, by J. C. Moyes and F. A. Gasquet, 210-39
  The *Risposta* Examined, 240-9
  Statistics given, 69, 78, 207-9
De Lugo, on the essential *forms* in Ordination, 52, 280, 281, 377
Decretum ad Armenos (Eugenius IV), 33, 95, 296-7, 306, 334, 335 (note), 357, 358, 360, 361

412 A ROMAN DIARY AND OTHER DOCUMENTS

Degradation of English Bishops, alleged, 32 (note), 34, 95, 212, 242, 243

Delehaye, Père, Bollandist, meeting with, 72

Denny, Edward, *Anglican Orders and Jurisdiction*, by, 4, 99 (note), 298 (note)
Association with the Author, 4, 5
Letters to T A. Lacey, 98, 126

Denzinger, *Enchiridion*, reference to, 289 (note)

d'Hulst, Mgr., visit to, 83

Diary, A Roman, 29-84
Author's retrospect, 21-4

Dillon, Mr, pressure brought to bear on, 37

Dissenters, origin of, 197

Dissertatio Apologetica de Hierarchia Anglicana, publication of. *See De Hierarchia*

Divine Office, The, in the English Church, 224

Dixon, *History*, references to, 33, 180 (note), 324 (note), 327 (note)

Donatists, method of argument, 54

Duchesne, Abbé, general references to, 6, 8, 19, 29, 30, 31, 33, 46, 47, 48, 51, 54, 57, 59, 71, 72, 81, 89, 95, 96, 100, 113, 114, 115, 128, 129, 130, 132, 134, 135, 254, 255, 299, 300, 306
Consultor to the Pope's Commission, 8, 31, 89, 254
Honorary Doctorate of Cambridge offered to, 71, 72, 129
View held by, as to the action of the Commission, 48, 59, 299, 300

Dudley, Lord R. (Simancas Correspondence), references to, 116, 117, 121

E

Eastern Churches—
Forms of Baptism, 289 (note), 290 (note)
Ordination, differing from Western use, 100, 279, 281, 295-7
Intercourse of English Church with, 203
Ordinations implicitly condemned by Leo XIII, 386
Recognition of, by Rome, 299-306
Reunion and, 203, 271

Edward VI, Bishops under, 196, 211, 242-5, 312-19

Edwardine Orders. *See* English Ordinal

Priests reconciled by unction, 65, 125, 360 (note)

Eirenicon, an, by Dr. Pusey, 204

Elizabeth, beginnings of, 77, 78 (notes), 124, 196, 212-18, 246, 247
Council of Trent, reply concerning, 61, 121-2
Question of the *Concilio*, 121, 122
Recusants under, 78 (note), 196, 216, 247
Simancas Correspondence, 116-25

Ely, Bishop of, reference to, 20, 29
Correspondence with T. A. Lacey, 89, 92, 93, 132

Embassy to Rome (confirmation of Pole's General Dispensation), 172 (note), 176, 344

Encyclicals, *Ad Anglos*, 6, 206, 341
Satis Cognitum, 63 (note), 83, 84, 133, 134

English Church, part of the Church Catholic, 12-14, 285-307

English Church Union, 9, 37, 247

English College, Library of, 38

English Ordinal, general references, 42-6, 58, 62, 87, 95, 105, 107, 123 (note), 124, 125, 171, 177, 280 (note), 311-28, 386
Marian Reaction and, 62, 99, 105, 113, 196, 212, 242-3, 322
Cardinal Pole's description of, 123 (note), 177, 280 (note)
Text of, 181-4
Interpretation of, 311-28, 350
Ordinal changes in 1662, 375
Paul IV and Julius III and, 171.
See also Barlow and Gordon cases, and De Augustinis, Fr, on
Preface to, 378
Words *Bishop* and *Priest* in, 311, 312, 328, 350, 375

Estcourt, and the Barlow Documents, 31, 34, 36, 96, 97, 127, 324 (note)

Eugenius IV, *Decretum ad Armenos*, 33, 95, 296, 297, 306, 307, 334, 335 (note), 357, 358, 360, 361, 387
Pole's Legatine Constitution, 94

Excommunication, discussion as to the nature of, 32

F

Fabre, M. Paul, on *De Hierarchia*, 17
references to, 38, 39, 49, 51, 71, 72, 79, 81

Farnese Palace, visit to, 30

INDEX

Feria Quinta, Session of the Holy Office on, 131, 266, 270
Ferrar, Bishop, case of, 31, 32, 33, 95, 96, 314, 321 (note)
  alleged degradation of, 32 (note)
Fête Dieu and Public Procession of the Blessed Sacrament, 79
Fleming, Fr. David, 8, 31, 88, 100
  Member of the Pope's Commission, 8, 31
Formosus, reference to, 357
Forms of Ordination (discussion of essentials in), 10–17, 41, 42–6, 48, 52, 54, 63, 93, 97, 98, 100, 101, 115, 128, 192 (note), 255, 258, 259, 263, 264, 267, 268, 274, 276, 278–82, 288–307, 317, 335–8
  Accipe Spiritum Sanctum, the form, 43, 44, 54, 97, 98, 100, 128, 192 (note), 268, 278–82, 317, 349, 357, 373
  Eastern and Western, differences in, 279, 281, 295–7, 331–8
  Imposition of the Gospel Text, 7, 16, 292 (note)
  Mainz, Council of, on, 43, 54, 83, 187–92
  Ordones Romani, 370, 371 (notes)
  Other Ancient Forms, 370
  Roman Rites, Ancient, 369
  Modern, 10, 369, 381
  Unalterable nature of a valid, 289–91
  See also Intention and Tradition of the Instruments
Fournier, Professor, reference to, 39, 49, 51
Fox, Bishop, Writ of Restitution, 160
Foxe, reference to, 32 (note)
Frere, Rev W. H., correspondence with T A. Lacey (Barlow documents), 101, 104, 112, 116, 135
  on the Marian Reaction, 62, 105, 322
  Reordinations by Bonner, 57, 58
Gairdner, *Catalogue,* reference to, 161. *Letters and Papers of Henry VIII,* 34, 36, 96, 97, 130
Galimberti, Cardinal, references to, 55, 58, 60, 62
  Death of, 62
Gardiner, Bishop, deprivation of, 212, 242
Gasquet, Dom—
  Discovery of the Bull and Brief of Paul IV, 6, 171, 176
  Edward VI and the Book of Common Prayer, by, 245

Gasquet, Dom—
  Member of the Pope's Commission, 8, 31
  Minor references, 30, 88
  O'Harte MS 98 (note), 99
  Risposta All'Opuscolo (De Re Anglicana), by, and J. C Moyes, 210–39
Gasparri, Mgr, general references, 5–8, 10, 14–17, 29, 30–3, 35, 38–42, 46, 47, 50, 51, 52, 54, 58, 83, 87, 88, 95, 102, 114, 115, 133, 254, 259, 273, 299, 303 (note), 304
  Boudinhon, Abbé, association with, 6, 14–17, 83, 259, 299
  Consultor to the Pope's Commission, 8, 29, 31, 89
  De la Valeur des Ord. Angl. by, 175 (note), 273, 299, 303 (note), 304
  Tractatus de Sacra Ordinatione, 46, 297 (note)
Genetti, Consultor to the Holy Office, 261
  Report on the Gordon case, 48, 261
German College, Mass at, 33
Gibson, Mandate for consecration in, 111
Gladstone, Rt. Hon. W. E , 49
  Correspondence with T. A. Lacey, 132, 134
  Memorandum by, on the validity of Anglican Orders, 139, 236, 237
  Minor references to, 18, 22, 23, 52, 53, 71, 72, 76, 77, 78, 80, 81, 82, 84, 236
  Message from Leo XIII to, 81, 82, 134
  Times, the, on the Memorandum, 237
Goodrich, Bishop, retains his See under Edward VI and Mary, 211, 242, 243, 314
  Vote on the English Ordinal, 313, 316 (note), 321 (note)
Gordon case, the, 42, 48, 100, 107, 108, 128, 129, 130, 135, 136, 259–71, 272–82, 346, 347, 362, 374, 388
  Text of the Decision, 273
  Inaccurate form of, 107
Great Schism (1416), 159
Greek Baptism, Gregory IX and, 331–3, 335, 338 (note)
  Ordinations accepted by Rome, 48, 100, 101, 264, 331, 337
  Gregory IX and, 331–8, 387

414 A ROMAN DIARY AND OTHER DOCUMENTS

Gregory IX and the Greek Ordinations, 264, 331-8, 387
Text of Decretal, 332-3
Gregory X, Greek Church received into communion by, 337
Greig, Rev. David, reference to, 80
Grey, Lady Jane, Proclamation of, 179
Guardian, The, Articles by T. A. Lacey in,
on Cardinal Pole's Description of the English Ordinal, 177
on the Gordon Decision, 272
Letters of Fr Ryder, on the Gordon Case, 264 (note)
Guthlin, Mgr. (Lucius Lector), reference to, 78

H

Halifax, Lord, correspondence with T. A. Lacey, 88, 92
Minor references, 9, 29, 47, 52, 57, 71, 84, 87, 89, 103, 141, 203
Hardouin, Eastern and Western Orders, 281
Heath, Bishop, deprivation of, 212, 242
Imprisonment of, 325, 326
Vote on the English Ordinal, 313, 315, 316, 319, 320, 324, 325
Henry VIII—
Royal Mandate for Barlow's Consecration. *See* Barlow Case.
Separation from Rome, 195, 210, 241
Hemptinne, Dom Hildebrand de, interview with, 37
Hippolytus, Canons of—
Form for ordination of Deacons, 16, 293, 294, 369, 370 (notes)
Primitive arrangements of the Roman Church, 64
Hodgekyn, Bishop, Consecration of Parker by, valid, 42
Hohenlohe, Cardinal, visit to, 51, 103
Holbeach, Bishop, reference to, 211, 242, 316 (note), 321 (note)
Holy Cross Day at Sta. Croce in Gerusalemme, 56, 57
Holy Office—
Archives of, inaccessible, 129, 135, 262
Commission of Cardinals on Anglican Orders, 59, 63, 80, 81, 114, 115, 127, 249, 256-63
Risposta and, 210-39, 240-9
Procedure of, 129, 130, 131
— *Feria Quinta,* 131, 266, 270

Hooper, Bishop, alleged degradation of, 32 (note)
Original Letters, 314
On the Prayer Book, 327, 328 (notes)

I

Ignazio, St., visit to, 35, 36
Armenian Mass at, 36
Imposition of Gospel Text, Ordination by, 7, 16, 292 (note)
Infallibility, Question of, 131, 266-72, 307 (note), 331
Decisions on *Feria Quinta,* 131, 266-70
Innocent III, Decretal, *de Presbytero non baptizato,* 289 (note)
Innocent IV, on Forms of Ordination, 11
Intention, Doctrine of, 44, 45, 60, 98, 103, 104, 128, 141, 258, 326-8, 351
Interpretation of the English Ordinal, 311, 350
Italian Government and Papal Court, relations between, 79, 80

J

Janssens, Dom, Prior of St. Anselmo, 53
Julius II, reference to, 65 (note)
Julius III and Paul IV, 41, 171-84, 343, 359
Commission to Pole, 73, 176, 343
Implicit recognition of English Orders, 46, 181

K

Keble, Rev. J., references to, 199, 204 (note)
An Eirenicon, addressed to (by Dr. Pusey), 204
King, Bishop, retains his See under Edward VI and Mary, 243
Reordinations by, 322, 326
Kitchin, Bishop, retains his See under Edward VI and Mary, 243, 244
Klein, Abbé, article in the *Revue Anglo-Romaine,* 131
Visit from, 84
Knox Little, Canon, reference to, 29

L

Labbe, reference to, 166, 360 (note)
Lacey, Bishop Royal Mandate for Consecration of, 159

INDEX

Lacey, Rev. T. A.—
A Roman Diary, 29-84
Correspondence, 89, 99, 101, 103, 112, 114, 129, 132, 135
See also articles and letters in the *Contemporary Review, Guardian*, and *Tablet*
De Re Anglicana and its critics, 195
Gregory IX and the Greek Ordinations, 331
Interpretation of the English Ordinal, 311
Introduction to the book, 3
The Royal Mandate for Barlow's Consecration, 153
Sources and theology of the Bull *Apostolicae Curae*, 253, 272, 285
Suppression of the article "De Unitate" by, 63
Visit to Rome with Fr Puller, on account of the Pope's Commission, 8, 29
Difficulties of the work, 4, 8-10, 14-20
See also De Hierarchia
Lapôtre, S J., Père, references to, 32, 71, 96
Lateran, Mass at, 69, 70
Museum, visit to, 73
Lathbury, D. C, *Correspondence on Church and Religion of William Ewart Gladstone*, 134
Launoy's Definitions of the Church, 50
Lawrence, Bampton Lectures, quoted, 123 (note)
Lazarists' House at Paris, visit to, 82, 83
Le Courayer (Gordon case), reference to, 261
Le Plat, reference to, 98
Le Quien, reference to, 135, 261, 363 (n)
Lee (Gordon case), reference to, 107
Lee, Bishop, Writ of Restitution, 160
Letters, A Series of, 87-136
See, under proper names: Amelli, Denny, Bishop of Ely, Frere, Gladstone, Halifax, Lacey, Lunn, Phillimore, Portal, Ross-Lewin, Wood
Levé, M., printer of the *Monde* and *Revue*, visit to, 82
Leo IV and the *Mouvement Centralisateur*, 49
Leo XIII—
The Bull *Apostolicae Curae*, 135, 136, 172 (note), 253, 285, 311
Sources of, 253-82
Theology of 285-307

Leo XIII—
Bull of Paul IV, inaccurate quotation of, by, 172 (note), 345, 359
Commission on Anglican Orders, *See* Anglican Orders
Eastern Orders implicitly condemned by, 386
Encyclicals · *Ad Anglos*, 6, 206, 341
Satis cognitum, 63 (note), 83, 84, 133, 134
Letter to Cardinal Richard, 249
Letter to the English Archbishops, 395
Message to Mr. Gladstone, 81, 82, 134
Personal Attitude of, 4, 6, 18-20, 47, 49, 60, 77, 96, 101, 254-7, 265, 266
Personal Piety of, 24
Reply of the English Archbishops to, 354
Unicitas and *Unitas*, on the difference between, 84, 133. *See also* Infallibility.
Lincoln, trial of the Bishop of, 37, 202, 229, 230
Lingard, treatment of the Barlow case, 21, 165
Lingens, Fr Emil, review of *De Hierarchia* by, 5
Llevaneras, Fr. José Calasanzio, Member of the Pope's Commission, (note) 31
Loisy, M , Essays of, reference to, 7
Loth, M. Arthur, editor of *La Vérité*, visit to, 83
Lunn, Rev J. R., Introduction to Bishop Barlow's *Dialoge*, 30, 314 (note)
Letter to T. A. Lacey, 93
Notes on Barlow's Opinion on Episcopal Consecration, 39, 47, 93
Lyon, ceremonial usages, 49, 50

M

Macaulay, on Apostolic Succession, 13
MacDevitt, Dr., on Conditional Reordination, 40
Mainz, Council of (1549), 43, 53, 83, 187
Text of—
De Sacramento Ordinis, 187
De Forma Sacramenti Ordinis, 188
De Materia Sacramenti Ordinis, 188
De Presbyteris, 192

416 A ROMAN DIARY AND OTHER DOCUMENTS

Manning, Cardinal, reference to Life of, 78 (note), 83 (note), 134

Marcellinus, Pope, history of, Dr. Bright on, 35 (note)

Marculfus, Indiculus of Frankish Kings, 166

Marian Reaction, the, 62, 99, 105, 113, 196, 212, 242–3, 322

Marini, Mgr. (Substitute of the Rota), the Reunion of the Eastern Churches, 82

Martinengo, Abbé, 117, 120

Mary, Queen, Beginnings of, 180 (note)
Bishops under, 125, 212, 242, 243
Reaction under, 62, 99, 105, 113, 196, 212, 242, 243, 322
Refusal to admit the Papal Nuncio, 121

Maskell, quoted for the order of Episcopal Consecration, 31, 96

Mazzella, Cardinal, general references, 22, 54, 55, 59, 60, 63, 95, 96, 129, 135, 262
Interview with, 65
Presentation of Report to the Pope, 76, 77
President of the Pope's Commission, 31, 54, 95, 96
Refusal to go behind the Gordon Decision, 135, 262
See also De Hierarchia Supplementum and the Royal Mandate

Mercer, Dom Cuthbert, reference to, 37

Merry del Val, Cardinal (now Cardinal Secretary of State), 34

Micronius, Martin, criticism of Ridley by, 314 (note)

Missionary Societies in the English Church, 209

Monophysites. *See* Eastern Churches

Montagu, Lord, embassy to Rome, 176

Monte Cassino, Prior of, letter to T. A. Lacey, 132
Visit to, 23, 66, 67

Month, The, article on the English Ordinal, by the Rev. Sydney Smith, 312, 322 (note)

Montorio, St. Pietro in, visit to, 32

Morinus, on the essential form of Orders, 280, 298

Moyes, Canon J. C —
on the Barlow Documents, 38, 39, 40, 41, 50, 51, 61, 94, 95, 101–3, 112, 113, 114, 157, 280 (note)

Moyes, Canon J. C.—
Member of the Pope's Commission, 8, 31
Minor references, 42, 46, 88, 135
and Gasquet, F A.—
Risposta All' Opuscolo, by, 210
Reply to, by T. A Lacey, 240

N

Nag's Head Fable, the, 40, 42, 261, 274

Neri, Feast of St Philip, 72

Nestorian Orders, recognized by Rome, 299

Newman, Dr. (afterwards Cardinal), references to, 22, 205, 2c6, 214
Letter to, by Dr. Pusey, *Is Healthful Reunion Impossible?* 206 (note)

Nicholas I, *Responsa ad Consulta Bulgarorum,* 290 (note)
Mouvement Centralisateur, and, 49
Baptism " in the Name of Christ " recognized by, 11

Nunziatura in Inghilterra, reference to, 177

O

O'Harte, Bishop, speech in the Council of Trent, 98

Orders, Holy, sacramental character of, 288, 289
Unalterable nature of, 289, 290
See also Anglican Orders

Ordinal, The *See* English Ordinal

Ordination. *See* Bishops and Forms of Ordination, and Reordination

Ormaneto, Mgr. Niccolò, Papal Nunzio to Court of Spain (1572–77), 77 (note)

Oughton, *Formularies,* reference to, 111

Oxenham, Mr., reference to, 33, 36, 62

Oxford Movement, the, 198, 199, 220, 221, 225

P

Paleotti, Acts of Council of Trent, reference to, 98, 99

Pantheon, visit to, 33

Parker, Archbishop, validity of the Consecration of, 42, 141, 276

Parma, Duchess of, letter of Bishop Quadra to, 122

Parocchi, Cardinal (Cardinal Vicar), celebration of the Mass on Holy Cross Day, 56, 57
Interviews with, 69, 73, 77

INDEX 417

Parson, *Reasons why Catholiques Refuse to goe to Church*, 247
Patrizzi, Cardinal (Abyssinian Decrees), reference to, 128
Paul IV (and Julius III), 171–84, 343, 345, 359, 362
   Breve *Regimini*, 31, 32, 171, 362
   Bull *Praeclara carissimi*, 99, 176–7, 359
   Inaccurately quoted by Leo XIII, 172–3 (notes), 345, 359
   Implicit recognition of Anglican Orders in, 41, 42, 171–6
   Nuncio of, refused by Mary, 121
Pastoral Office, duties of, 383
   Expressed in English Ordinal, 386
   in Eastern Formularies, 386
Pastoral work of the English Church, 209
   Alms of the Faithful, 209
Pecci, Cardinal, statement concerning, 55
Peckham's constitution concerning tabernacles, reference to, 94
Penning, Henry, letter sent from Cardinal Pole to Mary by, 180 (note)
Peter Martyr, references to, 195, 327 (note)
Peterborough, Bishop of, as representative of the English Church at Czar's Coronation, 58, 79
   Lecture on Queen Elizabeth, 61, 123
Phillimore, Sir Walter—
   on the Barlow Documents, 111, 164 (note)
   Interview with Cardinal Rampolla, 36, 37
   Visit from, 32
Pius IV, Bull of the *Concilio*, 116–25
Pius V, St, Bull *Regnans in excelsis*, 77–8, 197, 216, 246, 247
Pius X and the Bull *Apostolicae Curae*, reference to, 307 (note)
Pilkington, *Exposition upon the Prophet Aggeus*, 65, 126, 360 (note)
Pocock, Nicholas, Reference to, 214, 324 (note)
Pole, Cardinal, Acceptance of the English Ordinal, 29, 31, 33, 35, 46, 47, 62, 94, 95, 105, 113, 124, 171–84
   Powers granted by Julius III, 176, 177, 343
   by Paul IV, 171–7, 343

Pole, Cardinal—
   Description of the English Ordinal, 72, 73, 83, 177
   Date the Document reached Rome, 73, 178–81
   Form of the English Ordinal, 181
   Practice in regard to the English Ordinal, 359
Pope's Mass (Leo XIII), Fr. Puller and T A Lacey present at, 24, 81, 84
Porter, Fr. (Archbishop of Bombay), Reference to, 80
Porrection of the Instruments. *See* Tradition of Instruments
Portal, Abbé, general references, 3, 7, 23, 24, 29, 30, 38, 39, 41, 47, 49, 52, 55, 57, 58, 59, 63, 66, 69, 70, 72, 73, 77, 81, 82, 83, 87, 90, 99, 103, 114, 115, 129, 254, 255
   Discussion of Anglican Orders, 3
   Letter to T. A. Lacey, 87
   Memorandum of Mr. Gladstone, 49, 52, 72
   Revue Anglo-Romaine and, 7, 22, 63 (note), 73
   Interest in the Pope's Commission, 10, 22, 23, 29, 41, 59, 70, 81, 87, 90, 114, 129, 254, 255
Prayers, in Rite of Ordination. *See* Forms of Ordination
Protestant View of the English Ordinal, 311, 312
Puller, Fr, Article in the *Revue Anglo-Romaine*, 7
   Interview with Cardinal Vannutelli, 66, 80
   Les Ordinations Anglicanes, by, 88
   Letters to T. A. Lacey, 91
   Minor references to, 30, 35, 36, 50, 52, 54, 55, 57, 59, 65, 66, 71, 81, 82, 112, 123, 127
   Share in *De Re Anglicana*, 240, 241
   Visit to Rome in conjunction with the Rev. T. A. Lacey, 8–10, 18–20, 23, 29, 88, 89, 90, 91, 254
Puritans, Origin of, 197
Pusey, Dr, References to, 199, 204, 205, 206, 208, 233
   An Eirenicon, by, 204, 205
   Is Healthful Reunion Impossible, by, 206 (note)

Q

Quadra, Bishop, The Simancas Correspondence, 116–23
   Note on, 123

418 A ROMAN DIARY AND OTHER DOCUMENTS

R

Rampolla, Cardinal (Cardinal Secretary of State), Interviews with, 81
Fr Puller and the Rev. T. A Lacey requested to remain in Rome by, 19, 62, 63, 114, 115, 127
Memorandum from Mr. Gladstone, question of, 53, 60, 71, 72
Minor references, 35, 49, 59, 84, 127, 128, 134, 255, 272

Receive the Holy Ghost. See Forms of Ordination

Reconciliation. *See* Pole, Cardinal, Mission of, Reordinations, and Unction

Recusants under Elizabeth, 196, 216, 246, 247

Religious Congregations in England, 201, 207, 208, 225

Repps, Bishop, Royal Assent to the Election of, 62, 104, 126, 163, 168

Reordination, question of (1550–3), 57, 58, 116, 125, 126, 326
Conditional in the Roman Church, 48, 49, 101, 131, 139, 140, 255, 263, 264, 301

Reunion, Anglican Orders, recognition of, by Rome an absolute necessity for, 19, 20, 49, 60, 65, 131, 139–45, 254, 271, 285- 307
Effect of the Bull *Apostolicae Curae* on the Question of, 253–72, 285–307
Growing desire for, 4, 18, 19, 37, 47, 55, 60, 65, 73, 77, 78, 81, 82, 83, 92, 101, 132, 139, 204–6, 232–9, 256, 269, 271
Mr Gladstone's Memorandum, 139
Movement in the English Church, The *Risposta* on, 232–9

Revue Anglo-Romaine, issue of, by M. Portal, 7, 22
References to, 22, 63, 73, 82, 84, 204 (note), 258 (note)
Suppression of the article *De Unitate*, 63 (note)

Richard, Cardinal, Letter of Leo XIII to, 249

Ridley, Bishop, Degradation of, 32 (note)
Minor references, 211, 242
Vote on the English Ordinal, 313, 316 (note), 321 (note), 327 (note)

Riley, Mr. Athelstan, reference to, 29

Risposta all' Opusculo (*De Re Anglicana*), by J C. Moyes and F. A. Gasquet, 210-39
Reply to, by T. A. Lacey, 240–9

Ritual Controversies, Statements in the *Risposta* concerning, 202, 223, 233, 247–8

Rivière, s.j , Père, Meeting with, 72

Rochester, Bishop of, Reference to Speech of, 288

Rogation Days, not observed with abstinence in Roman Church, 49

Roman Church, Invariability of, 32 (note)
Mystic Life of, 24–6

Roman Commission on Anglican Orders. *See* Anglican Orders

Roman Diary, A, 29–84
Author's Retrospect, 21–4

Roman Rites of Ordination, Ancient, 369
Modern, 10, 369, 381

Royal Mandate for Consecration of a Bishop, The, 153
Memorandum by T. A. Lacey, 153–7
Letters to the *Tablet* by T. A. Lacey, 157–68
Prior to 1533, instances of, 159, 166

Ross-Lewin, Rev. Canon, Letter to T. A. Lacey, 65, 125

Rudini, Marchese di, Speech in the Italian Chamber, 79

Ryder, Fr , Correspondence in the *Guardian* on Conditional Reordination, 264 (note)

S

Sacconi, Confraternity of, 50

S. Agnese fuori le Mure, visit to, 69

S. Asaph's. *See* Barlow case

S. Clemente, Dominican Mass at, 70, 71
Miracle connected with, 71 (note)

S. David's. *See* Barlow case

S. Jerome, Tradition of the Church of Alexandria, 64

S Thomas Aquinas, View of the essential form in Ordination, 44, 280, 295
Greek Baptisms and Ordinations, 334, 337–8

Salcot, Bishop, Retains his See under Edward VI and Mary, 243

Sampson, Bishop, Documents for the Consecration of, 62, 112, 126, 163
Retains his See under Edward VI and Mary, 243, 244, 315
Vote on the English Ordinal, 313

INDEX

419

Sarum Pontifical, Ordinal of, 96

Scannell, Rev. J. B., on Anglican Orders, 38, 70, 135, 256
  Member of the Pope's Commission, 31
  Minor references, 70, 94, 96, 99

Scory, Bishop, Rehabilitation of, by Bonner, 58

Segna, Cardinal, Friendliness of, 80, 272
  Interview with, 65, 80, 272
  Minor reference, 63, 81

Shaxton, Bishop, references to, 211, 242
  Writ of promotion to Sarum, 162, 167

Sibley, Dom Dunstan, reference to, 68

Sights of Rome (Churches, etc.), comments on, 32, 33, 34, 35, 36, 37, 38, 39, 47, 48, 50, 53, 56, 59, 62, 66, 67, 69, 70-2, 73, 74, 78, 81

Sidney, Sir Henry (Simancas Correspondence), references to, 116, 121

Simancas Correspondence, extracts from, 116-23
  Note on, 123-5

Sinclair, Archdeacon, quoted in *Risposta*, 227, 247

Sixtus V, reference to, 77

Skyp, Bishop, Royal mandate for the consecration of, 40
  Vote on the English Ordinal, 313, 316 (note)

Smith, Fr. Sydney—
  Article on the English Ordinal (*Month*), 312, 313, 317, 321, 322, 324
  Pamphlet by, 39, 157, 161
  Tablet, reference to article in, by, 123 (note)

Smythies, Bishop, friendly relations with the Roman Bishop at Zanzibar, 63

Sneyd Cox, J G, biography of Cardinal Vaughan, 6, 8

Society of S. John the Evangelist, Cowley, 201, 207, 225

Sorbonne, the, view of the essential Form in Ordination, 280

Statistics of the English Church, statements in the *Risposta* concerning, 207-9, 231, 247, 248

Steinhuber, Cardinal, references to, 78, 79, 80, 81, 255

Stepney, Bishop of, Letter to *The Times* (Reordinations), 57, 58, 61, 125

Stubbs, *Reg. Sacr Angl.*, reference to, 322 (note)

Sulpicians, House of, visit to, 39, 81, 99

Swedish Church, question of the Ordinations of, used as an example, 15

T

Tablet, The—
  De Re Anglicana and the *Risposta* translation of, in, 240 (note)
  Letters on the Barlow documents, 99, 102, 129, 157-68
  — T A Lacey on the Royal Mandate, 157-68
  Minor references, 55, 123 (note), 258

Tavernier, M, Editor of *L'Univers*, visit to, 83

Taylor, Jeremy, on Holy Orders, 288

Theology of the Bull *Apostolicae Curae*, a Paper read at Sion College, 285

Thirlby, Bishop—
  Embassy to Rome, 176, 243
  Retains his See under Edward VI and Mary, 243
  Vote on the English Ordinal, 313, 316 (note), 322

Thirty-Nine Articles, 375 (note)

Thomas, Mgr, references to, 30, 78

Times, The—
  Bishop of Stepney (Reordinations), Letter in, 57, 58, 61, 125
  Encyclical of Leo XIII, abstract of, published in, 133
  Mr. Gladstone's *Memorandum* in, 78
  — on, 237

Tosti, Abbate, reference to, 53, 68, 134

Tractarians, references to, 199, 204, 205, 221, 233

Tradition of the Instruments, 38, 42, 51, 101, 178, 263, 264, 277, 279-81, 295, 301, 306, 380. *See also* Gordon case

Trent, The Council of (1562), 43, 45, 48, 61, 98, 99, 121, 122, 141, 199, 348 (note), 366, 370, 372, 373
  Elizabeth and, 61, 121, 122
  Formal definition on the Essential Matter in Ordination avoided by, 48, 98, 100, 298-300

Tuke, Letter to, from Cromwell, 34, 96-97, 127, 130

420 A ROMAN DIARY AND OTHER DOCUMENTS

Tunstall, Bishop, deprivation of, 212, 242
    Vote on the English Ordinal, 313, 319
Turton, Mr., reference to, 72
Tyrrell, Fr George
    Treatment of, by Rome, 25, 26

U

Unction, Place of, in the Sacrament of Order, 93, 380
    Priests reconciled by use of, 65, 125, 126, 360 (note)
Unicitas and *Unitas*, distinction between, 84, 133

V

Validity of Anglican orders
    See Anglican Orders, English Ordinal, and Names of Bishops
Vannutelli, Cardinal Serafino, references to, 63, 81, 129
    Interviews with, 66, 76, 80
Vannutelli, Cardinal Vincenzo, reference to, 62, 63, 76, 115
Vatican Council, reference to, 206.
    See also Holy Office
Vatican Library and Archives, 34 96, 98, 127, 177
Vaughan, Fr. Bernard, on Intention in Anglican Ordinations, 258
Vaughan, Cardinal, adverse attitude of, 6, 8, 9, 88
    Biography of, by J. G. Snead-Cox, 6, 8
    De Augustinis, Memoir of, 99, 100, 254
    Minor references, 61–133
    Vindication of the Bull *Apostolicae Curae*, 328
Venetian State Papers, references to, (30), 32, 34, 178 (note), 180 (note), 324 (note)
Vernacular Services, note on, 71
Victor, Pope, Action of, in the Paschal Controversy, 30

Voysey, Bishop, Deprivation of, 212, 242

W

Waggett, Fr., reference to, 36
Wakering, Bishop, Royal Mandate for the Consecration of, 159, 166
Weekly Register (Gordon case), reference to, 107
Wharton, Bishop, reference to, 104
    Retains his See under Edward VI and Mary, 243, 315
    Vote on the English Ordinal, 313
Wilkins, Pole's Legatine Constitution, 94, 95
Windsor Commission, 315, 316 (note)
Wiseman, Cardinal, references to, 22, 204
Wood, Rev. E. G., Correspondence with T. A. Lacey, 87, 94, 97, 99, 103, 106, 114, 127, 129, 130
    Discovery of the Barlow Documents, 50, 51, 61, 64, 106, 153
    On the form *Accipe Spiritum Sanctum*, 97, 128

Y

York, Archbishop of, reference to, in The *Risposta*, 235 (note)
Les Ordinations Anglicanes, by Fr Puller, Preface by, 88
    Letter to M. Portal, 29, 36, 91
    Mr Gladstone's *Memorandum*, addressed to, 71 (note), 78, 139, 236
    Prayer after the Litany, in the Ordination Service, 52, 63, 65, 115
    Roman visit, the, on, 88, 91
    Minor references, 29, 89
    See also Reply of the English Archbishops to Leo XIII

Z

Zeitschrift fur Katholische Theologie, Review of *De Hierarchie* in, 5

www.ingramcontent.com/pod-product-compliance
Lightning Source LLC
Chambersburg PA
CBHW070006010526
44117CB00011B/1447